Critical Choices

for

South Africa

An agenda for the 1990s

Edited by Robert A. Schrire

CONTEMPORARY SOUTH AFRICAN DEBATES

1990
OXFORD UNIVERSITY PRESS
CAPE TOWN

Oxford University Press
Walton Street, Oxford OX2 6DP, United Kingdom

OXFORD NEW YORK TORONTO
DELHI BOMBAY CALCUTTA MADRAS KARACHI
PETALING JAYA SINGAPORE HONG KONG TOKYO
NAIROBI DAR ES SALAAM CAPE TOWN
MELBOURNE AUCKLAND
and associated companies in
BERLIN IBADAN

ISBN 0 19 570574 2

© Oxford University Press 1990
OXFORD is a trademark of Oxford University Press

Cover
Cover illustration: detail from a mixed media collage entitled
Critical choices for South Africa by Willie Bester

Published by Oxford University Press Southern Africa
Harrington House, Barrack Street, Cape Town, 8001, South Africa

Page design & typesetting by Desktop design, Cape Town. Set in Stone.

Printed and bound by Clyson Printers, Maitland, Cape.

Preface

This book is the first to be compiled by the Institute for the Study of Public Policy of the University of Cape Town. It represents a major component of the research project entitled 'Critical Choices for South Africa'. We anticipate that the research will continue until the early 1990s, after which additional publications will follow.

This project was based on the assumption that the political debate in South Africa was entering a period of fluidity where the 'certainties' of the past were being replaced by a new openness and flexibility. Although the prescriptive and policy-orientated literature on South Africa is vast, and expanding rapidly, it tends to be of rather limited use. Some books advocate particular 'solutions', usually based on foreign models, which, it is claimed, would lead South Africa to a new utopia. Others sketch broad scenarios of possible futures, of which Clem Sunter's 'high road' and 'low road' is deservedly the best known.

None of these approaches, however, grapple in any detail with concrete problems, and they are usually written at a high level of generality. We felt it important to begin to fill this vacuum by looking at real world, and frequently more micro, issues. How can the health delivery system be improved? What are the major problems in the agricultural sector? How do we respond to massive urbanization pressures? These, and many other issues, were our primary interest.

To explore these issues, we commissioned more than fifty researchers from the scholarly community as far apart as Canada, Northern Ireland and Australia, in addition to South Africa, to undertake research. Fourteen policy papers have thus far been published in summary form and distributed widely to opinion leaders throughout South Africa and abroad. This volume contains a selection from the huge volume of research completed by the researchers. All but one chapter are original reports.

Throughout the project most of the papers were sent to anonymous referees for detailed comments and suggestions. We are grateful to them for their contribution. The reports were then sent to the authors who were given the opportunity to revise their chapters. Quite obviously, however, the chapters represent the view of the authors and not necessarily the view of the Management Committee or the Institute.

One cause for regret is our failure to enlist more contributions from the black community. Quite clearly, South Africa has moved beyond the stage where whites can monopolize the debate on options and priorities. Despite our best efforts, however, we were not successful. In part, this reflects the legacy of the apartheid system which has contributed to a reality where there are few black experts on technical issues, such as resource management and urbanization. In part it reflects the black priority, which is to work towards bringing about fundamental change in South Africa rather than speculate on policy options for a future socio-economic order. We believe, however, that the ideas developed in this book have a validity and vitality that is independent of the ethnic background of the authors.

In this book, we have adhered to the conventional South African terminology for describing the different people inhabiting the country. 'White' is used to describe those people descendant from European settlers, 'African' for members of the Bantu-speaking groups, and the term 'black' is used for all members of the society who are not white. 'Coloured' refers to those members legally categorized as being of mixed descent, and Indian/Asian refers to people descendant from the Asian traders and workers who settled in South Africa in the previous century.

Considerable costs were involved in commissioning research and publishing the findings. Because we did not wish to create the perception that the research project was influenced in any way by a particular donor, we followed a strict policy of limiting the contribution of each donor to a small percentage of total costs. In addition, we raised funds by encouraging corporations and individuals to subscribe to the policy series. We would like to thank the following corporations, which made the initial donations which enabled the project to be established:

The Chairman's Fund, Anglo American Corporation
Dart Corporation
Duracell
Foschini Limited
Liberty Life
Mobil
Sage Holdings
Shell
Standard Bank Investment Corporation
Tupperware

We would also like to thank the many individuals, corporations and consulates who made smaller financial contributions.

Finally, a very real debt was incurred to our editorial staff. Minnie Venter's all-round assistance — from editorial input, to liaising with authors and publisher, to standardizing and checking the manuscript — was invaluable. Tim Ross-Thompson, our senior editorial consultant, imposed his strong sense of style on the often eccentrically written chapters! Our sincere thanks go to both.

In a real sense this book is offered as a contribution to the debate about real options and choices. As such it simply starts a process which will, of course, be at the core of the politics of the new South Africa.

Hermann Giliomee
Robert Schrire
David Welsh

Management Committee
Institute for the Study of Public Policy
University of Cape Town

Contents

Contributors

ANN BERNSTEIN is Executive Director (Urbanization) of the Urban Foundation in Johannesburg. She was educated at the Universities of the Witwatersrand and California, where she took a Masters degree in architecture and urban planning.

ANTHONY MATHEWS is James Scott Wylie Professor of Law at the University of Natal in Pietermaritzburg. He was visiting scholar at Harvard Law School and Clare Hall, Cambridge, and visiting Professor in 1987 and 1989 at the College of Law, University of Florida.

AREND LIJPHART is Professor of Political Science, University of California, San Deigo. Educated in the Netherlands, he has written widely on the politics of plural societies.

BARRY STANDISH is a lecturer in the Economics Department, University of Cape Town. He studied at the Universities of Natal and Cape Town.

BOBBY GODSELL is the Industrial Relations Consultant with the Anglo American Corporation. Educated at Natal, Leyden and UCT, he recently co-directed the project 'South Africa beyond apartheid'.

CHARLES SIMKINS is an Associate Professor in the School of Economics at UCT and a consultant to the Urban Foundation. He holds a Doctorate in Economics from the University of Natal.

DAVID COOPER is an agriculturalist with the Environmental and Development Agency (EDA). He studied at the University of Natal and completed his M.Sc. at Reading University.

GAVIN MAASDORP is Research Professor and Director, Economic Research Unit, University of Natal, Durban. He spent his sabbatical at the Federal Institute of East European and International Studies, Cologne, and St Anthony's College, Oxford.

HERIBERT ADAM is Professor of Sociology and Political Science at Simon Fraser University in Canada. He received his education in Germany and has also lectured extensively in South Africa.

IRAJ ABEDIAN is a senior lecturer in Fiscal Policy in the Department of Economics, University of Cape Town. He studied economics at the University of Tehran, and later obtained a Masters degree from UCT.

JOHN BREWER is a Lecturer at Queen's University of Belfast. He was Visiting Fellow at Yale University in 1989. He previously held lecturing posts at the University of Natal in Durban and the University of East Anglia.

JOHN KANE-BERMAN, a former Rhodes scholar, is Executive Director of the South African Institute of Race Relations. He has written and lectured extensively on South Africa.

KEN HARTSHORNE is a consultant to the Centre for Continuing Education, University of the Witwatersrand. He was educated at the University of London, obtained his Masters degree from UNISA, and honorary Doctorates from the Universities of the Witwatersrand

and Natal. He has been involved in the education of black South Africans since 1938, as teacher, training college principal, and administrator.

LAURENCE BOULLE is Associate Professor of Law at Bond University, Queensland, Australia. Past Professor of Public Law and Dean of the School of Law at the University of Natal, Durban, he studied at the Universities of Natal, Stellenbosch, London and Michigan.

MARK SWILLING is a research officer at the Centre for Policy Studies, University of the Witwatersrand, where he received his higher education.

MICHAEL McGRATH is Professor of Economics, University of Natal (Pietermaritzburg). He was educated at the University of Natal and is an expert on the policies of income distribution.

MICHAEL SAVAGE is Professor of Sociology, University of Cape Town. He was trained at the University of Cape Town, London School of Economics and the University of Wisconsin, and is the founding editor of the journal *Social Dynamics*.

NEVILLE ALEXANDER is attached to the Health, Education and Welfare Society of South Africa (HEWSSA Trust). He studied at the University of Cape Town and the Tubingen University in West Germany, where he obtained his MA, and later his doctorate.

NIC OLIVIER is Professor in the Department of Roman Law and Legal Pluralism in the Faculty of Law, Potchefstroom University for Christian Higher Education. He studied at the Universities of Pretoria and Leyden.

PHILIP FRANKEL is Senior Lecturer in the Department of Political Science at the University of the Witwatersrand. He received his doctorate from Princeton University and consults widely for several multinational corporations.

PIERRE HUGO is Professor in the Department of Development Administration and Politics at the University of South Africa. He is a graduate of the Universities of Stellenbosch (MA), Bristoe (M.Sc.) and Zimbabwe (Ph.D.).

PUNDY PILLAY is an economist lecturing in the Academic Support Programme, University of Cape Town. He holds degrees from the Universities of Cape Town, Durban-Westville, South Africa and Witwatersrand. His research interests and publications are mainly in labour economics and the economics of education.

ROBERT SCHRIRE is Professor in the Department of Political Studies and Director of the Institute for the Study of Public Policy, University of Cape Town. He was educated at the University of Cape Town, the School of International Service, American University and obtained his doctorate from the University of California.

SOLOMON BENATAR is a graduate of the University of Cape Town, Medical School where he holds the Chair of Medicine. In addition to the practice of medicine, he has an interest in policy and social affairs.

WOLFGANG THOMAS is the Regional General Manager with the Small Business Development Corporation in Cape Town. He obtained his M.Com. from the University of Stellenbosch. He formerly lectured at several South African universities.

Introduction: Critical choices for South Africa

Robert Schrire

South Africa is today at the crossroads: the apartheid paradigm is dead as a guide to policy and a justification for state policies; yet no world view has yet emerged to replace it as the framework for a legitimate public order.

This intellectual vacuum is both a challenge and a danger. Public ideas are frequently more important in shaping policy than is appreciated. The present intellectual ferment creates opportunities to shape the public debate in important ways. The danger, of course, is that this vacuum will be filled by retrogressive or unworkable frameworks for policy or, as bad, that the vacuum will continue, which must negatively influence the prospects for negotiation and renewal.

Critical choices for South Africa has been published to provide a map for future state policies. It is an invitation to debate, a survey of choices, rather than a blueprint or 'solution'. Only politics in the real world can resolve problems: ideas are an aid to that process.

Policies are made and problems grappled with in several ways. The dynamics of events and international actions and decisions shape social realities. Secondly, and not always of the greatest significance, is the big decision, the 'rational' and self-conscious policy formulation. Governments are always only in imperfect control of situations and are not always the decisive participants. In analysing policy, it is therefore necessary to avoid too state-centric an approach.

While recognizing these realities, we have deliberately focused on state policies, but have not neglected the important role which will be played by groups such as extra-parliamentary opposition and business.

We have therefore conceptualized the critical issues which confront all South Africans as follows:

Critical issue one: Expanding the foundations of political participation while structuring and controlling state power.

Critical issue two: Balancing equalities and inequalities.

Critical issue three: Managing resources in a context of relative scarcity.

Critical issue four: Strategies of change.

Critical issue one: Expanding the foundations of political participation while structuring and controlling state power

We take it as axiomatic that any viable political order must be based on the principle of one-person-one-vote where each vote carries equal weight in free and fair elections. Without this, the system will not attain either domestic legitimacy or foreign acceptance. The other aspect that needs to be examined is the need to control and structure the exercise of state power.

State power always carries with it the possibility of corruption, abuse and repression. Indeed, one of the major barriers to genuine reform in contemporary South Africa is the not unrealistic fear of those who are presently in power that a change in the ruling élite would have adverse consequences for those groups and interests who presently benefit from the status quo. Clearly, South Africans need to think again about the realities of political power in a deeply divided society.

The principle of both universal participation and the control of state power can be realized through a wide range of institutional structures and procedures.

Arend Lijphart proposes a system of proportional representation which would permit the different interests within the electorate to be represented without the necessity of building in entrenched 'group rights' or making other invidious distinctions between members of the electorate.

Other scholars examine methods of controlling state power. Laurence Boulle discusses ways of limiting state power and increasing public participation in the governing process. He argues that the objective to provide political institutions which will give people the maximum possible freedom to take decisions affecting their own lives will ultimately lead to a state system that will be more democratic, responsive and legitimate.

The case for a bill of rights is made by Nic Olivier who surveyed several bills of rights in an international context, and, here, examines the possible impact of such a bill on the South African executive.

In his analysis of the imbalances between national security, freedom and reform, Anthony Mathews provides recommendations to increase freedom, and drastically reduce the grip of national security. He provides a detailed set of proposals to ensure a balance between the protection of human rights and the legitimate security needs of the state.

In the last chapter in this section, I examine a range of arrangements which would make government more accountable to the people.

Critical issue two: Balancing equalities and inequalities

Irrespective of how the power struggle in South Africa is ultimately resolved, the issues of equality and inequality cannot but become of increasing importance. By every indicator of economic welfare, be it personal income, land ownership or participation in the stock market, the population groups are characterized by vast and unsustainable inequalities. Clearly, the implications of inequality will have to be faced and a clear understanding of their causes, consequences and possible trade-offs developed.

The core of issues of income distribution are explored in detail by Michael McGrath.

South Africa's bureaucracy is staffed mainly by whites and provides limited advancement for blacks. A programme of equal opportunity and affirmative action within the bureaucracy is needed to address the inequality. Mechanisms for implementing such a programme and what affirmative action is needed are described by Pierre Hugo.

Other chapters widen the focus. An important issue with critical distributive consequences is the language issue. Language permeates every aspect of South Africa's political, economic and socio-cutural developments, as the 1976 unrest — sparked off by the language question — illustrates. The restrictions which are placed by language demands and the 'language planning' that is needed to address the dilemma are imaginatively discussed by Neville Alexander.

A key issue is the management and financing of our health care system. Mike Savage and Solomon Benatar relate the dilemma in health care to the political challenge facing South Africa and examine the strengths and weaknesses of the present health care system. They then propose new policies which would allow all communities participation in the health care service.

Finally, Ken Hartshorne explores some of the critical issues involved in African education. It is now widely accepted that the educational system is one of the major mechanisms for creating either inequalities or greater equalities and the tragic neglect of black education historically in South Africa continues to limit the future.

Critical issue three: Managing resources in a context of relative scarcity

All societies face critical issues of resource management. The problems which confront South Africa are aggravated by the distortions caused by white domination and the policies of apartheid. Rapid population growth has many negative consequences, but it is difficult to formulate and implement a practical policy because of the political implications involved. The important changes in the global economy — a new global economic system, rapid communications, the increasing importance of financial flows and the decreasing importance of commodities in world trade, all require rapid policy responses. The issues involved in economic growth thus become particularly important.

Gavin Maasdorp, in the introductory chapter, provides a comprehensive overview of the role of the state in the economy. He explores the different theoretical paradigms of political economy and explores some of their implications.

The chapters in this section also cover a wide range of functional policy areas. The country's population policy is discussed in terms of its socio-political and economic impact by Charles Simkins, who assesses the vast population growth against the background of rural neglect and restrictive urban legislation. The urban environment and its future imperatives are explored in detail by Anne Bernstein. In another chapter Wolfgang Thomas explores the issues involved in creation of employment.

Looking at relations between trade unions and business, Bobby Godsell analyses the question of whether industrial democracy, which unionization produces, will occur with or without economic growth. He argues that the relationship business must seek should be neither that of unrelenting opposition nor that of ally, but rather that of an advocate of its own agenda.

Pundy Pillay explores at micro level some of the institutional elements of a social democratic order. Embarking from the premise that neither of the two extremes — free markets and Soviet-type centralized planning — are economically tenable, he attempts to construct a social market economic strategy for South Africa, including as a minimum a non-racial, democratically elected government.

Abedian and Standish outline several economic development strategies, while, finally, the important and often neglected rural and agricultural sector is examined by David Cooper.

Critical issue four: Strategies of change

Many thinkers have produced 'solutions', 'constitutions' and 'principles' for a new South Africa. Few, however, have given much thought to the less glamorous but more important issues of strategies and tactics. How can sensible policy proposals be implemented? What are the strategic options facing the political and socio-economic participants?

John Kane-Berman provides a broad overview of the issues and the options. He summarizes the magnitude of the issues which are involved in putting South Africa together again.

More detailed studies follow: Philip Frankel on the role of the business community, Mark Swilling on strategies at the local and community level, and John Brewer on the strategic choices available to blacks in a context of a white-controlled state.

Finally, Heribert Adam examines many of the key issues involved in moving towards genuine negotiations and a viable political settlement.

Conclusion

All of the contributors illustrate the magnitude and complexity of the problems which confront South Africa. It would be easy to become despondent and to write South Africa off as a losing nation. Yet, this is far from the conclusion of any of our contributors. Without exception, every one of them believes that while there are no easy solutions, there is no reason why the status quo must be accepted as immutable. We do not need to suffer the future: the choice is ours to shape the future.

The new fluidity in South Africa, while clearly not meriting euphoria, gives ground for cautious hope. We need to move beyond the politics of rejection to the politics of ideas. We hope this book will contribute to this.

I

Expanding the foundations of political participation while structuring and controlling state power

1 Electoral systems, party systems and conflict management in segmented societies

Arend Lijphart

The electoral system is the most easily manipulated element of a political system and therefore a powerful tool for political engineering. There are strong arguments for proportional representation as a democratic, just and viable system in deeply divided societies. In this chapter it is argued that list proportional representation is its most desirable form for South Africa.

Introduction

This chapter will focus on the relationship between electoral and party systems and on the influence of electoral and party systems on the prospects of democratic conflict regulation in segmented (or plural) societies. I shall begin with a summary of what we know about the causes and consequences of electoral and party systems, with an emphasis on the contrast between the two most prevalent electoral methods: the plurality single-member district system (also frequently called the first-past-the-post system) and proportional representation (PR). Two major conclusions can be drawn from this well-established body of knowledge: firstly, the electoral system is the most easily manipulated element of a political system and therefore it is a powerful tool for constitutional engineering, and secondly, PR is clearly superior to the plurality method in segmented societies. I shall then discuss the other advantages and disadvantages of PR and plurality — which add up to a reinforcement of the case for PR in plural societies. Next, I shall argue that list PR in relatively large districts is the most desirable form of PR for segmented societies. And, finally, I shall try to rebut the argument, frequently stated by PR critics, that PR is not sufficiently democratic.

My point of departure will be the major conclusions of the Main Committee of the Human Sciences Research Council (HSRC) Investigation into Intergroup Relations. The committee argues that 'the political ordering of intergroup relations according to the original apartheid model has reached an impasse and that constructive relations cannot be developed further along these lines'. No specific alternative is proposed because the most appropriate system of government for South Africa's plural society 'should be the product of deliberation and negotiation between all the population categories', but the committee does specify that 'politically and constitutionally intergroup relations in South Africa must be given expression within a democratic framework'. Furthermore, the committee reports a widespread acceptance in South Africa of 'the right to democratic participation in decision making'.[1]

These conclusions — with which I find myself in full agreement — add up to the recommendation of a democratic system of government in an undivided South Africa. I also take them to imply that democratic elections should be held at all levels, including the election of the central parliament. The question that I shall address is: which electoral system should be used for these elections (in particular, the election of the lower house)?

Even though I shall argue in favour of PR, I should like to emphasize at the outset that the advantages of PR should not be exaggerated. PR cannot be regarded as either a necessary or a sufficient method for the satisfactory operation of democratic government in plural societies. It is not a necessary method because, while it is vastly preferable to plurality, it is not impossible that plurality will work reasonably well too; the plurality elections in ethnically and religiously divided India are a case in point. It is perhaps even more important to stress that PR is not a sufficient means to achieve viable democracy in plural societies. As I have argued elsewhere,[2] plural societies are best served by a set of interrelated formal and informal constitutional rules — such as broadly representative power-sharing cabinets, minority autonomy on a territorial and non-territorial basis, and so on — that together may be called 'consociational' or 'concensus' democracy. PR is an important ingredient of this kind of democracy and it tends to strengthen some of the other ingredients, but it cannot establish or maintain this kind of democracy by itself. My argument is that plural societies, like South Africa, need PR, but not that they need only PR.[3]

---

[1] Human Sciences Research Council, *The South African society: realities and future prospects* (HSRC Investigation into Intergroup Relations), Pretoria: HSRC, 1985, pp. 159, 163–4, 172–3.

[2] A. Lijphart, *Democracy in plural societies: a comprehensive exploration*, New Haven: Yale Univ. Press, 1977; and A. Lijphart, *Democracies: patterns of majoritarian and concensus government in twenty-one countries*, New Haven: Yale Univ. Press, 1984.

[3] See A. Lijphart, 'Power-sharing in South Africa', *Policy Papers in International Affairs no. 24*, Berkeley: Inst. of International Studies, Univ. of California, 1985.

Causes and consequences of electoral systems

Duverger's Law: the relationship between electoral and party systems

Figure 1.1 outlines the well-established chain of empirical relationships concerning the causes and consequences of PR and the plurality single-member district system. The best known proposition concerning electoral systems is still Duverger's Law. In Duverger's own most recent formulation, the Law states that: '1. the plurality method tends to lead to a two-party system; 2. proportional representation tends to lead to a system of many mutually independent parties; 3. the two-ballot majority system tends to lead to multipartism moderated by alliances.'[4] Let us focus on the first two parts of the Law since the two-ballot system has become a rare phenomenon in modern democracies — essentially limited to the Fifth French Republic. The explanation of the link between plurality and the two-party system is based on what Duverger calls 'mechanical' and 'psychological' factors: small parties find it difficult to elect representatives in plurality single-member districts and are therefore underrepresented by the plurality method; as a result, many of the voters favouring small parties will not vote for them because they do not want to waste their votes; the combined effect is that only two large parties tend to survive. In PR systems, these mechanical and psychological factors do not operate (or, since there always tends to be at least some discrimination against very small parties, they operate to a much more limited extent), and hence the pressures towards a two-party system are absent.

Figure 1.1:   Causes and consequences of electoral and party systems

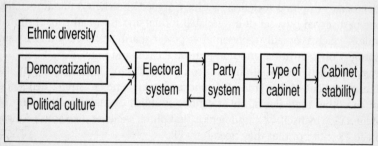

Two objections have been raised against Duverger's Law. One emphasizes the empirical exceptions to the law, especially the Austrian and Canadian cases. Canada's party system may be described as a 'two-and-a-half party

---

[4] M. Duverger, 'Which is the best electoral system?', in A. Lijphart and B. Grofman, eds., *Choosing an electoral system: issues and alternatives*, New York: Praeger, 1984, p. 35.

system'[5] in spite of the plurality method of elections, and Austria has a nearly perfect two-party system in spite of PR. However, most social science laws are not absolute laws, and what is remarkable about Duverger's Law is not so much that there are exceptions to it, but that there are so few exceptions. The two exceptions can be largely explained in terms of the plural character of the two countries. The Austrian two-party system reflects a plural society which happens to consist of two large segments. Canada's multipartism reflects its cultural and regional diversity which is sufficiently strong to overcome the deterrent effect of the plurality method. It is also clear that under PR Canada would have a much more pronounced multiparty system, and that under a plurality system Austria would have only the two large parties represented in parliament.

The second objection to Duverger's Law is that it misstates the causal direction of the relationship between electoral and party systems: electoral systems are said to be the effects instead of the causes of party systems.[6] This criticism is partly correct. A multiparty parliament elected by PR is not likely to decide in favour of plurality elections because of the risk that this would entail for most of the parties. Similarly, a two-party parliament does not have much of an incentive to adopt PR because plurality has very great advantages for the two largest parties. However, it would be wrong to conclude that this causal relationship eliminates the possibility of the reverse causal direction. In the British case, for instance, Butler has predicted that the plurality method will be abandoned before the end of the century; and the adoption of PR will certainly end the strict two-party system.[7] In none of the British general elections since World War II has the winning party received more than half of the total vote; clearly, if these elections had been held under PR, a two-and-a-half party system — and coalition governments — would have been the most likely outcome.

It is especially important to recognize the electoral system as a basic causal factor because it can be a powerful practical instrument for constitutional engineers. It is obviously much easier to influence the party system by means of the electoral system than the other way around. Sartori aptly characterizes electoral systems as 'the most specific manipulative instrument of politics'.[8]

---

[5] J. Blondel, 'Party systems and patterns of governments in Western democracies', *Canadian Journal of Political Science*, vol. 1, no. 2, June 1968, pp. 180–203.

[6] J. Blondel, *An introduction to comparative government*, London: Weidenfeld and Nicholson, 1969, pp. 204–6.

[7] D. E. Butler, 'Reflections on the electoral debate in Britain', in Lijphart and Grofman, *Choosing an electoral system*, p. 229.

[8] G. Sartori, 'Political development and political engineering', in J. D. Montgomery and A. O. Hirschman, eds., *Public Policy*, vol. 12, Cambridge, Massachusetts: Harvard Univ. Press, 1968, p. 273.

The strong mutual link between electoral and party systems is also demonstrated by the 'effective number of parties' that we find in plurality and PR systems in the period from 1945 to 1980. The 'effective number of parties' is a measure of multipartism that takes both the numbers and sizes of parties into account and which weighs large parties much more heavily than small ones.[9] In the four industrialized democracies with plurality systems (the United Kingdom, the United States, Canada and New Zealand) the average effective number of parties was 2,1 — close to a pure two-party system— but in the fifteen PR countries (for example, Israel, Austria, Belgium, West Germany and Switzerland), the average was 3,8 effective parties, almost twice as many.[10]

The next question is: if by means of choosing a particular electoral system we can influence the kind of party system a country has, which of the two types of party system should we try to encourage? My answer is that this depends on the type of society (homogeneous or plural) for which we are trying to engineer a suitable form of government. For reasonably homogeneous societies (such as the UK, Ireland, the Scandinavian countries, New Zealand and Japan), I am agnostic: it seems to me that good arguments can be made for both two-party and multiparty systems in these countries. For plural societies, however, the situation is quite different. As I have argued, in my writings on 'consociational' democracy, it is vital for peaceful conflict resolution in plural societies that all segments of that society be allowed to be represented by their own parties, if they so wish.[11] If a plural society consists of three or more separate segments, as most of them do, a multiparty system is preferable to a two-party system. Therefore, the appropriate electoral system for segmented societies is PR rather than plurality. In Lewis's colourful words, 'the surest way to kill the idea of democracy in a plural society is to adopt the Anglo-American electoral system of first-past-the-post'.[12]

Cabinet stability

One of the main reason why a two-party system is often considered desirable is that it tends to lead to one-party bare-majority cabinets; on the other hand, multiparty systems tend to lead to coalition governments and frequently to coalitions which are oversized, that is, coalitions that include more parties than are necessary to have majority support in parliament.

---

[9] M. Laakso and R. Taagepera, '"Effective" number of parties: a measure with application to West Europe', *Comparative Political Studies*, vol. 12, no. 1, April 1979, pp. 3–27.

[10] Lijphart, *Democracies: patterns of majoritarian and concensus government*, pp. 159–61.

[11] Lijphart, *Democracy in plural societies*, pp. 83–7.

[12] A. W. Lewis, *Politics in West Africa*, London: Allen and Unwin, 1965, p. 71.

This is the next empirical relationship indicated in Figure 1.1, and it is indeed a strong one. In my comparative study of twenty-one countries in the 1945–80 period, I found that countries with fewer than 3,0 'effective' parties were ruled by minimal majority coalitions 89 per cent of the time, those with between 3,0 and 4,0 parties, 70 per cent of the time, and those with more than 4,0 parties, only 28 per cent of the time.[13]

The question for the political engineer is: which type of cabinet should be encouraged? Here again, good arguments can be made for both options when we are talking about basically homogeneous countries. The British tradition obviously favours the minimal majority governments encouraged by two-party systems. For plural societies, the answer is not in doubt: these societies are best served by grand coalitions of all the major parties. Here we have another reason to prefer PR to plurality for segmented societies: PR encourages multipartism, which in turn encourages coalition government.[14]

To quote Lewis once more: 'One of the advantages of proportional representation is that it tends to promote coalition government.'[15]

The final empirical relationship on the right-hand side of Figure 1.1 provides the main reason why two-party systems and one-party majority cabinets are frequently admired: they are said to promote a high degree of cabinet stability. Cabinet stability is usually measured in terms of the period in which the same cabinet remains in office. Various operational definitions of what is meant by 'the same cabinet' can be used, but regardless of which of these is applied, there is a strong association between the type of cabinet and its durability: democracies with a tendency to minimal majority cabinets tend to have relatively long-lived cabinets; those that usually have oversized cabinets tend to have much less durable cabinets.[16]

This finding should be treated with caution, however, and it should certainly not lead to the conclusion that durable cabinets — and hence also minimal majority cabinets, two-party systems, and the plurality method of election — should be preferred to less durable cabinets and their concomitant party and electoral systems. The widely-held assumption is that cabinet durability means strong cabinets and a stable democratic regime. This assumption is only partly correct: durability does indicate strength,

---

13 Lijphart, *Democracies: patterns of majoritarian and consensus government*, p. 24.

14 Given the ethnically plural nature of South Africa, my assumption is that multipartism in a South African democracy will be a system of many *ethnically* based parties rather than what Giovanni Sartori calls the 'extreme multipartism' of a large number of *ideologically* polarized parties; see G. Sartori, *Parties and party systems: a framework for analysis*, Cambridge: Cambridge Univ. Press, 1976, pp. 131–45.

15 Lewis, *Politics in West Africa*, p. 79.

16 A. Lijphart, 'Measures of cabinet durability: a conceptual and empirical evaluation', *Comparative Political Studies*, vol. 17, no. 2, July 1984, pp. 265–79.

but only in the relationship between executive and legislature, not in the general sense of strong and effective government. Cabinets that exercise predominance over the legislature tend to be the most durable ones; if there is more of an executive–legislative equilibrium of power, the cabinets tend to have shorter lives.[17] What does this mean for segmented societies? I would submit that a compromise-oriented relationship between executive and legislature fits the needs of a plural society much better than that of a dominant majority cabinet supported by a docile legislature. This means that for plural societies all of the empirical consequences associated with PR, shown in Figure 1.1, are preferable to the consequences of the plurality system. Thus, constitutional engineers in a segmented society do not face a difficult choice between the two types of electoral system: the PR system is preferable.

Factors influencing the choice of electoral systems

Let us now turn to the three factors on the left-hand side of Figure 1.1. We have already seen that party systems influence the choice of electoral systems. In addition, there are three other factors that can be seen as causes of electoral systems: the presence of ethnic diversity, the process of democratization (that is, the adoption of universal suffrage), and the prevailing political culture, especially the contrast between Anglo-American and continental European political traditions. Rokkan has shown that there were two main reasons why PR was adopted in many European countries in the late nineteenth and early twentieth centuries. One was minority protection:

> It was no accident that the earliest moves toward proportional representation . . . came in the ethnically most heterogeneous countries: Denmark in 1855; the Swiss cantons in 1891; Belgium in 1899; Moravia in 1905; Finland in 1906. In linguistically and religiously divided societies majority elections could clearly threaten the continued existence of the political system. The introduction of some element of minority representation came to be seen as an essential step in a strategy of territorial consolidation.[18]

The second impulse toward the introduction of PR, occurring slightly later, was the extension of the suffrage. To quote Rokkan again, the victory of PR:

> came about through the convergence of pressures from below and from above. The rising working class wanted to gain access to the legislatures, and the most threatened of the old-established parties demanded PR to protect their position against the new waves of mobilized voters created by universal suffrage.[19]

---

[17] A. Lijphart, 'A note on the meaning of cabinet durability, *Comparative Political Studies*, vol. 17, no. 2, July 1984, pp. 163–6.

[18] S. Rokkan, *Citizens, elections, parties: approaches to the comparative study of the process of development*, Oslo: Universitetsforlaget, 1970, p. 157.

[19] Rokkan, *Citizens, elections, parties*, p. 157.

The third factor that can account for the adoption of PR or plurality is the contrast between Anglo-American and continental European political cultures. The relationship is an almost perfect one. Of the countries in the Anglo-American tradition, only one — Ireland — uses PR for the election of its lower house. Of the continental European countries, only one — France — does not normally use PR, although PR was used in the Fourth Republic and, more recently, for the 1986 National Assembly election as well as for the 1979, 1984 and 1989 elections of the French delegation to the European Parliament.

These three variables all provide good explanations for the adoption of electoral systems — but not equally good justifications. In line with what I have argued earlier about the need for PR in segmented societies, the ethnic diversity factor is both a good explanation and a proper justification for the introduction of PR. The extension of the suffrage can also be regarded as at least a partial justification for PR; not only the pure self-interest of existing parties, but also the general interest are served by permitting these parties to continue playing a role in the political system. But I would argue that the strength of a particular political culture is a poor reason for choosing an electoral system. This can be put more strongly: in a plural society, the anti-PR Anglo-American tradition is a major obstacle which constitutional engineers have to try to overcome.

Other advantages and disadvantages of PR and plurality

Let me briefly review the other advantages and disadvantages that PR and the plurality method can be given credit or blame for. In particular, I want to explore whether there are any considerations of this kind that weaken the recommendation of PR for plural societies. There are five points that should be given attention:

1. Apart from the alleged advantage of the plurality system that it encourages a two-party system — which, as we have already seen, is not an advantage for a plural society — the most frequently mentioned advantage of the plurality single-member district system is that it stimulates a close contact between the representative and the constituents of a district. Every voter has a clearly designated representative to whom they can turn. On the other hand, a voter's 'representative' will frequently be the candidate that the voter has voted against in the election — making the idea of close representation more a legal fiction than a political reality. This is especially a problem in a plural society in which voters prefer to be represented by a member of their own segment.

2. The plurality method is often said to have the advantage that it allows

the voter to vote for an individual candidate instead of for a group of candidates organized as a party list. However, one form of PR — the single transferable vote (STV), in which voters are asked to rank individual candidates according to their order of preference — has exactly the same vantage. And even in list PR systems, the voter can be given the option of not only selecting a party list, but also of selecting one or more individual candidates on the list.[20]

3. It is also often claimed that plurality is the simplest possible electoral system. This is true, but list PR is almost as simple. It is not much more difficult to pick one party list from among several lists than to select an individual candidate from a group of candidates.

4. A clear disadvantage of the plurality single-member district system is that the determination of the district boundaries is almost inevitably a difficult and contentious issue. In a plural society, gerrymandering in order to give advantages to a particular segment or segments is especially likely to strain peaceful social relations. One great advantage of PR — if applied in large districts of more than about six or seven representatives per district — is that it eliminates these distracting and gerrymandering problems altogether.

5. A final advantage of PR for plural societies is that it allows the representation of the segments without any need for a prior determination of which groups qualify as the constituent segments. This is especially important in plural societies, such as South Africa, in which there is very little agreement on the identity of any of the segments that comprise the plural society and indeed on the question of whether the society is really segmented at all. The advantage of PR is not just that it yields proportional results and that it permits minority representation, but also that it allows the segments to define themselves. This means that the divergent claims about the segmental composition of a plural society can simply be left to the electoral process and do not need to be sorted out in advance.[21]

---

[20] The West German system achieves the same goal by electing half of the Bundestag members in plurality single-member districts and the other half by list PR, and by giving each voter two votes. However, it is still mainly a PR system because the list PR votes determine the overall result. A disadvantage of the German system is that it is rather complex and that many voters do not fully understand it.

[21] One of the disadvantages of electoral systems that try to achieve proportional outcomes without using list PR or STV is that they require a predetermination of the minorities entitled to special treatment. This was one of the weaknesses of the Lebanese system of ethnically balanced states, although some authors have had high praise for it: see, for instance, D. L. Horowitz, *Ethnic groups in conflict*, Berkeley: Univ. of California Press, 1985, pp. 633–5. In general, my recommendation is that, if one wants to achieve proportionality, one should use one of the standard PR systems instead of various semi-proportional or 'mixed' methods; see A. Lijphart, R. Lopez Pintor, and Y. Sone, 'The limited vote and the single nontransferable vote: lessons from the Japanese and Spanish examples', in B. Grofman and A. Lijphart, eds., *Electoral laws and their*

List PR versus STV

Which form of PR is optimal for plural societies? The two main options are list PR, in which the voter chooses among lists of candidates, and STV, in which the voter rank orders individual candidates. The strong proponents of PR, such as Lakeman and Hallet, tend to be strongly in favour of the STV form of PR.[22] There are very few list PR enthusiasts. Although STV can, in some rare circumstances, yield disturbing logical paradoxes,[23] I am persuaded that it is indeed superior to list PR — but only for reasonably homogeneous societies. For plural societies, list PR is clearly the better method for three reasons:

1. Because STV requires the voters to rank order the candidates, it is not a practical method for districts that elect many representatives. The Irish STV system uses three-member, four-member and five-member districts, and in the Australian Senate elections by STV, the normal number of senators to be chosen is six. This number can probably be regarded as the upper limit for practical purposes. Districts with six or less representatives can be gerrymandered[24] — which is particularly undesirable in plural societies. List PR can easily be applied in much larger districts that are immune to gerrymandering.

2. The second disadvantage of the small districts of STV is that it limits the proportionality of the election outcome. As Rae has shown, the district magnitude, that is, the number of representatives a district elects, is clearly and positively related to the proportionality between party votes and party seats: the larger the district, the more proportional the electoral result.[25]

3. A less important reason for preferring list PR to STV in segmented societies is that list PR is simpler for the voters and much simpler for the vote counters. Because the electoral system should be above suspicion, the rather complicated counting procedures of STV are a slight disadvantage.

---

political consequences, New York: Agathon Press, 1986, pp. 154–69; and A. Lijphart, 'Proportionality by non-PR methods: ethnic representation in Belgium, Lebanon, New Zealand, West Germany and Zimbabwe', in Grofman and Lijphart, *Electoral laws*, pp. 113–23.

22 E. Lakeman, 'The case for proportional representation', in Lijphart and Grofman, *Choosing an electoral system*, New York: Praeger, 1984; G. H. Hallett (jun.), 'Proportional representation with the single transferable vote: a basic requirement for legislative elections', in Lijphart and Grofman, *Choosing an electoral system*.

23 S. J. Brams and P. C. Fishburn, 'Some logical defects of the single transferable vote', in Lijphart and Grofman, *Choosing an electoral system*.

24 R. S. Katz, 'The single transferable vote and proportional representation', in Lijphart and Grofman, *Choosing an electoral system*, pp. 138–9.

25 D. W. Rae, *The political consequences of electoral laws*, New Haven: Yale Univ. Press, 1967, pp. 114–25; and R. Taagepera and M. S. Shugart, *Seats and votes: the effects and determinants of electoral systems*, New Haven: Yale Univ. Press, 1989, pp. 112–25.

Consequently, the optimal PR system for plural societies is list PR in relatively large districts — or with a national pool of supplementary seats to maximize proportionality.[26]

List PR and democratic standards

The final question that should be addressed briefly is whether list PR is a sufficiently democratic electoral method. Several scholars — typically in the Anglo-American tradition — have argued that it is not. A recent example is Boulle's statement that 'proportional representation based on electoral lists controlled by party hierarchies' is a 'manipulative' instrument of élite control.[27] One answer to this criticism is that the implied contrast with the plurality method is greatly exaggerated. For instance, in the British plurality system we find a comparable degree of élite dominance: party leaders have usually been able to reserve safe constituencies for themselves and oppose the nomination of undesirable candidates by constituency organizations. If there is any difference in the degree of oligarchical control, it is a minimal one.

Three further points are worth making in this respect:

1. List PR is the electoral method used by a large majority of the world's democracies; the Anglo-American countries with their plurality systems are the deviant cases.

2. The trend is still towards PR; France and the Japanese upper house are the most recent examples of the adoption of PR. Moreover, there is a much stronger probability that plurality countries — especially the UK, Canada and New Zealand — will switch to PR as a result of widespread dissatisfaction with the operation of the plurality system, than that PR countries, in none of which there is any significant desire for the adoption of plurality, will abandon PR.

3. In Dahl's careful qualitative ranking of the world's democracies, the highest category includes eight countries: the four Nordic countries, the three Benelux countries, and Switzerland.[28] All eight use list PR. I do not want to argue that this proves the democratic superiority of list PR over plurality, but I do think that Dahl's finding makes it very hard to argue the opposite case.

---

[26] Such an allocation of seats at two levels in order to increase the proportionality of the election outcome is much more common than is frequently assumed. D. W. Rae refers to it as 'complex districting'; he lists Austria, Denmark, West Germany and Iceland as examples, but he overlooks Belgium and Italy. Since the publication of his book, Sweden has also adopted a two-tiered PR system. See D. W. Rae, *The political consequences*, pp. 20–1, 42–4.

[27] L. J. Boulle, *South Africa and the consociational option: a constitutional analysis*, Cape Town: Juta, 1984, p. 61.

[28] R. A. Dahl, *Polyarchy: participation and opposition*, New Haven: Yale Univ. Press, 1971, pp. 231–48.

Conclusion

To sum up, the electoral system that is optimal for segmented societies is list PR in large districts. The empirical evidence clearly supports this conclusion, and the test of democratic quality does not weaken it in any way. For constitutional engineers, in South Africa and elsewhere, this is a conclusion of great practical importance.

Acknowledgement

This is a revised version of a paper presented at the International Conference on Intergroup Relations of the Human Sciences Research Council, Pretoria, September 1985.

2

Limiting state power: opportunities for greater public participation in policy decisions

Where popular participation in public policy-making is manipulated by the state, hampered by lack of information and informal debate, and subject to overrule or ratification by the executive it can fail to satisfy any of the democratic or educative claims made for it. Much of the policy-making in South Africa is highly centralized, secretive and dominated by the political executive and higher reaches of the bureaucracy. In this chapter potential areas for development of greater public participation are examined.

Introduction

An important current community policy issue in South Africa involves the social desirability of a second nuclear power facility and its physical location. Following the controversy surrounding the first installation at Koeberg, the issue has attracted the attention of environmentalists, health organizations, consumer lobbies, local authorities and other interest groups. In terms of the Nuclear Energy Act 92 of 1982, the Atomic Energy Corporation has the sole right to produce nuclear energy in South Africa. The corporation is a registered company, its shares are wholly-owned by the state and it is managed by a board of directors, most appointed by the Minister of Mineral and Energy Affairs. Apart from its monopoly over production, the corporation is also the only body which can grant licences for the siting and operation of nuclear facilities. A separate body, the Council for Nuclear Safety, has the authority to veto the grant of a licence by the corporation. The members of the council are all appointed by the same minister to whom the corporation is responsible. The corporation can take the council's veto decision on appeal to the minister, whose decision on licensing matters is final. The minister is constitutionally responsible to parliament for such policy decisions, and there is a remote form of judicial control over his activities. No information about the siting, licensing or installation of nuclear facilities may be possessed or disseminated without the permission of the minister. The overall system is policed by the state and enforced through criminal sanctions.

The pattern of administrative decision-making here differs from that in many other cases, but its basic elements are not unique. It shows a highly centralized and secretive form of policy-making, dominated by the political executive and higher reaches of the bureaucracy, with only a few restricted outside influences.

It contains some checks and balances within that hierarchy, but it has only nominal political accountability for final policy outcomes, and virtually no legal or popular controls. It also accommodates no public participation in the decision-making process, despite the implications of the final decision for several interest groups and local communities.

Participatory democracy postulates a set of political institutions which gives people the maximum possible freedom to take decisions affecting their own lives. This chapter is concerned with the question of public participation in administrative policy-making.

Policy and policy-making

Modern governments are preoccupied with policy — its formulation, implementation and adaptation. This is evident in every sphere of social concern, from the control of the environment, to the education of children, to the accumulation of state revenue. As policy bears directly on the citizens of the state, it is debated, disputed, challenged and resisted by those whom it affects or frustrates. Ultimately, however, it can be applied and enforced through the coercive powers possessed by the state.

State policy is usually identified with the common good, that is, a public authority's plan for promoting the general interest. Needless to say, where basic constitutional rights are not evenly distributed, as in contemporary South Africa, state policy can assume a very sectional nature, even when promoted in collectivist terms.

The most formal manifestation of state policy is legislation, which in South Africa can be enacted by the central parliament, by sub-national bodies such as local or homeland authorities, and by executive and administrative agencies. However, while parliament as the primary policy-maker provides the broad guidelines, the executive, through its many agencies, plays the dominant role over time in implementing, developing and adapting state policy. In South Africa this means the cabinet, cabinet committees, such as the National Security Council, government departments and semi-state organs.

In reality, policy is the product of a wide range of political and economic forces. The actors involved include political office-bearers, a range of public administrators, various non-state economic and social interest groups, and, with increasing frequency, external sources of pressure. Moreover, policy-making is too dynamic and flexible to remain centred in parliament's law-making. The universal trend is for policy to be formulated and developed by the administrative arm of government. This is not only a hard reality, but also a defensible one. However, few would argue that the administration is a politically neutral force in government. Decisions by public authorities involve social and political choices in the fullest sense, yet they can be very isolated from direct social pressures.

Proposals to change this system have centred on new 'control' mechanisms appropriate to the administrative state. A bill of rights, judicial review, ombudsmen and other separation of powers-inspired institutions all involve more of the same and are premised on a limited understanding of how the constitutional system works.

But, if the centralized and secretive structures of decision-making can be transformed, it is possible to re-introduce control of government in a more positive form, namely through increased popular participation in policy-making. This has implications for the courts, political parties, caucuses and the mandate theory of government.

Once it is accepted that many of the policy decisions facing public authorities need not be subjected to 'expert' resolution, the way is opened for deciding them in a more legislative-type context involving the adjustment of competing claims by different interest groups, including the relevant state agency. In this way the accountability of government becomes a basic ingredient of the decision-making process. The best method of controlling state power is by making its exercise, in its many manifestations, more representative.

Participation: categories and objectives

Where popular participation is manipulated by the state, hampered by lack of information and informed debate, and subject to ratification or overrule by the executive, it can fail to satisfy any of the democratic or educative objectives claimed for it. But where it is widely pursued under conditions of extensive informed discussion and debate, and relatively free from state manipulation, it can enhance democratic and responsive government. Some of the variables in this context are outlined in the text that follows.

Manipulation

Manipulation in effect means non-participation. It occurs when public involvement in decision-making is rudimentary, qualified and designed by power-holders to 'educate' or 'cure' the participants. The main institutions of manipulation are nominated bodies with limited functions; participation in them is invariably controversial. There are several examples of manipulative 'participation' in South Africa's constitutional history, including the Natives Representative Council between 1936 and 1949, dubbed the 'toy telephone' by the participants because there was never any response to the submissions made through it, and, more recently, the President's Council, at least as far as some recommendations on the constitution and Group Areas legislation are concerned.

Consultation

Consultation provides citizens and interest groups with a more substantial platform from which to make representations, but under conditions which exclude the power to ensure that their recommendations will actually be heeded. There is little scope for follow-through and no assurance of changing the status quo. The process may be designed to placate those involved and their followers, without the state agency forfeiting its real decision-making power.

Co-optation

Co-optation is a more sophisticated form of consultation in that participants are party to actual decision-making processes and might have a marginal influence over policy, but the system's overall design ensures that the influence is limited. It is employed by the dominant group to achieve the political co-optation of opposition élites, thereby strengthening the dominant group and dividing and weakening opposition forces. Decision-making is usually secretive to avoid the scrutiny of constituency groups, themselves the ultimate objects of the co-optive tactics.

An example of this system is the national cabinet under the Tricameral Parliament on which the leaders of the majority coloured and Indian parties have served as junior partners without portfolio; they acquired constitutional responsibility but no political power. It is also evident in the homelands system and the proposed National Statutory Council.

Partnership

In a partnership arrangement citizens can negotiate and engage in consensual decision-making with traditional policy formulators. This involves a much higher degree of citizen power, best illustrated by the referendum mechanism. In South Africa in the educational field there are indications of the development of limited forms of partnership for white parents, dictated partly by the state's financial problems. There is also a partnership arrangement with some professional associations.

Delegation

The state may delegate policy formulation to private or semi-private agencies, with or without providing a framework within which they must operate. The system has been applied to professional organizations in South Africa and in the labour relations arena.

All these categories suggest that there can be forms of 'participation' in policy decisions without control slipping out of state hands. Whether participation is ritualistic or effective depends on the policy-making involved and the policy-maker.

Existing forms of participation in South Africa

The highest constitutional and legal form of policy-making, the central legislative process, does not provide a good example of participatory government. Parliament is predominantly unrepresentative of and out of touch with those for whom it legislates. The mandate principle of government has little force; the political executive dominates the legislative process. Some bills are published in advance in the Government Gazette and occasionally representations are invited from the public. In a few instances hearings are held, but generally the legislative process is tightly controlled and closed to outside influences.

In South Africa there is an extraordinary concentration of policy-making power in the hands of the central government. With few exceptions, most of the significant constitutional developments since Union have increased and consolidated Pretoria's power. This has affected the authority of parliament and severely diminished its effective policy-making functions. The following arrangements must be seen in the context of these historical tendencies and contemporary realities.

Elections

The most direct form of electoral participation in policy-making occurs in local government. In terms of the categories of participation already referred to, this can be classified as a delegation by the state of policy-making power to local white residents. However, the increasing pervasiveness of the central government's policies, particularly in matters such as residential segregation, planning and security, has detracted from the social and political significance of electoral participation in local government.

For those excluded from local government franchise because of their race, the state in recent years has attempted to provide some electoral participation, but the constraints on the various systems have rendered them predominantly of the co-optive/consultative type. In fact, the various institutions have not attained even these limited official objectives. There are few local authorities for Indians and coloureds, although legislation to cater for them has existed for over two decades. While a succession of urban councils, community councils and local authorities with increasing degrees of electiveness have been established for Africans, they have been fiercely resisted by their intended participants. Here the state's stringent conditions for African electoral participation have jeopardized their own initiatives.

Investigation

Where an administrative authority engages in structured investigations before making policy decisions it can introduce elements of indirect participation into policy-making, but often of a consultative/manipulative type. In South Africa investigations are regularly conducted through commissions of inquiry appointed in terms of the head of state's common law prerogative.

However, they provide only limited and indirect participation in administrative policy-making. Both commissions of inquiry and the permanent statutory bodies, such as the Group Areas Board, Housing Council and Law Commission, are appointed by the executive. Moreover, it is usually the executive itself which has the power and resources to formulate the final policy, in possible disregard of the participants' opinions and with little legal or political sanction. This has happened even to permanent, state-promoted, investigative bodies such as the President's Council, whose recommendations on aspects of the constitution and group areas have not modified government policies.

Consultation

Consultation is a prevalent feature of all modern systems of government and is provided for extensively in the South African constitutional system. The most direct form of popular consultation is provided for in the Referendums Act 108 of 1983. This empowers the executive, in its discretion, to hold plebiscites among white, Indian and coloured voters, or among any single group of the electorate or in any regional area of the country, on any policy matter. The electoral verdict is neither self-executing nor binding, and this consultative device has been used only once since its inception, and then only among white voters. As another example, the public authority is required to consult with a body representing a trade or profession or other interest group, ranging from the Estate Agents' Board to the Diamond Board, before it makes policy, often in the form of regulations. Wider consultation is provided for in the occasional statutory requirement that draft proclamations be gazetted for a certain period before coming into effect, with a notice inviting interested persons to make representations on them during this time.

The common weakness with consultation mechanisms is that they do not ensure that those involved will be able to influence the substance of policy decisions. The problem is compounded in the legal context in that the courts have interpreted the term consultation in the most formalistic of senses and so as not to impart any real control on the state authority. As consultation is often the most feasible way of accommodating public participation in administrative policy-making, its improvement, extension and enforcement would be an important element of constitutional change.

Mediation

Mediation involves an attempt to accommodate the opposing views of two or more parties through negotiation and reconciliation. The process is participatory in that the individuals or groups involved are part of the negotiation process and party to the final compromise. Mediation is encountered most consistently in the field of industrial relations where legislation provides for the compulsory appointment of conciliation boards and mediators in the case of management–labour disputes, instead of allowing for crude state intervention. However, in the conventional administrative process formal mechanisms for mediation are not conspicuous.

Initiation

There are few situations where the public has formal avenues for initiating changes in policy in South Africa, though the impact of informal pressure by powerful interest groups is undoubted, even on central legislation. This can be contrasted with the Swiss situation where formal public initiation of policy is one of the ingredients in a developed participatory system; for example, since the late nineteenth century a total of 100 000 voters have been able to petition the federal government for specific legislation and thereby initiate the law-making process.

In South Africa the closest equivalent is found in the competence of statutory bodies representing specific professional interests to initiate rule-making procedures. However, in most cases they lack the power to make them effective.

Autonomous policy-making

West German law guarantees the right of autonomous legislation to communities, universities, professional bodies, broadcasting establishments, and other similar institutions, each within its sphere of jurisdiction. There is no such guarantee in the South African context, though there are some similarities in certain areas. Certain bodies have either full or partial autonomous policy-making powers within a framework of state control. Industrial councils can decide on their own constitutions and their agreements constitute a form of domestic legislation within the industry concerned, though they are conditional on the minister's declaring them binding. The South African Teachers' Council for whites can issue regulations itself, though these are also subject to ministerial veto.

Adjudication

Much administrative policy is developed by boards, tribunals and officials through case by case adjudication. Where those affected by the decision are allowed to participate in the proceedings, the emerging policy becomes, to a small extent, susceptible to public influence. Inevitably this sphere is dominated by lawyers and the legal mode of thinking, which makes it inappropriate for some types of decision with a very high policy content. It is also an expensive method of influencing or modifying state policy.

Overall, the various South African procedures referred to in this outline of existing forms of participation do not have a high degree of effectiveness, legitimacy or political significance, for reasons which affect them all in some degree. Firstly, they exist in a political and institutional context which provides little support or incentive for public participation in policy making. Secondly, they are qualified in many instances by the peculiar conditions and restraints, sometimes racial, of the public law domain. Thirdly, there are no uniform procedures or minimal prerequisites which administrative bodies are required to follow. A reference to some comparative models of policy-making lends perspective to these institutions and their shortcomings.

Comparative models of participation

From the many comparative models of public participation in policy-making three relatively random examples have been chosen to illustrate possibilities for development in South Africa. Each is predominantly associated with a different constitutional/legal system.

Public inquiries

Investigation and inquiry is a prerequisite for good administrative policy-making; it also provides a useful mechanism for popular participation. In the United Kingdom the public inquiry is now a developed institution for determining state policy with the benefit of public involvement.

Unlike the South African situation, the procedures for public inquiries in the UK are more or less uniform. They are regulated by one general statute and the many specific pieces of legislation which stipulate their use. This treatment has obviated two of the shortcomings affecting South African commissions of inquiry, namely that affected and interested parties can be excluded from their investigations, and that they are not always held in public.

The range of state activities which are preceded by inquiries in the UK is very wide. It includes policy decisions on road and highway planning, the siting of power stations and airports, the compulsory acquisition of land, slum clearance and other major public works. Planning is the most frequent subject of the process, and even when a minister can make a decision which has a high policy content, an inquiry is required before the order can become legally effective. Thus, if the minister wishes to order the clearance of an area because of poor housing or slum conditions, the plan must first be advertised and made available for inspection. Owners and occupiers of the land as well as other potential 'victims' of the decision must be notified of their right to make objections; if there are any objections, a public inquiry must be held. While an inquiry's findings are not binding, it is politically difficult for a minister to ignore them.

While there are legitimate criticisms of the system, inquiries do perform a useful social function in modifying, constraining and, in some case, even thwarting state policy. They do so through a relatively uniform process which is accessible to the appropriate parties and contains internal checks on abuse of discretion and secrecy. Not only have the original reservations of the bureaucracy proved groundless, but the administrators have, contrary to their intuitive predictions, found that the procedures help good administration and enhance their own credibility, even though they may curb their discretionary powers. This is a positive factor for the possibilities of this institution in South Africa.

Participation in rules and regulations

Executive heads or their administrative subordinates are generally given the legal discretion to specify policy on matters of detail. In American public law this discretion has been controlled, restricted and guided through an extensive system of rule-and-regulation-making according to uniform procedures laid down in the Administrative Procedure Act and developed by the courts. Not only does this system uphold the elementary principle of justice that rules should be formulated prospectively, but it also accommodates significant public influence in the process of policy-making in matters ranging from environmental conservation to road safety and highway planning.

There are basically two kinds of rule-making, formal and informal. The formal type, which is not very prevalent, comprises a range of trial-type procedures such as an oral hearing, cross-examination by participating parties, and the submission of proposed findings and conclusions to the participants. The model for this system is the legal process.

For informal or notice and comment rule-making the model is the legislative hearing at which interest groups are allowed to petition for the issuance or amendment of rules. An agency must give public notice of proposed rule-making. Parties have the right to make written submissions on the draft rules and, in some cases, to participate at an oral hearing; agencies have to justify their final rules and inform the public of their purpose and scope.

The system upholds three basic values in the administrative process — fairness and accuracy of decisions; efficient, low-cost resolution of policy issues; and participant satisfaction. The advantages accrue to the agencies themselves, to the interest groups being directly regulated, and to other affected parties. One of the main criticisms of the system is that it allows for capture by well-organized, well-endowed and self-interested groups at the expense of smaller and poorer interests, and for potential capture of the legitimate public interest as well.

South Africa does not have the developed American system. There is, however, no lack of administrative discretion, which could be structured and guided through the rule-making process. Where public authorities, from the State President, to individual ministers, to subordinate officials, enact regulations there are some participatory elements: regulations must be publicized in the Government Gazette, the policy formulator may have to consult a statutory board or council on which interest groups are represented, and so on. These arrangements apply mainly in the environmental and planning fields, and in respect of the rules for professional associations.

However, although 'participation' is not wholly alien to the administrative rule-making process, it is limited in scope, effectiveness and significance. It is neither uniform nor accessible to deserving interests, and it operates in the context of massive restraints on political organization and official information. As there is likely to be a powerful executive and administrative branch for the long-term constitutional future of South Africa, regardless of political contingencies, rule-making constitutes an important way of making the exercise of discretion more democratic and accountable. Its extension would have distinct advantages for constitutional change in South Africa by providing for functional decentralization and enhancing political pluralism.

Direct legislation

Direct legislation goes further than public inquiry or notice and comment rule-making along the road of public participation in state policy-making. It also provides a far-reaching limitation on the power of the central government, as well as on political parties and caucuses. There are at least four institutional variations of this mechanism:

▷ *Direct initiative:* voters are allowed to make legislative proposals, which are voted into effect or rejected by the voters themselves.

▷ *Indirect initiative:* voters can petition the legislature for legislative change, which is then dealt with by the legislature.

▷ *Popular referendum:* voters have the automatic right to accept or reject laws passed by the legislature.

▷ *Legislative referendum:* the legislature can decide in its discretion whether or not to submit its proposals to the voters for ratification.

In all cases there is an assumption that citizens are better suited than elected representatives to decide policy questions.

Direct legislation, not a widespread practice, is often associated with the Swiss system of government. It operates at all three levels of government — national, cantonal and communal — in the form of both the initiative and the referendum.

There has also been an upsurge of direct legislation in the United States in recent years. It operates mainly in the form of the ballot proposition, in which voters at candidate elections are invited to indicate their preferences on specific policy issues, in particular taxation measures, education proposals and questions of nuclear power. It operates at state, county and city level, and twenty-six states now have some form of initiative or popular referendum at state level. (Direct participation does not exist at the national level of American government.) It is less élitist than traditional methods of determining policy and less alienating for those who will be affected by policy change.

Direct legislation is an important supplement to the normal legislative process. However, in South Africa direct legislation could become socially counter-productive if used by the white electorate to frustrate desegregation measures. Ultimately, this institution could not be implemented at the national level before the introduction of a system of candidate elections based on universal franchise.

Prerequisites for South African developments

Ultimately, a national political settlement in South Africa will be necessary to provide the cornerstone around which participatory mechanisms for policy-making can be constructed. Until that stage, reformist measures are not likely to be successful because they will be, or will be seen to be, manipulative or co-optive. Nevertheless, it is relevant to refer to other changes which would be necessary prerequisites for meaningful participation in administrative decision-making, whether locally or elsewhere. Three prerequisites are referred to in the text that follows.

Information

Access to state-controlled information is an absolute pre-condition for public participation in administrative decision-making. The limitations of official information in South Africa are notorious; they also constitute an incursion on many other civil rights.

Participatory mechanisms would require at least three major improvements in this area:

1. a political context in which there could be free and critical debate of state policies;

2. access to official information, statistics, plans, reports and proposals relating to specific programmes proposed by a public authority, including the right to copy relevant documentation; and

3. meetings which are open to the public and at which relevant evidence is aired and findings and recommendations, together with reasons, are provided.

Each of these developments would require fundamental changes to aspects of the state system and administrative practice.

Uniform procedures

An important element in participatory mechanisms would be the provision of a core of procedures common to all relevant kinds of policy-making. This would provide two advantages:

1. It would compel all tribunals, boards and other public authorities to satisfy minimum standards of participation, regardless of the subject matter of a particular policy decision or the whims of particular officials.

2. *Public familiarity:* if participatory procedures are unfamiliar and alienating for the public, an accessibility problem will arise. The American Administrative Procedure Act provides a precedent. A supervising agency, or participatory ombudsman, could provide an internal check over compliance with standardized procedural requirements.

Public funding

As administrative policy-making shifts from an 'expertise' model to one of pluralistic participation, the problem of the under-representation of indigent and unorganized interests is accentuated. Even minimal funding could be problematic for some interests. To prevent the 'public interest' being captured by well-organized and well-funded bodies it would be essential in certain circumstance to provide public funding. Uneven distribution patterns in South Africa make this requirement paramount.

Areas of possible development

In examining areas in which the development of participatory programmes might be considered it is assumed that for the foreseeable future a strong centralized executive authority in South Africa will not lightly relinquish control over many strategic areas of policy-making, including security, foreign policy, public finance and economic affairs. Those referred to in the text that follows already show some participatory tendencies.

Planning

Planning is present at all levels of government in the modern administrative state and provides an appropriate site for public participation. Successful planning, moreover, depends largely on its popular acceptability. It is regarded as one of the most successful areas of participation in the UK where regular use is made of the public inquiry in the planning process.

In South Africa there are two important statutory sources of planning regulation. At the national level the Physical Planning Act 88 of 1967, as amended, empowers the minister to establish a guide-plan committee to compile a draft guide-plan for the future spatial development of a specific area. The committees are intended to represent the three tiers of government and various other institutions. Any person, including a local authority, may submit proposals and at a later stage make representations on the guide-plan.

At the sub-national level town planning schemes are regulated by different ordinances in each province. In day-to-day planning these schemes are of paramount importance. In the Transvaal, for example, schemes can be proposed by a local authority after investigations by a town planning committee involving some public representation.

A major limitation is that all local planning is subject to the unilaterally imposed Group Areas Act and other central laws affecting the use and ownership of land. Planning measures also do not affect those living in informal housing areas; in some metropolitan centres this means most of the inhabitants. In this context note should be taken of the very informal planning negotiations which have taken place in some areas of Natal; they have involved public authorities and community organizations representing those living in informal housing settlements. Residents, assisted by professional town planners, have succeeded in co-structuring upgrading plans for their areas on a very low-key level. With informal urbanization so prevalent in South Africa, participatory initiatives such as these need to be developed.

Environmental affairs

Environmental policy is linked to planning: however, there has not been much progress in this field in South Africa, partly because of the late emergence of active conservation and environmental lobbies. In other countries the area has long been contested by relevant interest groups.

The Environmental Conservation Act 100 of 1982 reflects the South African state's attitude to participation in this field. The act empowers the Minister of Environmental Affairs to make a wide range of regulations relating to matters such as solid waste control, littering and noise pollution, after consultation with the Council for the Environment. Public participation is limited and constrained. The council is a nominated body and has no necessary influence on the regulations; public representations can be made only late in the process and do not have to be actively considered by the policy-makers. Even local authorities have no special input into the drafting process, despite the fact that regulations can be made binding in particular municipal areas and require certain actions from local councils.

The Council for the Environment advises the minister on a range of matters affecting the environment, including the introduction of legislation. It can, at its discretion, receive representations from any party on such matters, provided a memorandum has first been presented to it. There is also some public input into policy on declared nature areas.

As some aspects of environmental policy are well-suited to local variation, this should be an appropriate area for the introduction of extensive public participation. Public inquiries, the disclosure of proposed policy and programmes, and the funding of participants would improve the quality of decision-making and enhance its credibility among different interest groups. They might also help to conserve and improve the natural and built environments.

Education

Since the early reign of the present government, tight national controls have been maintained over educational policy, which has been modified and amended to reflect its ideology. Tertiary education has been something of an exception in that universities have enjoyed autonomy over their curricula and internal statutes (the latter still requiring ministerial approval and parliamentary tabling), while being dependent on the state for both their funds and the definition of who might teach and be taught in their lecture rooms. Non-tertiary education was of provincial concern in terms of the Union constitution, but over time has come to be extensively controlled from Pretoria.

In 1986 legislation was introduced to 'provide greater participation by the organised teaching profession and organised parent community in the education in schools and the training of teachers'. In formulating education policy the minister must consult the education councils in each province. These comprise local education officials, ministerial nominees, and representatives of the organized teaching profession and organized parent community in the province. All proposed legislation relating to education must be referred to the provincial education councils. As before, however, final control remains in Pretoria, subject to parliament's guiding principles.

Committees exist in each province to allow some public input into white educational matters. At every provincial school a committee must be established to exercise specific functions. In each province there are also a number of regional committees, with a range of financial and advisory powers, which are elected through a ward system by the relevant school committees.

In comparison with past arrangements, these regulations provide a new approach to participation in education matters. While tight state control is kept over major policy issues, the consultative mechanisms have been expanded and some autonomous decision-making, particularly in financial matters, is delegated to bodies representing predominantly parental interests. Yet, even after these reforms, the system is far removed from the extensive local control over education which exists in some countries. Furthermore, it leaves quite unaffected the whole spectrum of black school education which is more rigidly controlled by the central state and suffers from acute problems of quality, organization and legitimacy.

Conclusion

A national representative institution will be an essential feature of a future political settlement in South Africa. The most important issues of national policy should be settled by this body and be embodied in statutory form. However, for the newly-enfranchised electorate the choice of legislative representatives must be complemented by active choices of policy. This will require forms of public participation in administrative decision-making more substantial and more varied than those which presently exist.

They will promise several advantages. Participation will broaden the official perspective on issues of policy, which should lead to better decision-making. If the participation is authentic, it will increase the legitimacy and acceptability of government actions. It will allow for issue fragmentation and the bypassing of powerful and undemocratic party structures, which at present manipulate the limited popular participation in government. It will allow for decentralization and regional and local variation in policy-making. And it will provide an educational process to transform individuals from subjects of the state into political citizens.

The potential difficulties include citizen apathy and ignorance, prohibitive expense, and delay in the governing process. However, if a basic premise of democratic constitutionalism is that it can only be sustained by democracy in institutional detail, then the disadvantages must be regarded as inescapable costs of the system. It is also significant that subordinate groups are now not only demanding the vote, but also full participation in all areas of government.

Participatory mechanisms should be more seriously considered in the South African debate on restructuring the state system. The objective should be to provide political institutions which will give people the maximum possible freedom to take decisions affecting their own lives. These recommendations are therefore tentative suggestions for redesigning the state system in the interests of more democratic, responsive and legitimate policymaking. In the process, law would not replace politics, as some advocates of judicial review and other separation of powers institutions would have. Instead, rejuvenated legal institutions would be used to facilitate policymaking and provide the best circumstances in which political choices could be made. The 'control' of government would have more of a positive than a negative orientation.

The decision on the location of a nuclear power facility at Burgtownville in the 1990s, and on the conditions under which it will operate, was taken in terms of the Nuclear Energy Act 37 of 1990 in the following way: A committee of the Atomic Energy Corporation, a public company with equal state and private shareholding and managed by a board elected by shareholders, conducted a preliminary survey into possible sites and reported to the main body. The corporation, after consultation with the Department of Health and Environmental Affairs, identified four possible sites in the light of the report's findings. These locations were advertised in the Gazette and media, together with a policy statement from the corporation on the feasibility of each site. Public inquiries, at which all interested parties were allowed to participate, were held close to each potential site. The participation of local authorities below town council status was funded by the department, as was that of indigent applicants whose credentials were approved by the participation ombudsman in the Department of Consumer Affairs. An environmental impact study, as well as all documentation before the inquiry committee, was made available to participants. The committee's recommendations were submitted to the corporation, which took a preliminary decision on the siting and submitted it to the Council for Nuclear Safety, a body of nominated and elected members representing scientific, consumer, environmental and health interests and falling under the office of the State President. As a consequence of the council's first recommendation, the corporation was required to file further health and financial reports. The corporation's decision, together with the council's final recommendation, was submitted to parliament for ratification and subsequent proclamation by the head of state. The conditions of operation and regulations controlling hazardous waste were finalized after notice and comment procedures involving participation by interested parties; they included provision for the waste disposal requirements to be judicially enforced at the suit of private bodies such as the 'Nuclear Watchdog Committee'. As the provisions of the new Code of Administrative Procedure and Openness in Government Act had been complied with throughout, no judicial review of the decision-making record was instituted.

Bibliography of principal references

Baxter, L. G., *Administrative law*, Cape Town: Juta, 1984.

Berry, W. G., *Local government law in the Transvaal*, Durban: Butterworths, 1983.

Boulle, L. J., *Participatory democracy and the administration — South African prospects*, Pretoria: HSRC, 1984.

Craig, P. P., *Administrative law*, London: Sweet and Maxwell, 1983.

Dessemontet, F. and Anstey, T., *Introduction to Swiss law*, Deventer: Kluwer, 1983.

Flick, G. A., *Federal administrative law*, Sydney: The Law Book Co. Ltd., 1983.

Fuggle, R. F. and Rabie, M. A., *Environmental concerns in South Africa: technical and legal perspectives*, Cape Town: Juta, 1983.

Ganz, G., *Administrative procedures*, London: Sweet and Maxwell, 1974.

Hughes, C. J., *The parliament of Switzerland*, London: Cassel and Co., 1962.

Kahn, M., *Planning, process and participation*, Pietermaritzburg: Univ. of Natal Press, 1982.

Magleby, D. L., *Direct legislation. Voting on ballot propositions in the United States*, Baltimore: John Hopkins Univ. Press, 1984.

McAuslan, P. and McEldowney, J. F., *Law, legitimacy and the constitution*, London: Sweet and Maxwell, 1985.

Pateman, C., *Participation and democratic theory*, Cambridge: Cambridge Univ. Press, 1970.

Singh, M. P., *German administrative law in common law perspective*, Berlin: Springer-Verlag, 1985.

Sout, R. M., *Administrative law in Ireland*, Dublin: Inst. of Public Administration, 1985.

Turner, R., *The eye of the needle. Towards participatory democracy in South Africa*, Johannesburg: Ravan Press, 1980.

Wade, H. W. R., *Administrative law*, Oxford: Clarendon Press, 1982.

Walker, G., *Initiative and referendum: the people's law*, Sydney: Law Book Co. Ltd., 1987.

3 A bill of rights

Nic J. J. Olivier

> At the request of the government, the South African Law Commission has drawn up a working paper on group and human rights in South Africa, including its proposals for a bill of rights. This chapter examines human rights in general as a prelude to its discussion of the proposed bill, and includes relevant sections from other human rights documents.

Introduction

It is generally accepted that contemporary Western doctrines of human rights derive from John Locke,[1] who argued that a treaty was entered into between members of the community to create a state community. Thereafter, a second treaty (the social contract) was concluded between the members of the community and a specific body or person which created a legitimate authority, that is, government. The subjects could unilaterally end the contract and appoint a new authority if this government failed to fulfil its obligations.

It was, however, recognized that the so-called 'inalienable rights' could not exist as absolutes, and would have to be balanced with the interests of the state. Human rights could thus be limited by the state.

The classical humanist view was embodied in Western enactments of human rights until after World War II. In these enactments (for example, the American Declaration of Independence of 1776 and the Bill of Rights of 1791) the question arises of the limits of state authority, particularly the negative limitation of state actions in the private sphere. Since 1945 the **account** in the newer Humanism has been on the relativistic approach to the protection of human rights. For example, the West German constitution of 1949 contains a number of inalienable fundamental rights, but also a

---

[1] Refer to the example of J. D. Van Der Vyver, 'The concept of human rights: its history, contents and meaning', in C. F. Forsyth and J. E. Schiller, eds., *Human rights: the Cape Town Conference*, Cape Town: Juta, 1979, pp. 10–32; and E. De Villiers, *Die geskiedenis van menseregte*, Cape Town: Tafelberg, 1984, pp. 9–38.

summary of limitations. These rights may not be abrogated, nor may their substance be altered.[2]

Marxist-Leninist theories of human rights

Because individualistic theories of human rights could not eradicate exploitation and inequality, Marxist-Leninist writers criticized them sharply. Karl Marx in his *Zur Judenfrage* (1843) viewed the classical theory of rights as describing the egoistic man able to withdraw to his own private sphere to the prejudice of others to enjoy and dispose of his accumulated wealth. Marx believed that real freedom of man could only be realized through involvement with the community.

This does not mean that human rights are rejected by Marxists. The idea of equality should be embodied in the economy and welfare policy. The constitutions of socialist countries emphasize this approach, protecting these rights and differentiate between:

▷ primary social rights, for example, the rights to labour and to education; and

▷ secondary classical human rights, which may be exercised only in so far as they do not conflict with the community interest.

Third World human rights theories

The Third World approach is based on a strong anti-colonialist perspective. The most important rights recognized are the so-called social rights and the right to self-determination. Although this appears analogous to the socialist approach, the fundamental difference is that human rights should be utilized not only to eradicate the disadvantages caused by colonialism, but also to prevent further disadvantages. Third World theory holds that some social rights and the right to self-determination should also be recognized in terms of which the international economic order should be radically restructured.

The United Nations[3]

The Charter of the United Nations has as its object in Article 55 the promotion of 'universal respect for, and observance of, human rights and fundamental freedoms for all without distinction as to race, sex, language or religion'.

---

2 See amongst others J. D. Van Der Vyver, *Die beskerming van menseregte in Suid-Afrika*, Cape Town: Juta, 1975, pp. 8–9; and De Villiers, *Die geskiedenis van menseregte*, p. 22.

3 See in general Van Der Vyver, *Die beskerming van menseregte*, pp. 35–7; J. D. Van Der Vyver, *Seven lectures on human rights*, Cape Town: Juta, 1976, pp. 27–138; and De Villiers, *Die geskiedenis van menseregte*, pp. 19–27.

Article 56 of the Charter states that the signatories undertake 'to take joint and separate actions in cooperation with the organisation for the achievement of the purpose set forth in Article 55'.

Although it is generally accepted that this international document is not binding (one reason being the absence of effective enforcement), it is commonly viewed as an instrument for the promotion of human rights, and thus has moral persuasive power.

Because no human rights charter existed at the establishment of the United Nations, a Commission on Human Rights was created to formulate the following:

▷ a universal declaration of human rights;

▷ a treaty for the recognition of human rights in international law; and

▷ a treaty for the effective recognition and protection of human rights.

The Universal Declaration of Human Rights of 1948 was ratified by most members of the United Nations. Article 2 of the Declaration contains the equality principle:

> Everyone is entitled to all the rights and freedoms set forth in this declaration, without distinction of any kind, such as race, colour, sex, language, religion, political or other opinion, national or social origin, property, birth or other status. Furthermore, no distinction shall be made on the basis of the political, jurisdictional or international status of the country or territory to which a person belongs, whether it be independent, trust, non self governing or under any other limitation of sovereignty.

The declaration contains classical liberal human rights (Articles 3–21) as well as social rights (for example, the rights to social security, remuneration, labour and recreation — Articles 22–7). It can thus be said that the declaration is the first human rights document to contain Western as well as socialist views on human rights.

However, its provisions lack instruments of enforcement and are therefore non-binding.

As regards the Commission's second aim (the formulation of international law treaties) the United Nations approved two conventions in 1966:

1. the International Convention on Economic, Social and Cultural Rights, which contains the typical social rights that are predominant in the human rights approaches of the socialist and Third World countries; and

2. the International Convention on Civil and Political Rights, which is based on the classical liberal Western human rights tradition.

The Third World human right of self-determination of national units was embodied in both treaties. This resulted in the lack of any real progress with the Commission's third aim — to formulate a treaty for the effective enforcement of human rights.

South Africa voted against the adoption of two treaties dealing with the elimination of discrimination: the International Convention on the Elimination of all Forms of Racial Discrimination (1965), and the International Convention on the Suppression and Punishment of the Crime of Apartheid (1973).

South Africa has steadfastly refused to endorse either the UN Declaration or these two conventions. The reason is self-evident; the policy of apartheid violates all these human rights provisions.

The European community[4]

The European Convention of Human Rights of 1953 contains measures which recognize certain human rights as well as an institutionalized system to protect and enforce them. In its preamble those fundamental freedoms that form the basis of justice and peace are recognized. It aims further to take the first steps for the collective enforcement of certain of the rights stated in the Universal Declaration (of human rights).

In contrast with the Universal Declaration of Human Rights' vague and unqualified terminology, the European Convention of Human Rights describes the particulars and limitations of the various rights and freedoms.

Section 1 of the European Convention contains an inventory of human rights. It was supplemented by a first protocol in 1954 and a fourth in 1968.

They may be limited by statutory provisions whenever it is necessary for the survival of democratic society: in the interest of national security and of public safety, for the maintenance of 'public order', for the prevention of crime, for the protection of rights and freedoms of others.

Although the classical view of human rights is predominant in several of the older human rights charters, recent bills of rights indicate a change in the direction of qualified protection, especially with regard to public interest.

In Second and Third World constitutions the so-called social rights (which influence the political, economical, cultural and social community life) and the right to self-determination are perceived to be more important than the classical freedom rights.

In recent national bills of rights, as well as regional and international treaties, the more recent Western and socialist as well as the Third World approach can be recognized.

Effective mechanisms for the enforcement and protection of human rights are, however, (with a few exceptions) non-existent.

---

[4] See Van Der Vyver, *Die beskerming van menseregte*, pp. 152–4; Van Der Vyver, *Seven lectures*, pp. 152–3; F. Ermacora, 'The system of the protection of human rights within the framework of the Council of Europe', in Forsyth, and Schiller, *The Cape Town Conference*, pp. 236–47; and Article 2.3 of the European Convention of Human Rights.

Classification

One way of classifying human rights is as follows:

▷ individual or substantive human rights (including the general, civil and cultural human rights);

▷ procedural human rights (due process of law);

▷ socio-economic rights;

▷ group rights.

These categories contain among other items the specific human rights that are outlined in the text that follows.

Individual human rights[5]

1. General

▷ Right to human life and liberty

▷ Freedom of assembly

▷ Freedom of association

▷ Freedom of conscience

▷ Non-discrimination (equality)

▷ Right to property

2. Civil rights[6]

▷ Right not to render military service

▷ Right to choose one's place of residence

▷ Right to citizenship

▷ Right to claim compensation

▷ Right to claim redress

▷ Right to criticize

▷ Right to express one's opinion

▷ Right to freedom of conscience

▷ Right to freedom of movement

▷ Right to freedom of religion

▷ Right to freedom of speech and of the press

▷ Right to freedom of thought

---

5 Van Der Vyver, *Die beskerming van menseregte*, pp. 5–40, 58–60, 74–5, 89–99, 130–4, 148–56; and Van Der Vyver, *Seven lectures*, pp. 59–65, 78, 112–26, 149. See, for the position in South Africa, amongst others, J. Dugard, 'Human rights in South Africa: retrospect and prospect', in Forsyth, and Schiller, *The Cape Town Conference*, pp. 263–85.

6 Van Der Vyver, *Seven lectures*, pp. 17–23, 53–78, 85–8, 110–14, 125–6, 139–41; A. S. Mathews, *Freedom, state security and the Rule of Law*, Cape Town: Juta, 1986, pp. 124–39; and Van Der Vyver, *Die beskerming van menseregte*, pp. 5–6, 16, 21–39, 71–3, 96, 114–36, 103–104, 147–9, 168, 178, 183.

▷ Right to have a present situation maintained intact
▷ Right to have recourse to a court
▷ Right to have the environment preserved
▷ Right to information
▷ Right to integrity of one's personality
▷ Right to keep and bear arms
▷ Right to liberty
▷ Right to life
▷ Right to privacy
▷ Right to publish
▷ Right to require a check on scientific development and technical progress
▷ Right to secrecy of post and telecommunications
▷ Right to use one's language
▷ Right to use public amenities

3. Cultural rights[7]

▷ Right of access to arts and sciences
▷ Right of copyright
▷ Right to education
▷ Right to free development of one's person
▷ Right to freedom of expression
▷ Right to incorporeal things
▷ Right to write

4. Political rights[8]

▷ Right of asylum
▷ Right of citizenship
▷ Right to demonstrate
▷ Right to free elections
▷ Right to participate in government
▷ Right to participate in politics
▷ Right to petition the government
▷ Right to form political parties
▷ Right to vote

---

[7] Van Der Vyver, *Die beskerming van menseregte*, pp. 5, 16, 40, 27–8, 35–6, 114–30; Van Der Vyver, *Seven lectures*, pp. 58, 63–6, 112, 116; and Dugard, 'Human rights in South Africa' pp. 263–85.

[8] Van Der Vyver, *Seven lectures*, pp. 6, 26, 33–4, 59, 63–6, 74–7, 110–12; Dugard, 'Human rights in South Africa' pp. 263–85; and Van Der Vyver, *Die beskerming van menseregte*, pp. 37, 61, 114, 121, 105–7, 130–4, 143–7, 164, 175–7.

Socio-economic rights[9]

1. Economic rights

- ▷ Consumer rights
- ▷ Right of recourse
- ▷ Right to form trade unions
- ▷ Right to choose one's place of work
- ▷ Right to choose one's trade or profession
- ▷ Right to conclude a contract
- ▷ Right to exact performance of an obligation
- ▷ Right to housing
- ▷ Right to food and clothing
- ▷ Right to inherit
- ▷ Right to legal aid
- ▷ Right to make a will
- ▷ Right to minerals
- ▷ Right to property (and ownership)
- ▷ Right to reasonable remuneration
- ▷ Right to services of employee
- ▷ Right to social security
- ▷ Right to work

2. Social rights

- ▷ Right to a family
- ▷ Right to assemble peaceably
- ▷ Right of parent
- ▷ Right to associate with one's fellow man
- ▷ Right to found or participate in association
- ▷ Right to health care
- ▷ Right to integrity of one's reputation
- ▷ Right to marry
- ▷ Right to pursue happiness

---

9 Van Der Vyver, *Seven lectures*, pp. 34, 24–5, 48, 58–9, 62–6, 70, 77–8, 85–8, 112, 116, 138–9, 149;
 Van Der Vyver, *Die beskerming van menseregte*, pp. 12, 36, 40, 50–60, 69–71, 74–5, 80, 97–9, 114,
 116, 130–4, 148, 155–6; and see A. J. Rycroft, 'The protection of socio-economic rights', in H. Corder,
 ed., *Essays on law and social practice*, Cape Town: Juta, 1988, pp. 267–84.

Procedural human rights (due process of law)[10]

▷ Right not to be arrested and detained arbitrarily

▷ Freedom from inhuman treatment

▷ Right of recourse to legal proceedings

▷ Right not to be a witness against oneself

▷ Right not to be subjected to double jeopardy

▷ Right not to be subjected to cruel punishment

▷ Right not to be subjected to punishment not prescribed by law

▷ Right not to be subjected to retroactive law

▷ Right not to be subjected to unreasonable searches and seizures

▷ Right not to give evidence

▷ Right to appeal

▷ Right to be confronted by witnesses against oneself

▷ Right to be presumed innocent

▷ Right to defend oneself

▷ Right to a fair trial

▷ Right to give evidence

▷ Right to *habeas corpus* procedure

▷ Right to be informed of charges against oneself

▷ Right to legal representation

▷ Right to the necessities of life while being detained

▷ Right to obtain witnesses in one's favour

▷ Right to prepare one's defence

▷ Right to a public trial

▷ Right to speedy trial

▷ Right to trial by an independent and impartial tribunal

▷ Right to witness fee

---

10   See, for the position in South Africa, amongst others, Dugard, 'Human rights in South Africa'; Van Der Vyver, *Seven lectures*, pp. 16, 28, 57–77, 83–114, 122–3, 156; Van Der Vyver, *Die beskerming van menseregte*, pp. 21–33, 37–41, 114, 121, 137–82.

Group rights[11]

▷ Freedom of religion

▷ Language rights

▷ Right to form cultural association

▷ Right to preserve cultural identity

As far as human rights in South Africa are concerned, comment in this chapter centres on equality and race, the limits of government, the freedom of the press and the effect of the declaration of the State of Emergency.[12]

Since 1945 the concept of equality or non-discrimination has been the subject of international human rights discussion and protection,[13] aimed particularly at the eradication of discrimination based on origin, sex and race. Racial discrimination, and in particular the policy of apartheid, has been declared a crime against humanity.

In South Africa, race forms the basis of the structure of society[14] and the Population Registration Act 30 of 1950 plays a pivotal role. Participation in the Tricameral Parliament is dependent on classification as a member of a specified racial group. In South Africa the acquisition of substantive private law rights depends in many cases on the particular individual's (compulsory) racial classification. The Group Areas Act 36 of 1966, which prescribes separate residential areas for the various population groups, is perhaps the best-known example of such race-based legislation. In the field of public amenities the Reservation of Separate Amenities Act 49 of 1953 provides for the exclusive use and enjoyment of facilities such as parks, beaches, buses and swimming pools by members of specific race groups. (This law will probably be repealed during the 1990 parliamentary session.)

There is no clear demarcation of the relationship between government and the individual. This has resulted in a large number of legislative and administrative measures that infringe on basic human rights. The subject of the limits of government will play an important role in the discussion on the future of human rights in South Africa.

Another field in which substantial inroads have been made is the freedom

---

11 L. C. Blaauw 'The constitutional tenability of group rights, unpublished, 1989; L. C. Blaauw, 'Groepsregbeskerming in die KwaZulu-Natal Indaba se grondwetlike voorstelle', *SA Public Law*, pp. 232–43; and L. M. Du Plessis, ''n Regsteoreties-regspolitiese peiling van die menseregtehandves-debat in Suid-Afrika', *Tydskrif vir regswetenskap*, vol. 12, no. 2, pp. 124–44, 133.

12 W. Du Plessis, 'Die reg op inligting en die openbare belang', unpublished LLD thesis, Potchefstroom Univ. for CHE, 1986; and A. Rycroft, *Race and the law in South Africa*, Cape Town: Juta, 1987.

13 Du Plessis, 'Die reg op inligting en die openbare belang'; and Rycroft, *Race and law*.

14 N. J. J. Olivier, 'Regspluralisme in Suid-Afrika', *Tydskrif vir Regswetenskap*, 1988, pp. 60–79; and Rycroft, *Race and law*.

of the press.[15] The press is controlled by a large number of complicated legislative measures which have been aggravated by the restrictions imposed by the various emergency proclamations. Newspapers have been prohibited from publishing reports on unrest situations without consent of the minister. The banning of newspapers is also authorized; this has happened in some cases. The very real dangers inherent in muzzling the press are apparent — only when the public is informed, can informed critical choices be made.[16]

The declaration of the partial Emergency in 1985 and subsequent existence of a general Emergency since 1986 has had the effect that the already severely limited human rights situation in South Africa is in a critical phase. Many procedural and substantive human rights have been abrogated, and in some areas the powers of review of the Supreme Court have explicitly been excluded (for example, various provisions of the Emergency regulations). Because the Emergency has been in existence for more than four years, there is a very real danger that Emergency measures will be perceived as part of everyday legal life. In addition, the courts can no longer fulfil their function as watch-dog and custodian of civil liberties.

The SA Law Commission's proposed bill of rights

The South African Law Commission was established by the South African Law Commission Act 19 of 1973. It consists of judges, members of the Bar and Law Society, academics and officials of the Department of Justice. From time to time *ad hoc* members are appointed if the Commission deems their specialized knowledge to be indispensable for the proper conduct of a particular research project. The Commission is also assisted by a number of full-time officials who are responsible for research and the compilation of reports as determined by the Law Commission.[17]

The Law Commission published *Working Paper 25 on Project 58: Group and Human Rights* in March 1989 as the result of a request in April 1986 by the Minister of Justice, Mr H. J. Coetzee, to the SA Law Commission:

> to investigate and make recommendations on the definition and protection of group rights in the context of the South African constitutional set-up and the possible extension of the existing protection of individual rights as well as the role the courts play in connection with the above.

The project leader was Mr Justice P. J. J. Olivier. The basic point of departure was as follows:[18] 'The subject of fundamental human rights, a Bill of

---

15 A. Lewis 'Freedom of the press', in Forsyth and Schiller, *The Cape Town Conference*, pp. 251–60.

16 *Working Paper 1*, 1989; and *Hansard*, 1986, cols. 4014–15.

17 *Working Paper 1*.

18 *Working Paper 181*.

Rights, and group rights is a controversial one. We have tried to approach the matter as objectively as possible, from a practical legal point of view.'

Findings

In its discussion of the protection of human rights in South Africa, the Commission examined the content, influence and validity of the so-called doctrine of the sovereignty of parliament and concluded that the idea of unchecked parliamentary sovereignty[19] was foreign to South African law. On account of this doctrine the South African courts have been loath to invalidate parliamentary legislation.

The Republic of South Africa Constitution Act 110 of 1983 provides for a formal testing competency of legislation concerning the entrenched provisions as well as all other legislation. Provincial ordinances (nowadays provincial proclamations promulgated by the Administrator) are deemed to be original legislation. The result of this attitude is that parliamentary and provincial legislation can be questioned only on the grounds of non-compliance with procedural provisions as to the prescribed legislative process. As far as the competence of South African courts to inquire into the validity of delegated legislation is concerned, the Commission states that the present position is that 'the testing right yields no more than an *ultra vires* inquiry — here there is no substantive testing right either'.

The primary criterion is the wording of the enabling provision as contained in the legislation concerned.

This general belief in the supremacy of parliament and the concomitant narrow view of the courts' inherent powers to review parliamentary and subordinate legislation has resulted in a strong tendency to acquiesce in the extension of the powers of the legislature. The result has been an unwillingness by the courts to use their powers of review and testing powers to protect and to promote human rights. This has been severely criticized in recent years. The Commission concludes that:

> In view of our system of parliamentary sovereignty and the denial of a testing right for the courts on the basis of fundamental human rights, the courts are severely hampered as regards the protection of individual and group rights in the face of legislation which curtails these rights.[20]

Recommendations

The main recommendations of the Working Paper are as follows:

---

19 Based on the (erroneous) assumption that this doctrine forms part of the British constitutional heritage that has been taken over in South Africa and forms the basis of South African constitutional law with regard to the powers and privileges of parliament. In Britain the powers of parliament are limited by *inter alia* various conventions and the existence of unwritten human rights.

20 *Working Paper 1.*

1. A bill of rights should be enacted.

2. Powers of review should be granted to the courts to uphold the rights contained in the bill of rights and to invalidate legislation and executive acts contrary to the provisions of the bill.

3. A plan of action should be drawn up to make the public aware of the contents of the proposed bill of rights, to elicit discussion and to obtain public participation in the process of finalizing the bill.

The Commission argued that the established fundamental rights (individual rights and procedural rights) should be included in a bill of rights, but that the enactment of socio-economic rights and duties of citizens to the state, was not warranted. Group rights, it stated, could not be protected by legislation, but political rights could be based on group affiliation. However, the Commission did not make recommendations on the future constitution or on the principles of representation. Cultural rights such as language rights should be protected. In line with the general thrust of the Human Sciences Research Council's Project on Intergroup Relations, the Commission rejected rigid group classification and supported freedom of association (which includes the right to disassociate).

Government reaction before the 1989 elections was understandably low key. However, the National Party in its election Action Plan stated unequivocally that it was in favour of the introduction of a bill of rights enforceable by the courts. Its conception of the place and role of group rights differs fundamentally from the Commission's. Despite government acceptance of a so-called 'open group' and hesitant acceptance of the principle of voluntary association (and disassociation), the group concept still remains pivotal in official policy.

Content

The contents of its proposed bill of rights (Chapter XIV of the Working Paper) comprises sections on fundamental freedoms (individual rights), procedural rights (due process of law) and a general section on the inviolability and the justiciability of the specific rights as well as of the bill of rights itself. This includes those that are listed in the text that follows.[21]

---

[21] The articles are quoted directly from the proposed bill of rights. It is ironic that, in the light of what is said in Article 2, the masculine pronoun has been used throughout the document.

Substantive human rights

Part A: fundamental rights

The rights set out here are fundamental rights to which every person in the Republic of South Africa shall be entitled and, save as provided in this Bill, no legislation or executive or administrative act of any nature whatever shall infringe these rights.

ARTICLE 1: The right to life: Provided that legislation may provide for the discretionary imposition of the sentence of death in the case of the most serious crimes.

ARTICLE 2: The right to human dignity and equality before the law, i.e. there shall be no discrimination on grounds such as race, colour, language, sex, religion, ethnic origin and social class. However, legislation, executive or administrative acts, (in the short-term) to improve the position of persons or groups who find themselves disadvantaged, shall be permissible.

ARTICLE 5: The right to be recognised legally, economically and culturally as having rights and obligations and as having the capacity to participate in legal, commercial and cultural affairs.

ARTICLE 6: The right to privacy, which shall include protection from arbitrary search.

ARTICLE 8: The right to freedom of speech and to obtain and disseminate information.

ARTICLE 10: The right to freedom of choice with regard to education and training.

ARTICLE 11: The right to the integrity of the family, freedom of marriage and the upholding of the institution of marriage.

ARTICLE 12: The right to move freely within the Republic of South Africa and therein to reside, to work, or to carry on any lawful business, occupation, trade or other activity.

ARTICLE 14: The right, freely and on an equal footing, to engage in economic intercourse, which shall include the capacity to establish and maintain commercial undertakings, to procure property and means of production, to offer services against remuneration and to make a profit.

ARTICLE 15: The right to private property: Provided that legislation may in the public interest authorise expropriation against payment of reasonable compensation which shall in the event of a dispute be determined by a court of law.

ARTICLE 16: The right to associate freely with other groups and individuals.

ARTICLE 17: The right of every person or group to disassociate himself or itself from other individuals or groups: Provided that if such disassociation constitutes discrimination on the ground of race, colour, religion, language or culture, no public or state funds shall be granted directly or indirectly to promote the interests of the person who or group which so discriminates.

ARTICLE 18: The right of citizens freely to form political parties, to be members of such parties, to practise their political convictions in a peaceful manner and to be nominated and elected to legislative, executive and administrative office, and to form and become members of trade unions: Provided that no person shall be compelled to be a member of a political party or a trade union.

ARTICLE 19: The right to assemble peacefully, to hold demonstrations peacefully and to obtain and present petitions.

ARTICLE 20: (a) The right of all citizens over the age of eighteen years to exercise the vote on a basis of equality in respect of all legislative institutions at regular and periodic elections and at referendums.

ARTICLE 21: The right of every person, individually or together with others, freely to practise his culture and religion and use his language.

ARTICLE 22: The right of every person to be safeguarded from discrimination against his culture, religion or language and to be safeguarded from preferential treatment of the culture, religion or language of others.

Procedural human rights

ARTICLE 23: The right to personal freedom and safety, which shall also mean that no person shall be deprived of his freedom, save in the following cases and in accordance with a generally applicable prescribed procedure whereby his fundamental rights to spiritual and physical integrity are not denied:

(a) Lawful arrest or detention of a person effected in order to cause him to appear before a court of law on the ground of a reasonable suspicion that he has committed a crime or whenever it may on reasonable grounds be deemed necessary to prevent the commission of a crime;

(b) Lawful detention upon conviction by a court of law or for non-compliance with a lawful order of the court.

(c) Lawful detention of a person in order to prevent the spread of infectious disease;

(d) Lawful detention of a person who is mentally ill or one who is addicted to narcotic or addictive substances, with a view to his admission, in accordance with prescribed procedure, to an institution or rehabilitation centre.

(e) Lawful detention of a person in order to prevent his unauthorised entry into or sojourn in the Republic of South Africa or with a view to the extradition or deportation of a person in accordance with prescribed procedure.

ARTICLE 24: It shall be the right of every person under arrest:

(a) To be detained and fed under conditions consonant with human dignity;

(b) To be informed as soon as possible, in a language which he understands, of the reason for his detention and of any charge against him;

(c) To be informed as soon as possible that he has the right to remain silent and that he need not make any statement and to be warned of the consequence of making a statement;

(d) Within a reasonable period of time, but not more than forty eight hours or the first court day thereafter, to be brought before a court of law and in writing to be charged or in writing to be informed of the reason for his detention, failing which he shall be entitled to be released from detention, unless a court of law, upon good cause shown, orders his further detention;

(e) Within a reasonable period after his arrest, to be tried by a court of law and pending such trial to be released, which release may be subject to bail or guarantees to appear at the trail, unless a court of law, upon good cause shown, orders his further detention;

(f) To communicate and to consult with legal representatives of his choice;

(g) To communicate with and to receive, in reasonable measure, visits from his spouse, family, next of kin or friends, unless a court of law otherwise directs;

(h) Not to be subjected to torture, assault or cruel or inhuman or degrading treatment.

Aʀᴛɪᴄʟᴇ 25: The right of every accused person:

(a) Not to be convicted or sentenced unless a fair and public trial before a court of law has taken place in accordance with the generally applicable procedural and evidential rules;

(b) To be treated as innocent until the contrary is proved by the state;

(c) To remain silent and to refuse to testify during the trial;

(d) To be assisted by a legal representative of his choice and, if he cannot afford this, and if the case is a serious one, to be defended by a legal representative remunerated by the state;

(e) Not to be sentenced to inhuman or degrading punishment;

(f) Not to be convicted of an offence in respect of an act or omission which did not constitute an offence at the moment when it was done and not to receive a penalty heavier than that which was applicable at the time when the offence was committed;

(g) Not to be convicted of a crime of which he was previously convicted or acquitted, save in the course of appeal or review proceedings connected with such conviction or acquittal;

(h) To have recourse by appeal or review to a court superior to the court which tried him in the first instance: Provided that if a Division of the Supreme Court of South Africa was the court of first instance it may be prescribed that leave to appeal shall first be obtained from that court or from the Appellate Division;

(i) To be informed as to the reasons for his conviction and sentence.

Aʀᴛɪᴄʟᴇ 26: The right of every person convicted of a crime and serving a term of imprisonment in accordance with a sentence of a court of law:

(a) Not to be subjected to torture, assault or cruel or inhuman or degrading treatment;

(b) To be detained and fed under conditions consonant with human dignity;

(c) To be given the opportunity of developing and rehabilitating;

(d) To be released upon expiry of the term of imprisonment imposed by the court of law.

Aʀᴛɪᴄʟᴇ 27: The right to cause civil disputes to be settled by a court of law and to appeal to a court of law by way of review against executive and administrative acts and against quasi-judicial decisions.

ARTICLE 28: The right to have the rules of natural justice applied in administrative and quasi-judicial proceedings and to have reasons furnished for any prejudicial decision.

ARTICLE 29: The right that the South African law, including the South African international private law, shall apply to all legal relations before a court of law: Provided that legislation may provide for the application of the law of indigenous groups or the religious groups in civil proceedings.

General section

Part B

ARTICLE 30: The rights granted in this Bill may by legislation be limited to the extent that is reasonably necessary in the interests of the security of the state, the public order, the public interest, good morals, public health, the administration of justice, the rights of others or for the prevention of disorder and crime, but only in such measure and in such a manner as is acceptable in a democratic society.

ARTICLE 31: The Supreme Court of the Republic of South Africa shall have jurisdiction upon application by any interested person acting on his own behalf or on behalf of a group of interested persons to determine whether any legislation or executive or administrative act violates any of the rights herein set forth or exceeds any of the limitations herein permitted and, if so, to the extent that the violation or excess takes place, to declare invalid the legislation in question or to set aside the executive or administrative act in question: Provided that finalised executive and administrative acts by which effect has been given to legislation declared invalid and which are not the subject of the proceedings concerned, shall not automatically become void.

ARTICLE 32: The provisions of this Bill shall apply to all existing and future legislation and to all executive and administrative acts done after the date of the introduction of this Bill.

ARTICLE 33: The provisions of this Bill, including this article, shall not be amended or suspended save by a three-quarter majority of those members who are entitled to vote in each House of Parliament and who have been directly elected by the electorate: Provided that the addition of further fundamental rights or the extension of existing fundamental rights may be effected by a simple majority.

Socio-economic rights

The Commission considered that the socio-economic rights embodied in Article 14 of the bill of rights were sufficient. The right to property as well as to compensation in the case of expropriation was recognized in Article 15.

Group rights

The bill of rights provided in Articles 21 and 22 for the protection of cultural, religious and language rights that may be exercised by individuals. The Commission accepted that these were individual rights enjoyed by individuals.

Political rights

Although the Commission rejected group classification and accepted freedom of association (and of disassociation) as the basis of society, it nonetheless concluded that political participation could be group based. The Commission did not, however, specify how this was to be implemented.

Relationship with existing and new legislation

Article 23 provides for the invalidation of all existing and new legislation as well as of executive and administrative acts that are contrary to the provisions of the bill of rights.

Justiciability

The Supreme Court is empowered to inquire into the validity of all legislation, executive and administrative acts if the rights contained in the bill of rights have been violated or if the limitations (to those rights) have been exceeded. This power of review can only be exercised if an application is brought; the Supreme Court is not empowered on its own to invalidate legislation or executive and administrative acts.

Amendability

In terms of Section 33 the bill of rights may be amended or suspended only if two-thirds of the directly elected members of parliament vote in favour of such a proposal. This is to prevent the recurrence of the enlargement of parliament (as happened in 1955). Extension of existing rights and the addition of new rights may, however, be effected by a simple majority.

Evaluation

The Law Commission's proposed bill of rights is an impressive document that embodies substantive and procedural human rights. Nonetheless, it raises a few as yet unresolved issues:

1. The possible introduction of more socio-economic rights and of obligations (duties).

2. The implied contradiction between the foundations of cultural rights (language, religion and culture) on the one hand and political rights on the other. The group concept was rejected for cultural rights; however, the Commission concluded that political rights could be protected on a group basis and a future constitution structured on the (prescribed?) group affiliation of citizens.

3. The limitations mentioned in Article 30 (state security, public order, public interest, good morals, public health, the administration of justice, the rights of others and the prevention of disorder and crime) are similar to those found in contemporary Western charters. The yardstick to be applied in such cases is that which is 'acceptable in a democratic society'. Opinions on what constitutes a democratic state and what is deemed to be acceptable differ greatly.

Charters of other South African organizations

Several South African organizations have formulated their own bills of rights. All of them contain references to socio-economic rights and/or duties to the state, and accept equality and non-discrimination as basic premises. They differ, however, on whether the right to private property should be protected; the African National Congresses's Freedom Charter, for example, provides for the expropriation and nationalization of mines, banks and land.

African National Congress (ANC)

The relevant articles of the ANC's Freedom Charter are given in the text that follows.

The people shall govern!

▷ Every man and woman shall have the right to vote for and to stand as a candidate for all bodies which make laws;

▷ All people shall be entitled to take part in the administration of the country; the rights of the people shall be the same, regardless of race, colour or sex;

▷ All bodies of minority rule, advisory boards, councils and authorities shall be replaced by democratic organs of self-government.

All national groups shall have equal rights!

▷ There shall be equal status in bodies of state, in the courts and in the schools for all national groups and races.

▷ All people shall have equal right to use their own languages, and to develop their own folk culture and customs.

- ▷ All national groups shall be protected by law against insults to their race and national pride.
- ▷ The preaching and practise of national, race or colour discrimination and contempt shall be a punishable crime.
- ▷ All apartheid laws and practices shall be set aside.

The people shall share in the country's wealth!

- ▷ The national wealth of our country, the heritage of South Africans, shall be restored to the people.
- ▷ The mineral wealth beneath the soil, the banks and monopoly industry shall be transferred to the ownership of the people as a whole.
- ▷ All other industry and trade shall be controlled to assist the well-being of the people.
- ▷ All people shall have equal rights to trade where they choose, to manufacture and to enter all trades, crafts and professions.

The land shall be shared among those who work it!

- ▷ Restrictions of land ownership on a racial basis shall be ended, and all the land re-divided among those who work it to banish famine and land hunger.
- ▷ The state shall help the peasants with implements, seed, tractors and dams to save the soil and to assist the tillers.
- ▷ Freedom of movement shall be guaranteed to all who work on the land.
- ▷ All shall have the right to occupy land wherever they choose.
- ▷ People shall not be robbed of their cattle, and forced labour and farm prisons shall be abolished.

All shall be equal before the law!

- ▷ No-one shall be imprisoned, deported or restricted without a fair trial.
- ▷ No-one shall be condemned by the order of any Government official.
- ▷ The courts shall be representative of all the people.
- ▷ Imprisonment shall be only for serious crimes against the people, and shall aim at re-education, not vengeance.
- ▷ The police force and army shall be open to all on an equal basis and shall be the helpers and protectors of the people.
- ▷ All laws which discriminate on grounds of race, colour or belief shall be repealed.

All shall enjoy equal human rights!

▷ The law shall guarantee to all their right to speak, to organise, to meet together, to publish, to preach, to worship and to educate their children; The privacy of the house from police raids shall be protected by law; All shall be free to travel without restriction from countryside to town, from province, and from South Africa abroad;

▷ Pass Laws, permits and all other laws restricting these freedoms shall be abolished.

There shall be work and security!

▷ All who work shall be free to form trade unions, to elect their officers and to make wage agreements with their employers; the state shall recognize the right and duty of all to work, and to draw full unemployment benefits;

▷ Men and women of all races shall receive equal pay for equal work.

▷ There shall be a forty-hour working week, a national minimum wage, paid annual leave, and sick leave for all workers, and maternity leave on full pay for all working mothers;

▷ Miners, domestic workers, farm workers and civil servants shall have the same rights as all others who work;

▷ Child labour, compound labour, the tot system and contract labour shall be abolished.

The doors of learning and of culture shall be opened!

▷ The government shall discover, develop and encourage national talent for the enhancement of our cultural life;

▷ All cultural treasures of mankind shall be open to all, by free exchange of books, ideas and contact with other lands;

▷ The aim of education shall be to teach the youth to love their people and their culture, to honour human brotherhood, liberty and peace; Education shall be free, compulsory, universal and equal for all children; Higher education and technical training shall be open to all by means of state allowances and scholarships awarded on the basis of merit; Adult illiteracy shall be ended by a mass state education plan;

▷ Teachers shall have all rights of other citizens;

▷ The colour bar in cultural life, in sport and in education shall be abolished.

There shall be houses, security and comfort!

▷ All people shall have the right to live where they choose, be decently housed, and to bring up their families in comfort and security;

▷ Unused housing space to be made available to the people; Rent and prices shall be lowered, food plentiful and no-one shall go hungry;

▷ A preventive health scheme shall be run by the state; Free medical care and hospitalisation shall be provided for all, with special care for mothers and young children;

▷ Slums shall be demolished, and new suburbs built where all have transport, roads, lighting, playing fields, creches and social centres;

▷ The aged, the orphans, the disabled and the sick shall be cared for by the state;

▷ Rest, leisure and recreation shall be the right of all;

▷ Fenced locations and ghettoes shall be abolished, and laws which break up families shall be repealed.

There shall be peace and friendship!

▷ South Africa shall be a fully independent state, which respects the rights and sovereignty of all nations;

▷ South Africa shall strive to maintain world peace and the settlement of all international disputes by negotiation — not war;

▷ Peace and friendship amongst all our people shall be secured by upholding the equal rights, opportunities and status of all; The people of the protectorates — Basutoland, Bechuanaland and Swaziland — shall be free to decide for themselves their own future;[22]

▷ The right of all the peoples of Africa to independence and self-government shall be recognized, and shall be the basis of close cooperation.

KwaZulu–Natal Indaba

The KwaZulu–Natal Indaba has formulated a bill of rights containing all the usual human rights. Several of the articles focus on socio-economic rights and the duties of citizens toward the state.

4(1) No one shall be held in slavery or servitude.

(2) No one shall be required to perform forced or compulsory labour: Provided that this does not include:

(a) Any normal work required to be done in the ordinary course of detention under the provisions of subsection (3) or during conditional release from such detention:

---

22 Basutoland, Bechuanaland and Swaziland (Lesotho, Botswana and Swaziland) have been independent from British colonial rule since the 1960s.

(b) Any service of a military character in terms of a law requiring citizenship to undergo military training;

(c) Any service exacted in case of emergency or calamity threatening the existence or well-being of the Province;

(d) Any work or service which forms part of normal civic obligations imposed by law.

7(1) Everyone has the right to lawfully own and occupy property anywhere in the Province.

(2) No one is to be deprived of his property without due process of law, and expropriation may only be authorised in terms of a law if it is in the public interest and if equitable and fair compensation is promptly paid.

(3) Land and natural resources shall not be expropriated except for the common good and in accordance with laws providing for equitable compensation.

13(1) Everyone shall be entitled to equal work opportunities and to free choice of employment.

(2) Everyone with legal capacity shall have freedom to contract and to conclude agreements with others in the voluntary exercise of his rights and freedoms and generally for the promotion of his interests.

FCI Bill of Rights

The South African Federated Chamber of Industries has also formulated its own bill of rights providing for the classical individual and procedural rights. The following articles refer to socio-economic rights:[23]

6. Everyone has the right to own property, alone as well as in association with others including communal ownership as found in traditional communities. No one shall be deprived of his property without due process of law.

7. Everyone has the right to the rewards of his endeavours and this right shall be subject only to such limitations as are prescribed by law and are necessary in a democratic society in the public interest and the promotion of the public wealth and well-being.

8. Everyone has the right freely to employ labour and to own or manage a business in accordance with the rights and principles set out in this Charter. Everyone has the right to work and to free choice of employment. Everyone, without discrimination, has the right to equal pay for equal work. Everyone who works has the right to fair remuneration.

---

23 Note that the FCI Bill of Rights also makes use of the masculine pronoun.

Everyone has the right to form or join trade unions, or commercial, industrial or other associations of his choice for the furtherance or protection of his economic interests; however, no one may be compelled to join such a union or association.

9. The people, may, themselves for their own ends or through the institutions of democratic government, freely dispose of their natural wealth and resources without any prejudice to any obligations arising out of international economic cooperation, based upon the principle of mutual benefit and international law; in no case may a person be deprived of his own means of subsistence.

Why a bill of rights is necessary

The status of human rights in South Africa is very problematic as a result of a number of factors, including:

1. the doctrine of parliamentary sovereignty;
2. the curtailment by legislation of the inherent powers of review of the Supreme Court;
3. the increase in parliamentary and subordinate legislation that infringes basic human rights;
4. the granting of vast powers to the executive and the administration;
5. the absence of consensus that human rights are important and that they can function effectively;
6. the central role that the group concept (and race in particular) has played in South Africa
7. the unequal division of land in South Africa;
8. the existence of statutory discrimination;
9. the existence of legislation that is not in accordance with basic human rights;
10. the declaration and renewal on a yearly basis of the State of Emergency; and
11. the exclusion of a large part of the working population (for example, farm workers and domestic servants) from the limited protection offered by existing legislation.

However, there are a number of encouraging signs. They include:

1. the Working Paper of the South African Law Commission that on the whole contains a balanced exposition of the basic rights that need protection;
2. the increase in public discussion on human rights and the merits and content of a human rights document;

3. the formulation of various bills of rights by organizations that differ sharply in ideological content and strategy (However, one can identify a substantial middle ground of shared values on the basic substantive (individual) and procedural rights, and a number of socio-economic rights. Major differences exist, however, regarding issues such as private property and the redistribution of wealth, the nationalization of mines, minerals and land, the role of national goals superimposed on human rights, the role of obligations towards other citizens and the state, and the limitations on (and exceptions to) human rights); and

4. the growing opposition to measures infringing on human rights, ranging from law societies to members of the public.

Through the centuries it has become clear that there is a world-wide need to strike a balance between the powers of the state and the interests of the individual. This implies that a restraint be placed on (a) the legislative powers and (b) the executive and administrative acts of governments. Provision must also be made for the control of the validity of legislation and executive and administrative powers by an independent judiciary using the yardstick of an entrenched bill of rights that can only be amended under predetermined circumstances if certain prescribed conditions have been met.

History has shown that an entrenched bill of rights is the only effective way by which this balance can be maintained and fundamental freedoms be guaranteed. Such a bill of rights — if implemented fully and enforced vigorously — also has the effect of:

1. moulding the perceptions of the legislature and the administration that they should not possess vast and unlimited powers;

2. teaching the public of the unquestionable need for the existence, protection, enforceability and justiciability of such freedoms;

3. giving effect to the principles underlying democracy; and

4. establishing and providing for the continued existence of the principle of government subject to law.

The introduction and subsequent entrenchment of such a bill of rights guaranteeing fundamental freedoms and enforced by an independent judiciary will have the effect of eradicating both the racial basis of the South African legal system (and thus to a large extent also of the present South African social system) and the inequality of the present system.

In the long term the bill of rights will become part and parcel of the South African legal system and will be deemed to be an inalienable fundamental right to be protected against all attempts to diminish its role as final check on government powers and ultimate custodian of individual freedoms.

Conclusion

To accelerate progress, the following is proposed:

1. holding representative discussions to formulate a bill of rights on a basis of consensus;

2. enacting the bill of rights as an enshrined charter that may be amended only if stringent conditions have been complied with;

3. repealing all discriminatory legislation;

4. repealing legislation that is contrary to the bill of rights;

5. educating the public about the meaning, content and worth of human rights;

6. educating and training officialdom to act in accordance with the provisions of the bill of rights;

7. restoring and extending the powers of review of the South African Supreme Court;

8. ensuring the power of enforcement of this bill of rights by the South African Supreme Court;

9. adapting South African administrative law so that it accords with the bill of rights;

10. drafting a new constitution by representatives of all concerned; this constitution should provide for participation on the basis of equality;

11. repealing the Emergency; and

12. implementing affirmative action to redress past injustices.

4 National security, freedom and reform

Anthony S. Mathews

As important as are the individual concepts of national security, freedom and reform, it is even more crucial that they should operate in a balancing cohesion for the orderly well-being of any society. This chapter stresses the need for a full understanding of their complex interrelationship in any policy formulation for South Africa.

Introduction

The three parts of the triad of national security, freedom and reform represent important social goals for any society. While there are plenty of advocates for each in South Africa, there is a limited appreciation of even that which is commonplace of their interrelationship. Among that which is considered commonplace are the propositions that the enjoyment of freedom requires a framework of social order and stability, that national security programmes must be kept in bounds if they are not to undermine freedom, and that over-ambitious reforms may jeopardize both liberty and security.

The advocates of law and order tend to be blind to the impact of their policies on freedom, while the cadres of the liberation struggle display a complementary myopia towards the social need for peace and stability.

In the clamour of the public debate one may clearly discern the hysterical shrieking of the law-and-order lobby, the vociferous cry of the liberators, and the boisterous demands of the total-reform-now movement.[1] What is seldom heard, even when occasionally expressed, is the voice of the believer in the full trinity of order, freedom and reform — the voice of the advocate of a rounded social programme as opposed to the cries of single-minded zealots, whether in or out of public office.

---

1 In fairness to those whose cry is for liberation and reform, it must be recorded that their single-mindedness is a kind of matching madness to the fanatical pursuit of domination through 'law and order' by those in public office. Moreover, not all liberationists are included in the criticism expressed in the text at this point. The liberators who particularly deserve censure are those who advocate an instantaneous and totally unqualified transfer of power to the majority in the belief that this will banish all the ills of a troubled society like our own.

There is undoubtedly potential for conflict between the goals of security and freedom. While even the mildest of security legislation restricts freedom, full-blown national security programmes of the South African variety suspend or qualify every one of the basic rights, and even may be said to annihilate liberty. On the other hand, too much freedom (especially organizational freedom for antisocial groups) may threaten stability to the point where social order disintegrates.

The conflict potential of security and freedom tends to predominate in debate and to obscure an equally important truth about the relationship — the truth of their interdependence and mutually-sustaining nature.[2] The institutionalization and social enforcement of basic rights implies and requires a stable system; and a stable system depends in part on the enjoyment of those rights by the masses.

The relationship between the social goal of reform, and security and liberty is equally subtle and displays the same paradoxical mix of conflicting and mutually sustaining elements. Reform programmes ought to extend freedom and may even re-establish a disintegrating social stability; but reform policies, formulated blindly and pursued obsessively, are likely to usher in an era in which neither freedom nor stability is attained to a satisfactory degree.

Neither security, freedom nor reform can be promoted in isolation. They stand towards each other in an intimate, complex and shifting relationship which is characterized by both conflict and dependence. Policy formulation for any society requires an understanding of the state of the relationship, and of the particular balance or imbalance that characterizes it. It also requires an assessment of the balance or emphasis dictated by the needs of the moment.

Social and political conditions have a direct bearing on the framing of the policies and strategies needed to bring into a state of equilibrium the goals of freedom, security and reform. If, for example, social and political inequalities are great, reform will have a high priority; but such inequalities usually engender political strife and this, in turn, calls for an emphasis on control measures. There is a danger, however, that these measures will become an end in themselves and stifle both the development of freedom and the prospects of successful reform.

Only a thorough-going evaluation of underlying social and political realities can avoid the danger of one goal — whether it be security, freedom or reform — being so elevated in policy formulation that it destroys the others. There is no universal state of equilibrium, only a mix appropriate

---

[2] The truth is not claimed to be universal and certainly does not hold for totalitarian societies in which there is no public ethic of individual freedom.

to a given situation.

The present balance between freedom, security and reform

Policy formulation for South African society requires a clear understanding of the present balance that official policy strikes between the goals of freedom, national security and reform. First, political liberty, in the words of Dahrendorff, means 'the right to participate in the exercise of political power, as a member of a body vested with political authority or as an elector of the members of such body'[3] and liberty in this sense is closely associated with and incorporates civil rights such as the freedom of the person, of movement, speech, assembly and association.[4] Reform implies democratic reform — a movement towards political liberty and the associated civil rights for all South Africans, especially for those presently excluded. We need to determine the relationship between freedom and reform in the senses just described, and national security as expressed in South African security laws and practices.

The primary impact of the national security programme is upon civil rights associated with political freedom. While the right to vote is not directly touched by internal security legislation, persons restricted under provisions of the Internal Security Act are precluded from holding certain public offices, even if elected to them.[5]

In the main, political participation is indirectly affected by security action against those who campaign for full political rights. Civil rights, on the other hand, are directly removed, suspended or modified by such legislation. Freedom of the person has become the victim of a variety of detention-without-trial provisions; freedom of expression, the victim of far-reaching censorship powers; and freedom of assembly and association, the victim of virtually unchecked banning powers. These are some examples of the deep and drastic inroads made by security laws into basic civil rights.

It is now impossible to speak of civil rights. What used to be civil rights are precarious privileges enjoyed only by favour of the ruling party. The notion of balance between national security and civil rights has been replaced by a relationship of total subjugation.

The features of security legislation which indicate that balance has been replaced by subordination are the following:

---

[3] R. Dahrendorff, *Society and democracy in Germany*, New York: Doubleday, 1967, p. 70.

[4] Dahrendorff, *Society and democracy*; see also J. Rawls, *A theory of justice*, Oxford: Oxford Univ. Press, 1972, p. 61.

[5] See Section 33 of the Internal Security Act 74 of 1982. The same applies to persons convicted of certain offences.

▷ There is an absence of specific criteria to which official action that affects basic freedoms must conform. Ministerial power to ban meetings is a clear example of the lack of governing standards. The power to ban may be exercised if the minister deems the prohibition necessary or expedient in the interests of the security of the state, the maintenance of public peace or the prevention of intergroup hostility.[6]

The already imprecise standards of broad expressions like 'security of the state' are rendered almost meaningless by the subjective power vested in the minister to determine whether the criteria of the law are satisfied in a given case. Provisions of this kind abound in security legislation, concealing a vacuum in standards and criteria.

▷ Even when standards are specified, there is usually no power vested in the courts or other independent tribunals to enforce compliance with them. Subjective discretion clauses (which make the exercise of power dependent on opinion or belief), provisions limiting or excluding court jurisdiction, and indemnity clauses have almost rendered the courts powerless to enforce compliance with the criteria that do appear in security legislation. Thus, with reference to a ministerial ban on meetings in the alleged interest of security or public peace, the normally activist Natal court has declared that the minister's actions are beyond judicial control.[7]

▷ The state's ability to withhold information even from the courts[8] frequently makes it impossible to determine whether the statutory criteria that do exist have been met in a particular case. Attempts to elicit information through the courts in security cases (other than prosecutions) are invariably unsuccessful whether the case concerns banning,[9] detention[10] or some other form of arbitrary restriction.

The lack of standards, or court inability to compel compliance with them where they do exist, destroys any notion of balance or equilibrium between national security and basic liberties. Liberties must be converted into civil rights before we can speak of an institutional balancing of security and freedom; and civil rights do not exist unless the law sets enforceable standards according to which they may be withdrawn or vindicated. There can be no argument, moreover, that security and freedom are kept in a state of

---

6 Section 46(3) of the Internal Security Act 74 of 1982.

7 *Metal and Allied Workers Union v. Castell*, No, 1985 (2) SA 280 (D).

8 Particularly under Section 66 of the Internal Security Act 74 of 1982.

9 See, for example, *Minister of Justice v. Alexander*, 1975 (4) SA 530 (A).

10 Even where the detaining authority is required to justify a detention according to objective criteria, attempts to uncover factual information are generally abortive: see *Manning v. Minister of Law and Order* (case no. 2517/87 of the Durban and Coast Local Division of the Supreme Court).

equilibrium in practice even though the equilibrium may not be reflected in the formal political and legal arrangements of the society.

With detentions, until recently, running into hundreds, if not thousands, every year[11] with over sixty organizations banned, with all open-air meetings illegal unless officially sanctioned, and with heavy censorship of opinion and information over great areas of public life, there is simply no room for the notion that the basic liberties of person, speech, assembly and association enjoy actual, if not formal, recognition in South Africa. National security is in total ascendancy, in theory and in practice.

Those responsible for the national security programme in South Africa frequently argue that its measures are essential to protect and further democracy and freedom in South Africa.[12] Though this is clearly a baseless proposition, it has acquired a meretricious attractiveness because the security laws are sometimes used against people whose conduct indicates a hostility to, or complete lack of understanding of, free and democratic institutions.

The first difficulty with this argument is that it seems impossible to reconcile so total a subordination of freedom to national security with an intention to further liberty and democracy. If that was an important objective of security policy, one would expect some limits to be placed upon security powers and some recognition of the legal right to basic freedoms. In fact, the ascendancy of security over freedom is so complete that we are in effect being told that a programme for the total destruction of civil rights is necessary for their preservation. It does not make logical sense to tell the people: 'We want you to be free; therefore we are assuming total power over you.'

A security policy intended to further liberty and democracy would not put basic freedoms at the uncontrolled mercy of officials of state.

It would not inform members of the security forces, down to the newest recruit, that they may use lethal force to disperse gatherings simply because they think it necessary, not because there are reasonable grounds for so acting.

It would not sanction grave deprivations of liberty like detention-without-trial and banning because some official declares that these are required for peace and order without having to establish that this is so. It would not authorize suspension of the basic right of assembly because a minister, who

---

11 It has been estimated that between 12 June 1986 (the day on which the first full State of Emergency was proclaimed) and the beginning of October 1987, at least 13 989 persons were detained (*Weekly Mail*, November 20, 1987). The total number of persons detained since peace-time detention was introduced in 1963 is just under 70 000.

12 A good example of an attempt to invest security laws with democratic legitimacy is the paper given by Dr Stoffel van der Merwe, Deputy Minister of Information and Constitutional Planning, to the Star Centennial Conference on the Press on 8 October 1987, Bureau for Information, Pretoria.

is dealing with his own political opponents in banning meetings, feels that such action is required.

In short, the laws themselves bear no testimony to a commitment to democracy or to democratic rights. Quite the contrary, they speak of a deep and enduring hostility to free and democratic institutions.

Analysis of the national security programme shows that official talk about furthering democracy and freedom is an attempt to legitimatize laws whose real objective is to consolidate sectarian power and privilege. Evidence for this is to be found in the laws themselves and in their application. The formal laws provide both indirect and direct evidence of anti-democratic objectives.

The indirect evidence consists of the deliberate removal from the security laws of enforceable standards which would restrict their use to anti-democratic persons or activities — to people or programmes that seek to bring about change by spreading violence or disorder or by overturning the government of the day. The abolition of standards that by and large serve to confine security law to real security threats clearly implies that other threats are covered, and were intended to be. The direct evidence is to be found mainly in the scope of security crimes, like subversion and sabotage, which by definition are directed at extra-parliamentary dissent.

When we turn to the application of security laws, their anti-democratic character becomes overwhelmingly clear. Thousands of people who neither in thought nor deed have committed themselves to violence, disorder or the overthrow of government, have been dealt with under 'security' legislation. Sometimes the authorities provide revealing, though unintended, proof of the underlying function of security law control. For example, it is common for the following restrictions to be placed upon emergency detainees on their release from detention:

> . . . you shall not during the period from the date of your release for so long as the said regulations remain in force or these conditions remain in force . . . attend any gathering which has been convened, advertised or is otherwise brought about to attack, criticise or protest against any campaign, project, programme, action or proposed action by the government of the Republic of South Africa.[13]

There could hardly be clearer testimony of the government's intention to control opposition to everything it does or proposes to do by means of 'security' laws. This kind of restriction cannot be reconciled with democratic objectives; on the contrary, it discloses underlying political control purposes that are destructive to a democratic resolution of conflict in South Africa.

The relationship between national security and political reform is also

---

[13] Since this chapter was written, this particular restriction was declared *ultra vires* in *Visagie v. Security Police* 1989 (3) SA 859 (A).

grotesquely asymmetrical. Whatever the position may have been in the past, the South African crisis of the present and the future centres on political reform. Socio-economic reform, while still clearly necessary and desired, has been displaced by the demand for political rights, partly because the disenfranchised perceive correctly that comprehensive improvements to basic living conditions depend directly upon access to political power.

There is another reason why political reform is crucial. Disorder and instability in South Africa are directly related to the failure of the political system to respond to the heightened aspirations and demands of the newly mobilized black masses.[14] It follows that the attainment of security is as much dependent on political reform as the goal of freedom is. However, this is a truth which current security policy-making, as reflected in national security legislation, obdurately refuses to acknowledge.

National security laws have closed off the spaces in public life in which new initiatives in political reform may be generated. While other laws have denied access to the vote and to political office for the black masses, and while the government's political reform programme adds up to little more than a cynical blend of minority co-option, tokenism towards blacks and the centralization of the power of the ruling group, security legislation has smothered the exercise of the civil rights associated with formal participation in decision-making.

By its indiscriminate attacks on both democratic and anti-democratic individuals and groups in society, and by the denial of civil rights to the whole spectrum of extra-parliamentary political movements, this legislation has undermined the development of stable, well-led and responsible groups that are a pre-condition of ordered progress to political power-sharing. It has eliminated black leadership (whether responsible or irresponsible), created or stimulated undisciplined, warring factions, and raised group conflict to a frighteningly destructive level.

Our security law is systematically destroying the conditions for evolutionary and stable political change. As in the case of the relationship of security and freedom, there is no compromise between competing interests. The goal of political reform has fallen victim to the security apparatus's insatiable appetite for power.

There is in fact no balance between security, freedom and political reform in South Africa. Security law has pre-empted the entire field by its denial of the goals of freedom and political reform and its hostility to them. Security in South Africa has evolved into an elaborate and powerful mechanism of political control which by its very nature has contained the competing interests of freedom and political change.

---

[14] S. P. Huntington, *Political order in changing societies*, New Haven: Yale Univ. Press, 1968, pp. 53–4.

A pre-condition, therefore, of a healthier relationship between security, freedom and reform is the limitation of security law to legitimate security objectives so that it ceases to be a vehicle for political hegemony. There are many who believe that the only acceptable correction is to reverse the ascendancy so as to give liberty and reform total sway over security interests.

For South Africa, at any rate, such a reversal is an unrealizable dream, however seductive its appeal. The reasons lie in the socio-political realities of the society to which we now turn to determine how and to what degree the parts of the triad that are the concern of this chapter may be brought into harmony.

Socio-political realities

There is hardly need to review those features of society that underline the need for reform in South Africa. (Topics that are dealt with elsewhere in this book include those outlined in the text that follows.) Gross disparities of income and wealth between black and white South Africans still exist and have not been substantially mitigated by social and economic reform programme (see Chapter 6); legalized discrimination, especially in the sphere of land ownership and occupation, remains entrenched; Africans (outside the homelands) have no voice in central decision-making, and even in regional and local government there has been a devolution of functions rather than powers being given to black representatives.

What is not generally appreciated, however, is that current social realities point ineluctably towards the primacy of political reform, because of the convergence of two broad trends in society. The first trend is an outcome of the limited programmes of socio-economic reform that have been inaugurated recently. These programmes, far from satisfying the appetite for change, have generated new demands and, as the crucial linkage between socio-economic improvement and political rights has become apparent, have increased pressures for broader political involvement and participation.

The second trend, the so-called modernization process, has produced the same result. The movement of blacks from traditional society into a modern economy, and the improved educational opportunities and general social awareness that has gone with it, have generated both a demand and a need for political rights.

The demand for political participation is articulated by every significant black organization or grouping in South Africa, from the most conservative to the most radical. This demand flows directly from the understandable perception of blacks that the denial of full citizenship is a denial of their human worth. The need for an extension of political rights is an outcome of this perception but is also the result of tension between the heightened aspirations and grievances of the black masses as a consequence of modernization and the absence of viable political institutions through which those grievances and aspirations can be channelled and accommodated.[15] This tension, now acute, is the main reason for the present unrest and instability in South Africa.

Recognition of the urgency of political reform leads to what it implies. Political reform can have no meaning unless it incorporates, as a basic preliminary step, the restoration, and in some instances creation, of the civil aspect of political freedom. This means allowing all South Africans the right to express their views, to associate and organize freely, and to elect truly representative leaders. It is only by permitting, indeed encouraging, the exercise of these rights that we can begin the process of determining how political power should be extended and shared, and what the main features of a new political and constitutional dispensation should be.

If the government is serious in its oft-repeated assurance that it does not wish to prescribe political solutions, it must restore the freedom necessary for all groups to discuss, formulate and strive for their visions of political accommodation, if not salvation. The continued denial of that freedom will perpetuate the conflict that the current State of Emergency is merely holding in check.

How possible and desirable is it to re-establish freedom under law in South Africa? The very societal conditions that underline the need for civil rights may also require the limitation of the freedoms that are to be restored. Certainly, South Africa's social situation makes the early achievement of the optimum goal of a civil rights programme unlikely, if not impossible, even under a transitional or new political order.

The optimum goal would be the full legal guarantee of all civil rights for all citizens in normal times, subject only to the partial abrogation of these rights during declared short-term emergencies. There is no known conflict society today in which that happy state of affairs has been substantially, let alone fully, realized. The governments of such societies have all been obliged to adopt, more or less permanently, special security measures that infringe on civil liberties.

Special measures, of varying degrees of stringency, have been in force in Northern Ireland since 1968;[16] Israel has been under declared emergency rule since independence in 1948; both pre- and post-liberated Zimbabwe has enforced drastic security measures on a continuous basis. While

---

15 Huntington, *Political order*, p. 47.

16 The year that marks the starting point of the present crisis there. Of course, special measures (of a more drastic kind) were employed in earlier crisis periods.

South Africa can certainly improve on its deplorable civil rights record, it is unlikely to be able to do better than the best of the other societies just mentioned. It is characterized by too many societal conditions that will necessitate coercive measures (and the consequent restriction of basic liberties).

The first of these is its racial and ethnic pluralism. Reluctant though one may be to admit it, the presence within a single society of large racially and culturally distinct groups is an almost certain source of at least some measure of social strife and disorder. Latent conflict in divided societies may be exacerbated or moderated by various factors, particularly style and content of policies implemented by the ruling group.

The second 'societal condition' is the modernization process to which the masses in South Africa have been exposed for some decades and which they will continue to experience for a considerable time. The process involves urbanization, large jumps in literacy, and education and media exposure. This in turn creates an awareness of the possibility of better living standards and of present disadvantages and deprivations attaching to excluded groups. New or heightened aspirations and political repression or exclusion are a dangerous, if not explosive, combination.

Finally, there is the impact of ruling group policies and practices on ethnic conflict and on the consequences of modernization. As already observed, governmental management may either heighten or mitigate the conflict potential of a divided society that is undergoing rapid modernization. Ironically, the policy of apartheid, designed to bring racial peace and harmony to the country, is now revealing its disastrous consequences for all in 'the beloved country'. Racial conflict has never been higher and is grimly expressed in the annual statistics of riots, political deaths, property destruction and urban terrorism.

However much the semantic gerrymandering of official propaganda may seek to present this conflict in non-ethnic terms, it is patently a struggle between black and white South Africans for power, status, wealth and opportunity. The ways in which government policy has intensified the ethnic dimensions of this conflict are clear. The official policy of apartheid has ensured that the benefits of modernization have been differentially distributed between the major ethnic groups.

While modernization has awakened among the black masses new hopes, visions and aspirations, apartheid has simultaneously limited black chances of attaining the anticipated benefits. Apartheid has reinforced what Horowitz found to be a major factor in ethnic conflict in Asia and Africa — the juxtaposition of less-developed and more-developed/developed groups within the same society. Under apartheid policy, being less developed (in terms of power, wealth and status) is officially a condition of being black, and whiteness is officially a condition of being more developed/developed (in the same terms).

No doubt these conditions would have tended to run along ethnic lines even without apartheid. However, a different policy could have mitigated and perhaps eliminated the differential distribution of the advancement of modernization.

Implicit in ruling group policy, moreover, is the will to rule permanently, which puts South African ethnic conflict into the 'zero-sum category' and rules out opposition policies or strategies of moderation. Even the rhetoric of the political reform policy of the government goes no further than sharing power without losing it. Official policy defines moderation out of existence. Then again, the entire party political system is conducted on ethnic lines — a feature which the recent repeal of legislation requiring party politics to be conducted on ethnic lines has barely affected.

Finally, in this brief review of the impact of government policy on ethnic conflict, we need to record the effect of the official denial of legitimacy to black groups (expressed in banning or other forms of repression) on the nature of opposition to official policies. The black indigenous group has been made to 'feel under siege in their own home, a powerful feeling that often calls up determined and violent political activity'.[17]

There is another aspect of white Nationalist policy in South Africa that is playing a largely unrecognized role in furthering conflict in the community, particularly ethnic conflict. National security policy in South Africa, tricked out as a 'law and order' programme, has become a divisive and strife-engendering instrument of political control. The main reason for this is that apartheid, which lacks all vestige, or even the hope of a vestige, of legitimacy among black South Africans, can be maintained only by brute force repression. State coercion provides the buttress that legitimacy would normally give to the basic policies of the society.

The law-and-order machinery is there to provide protection primarily for the white ethnic group and for those whom it has managed to co-opt into collaboration with it. Other groups not only fail to get that protection — they are also the principal victims of an increasingly lawless security programme that is directed indiscriminately against those who oppose ruling policies by non-violent or violent means. It has become a prime source of ethnic strife and general disorder in the country.

No security policy, as the McDonald Commission in Canada has declared, can be effective unless it has the broad backing and trust of the whole

---

17 D. Horowitz, *Ethnic groups in conflict*, Berkeley: Univ. of California Press, 1985, p. 213.

society.[18] The corollary is that a security system characterized by sectarian objectives and partisan application will undermine stability, creating lawless rival factions, vigilante groups and guerrilla armies.[19] That these are now a permanent part of the South African social scene can be blamed largely on a sectarian and lawless security system.

While ruling group policies and practices are directly responsible for social conflict and the denial of civil rights, as a social force they lack the inevitability of the other factors reviewed in this chapter. The ethnic plurality of the society must be accepted as given in the light of the total impracticability of partition schemes; modernization is something which could scarcely have been avoided in the past or arrested in the future.

Nevertheless, even though governing policies appear in this sense to be different and to be amenable to change or abandonment, their consequences may take generations to work through and out of the system. The divisions and hostilities they have created, and the ready resort to violence and destruction which they have fostered, will certainly not disappear overnight even under a new order characterized (presumably) by policies that are more socially therapeutic.

This is a problem which policies of political reform directed at the restoration of basic rights cannot ignore or underestimate; nor can such policies neglect the force of De Tocqueville's famous observation that it is precisely in times when a repressive order is lifted that pent-up dissatisfactions are wont to be expressed in strife and conflict.

There is a feature of ruling party repression in South Africa that is likely to give De Tocqueville's axiom added validity — the destruction of black leadership under National Party security laws. During a period of change there will inevitably be violent jostling to fill the vacuum in leadership positions, and ones filled to capture the advantages of power under the new order. Everything appears to point, therefore, to a continuing need to devise control measures to contain intergroup conflict with the consequence that there will be some measure of restriction over basic rights.

The restoration of basic rights faces a further difficulty in South Africa. The basic values which underlie a system of civil rights appear to have shallow cultural roots among almost all the major groups. The first of these values is that of the individual as an autonomous person and therefore that the person rather than the group is the primary legal concept.[20] The second

---

18 *Freedom and security under law*, (The McDonald Report) vol. 1, 2nd report of the Commission of Enquiry concerning certain activities of the Royal Canadian Mounted Police, Ottawa: Canadian Government Publishing Centre, 1981, p. 15.

19 P. Wilkinson, *Terrorism and the liberal state*, London: McMillan, 1977, p. 124.

20 See A. B. Bozeman, 'Human rights and national security', in *Yale Journal of World Public Order*, vol. 9, 1982,

is the notion of the 'law-directed state' in which people are viewed not as subjects but citizens with all the rights essential for active participation in government.[21] These values are not deeply grounded in the belief systems of any group in South Africa, except perhaps the English community.

Four decades of Afrikaner Nationalist rule have demonstrated how dispensable these two values are. Legislation passed by the ruling party has converted citizens into submissive, rightless subjects and the *rechtsstaat* or law-directed state has been undermined. If the idea of the autonomous individual governed by law was ever incorporated into the belief system of the Afrikaner group, it has certainly now ceased to be part of their cultural ethic.

The hold of these same values is clearly also fragile among indigenous African communities. As Bozeman says, there is 'not even a voting majority in the modern society of states to support the twin notions of the individual as an autonomous person and citizen'.[22] To be realistic, Africa can barely boast of a voting minority, let alone majority, for the ideas under discussion.

A reform programme aimed at creating an order characterized by legally-protected individual rights will lack a cultural support base among the major contenders for power in South Africa. The process of creating a viable system in which the individual will be respected and government authorities legally controlled will clearly be a long and tortuous one.

Future reform

From this socio-cultural analysis of South African society it is clear that the present lack of rights that characterizes the society will not and cannot be replaced in the short term, even under the best imaginable of new governments, with a system characterized by full-blown individual rights and the strict subjection of public authority to legal rules.

The available studies of the most successful strategies of change from despotic to democratic rule support this. In Brazil, for example, liberalization has been a fluctuating rather than a linear process[23] 'characterised by a series of changes that have improved the context of human rights and enlarged the forum for political activities, and by tight government controls designed to limit the consequences of the process.'[24]

---

pp. 40, 42.

21 Bozeman, 'Human rights', p. 43.

22 Bozeman, 'Human rights', p. 44.

23 T. G. Sanders, 'Human rights and political process', in H. Handelman and T. G. Sanders, eds., *Military government and the movement towards democracy in South America*, Bloomington: Indiana Univ. Press, 1981, p. 185.

24 Sanders, 'Human rights', p. 184.

Though the 'two steps forward one step backward' approach to democratization was a conscious process in Brazil, it is clearly one dictated by social factors that are also present in South Africa, such as the resistance of conservative groups to too rapid a process of change, and the social conflict that tends to arise when security controls are lifted.

While studies of the more successful strategies of liberalization emphasize the importance of controlling the process by the use of 'repressive' measures, they provide no support for the type of repression characterized as 'emergency law' in South Africa. We can accept, however, that the process of liberalization will inevitably be accompanied by programmes of control, hopefully characterized by more rationality, moderation and humanity than the current South African version.

The establishment of complete freedom under law is an option precluded both to power-holders (who, in any event, do not desire it) and to their challengers and successors. On the other hand, adherence to present policies is also out of the question. Repression under the guise of national security is a viable choice only in the minds of those who cannot, or refuse to, comprehend social realities. These policies guarantee a future of conflict within the society and between South Africa and the outside world. Moreover, present policies are leading the country away from, not towards, a democratic resolution of social problems.

The rejection of the extremes represented by the status quo and by its reversal brings intermediate solutions into focus — beefing up of citizen rights and considerably less muscle for the security arm of government. Freedom and order can be brought into a kind of equilibrium by a better directed and controlled security system and by institutional protection for basic political freedoms. The method or model by which this can be achieved is best described as a qualified due process model. This gives due weight to political reform since it envisages the recognition of civil liberties and their enforcement or withdrawal according to the needs of the time as determined by disinterested officials or tribunals.

The prospects of political reform can be enhanced by requiring the regular review of measures which further or retard political and individual liberty. In this way the skewed relationship between freedom, order and reform should be replaced by one in which all the parts of the triad are recognized and accorded institutional protection, even though the balance between them may be a shifting one according to the needs and pressures of the time.

Some cautionary remarks about the qualified due process model:

> It will have relatively low appeal to the politically extreme groups spawned by ethnic confrontation and conflict in South Africa — it will seem as pallid to the law-and-order lobby as it will to the radical

liberationists, yet only such models of compromise and concession can alleviate the social ills of ethnically divided societies.

▷ The model is incompatible with the politics of both white and black domination. Its adoption, even in stages, implies a commitment by the power-holders to relinquish absolute control and by their challengers to forego claims to sole authority to determine the fate of each and every subject. It is therefore less attractive now than it will be when political incumbents and challengers have been brought to virtual stalemate by a long war of attrition.

▷ The model is a fairly sophisticated one which will require time to be learnt, absorbed and given proper institutional embodiment. The sooner the process is begun, the greater the chance of creating a system in which freedom, order and reform will be complementary rather than mutually destructive.

Any due process model, whether qualified or not, must prescribe legally enforceable standards for national security operations. To do this, a prior question must be asked and answered: what does the national security programme seek to protect and what is it required to guard against? This question was never squarely faced by the Rabie Commission in its seemingly exhaustive investigation into internal security legislation in South Africa.[25] The McDonald Commission in Canada, in one of the most comprehensive and profound studies of national security in a free society, did not commit the elementary blunder of ducking it.[26] The objective of the national security programme in Canada, the Commission said, should be to protect the system of democracy, the main components of which it declared to be 'responsible government, the rule of law and the right to dissent . . .'.[27]

Freedom, democracy and the rule of law have been the chief casualties of four decades of National Party rule and the objective of the present security programme is manifestly not to protect those values and institutions. However, this chapter is concerned with reform choices. The McDonald Commission's statement of underlying values can be reformulated for a programme of change in South Africa. The chief objectives of a security system of the future should be to protect those citizen freedoms that remain and, more importantly, to create a framework within which freedom may progressively be broadened under the control of the law.

The role of a reformed security system will emerge more clearly if we turn to the second part of the question posed earlier: what does a national

---

25 *Die verslag van die kommissie van ondersoek na veiligheidswetgewing,* (RP 90/1981).

26 The McDonald Report.

27 The McDonald Report, pp. 39–44.

security programme seek to guard against? According to the McDonald Commission, the threats against which national security operations may legitimately be directed are espionage, foreign and clandestine interference in local politics, terrorism and political violence, sabotage (narrowly defined) and revolutionary subversion (ideologies or programmes that envisage the overthrow of the liberal democratic state).[28]

In the South African context, this statement of the threats which security legislation may legitimately counter is significant mainly for what it omits. The McDonald Commission made it clear that it should be no part of a security system, as it is in this country, to suppress political dissent, or to deal with opposition to government policies or with unpopular ideologies or ideas.

South African national security legislation, while covering the threats envisaged by the McDonald Commission, also extends to the control of opposition and dissent. Reform clearly implies the removal of illegitimate objectives without, of course, nobbling the security forces in operations against espionage, terrorism and the like. In short, reform means the removal of the ideological and political control objectives of current security laws.

Once the broad goals of security law have been established, they must be translated into enforceable legal prescriptions — a charter which would specify what operations the security forces may legitimately undertake and what activities lie outside the scope of their mandate. It should also provide mechanisms for holding the security forces to their mandate. These should include judicial review and may also extend to internal review procedures, parliamentary control and the establishment of an ombudsman or a tribunal with a similar function.

The main function of the charter should be to lay down standards or criteria against which the propriety or validity of security force actions might be judged, ranging from criteria for guilt under the code of security crimes, to legal justifications for detaining individuals or banning meetings or organizations.

It goes without saying that the crimes created by the charter will accord with the principle of legality and will not permit the conviction of citizens in terms of criminal prohibitions that are excessively vague or sweeping. Nor will the charter permit the security authorities, whether at ministerial level or otherwise, to be the sole judges of who should be detained or what organization or meetings should be outlawed. It is quite unacceptable that government officials should be able to act as uncontrolled despots in respect of such decisions, as they do under present law.

---

[28] The McDonald Report, p. 431, *et seq.*

The prescription of standards will be pointless unless independent tribunals are created with powers to enforce them. Wherever possible, the ordinary courts should have jurisdiction over crimes, and possibly over other matters such as detention.[29]

It will not be sufficient to increase the jurisdiction of the ordinary courts since their present composition and functioning reflects the current state of political inequality and the distorted distribution of decision-making authority. The structure and functioning of the judiciary will have to be reviewed in the period of change. Where jurisdiction is granted to non-judicial bodies, they must have factual and visible independence both in terms of their membership and their constitution.

Particularly to be avoided is the South African tendency of granting the courts the appearance rather than the substance of jurisdiction in security matters. For example, under almost all detention laws in South Africa[30] the courts have a negligible power of intervention since the power to detain is legally dependent on the detaining authorities' subjective opinion. Where the exercise of that power is based on a genuinely-formed opinion, the courts tend to uphold it, however groundless it may be. Intervention by the courts is limited to gross misuse or abuse of the detention power, a limitation which has ensured that few detainees receive justice in South Africa.

Increased court involvement does not involve the substitution of court judgment for that of the executive in the administration of security law. There is a well-established legal formula which avoids casting the judge as either eunuch or usurper in security matters. This formula would limit court intervention to cases in which no reasonable man could have arrived at the decision taken by the relevant security authority. The judge does not retry the merits of security cases; rather, he overrules those that are patently without merit.

Greater power for courts or independent tribunals in security matters also involves adherence to procedural justice or due process. Restrictions of liberty, even in the asserted interests of national security, should generally be preceded, or in cases of extreme urgency certainly be followed, by a hearing in which the basic elements of natural justice are observed.

The main requirements of natural justice are an unbiased and independent judge, presentation of at least the outline of the state case against the affected person, and legal representation. Not all the due process requirements of a criminal trial need be observed where restrictions such as

---

29 They have such jurisdiction in Israel, as will be explained further on in the chapter.

30 Section 29 detention has been an exception since the judgement in *Minister of Law and Order v. Hurley*, 1986 (3), SA 568 (A).

detention or banning are imposed. The guiding principle should be that every requirement of procedural justice that will not clearly undermine legitimate security operations should be observed by the authorities.

To sum up, a qualified due process model of security control implies that national security operations will be controlled by legal standards under the guidance of independent courts or tribunals applying the basic rules of natural justice wherever possible.

Israel provides a concrete example of the application of this model in a society subject to national security threats at least as formidable as in South Africa. The due process model of preventive detention was adopted[31] in 1979 to replace the executive model introduced by the British mandatory power in 1945. The new Israeli preventive detention law[32] accords with procedural justice in the following ways:

▷ Every detainee must be brought before a superior court within 48 hours of detention, failing which his detention becomes invalid.

▷ The court conducts a hearing on the detention at which the detainee may be present and legally represented.

▷ After hearing both the state case and that of the detainee, the court may either confirm or set aside the detention order.

▷ If the court confirms the order, it must periodically review the necessity for detention under the same rules of procedure.

However, there are several departures from the strict requirements of procedural justice:

▷ The criteria for detention (that it is required 'for reasons of state security or public security') are not specific enough.

▷ The detainee and his legal representative may be excluded from the hearing by the court during the presentation of sensitive evidence (although they will later be told of the gist of the evidence).

▷ The strict rules of evidence in criminal cases need not be observed.

▷ Only lawyers authorized to appear before an army court martial may represent the detainee.

The Israeli due process detention model illustrates that it is possible to bring the courts into the detention process and to render substantial justice to the detainee without dereliction of national security requirements. The courts have confirmed some detention decisions but set aside others, and they appear to be striking a reasonable balance between the demands of security and considerations of liberty in a conflict-ridden society.

---

[31] In Israel proper, as distinct from the occupied territories.

[32] Emergency Powers (Detention) Law no. 5739, 1979.

In another such society — Northern Ireland — the balance has recently been struck at a point more favourable to liberty without any increase in insurgency or unrest. Preventive detention has not been employed in Northern Ireland since 1975 and interrogational detention is strictly circumscribed by law, being limited to a maximum of seven days and subject to effective procedures to prevent the abuse of detainees.

Interrogational detention in Northern Ireland provides a good model for reform of the same institution in South Africa which, on account of its indefinite duration and lack of proper controls, has led to numerous detainee deaths and the extensive practice of torture.

No model need be followed slavishly; but if there is a will to reform and to extend freedom without neglecting the legitimate demands of security, there is much that can be learnt from divided societies like Israel (excluding the occupied territories) and Northern Ireland. In neither of these countries has the introduction of more due process elements into security law aggravated security threats. On the contrary, in Northern Ireland there is clear evidence that unrest incidents declined after preventive detention was abolished.

On the positive side, there were undoubtedly political gains flowing from the reforms in both societies: they invested government in both societies with greater internal and external legitimacy. Greater legitimacy is a political advance which South African society is sorely in need of.

These examples do not exhaust the usefulness of the qualified due process model, which can be adapted to many other security functions. The banning of individuals could be subject to due process requirements similar to those now required for detention in Israel. For example, the courts there have the power to examine all the information which influenced the state authorities in imposing a banning order and to order release of such information to detainees.

Security provisions relating to the right of assembly are virtually devoid of due process elements in South Africa: at present the minister's power to ban meetings of two or more persons on public or private property is absolute. Even where the minister has authorized magistrates to grant exemptions to the sweeping ban on open-air meetings, the magistrates' decisions are effectively beyond judicial control.[33]

Security law on the right of assembly in South Africa constitutes a standing invitation to the governing party to suppress opposition to itself. There is clearly a need in conflict societies to regulate the right of assembly, particularly in public places, but the decision to ban or to subject meetings to

---

33 *Castel NO v. Metal and Allied Workers Union*, 1987 (4), SA 795 (A).

controls should be vested in more disinterested persons or bodies with a right of review on the merits to the courts.

Conclusion

The central proposition of this chapter has been that freedom and reform on the one hand, and security on the other, can be balanced so that the needs of each receive the weight and emphasis demanded by the social conditions of the time. Though the balance will be a shifting one, the goal of social policy should be the extension of freedom through reform and the reduction of coercive powers which inhibit the enjoyment of fundamental civil liberties.

It is a pre-condition of the achievement of that goal that security law should not be an instrument of sectarian political control, as it is at present, but rather a mechanism that permits all contending groups to settle their differences peacefully. The proposal that the scope of security law be reduced is not based on any under-estimation of the importance of maintaining peace and order in a divided society. The basic nature of the human need for security makes it all the more reprehensible that it has been grievously exploited in South Africa.

It is not freedom that has got out of hand in South Africa, but security. Unless the rapaciousness of the security machine is brought under control, the prospects for liberty and reform are dim, if not non-existent. But security power has to be tamed, not eliminated. Legislation to preserve security is essential in all societies, and of high importance in a divided one.

5   The public bureaucracy: reform and accountability

Robert Schrire

> *This chapter explores the relationship between bureaucratic power and public policy-making in contemporary South Africa, and then speculates on the possible role of the public bureaucracy should genuine reform become the policy of the government of the day. By reform is meant a broadening of the recruitment base of political participation, with the consequent incorporation of blacks into the ruling élite.*

Introduction

Former State President P. W. Botha's major political legacy is the institutionalization of a massive, centralized and authoritarian state structure. From the State Security Council to Joint Management Centres, the system is bureaucratic, with most aspects of its operations conducted behind closed doors.[1]

Indeed, the last decade has been characterized by the implementation of a policy based upon secrecy, and the restructuring of state organizations. The government has argued that policy should be developed from the top, which it has then imposed upon an increasingly unwilling and even hostile population. Committee government has become the norm, with the consequent characteristics of power struggles, hierarchy, secrecy and limited access to authority.

In this process, the permanent officials of the public service have exercised unparalleled power. The Office of the State President is unique to South African politics and has become the key to both policy making and implementation. Functions such as information and administration are performed by ministers directly responsible to the President. Key bodies such as the National Intelligence Service and the National Priorities Committee are also located within the presidency, while a powerful secretary-general services the system.

---

1   The Botha system is analysed in B. Pottinger, *The imperial presidency*, Johannesburg: Southern, 1988. See also Centre for Policy Studies, *South Africa at the end of the eighties*, Johannesburg: The Penrose Press, 1989.

The system of committee government has given bureaucrats unique access to policy. The size of government involved in the new system gives them influence over the presidency not enjoyed under a prime-ministerial system. Bureaucrats now participate directly in key bodies such as the State Security Council; they also play a vital role in servicing the other cabinet committees. Inevitably, the imperial presidency has created a new system of power relationships in which bureaucracy has flourished.

An important consequence has been a reduction in public support for the institutions of government, as well as in their legitimacy. Another has been a dramatic decline in the degree to which administration is accountable to the people.

One of the most urgent tasks facing President de Klerk is to restructure the state administrative apparatus. The almost exclusively white administration will have to become more broadly representative of the general population, a concept explored in Chapter 7 by Hugo. Secondly, the administrative organs of the state must be made accountable to the citizenry and more compatible with reform policies.

Before policy proposals to make administration more reformist and accountable can be formulated, it is necessary to summarize the present weaknesses of the state structures. The most important include the following:

▷ There is a focus on control rather than development or welfare. Historically, a major function of the state has been to protect minority interests, including the state structures themselves. This has entailed excluding blacks from the political system, including the higher levels of the public service, and implementing a maze of repressive laws regulating, among others, Group Areas, population mobility and private sexual choices. In ethos and structure, control has been the fundamental driving force of the political system.

▷ There has been a failure of the polity, as represented by an exclusively white electorate, to contribute to a circulation of élites through regular changes in government. Since 1948 the National Party has exercised uninterrupted power; at no time has it been seriously challenged either by its parliamentary rivals or by extra-parliamentary forces. Thus the regular changes in government, which are supposed to characterize a Westminster system, have not taken place — with important consequences for bureaucratic behaviour.

Where changes of government are relatively frequent, such as in the United Kingdom, there is a healthy tension between political and administrative élites.[2] Political parties, especially when in opposition, are

---

2 A lot of literature on this topic exists. See especially, S. Beer, *Modern British politics*, London: Faber and Faber,

a major source of new initiatives — indeed they seek office largely on a platform of rejecting important elements of the policies of the day.[3] Naturally, upon taking office they usually have some reservations about those senior civil servants who implemented the policies of their predecessors.

However, the continuity in office of the National Party, allied to the close socio-cultural similarities between political and administrative élites, has tended to diminish, if not eliminate, this natural tension between politicians and administrators. Indeed, political-administrative co-operation has probably been powerfully reinforced by the opposition to 'Afrikaner government' from important groups in South Africa and by the external pressures focused on official policies. Since 1948, then, the relationship between administrator and political figure has been one of partnership.

▷ A closed, hierarchical and authoritarian mode of decision-making and implementation is a feature of government. Policy-making is a closely held monopoly enjoyed by a handful of political and administrative élites. The process of decision-making is deliberately kept secret: participants, the options considered, and the reasons for a decision are seldom publicly revealed. Power inequalities are a dominant characteristic of the process and the role of the presidency is critical. The public is largely excluded from the process and a wide range of interests are not taken into account.

▷ Policy-making and its implementation favours white interests over those of blacks. By any criterion of policy evaluation, be it resource allocation or issues of values and symbols, black interests are disadvantaged relative to white interests and, at worst, are completely rejected.

In future the key issue will be the role of the bureaucracy in the process of genuine reform. Until now the bureaucracy has been a reasonably effective instrument of administration, for at least three reasons:

1. the similarities in culture, values and interests between the political and administrative élites;

2. the dominant position of the National Party-controlled cabinets, as a result of their secure hold on power; and

---

1980; F. F. Ridley, ed., *Government and administration in Western Europe*, Oxford: St Martin's Press, 1979; J. J. Richardson and A. G. Gordon, *Governing under pressure*, Oxford: St Martin's Press, 1979; J. J. Richardson, ed., *Policy style in Western Europe*, London: Allen and Unwin, 1982; and B. Smith, *Policy-making in British government*, Oxford: St Martin's Press, 1976.

3 An interesting model built upon this assumption is contained in A. Downs, *An economic theory of democracy*, New York: Harper and Row, 1957.

3. the limited nature of the reforms so far, with the consequent continuation of a basic political-administrative system which strongly favours white interests.

Put simply, a largely united political élite, under strong leadership, has worked effectively with a set of public officials sympathetic towards the interests and values of the political élite, which they also share. In large measure, both groups have seen their task as serving the interests of their larger outside constituency — the white electorate.

The bureaucracy and reform

The process of genuine reform will have to entail many fundamental changes, including the following:

▷ increasing demands from black groups for public services;

▷ increased black participation in elective politics;

▷ a weaker government, which will attempt to balance the interests of its different constituencies;

▷ rapid change in a wide range of political, economic and social practices and institutions;

▷ increased community conflict and lack of consensus, both within the white community and between different politically defined groups and factions; and

▷ increased recruitment of blacks into all levels of the public service. (See Chapter 7.)

Under these probable conditions what role will the public service play in the political process? Much will depend on the general political circumstances under which reform takes place and also on the nature of the reforms and the consequent political demands made upon the bureaucracy.

The present structure and performance of the public bureaucracy reflects the political alignment of forces in the larger polity. An essentially white-controlled set of institutions, sharing the interests and values of the dominant forces in the polity, performs basic control functions over blacks.

How, one may ask, is this bureaucratic system likely to react to genuine reforms which place increasing political power in the hands of blacks and which lead to changes in the distribution of costs and benefits between the state's ethnic groups? Much will depend on the type of policy advice emerging from within the bureaucracy, the bureaucratic reactions to political decisions in the areas of implementation and administrative discretion, and the relationship between bureaucrats and the public and within the bureaucracy itself.

Policy advice

It is accepted that senior bureaucrats will inevitably exercise significant influence on policy-making. Indeed, one of the factors which has greatly limited the policy influence of coloured people and Asians participating in the Tricameral Parliament has been the absence of black people from senior levels of the public service.

Of all the forms of potential influence exercised by bureaucrats, the most susceptible to political controls is the advice function. The political élite has several mechanisms it could use to ensure that non-bureaucratic sources of information and analysis are incorporated into the policy process:

▷ The use of political parties as a source of policy initiatives: in the Westminster model, political parties are one of the major sources of policy initiatives, because the system is based upon constructive opposition. It is incumbent upon the parties in opposition to devise credible policy alternatives on which they can base their campaigns for office.

▷ The use of outside experts and policy institutes: in countries such as the US, where weak or non-existent political parties are a feature, a major source of policy expertise comes from policy professionals. A significant segment of the intellectual community is involved in a wide range of policy debates, and specialized institutions such as the Rand Corporation and the Brookings Institution exist to explore public policy issues and to propagate policy recommendations.

Far too few organizations or institutes in South Africa are actively involved in policy debates, although this is slowly changing. Organized interests such as commerce ought seriously to be financing independent think-tanks; government should contract with outside groups and experts not only to explore new policy initiatives, but also to monitor its own performance.

▷ The restructuring of the public service to permit the utilization of non-career officials in departmental affairs: in the US this is achieved by creating a layer of partisan positions within each department, which may be temporarily filled by each new administration.[4] The task of these officials is to ensure that the permanent bureaucrats respond to the policy of the administration, and to provide policy perspectives which do not reflect bureaucratic priorities. In France, each minister may appoint his own departmental cabinet from outside the permanent bureaucracy to serve similar functions.

---

4 For the United States experience, consult H. Heclko, *A government of strangers*, Washington, DC: Brookings Inst., 1977; K. Meier, *Politics and the bureaucracy*, North Scituate, Massachusetts: Duxbury Publishers, 1979; and D. Nachmias and D. Rosenbloom, *Bureaucratic government USA*, New York: St Martin's Press, 1980. E. Suleiman, *Élites in French society: the politics of survival*, Princeton Univ. Press, 1978 is the best source on the French system.

▷ The establishment of policy-orientated staff within the executive branch, either located in a special planning unit or appointed to members of the presidential staff: in the United States government, the President appoints a large number of experts, whose major function is to provide him with advice and analysis. In addition, major departments have their own policy-planning staffs, and at the federal level the National Security Council (NSC) and the Office of Management and the Budget (OMB) are designed to provide non-departmental perspectives on national issues.

Government needs to accept the desirability of 'multiple advocacy' in terms of which a system of institutionalized dissent is built into the policy framework.[5] This means that at all levels decision-makers are exposed to competing assessments of the nature of the problem; the options, costs and benefits of different scenarios. This limited adversarial structure should enable government to choose between conflicting alternatives with a greater understanding of the complexity of competing interests and perceptions.

Political leaders have the means to ensure that they are not exclusively dependent upon the bureaucracy for expertise. In addition, bureaucrats are sensitive to the views of their political masters and are perhaps more likely to tailor their advice to the assumed purposes of their political superiors than to impose their own policy preferences.

Implementation and discretion

A key power of the bureaucracy, and difficult to limit, is that which is inherent in the administrative function.[6] Most legislative measures will be vague, and even comprehensive measures cannot outline in exhaustive detail how the ends are to be realized. The choice of means is therefore inherently political and may indeed have substantial impact on the attainment of objectives.

Although many scholars have recognized the political importance of administrative discretion, none has devised satisfactory solutions.[7] Discretion is inherent in administration and an unavoidable element which cannot be fully controlled. However, certain measures can limit the negative consequences of this discretion:

---

5 This concept has been developed in greatest detail in the writings of Alexander George of Stanford University. See also the work of Graham Allison and Irving Janis.

6 See C. Ham and M. Hill, *The policy process in the modern capitalist state*, New York: St Martin's Press, 1984; and E. A. Nordlinger, *On the autonomy of the democratic state*, Cambridge, Massachusetts: Harvard Univ. Press, 1981.

7 The most ambitious set of proposals remain those in K. C. Davis, *Discretionary justice*, Urbana, Illinois: Illinois Univ. Press, 1977.

▷ The legal framework must be created which makes administrators responsible for their actions. This could include laws obliging bureaucracies to provide detailed information from their files according to criteria which balance organizational effectiveness and public responsibility.

South Africa could do worse than copy the United States in passing a 'Freedom of Information Act' which would grant individuals reasonable access to government-held information. Laws that protect the right to privacy could also be passed to protect citizens from the misuse of private information obtained by government on, for example, religious or political affiliations.[8]

▷ The courts can be used to give aggrieved parties the opportunity to redress bureaucratic errors and bias. This could be achieved through the existing courts or by the creation of specialized tribunals to deal with administrative and other issues.

The doctrine of judicial review requires strengthening. There are virtually no countervailing powers to government to enable citizens, with a minimum of delay and cost, to obtain fairness in both procedures and substantive decisions. The right to challenge unfair or arbitrary government decisions must be both accepted in principle and made feasible in practice.

▷ Legislative authority must be strengthened to enable it to have some control over the implementation of policy. This would require greater use of a committee system incorporating members of the legislature. Although this system of legislative oversight is probably incompatible with a Westminster system, the 1983 Constitution contains the seeds of greater separation between the legislature and the executive.

▷ A supervisory capability must be created within the political executive. Although it is recognized that attempts by a political executive to take over the implementation of policy from the careerists are costly, and usually ineffective, nevertheless, the executive should have the capacity to ensure that bureaucrats implement policy in a way which is compatible with the goals of its programmes.

This capacity could be created in several ways. The Office of the President could be expanded to give the President supervisory power. For example, a group of experts could be appointed with skills in economics, finance and foreign policy to monitor the performance of these departments. The President could also employ personal aides to assist him in his executive functions. Alternatively, this capacity could

---

8 An excellent discussion is contained in B. Rosen, *Holding government bureaucracies accountable*, New York: Praeger, 1982.

be formalized in executive agencies with broad supervisory powers, equivalent to the OMB or NSC in the United States.

Perhaps the most important factor determining the behaviour of the bureaucracy is its perception of basic government attitudes and orientations. Take, for example, the agencies of the state where discretion is most unavoidable and dramatic — the police and the security services. In their case the measures outlined above would, at best, be only partially effective. There are usually few reliable witnesses to the relevant events, and generally the word of a police officer stands against the assertions of an alleged victim.

Yet the responsiveness and integrity of the police and security forces do differ from state to state, although the formal institutional structures of control may be very similar. It is generally accepted that in South Africa white prisoners receive better treatment than black prisoners; and the police are generally more circumspect in dealing with white protesters than with black.

The evidence that torture and the physical and mental abuse of prisoners are fairly widespread seems to be irrefutable. Perhaps a major reason why the government has not been effective in reforming the security system is that government and its officials have similar values and interests. Both sets of officials share the basic racial prejudices of society, both place a higher premium on white rights than on black rights, and both regard the infringement of black rights as less serious than that of white rights.

As a result, government statements against the abuse of prisoners are not taken as seriously as might be expected — not because the government is cynical, but because officials do not perceive signs of genuine concern or a genuine political commitment to the improvement of black rights.

The bureaucracy and the public

To a considerable degree, attitudes of the public towards government are shaped by their experiences in dealing with bureaucracy. Civil servants are in daily contact with the public and influence public perceptions of policy in important ways. A corrupt, inefficient or hostile bureaucracy will undermine public support for the authorities and their policies, irrespective of their merits.

The white experience will differ dramatically from the black experience. Blacks experience the bureaucracy mostly in its role as the implementor of the control policies of government. As such, they have to suffer the corruption, inefficiency and racial arrogance of officials in their day-to-day enforcement of influx control (now substantially modified), allocation of housing, implementation of education policies — in fact, all the devices making up the general bureaucratic web which ensnares them from cradle to grave.

Changing attitudes and consequent patterns of behaviour will be the most difficult challenge facing the reform élite. It is also the most difficult to monitor. Of the limited options available, the following would be the most effective:

▷ First, the composition of the bureaucracy should be broadened, especially its higher echelons. Considerable literature on the representative bureaucracy exists — most of it inconclusive.[9] However, in a plural community with deep ascriptive divisions, a public sector which reflected these constituencies would have several important advantages.

One is an urgent need to break the white domination of the senior levels of the present bureaucracy. Black input at all levels would, if nothing else, improve communications between bureaucrat and client. Another is that, from a political perspective, blacks would be given visible evidence of the significance of reform.

Increased black recruitment into policy levels of the public service would be a dramatic sign of the realities of reform. This could help legitimize the system and dampen demands from the have-not sectors.

▷ The second opportunity is to create a mechanism for handling individual complaints. This could include an office of ombudsman. The literature indicates that this should be located outside the regular public service and be under direct political control.[10] The mechanisms for bringing items to the attention of the ombudsman and working procedures should be as simple as possible. It may also be preferable to create a series of small, specialized offices rather than a large, complex department.

The office of ombudsman should serve two purposes: to provide citizens with information about government programmes and how to approach government officials, and to provide a means of action when citizen complaints require further investigation.

▷ In addition, the role of the citizenry in policy should be expanded and institutionalized, a topic explored in greater detail in Chapter 2 by Boulle. The legislature should consider instituting 'Sunshine' laws which grant citizens the right to know how decisions were made, who participated in the process and the source of the information.

The expansion of public participation could help defuse conflict issues, and contribute to the legitimation of new reform institutions. In the critical area of police–citizen relations, for example, where tensions and suspicions exist, a useful start could be made by setting up

---

9 See S. Krislov, *Representative bureaucracy*, London: Prentice-Hall, 1974.

10 See S. V. Anderson, *Ombudsman readings*, Edmonton, Alberta: International Ombudsman Inst., Univ. of Alberta, 1980; and F. Stacey, *Ombudsman compared*, Oxford: Oxford Univ. Press, 1978.

joint committees comprising local residents and law enforcement officers. Their task would be to investigate citizen and police grievances, thereby starting a process of increasing co-operation. Public hearings, report-back meetings and the greater use of radio and television could all be used to increase the possibilities for citizen involvement.

In the final analysis, the most significant factor will be the attitude of the political élite towards reform. If the government is genuinely determined to implement reforms, this attitude will influence bureaucratic behaviour. If, on the other hand, bureaucrats detect a basic ambivalence, they will seize the opportunity to continue their traditional attitude towards their largely black clientele.

Relationships within the bureaucracy

The increased recruitment of blacks into all sectors of the public service will have profound consequences at all levels of organizational performance. The present homogeneity will be destroyed and the public bureaucracy will gradually mirror the pluralism of the larger society. This will produce at least two major changes: the relationship between the bureaucracy and the public will change (as indicated above); and personnel relations within the bureaucracy will change.[11]

The end of an Afrikaner bureaucracy and the creation of a representative set of institutions will be a significant development. More diverse interests and values will be reflected at all levels. New conflicts will emerge, both over scarce resources and over policy positions. Human relations within the organizations of the state must inevitably deteriorate, as government has to transform itself from an artificially segregated élite body to one which has greater ethnic diversity.

The bureaucracy will thus lose some of its effectiveness and unity of purpose. It will itself become one of the sites of conflict and the spoils of political victory; and in the process become politicized to a greater degree than at present. These changes, however, will be inevitable if genuine reform takes place. The maintenance of an Afrikaner bureaucracy in a de-racialized society, with some form of political power-sharing, will be an impossibility.

Conclusions

Bureaucracies are inherently blunt instruments, more suited to the administration of a static status quo than of dramatic innovation or political reconciliation. They are inherently conservative, both because of the kind

---

[11] See H. Adam and H. Giliomee, *The rise and crisis of Afrikaner power*, Cape Town: David Philip, 1979.

of people attracted to the security of a bureaucratic career and because of their size, structure and internal dynamics. There is always some tension between a democratic polity on the one hand, and an administrative order on the other.[12]

However, although there will always be a gap between promise and performance, and aspirations and achievements, bureaucracies are more effective for organizing resources and providing the ordered framework necessary for community existence than any other known system. At the same time, it is necessary to structure the bureaucracy to serve the larger interests of the polity. The South African bureaucracy cannot be faulted, because it does what it has been designed to do — administer the status quo, which implies furthering white interests and acting as the instrument of control over blacks.

The reform of South Africa's institutions of representative government are clearly of pre-eminent importance in the process of reform. Changes in the bureaucracy cannot be a substitute for extending the franchise; indeed, reform of the bureaucracy will fail unless the larger issues of power and privilege are simultaneously addressed.

At the same time, reform of the institutions of representation are unlikely to succeed unless accompanied by changes in the administrative framework. A basic reality is that the level of government which most people come into contact with most often is the public official administering the policies of the state, and, to a large extent, citizens will judge national politics on the basis of these experiences.

The politics of reform will demand a fundamental reorientation of the bureaucracy. Its basic functions will have to change from control to interest representation and political reconciliation. This will entail not only changes in basic policy — the prerogative of the political élite — but changes in the form and style of service delivery, and change in the racial composition of the bureaucracy itself.

Many of the changes necessary to reform the bureaucracy will demand more far-reaching political changes. It is vital for the legislature to play a far more important role in controlling state officials than is possible under the present constitution. The legislature should have the powers to launch independent investigations and hold hearings, to review policy implementation, to have an independent research and expertise capability in areas such as budgeting policy, and to have some influence, perhaps through a confirmation process, over the choice of key public officials such

---

12 For analysis which deal with these issues, see G. E. Berkley, *The craft of public administration*, Boston, Massachusetts: Allyn and Bacon, 1978; and C. J. Friedrich, *Man and his government*, New York: McGraw-Hill, 1963.

as the heads of the police, intelligence service, and central bank. Clearly then, the reform of the bureaucracy will have to be part of a process away from the present centralized system to one of greater decentralization and deconcentration.

Reform élites have to balance the political demands for reform with the equally important need to ensure that the bureaucracy remains efficient and effective. Broadened recruitment, the Africanization of some of the basic organizational procedures, and inevitable politicization will, at least in the short-term, adversely affect narrowly defined efficiency.

As long as the trains still run, perhaps it is better for them to have less efficient, multiracial operating teams than more efficient, traditional white operators. Reform, as cited above, is thus likely to weaken the bureaucracy because part of its organizational coherence stems from its unrepresentative ethnic composition and conservative operating procedures. In a multi-ethnic and multi-cultural society the public bureaucracy stands out as a symbol of white, and especially Afrikaner, domination, because indeed it is predominantly both.

A reform bureaucracy will be less efficient than its predecessor, less effective in a technical sense and probably corrupt in different ways. Politicization may mean that some groups will receive preferential treatment while others will be discriminated against. Basic relationships between the organization and its clients will change — not always for the better.

Moreover, this chapter has stressed that the polity has the means to control its bureaucracy. A government genuinely dedicated to reform will have the means to ensure that its permanent officials comply with its dictates. A divided government, or one that is ambivalent about its reform policies, will create opportunities for bureaucracies to impose their own values on policies and their implementation.

Reform is always an uncertain process and will have untidy elements. New groups and interests will benefit; old beneficiaries will lose. However, there is one major advantage that reform will have from an organizational perspective: the deregulation of society, for example, ending all influx control measures, deregulating the economy and abandoning Group Areas, are administratively easy to implement.

While the politics of regulation places heavy burdens on the bureaucracy and creates many opportunities for corruption, favouritism and inefficiencies, the politics of deregulation decreases the burden on the state and places it where it belongs — on the individual citizen.

Perhaps the solutions to South Africa's problems coincide with the interests of an efficient public service — a society where the state sheds most of its control functions and limits itself to those important welfare functions which only it can do, and hopefully can do well.

Acknowledgement

Parts of this chapter were previously published in the *Journal of Contemporary African Studies*, Pretoria: Africa Institute of South Africa, 1986. Permission to use this material is gratefully acknowledged.

II

Balancing equalities and inequalities

Income redistribution: the economic challenge of the 1990s

Michael D. McGrath

In this chapter the major dimensions of income inequality in the South African economy are identified, with reference to the moral and pragmatic social stability needed for affecting a redistribution of incomes. Active policies for redistribution are examined against the constraints prevalent in the South African economy.

Introduction

Even though racial income inequality in South Africa has narrowed in the last two decades, it still remains so large that it is a major obstacle to the survival of the capitalist economic system in South Africa in the long run. Much concern has been expressed about the stagnation of economic growth in the South African economy in the 1980s. Economic growth, however, is not an end in itself, but simply a means to achieving higher levels of economic welfare and the distribution of incomes is also an important determinant of welfare. We might remember Keynes' words in this context:

> For my own part, I believe that there is social and psychological justification for significant inequalities of incomes and wealth, but not for such large disparities as exist to-day. There are valuable human activities which require the motive of money-making and the environment of private wealth-ownership for their full fruition . . . But it is not necessary for the stimulation of these activities and the satisfaction of these proclivities that the game should be played for such high stakes as at present. Much lower stakes will serve the purpose equally well, as soon as the players are accustomed to them.[1]

Here Keynes is stating that the economic inequalities of his time were unacceptable, and that a less unequal distribution of incomes would not dampen the performance of the economy. However, it is even conceivable that welfare could be maximized by trading off some economic growth for a more equitable distribution of income if an aversion to income inequality was weighted heavily in society's welfare function.

---

[1] J. M. Keynes, *The general theory of employment, interest and money*, London: Macmillan, 1937, p. 374.

In the terminology of modern welfare economics, for economists who are concerned with issues of social justice, the level of social welfare (W) depends not only on the absolute level of income (Y), but also on the distribution of the rewards from economic activity (G) and the level of absolute poverty (P). We can thus write this general welfare function as:

$$W = W (Y, G, P).$$

Economic growth which raises Y would raise W, *ceteris paribus*, but so too would reductions in G and P also be likely to raise welfare, especially if Y was not reduced. At the high average real economic growth rates of around 5 per cent per annum which were experienced in South Africa in the 1960s a trade-off between improved distribution and a small lowering of the growth rate might have been contemplated. In the 1980s, however, pressures of disinvestment on capital flows, the threat of potential sanctions, and a current international gold price of around $400 have acted to severely constrain the growth path which the South African economy now faces to between 2 and 2,5 per cent per annum. On this low growth path there are not a range of growth rates over which trade-offs with improved income distribution can be made, and policies must be sought which enhance the growth performance of the economy, and simultaneously improve income distribution.

It has also come to be accepted by most South Africans that a majority black government will come to power in South Africa in the future, and many people recognize that this future is not all that far away. The extent to which that government adopts radical economic programmes will be very largely determined by the events which lead up to the change of government. A long period of military struggle, high levels of internal repression and domestic economic stagnation would all augur badly for the new government following the free-enterprise route. Indeed, it is realistic to assume that any future new majority government in South Africa will implement some 'socialist policies' in the form of nationalization of industry and expropriation and redistribution of agricultural land. The degree of socialism is, however, a variable, the extent of which may be partly determined by the economic policies of the 1990s in South Africa. All other things being equal, it would not seem unreasonable to hypothesize that the smaller the racial inequalities in the distribution of incomes, and the less the extent of poverty, at the time of a change of government, the less will the need be for radical economic policies by the new majority government. Further, there is an urgent need for improving the distribution of income in South Africa based purely on the moral judgment that the present magnitude of inequalities are too large. However, this view is not inconsistent with the pragmatic need to reduce income inequalities to ensure the survival of capitalism.

Therefore, this chapter proceeds on the belief that the major economic challenge of the 1990s is to narrow the vast income inequalities which characterize the South African economy while at the same time not eroding any economic growth which can be achieved within the stagnating South African economy.

Income inequality in the economy

The broad magnitudes of the income inequalities in South Africa are widely accepted amongst economists.[2] They are:

1. A Gini coefficient for 1975 of 0,68, contrasted with Ginis of 0,5 — incomes 0,6 for most semi-industrialized economies.

2. A very skewed racial distribution of income with the white share in incomes in 1980 still exceeding 65 per cent of personal income. In per capita terms for 1980 white incomes were respectively 12,9; 3,9 and 5,3 times greater than African, Indian and coloured incomes. Table 6.1, showing the size distribution of incomes by race group in South Africa, illustrates the skewed racial distribution of incomes very clearly.

   As the table shows, in 1985 less than 5 per cent of African households had incomes in excess of R16 000 per annum, compared with 83 per cent of white households. At the bottom end of the income spectrum, African households accounted for the vast mass of the group in poverty (for example, the households with incomes less than R5 000 per annum). However, African households accounted for 10 per cent of the group in the highest income class shown in the table, and made up 38 per cent of the next highest income class, exceeding respectively the number of coloured and Indian households in both these income classes.

3. Wide urban–rural inequalities: for the mid 1970s per capita incomes of African households in the metropolitan regions were 2,2 times as great as per capita incomes in the black states, and 3,7 times per capita incomes of African households in the white rural area.

4. The high levels of racial income inequality and the wide urban–rural differentials in income would indicate that poverty will be widespread in the African population, and that it will be particularly prevalent in the non-metropolitan regions. In the mid-1970s approximately 30 per cent of African households in the metropolitan regions fell below their poverty line income, and approximately 62 per cent of the African

---

[2] Income and wealth distribution data is drawn from M. D. McGrath, 'The distribution of personal income in South Africa in selected years over the period from 1945 to 1980', unpublished Ph.D. thesis, Univ. of Natal, Durban, 1983.

population of the black states (excluding the overlapping segments of the metropolitan areas) and approximately 74 per cent of the African households in the white rural areas would have been in poverty. Estimate for the black states includes incomes in the urban non-metropolitan areas, and if these urban incomes were excluded, the incidence of poverty in the remaining rural areas would be even higher. These estimates of poverty are very crude since they do not take into account differences in household sizes within the regions, and they measure poverty solely in terms of a 'head count', that is, the proportion of the population in poverty. Nevertheless, they do highlight the vast extent of poverty among Africans in the economy, and the very high incidence of poverty in the rural areas. In 1975, by contrast, approximately 4 per cent of white families, over 24 per cent of Indian families and 50 per cent of coloured families were living in poverty.[3]

Table 6.1:   The size distribution of incomes in the economy, 1985*

	Percentages**				
Income class	White	Coloured	Indian	African	All
0–2 999	2 (2)	26 (12)	5 (1)	38 (85)	24
3 000–4 999	1 (2)	?? (16)	8 (2)	2 (80)	17
5 000–7 999	2 (4)	19 (17)	14 (4)	10 (75)	17
8 000–10 499	2 (8)	7 (13)	13 (8)	8 (72)	7
10 500–15 999	10 (36)	12 (18)	18 (9)	5 (38)	8
16 000+	83 (79)	14 (6)	42 (6)	5 (10)	30
	100 (28)	100 (12)	100 (4)	100 (56)	100

Source:
Estimated from Bureau of Market Research income and expenditure data.
Notes:
* Excluding African households in white control non-metropolitan areas (i.e. white towns and white farms).
** Figures in parenthesis are row percentages.

The causes of the income inequalities lie partly in the labour market and in the structure and rewards for occupations, and partly in access to employment in the high wage sector of the economy, in the unequal racial distribution of income from wealth and entrepreneurship, and in a higher dependency ratio among Africans. Policy to narrow inequality will have to encompass all these factors.

The cleavages in the labour market resulted from a historical growth path of the economy in which whites were able to command education,

---

[3] A comprehensive treatment of poverty is to be found in F. Wilson and M. Ramphele, *Uprooting poverty: the South African challenge*, Cape Town: David Phillip, 1989.

and hence skilled and managerial occupation, while blacks generally were crowded into less skilled occupations and many Africans were forced by influx control to remain in rural areas. This limited the growth rate of urbanization and consequently rationed the demand for urban infrastructure in the form of housing, health services, and education, lowering the infrastructural costs associated with urbanization. Until recently Africans have faced constitutional constraints on the ownership of capital, for example, through the prohibition of freehold in the main urban areas, and African entrepreneurs have faced severe obstacles. High white wage incomes and profits have resulted in a distribution of personal wealth for 1975 (excluding land in the homelands) in which the top 5 per cent of the population as a whole owned 88 per cent of personal wealth. Low economic participation rates in rural areas and high dependence ratios also contribute to the relatively low levels of African incomes.

Economic stagnation and income distribution

For economists, the stylized relationships between economic growth and income distribution originates in the works of Kuznets,[4] in which income inequalities only narrow when a relatively high level of industrialization has been achieved and the labour surplus of the economy has been absorbed into employment in the industrial section. Similar 'trickle down' mechanisms operate in Knight's model for the South African economy, which predicts that market forces, given the political and economic institutions that keep white labour scarce and provide it with skills, will operate to widen income inequality with the passage of economic growth as long as there is a labour surplus.[5] Rapid economic growth will therefore widen racial income inequalities, but is paradoxically also a condition for the later narrowing. The narrowing of income inequality in the final step of the Kuznets' process requires the attainment of a growth path in which labour is absorbed rapidly from the traditional sector, labour's bargaining power rises, and the benefits from growth are shared with labour. The experiences of many developing countries, including the South African economy, show that the path of trickle down is far from inevitable. In the South African case the rate of growth of investment and employment since the 1970s has been inadequate to generate trickle down and there have also been strong urban biases, in the form of access to employment, education, health services, training and higher skilled occupations,[6] which have limited the spread of

---

[4] S. Kuznets, 'Economic growth and income inequality', *American Economic Review*, vol. 45, 1955, pp. 1–28.

[5] J. B. Knight, 'A theory of income distribution in South Africa', *Bulletin of the Oxford Institute of Economics and Statistics*, vol. 26, 1964, pp. 289–310.

[6] The tightened application of influx control regulations and penalties after the Riekert Commission Report

the gains from growth to rural areas.

The growth rates of employment which are necessary to achieve trickle down have not, however, occurred since 1975. The 1978–87 Economic Development Programme shows that real growth rates of gross domestic product (GDP) in excess of 5 per cent per annum must be achieved in order to hold constant the absolute level of unemployment.[7] With real GDP growing at 5 per cent per annum, employment would grow at 2,5 per cent per annum, contrasted with a 2,6 per cent per annum growth rate of work-force. Between 1980 and 1985, however, the index of modern sector employment (excluding agriculture) has grown by less than one per cent per annum, falling far short of the rate needed to create a scarcity of unskilled labour over the same period, while real remuneration per worker increased in total by 9 per cent. Between 1981 and 1985 coloured average real wages increased most, growing at an annual rates of 3,3 per cent, as against 1,6 per cent per annum for Africans and Indians and 0,4 per cent for whites,[8] and the wage gap closed, even though the economy was not absorbing its labour surplus.

A decomposition analysis to determine by race the effect of the grade composition of employment, and the effects on differences in pay structures, can shed light on the economic importance of the changes which were taking place in the labour market. The decomposition analysis revealed that the extent of racial pay discrimination was reduced by roughly half between 1976 and 1985. In 1976 coloureds, Indians and Africans received respectively 37,8; 33,0; and 42,9 per cent less pay than whites on account of their race alone, that is, standardizing for sex and grade. The corresponding figures in 1985 were 21,2; 12,7 and 21,8 per cent respectively,[9] and by 1989 the extent of racial discrimination in pay had diminished even further to 20,1; 10,6 and 15,3 per cent respectively.[10]

The decomposition analysis showed that racial differences in the distribution of workers among grades accounted for 57 per cent of the difference in racial mean wages in 1976 and for no less than 84 per cent in 1985. The residual, after standardizing for job grades and gender — which could reflect wage discrimination — represented 45 per cent of the wage difference

---

in 1979 heightened the dichotomy in the black labour force between urban insiders and rural outsiders.

7 *Economic development for the Republic of South Africa 1978–1987*, Pretoria: Office of the Economic Adviser to the Prime Minister, 1979.

8 Estimated from *South African statistics 1988*, Pretoria: Central Statistical Services, p. 76; and *South African Reserve Bank Quarterly Bulletin*, Sept. 1989, p. S104.

9 J. B. Knight and M. D. McGrath, 'The erosion of apartheid in the South African labour market: measures and mechanisms', *Applied Economics discussion paper no. 35*, Oxford: Oxford Institute of Economics and Statistics, Sept. 1987.

10 Estimated from Peromnes Salary survey for Feb. 1989, supplied by FSA.

in 1976, but only 21 per cent in 1985. In other words, differential grade attainment has become relatively more important and segregated wage determination processes less important in explaining the racial wage gap in South Africa. The change in the African and white mean between 1976 and 1985 has also been decomposed into the effects of changes in the occupational distribution and those changes in the wage determination process. This exercise reveals that 89 per cent of the increase in white pay was due to the improvement of the white occupational distribution, while some 60 per cent of the increase in the African real wage was due to an improved grade composition of employment. Signs of an emerging integration of the labour market are quite clear. However, African workers still remain crowded into lower skilled occupations, while white workers dominate in the managerial, technical and supervisory grades of employment. Levels of education attainment have become the most important determinant of the occupational structures.

Government has abandoned many of its restrictive policies in response to the economic growth crisis. Faced with the reality of the presence of large-scale urbanization following the abolition of influx control in 1986, government has moved to allow more scope for informal sector growth, and has allowed greater freedom of competition in areas of the economy such as black transport.[11] At the same time, government has prepared itself to expand the tax base to capture a larger share of the growth in income from informal activities by adopting the Margo Commissions' recommendation that the tax base should be widened and more reliance should be placed on indirect taxation.[12]

The stagnation of the South African economy in the 1980s has eliminated any possibility of the economy absorbing all its economically active population into modern sector employment for years to come. It is, however, most probable that the trend to an integration of jobs and wage structures which started in the 1970s will continue. Thus, within the metropolitan regions the future is likely to show reducing inequality between the participants in modern sector occupations.

However, the incidence of poverty in the metropolitan regions will also increase. The slowing growth of employment opportunities, and the abolition of influx controls and of restrictions on employment of African workers have removed the protection which the migrant labour system gave to workers from rural areas, and this segment of the labour force will rapidly

---

[11] For expression of this change in philosophy, see *White Paper on privatisation and deregulation in the republic of South Africa*, WPG 87, Govt. Printer.

[12] *White paper on the Report of the Commission of Inquiry into the tax structure and deregulation of the Republic of South Africa*, (Margo Report) WPC 88, Govt. Printer.

disappear. The termination of the migrant labour system will push these workers into the urban areas (most probably to be joined by their families at a later stage). Competition for unskilled jobs in urban areas will intensify and unskilled wages will stagnate and may fall in real terms. Income short-falls will be augmented by various subsistence activities, creating informal sector growth. Thus the wide urban–rural income gaps of the period prior to the 1970s will be deflected to the urban areas.

The gains from economic growth have become more unequally distrib-uted within the African population, and this process will continue to occur, with African households with access to modern sector jobs probably expe-riencing the greatest relative gains from economic growth. This group will remain a relatively small élite and will probably become a falling proportion of the African population.

Even if average differentials between whites and blacks continue to nar-row during the coming decade, the gap in income from other sources will take a long time to begin closing, for it is to be expected that consider-able time will have to elapse before the income generated by the savings of blacks constitutes a substantial component of black incomes.[13]

For the future, with its present economic institutions and situated on its current growth path, the South African economy will continue to exhibit a distribution of incomes in which the present racial cleavages will exist, with the incomes of the white group dominating the upper deciles, although there will be a greater number of blacks in both the higher and the middle ranges.

Stimulating redistribution and growth

From the analysis above it is clear that the market by itself will not bring about a major redistribution of incomes, given the slow expected growth rates of employment. A question thus arises about the potential for active redistributive policies by government. Will policies directed at redistribu-tion lower the growth rate of incomes, and how much chance do they have of succeeding?

The relationship between the pattern of income distribution and the level of output and employment received attention in the Keynesian liter-ature where the concern was the lack of aggregate demand. Redistribution of income from groups with a low marginal propensity to consume (MPC), that is, the rich, to groups with a high MPC, that is, the poor, would in-crease aggregate demand and thereby the level of output and employment.

---

13 The intransigent nature of the black/white income gap is shown in van der Berg's simulation to the year 2000 under low and high growth rates of GDP. See S. van der Berg, 'An interacial income distribution in South Africa to the end of the century', *The South African Journal of Economics*, vol. 57, 1989, pp. 35–51.

However, fears were held that a redistribution of income in favour of the poor would lower savings and therefore the rate of capital accumulation. Since capital was assumed to be the major growth constraint, it follows that output and employment would be lowered with redistribution. Redistribution of income affects not only the level but also the composition of demand. Thus, if there are variations in the factor intensity of goods consumed by different income groups, factor requirements for a given level of output could be altered by income redistribution. In general, goods consumed by the poor tend to be relatively more labour-intensive than those consumed by the rich. A more equitable distribution would increase employment and reduce the amount of capital, and thereby savings, required by a given level of output. The level of imports could also be reduced if the marginal propensity to import by lower-income classes is lower than that of higher-income groups.[14]

Employment, capital requirements and foreign exchange availabilities are thus all potentially affected by income redistribution. Moreover, redistribution might also have qualitative effects for general health and nutrition, and consequently the productivity of the population might be increased. Entrepreneurial incentives might, however, be lowered. A redistribution of income in favour of the poor might thus set in motion growth-hindering and growth-fostering forces, and the relative strength of each is an empirical matter.

In recent years a number of studies have attempted to simulate the effect of income redistribution on economic growth. The earlier versions of these models found that these effects are small, with the actual magnitude depending on the size of the redistribution.

These simulations indicate that there may not be growth and equity trade-offs and that income redistribution policies can be followed without sacrificing growth. Various ILO reports show that the two might be positively related since promoting the growth of the informal sector in which the poor are located would reduce inequality and at the same time increase growth. Workers have very little embodied human capital. The informal sector does not, therefore, compete with the modern sector for the limited capital (especially imported) and human resources. Promoting the growth of this sector will not only foster growth of output and employment, but also increase the absolute as well as relative incomes of the poor, and one way to foster the growth of the sector is to redistribute income in favour of

---

[14] For overview see W. Cline, *Potential effects of income redistribution on economic growth: the Latin American case*, New York: Praeger, 1972; and D. Chin, 'Distribution, equality and economic growth: the case of Taiwan', *Economic Development and Cultural Change*, vol. 26, 1977.

the poor, whose consumption patterns favour its output.[15]

The main objective of more recent models is to investigate the effectiveness of different policies for redistributing incomes. A sophisticated model of Adelman and Robinson, tested for the Republic of Korea, found a remarkable stability of the time path of the size distribution of incomes. They conclude: 'Given the deterioration in income distribution observed in the basic path, reducing poverty is most difficult. Indeed, of all the hoped-for ends of economic policy, a steady reduction of deprivation may be the hardest to achieve.'[16]

The distribution of income to different classes of recipients is surprisingly found to be sensitive to policy intervention despite the relative stability of decile shares of income. Policy can therefore be powerful in reshuffling the incidence of poverty. The model lends the further observations that:

> First, contrary to popular belief, increasing the share of wages does not necessarily imply either a more equitable distribution of income or a reduced incidence of poverty in the economy. Second, since the relations among socioeconomic groups are of immense political concern, the ability to manipulate the functional distribution of income is politically more significant than the inability to change the more socially neutral size distribution. Third, significant improvements in equity and reductions in the incidence and degree of poverty cannot be made without massive efforts involving programmes far more sweeping than any usually contemplated in the developing nations. Finally, because of the sensitivity of the functional distribution of income to policy interventions, such programmes are like to cause substantial social unrest.[17]

Adelman and Robinson also find that most anti-poverty policies eventually help the rich and middle groups more than the poor. Even when the rich are taxed quite progressively, many of their simulations produced evidence of a trickle up effect. The simulations also indicated for a wide range of policies that it is easier to worsen income distribution than to improve it.

Economic policy choices

Within the framework of a capitalist economic system three broad approaches can be identified for meeting the dual objectives of reducing poverty and narrowing income inequality, namely:

1. high rates of economic growth and trickle down;

---

15 See, for example, *Towards full employment: a programme for Colombia*, 1970 and *Employment, incomes and equality: a strategy for increasing productive employment in Kenya*, 1972, Geneva: International Labour Office; and also M. Urrutia, *Winners and losers in Colombia's economic growth of the 1970s*, Oxford: Oxford Univ. Press, 1986.

16 I. Adelman and S. Robinson, *Income distribution policies in developing countries*, Oxford: Oxford Univ. Press, 1978, p. 190.

17 Adelman and Robinson, *Income distribution policies*, p. 191.

2. static redistribution; and

3. redistribution with growth.

The mechanism of trickle down has already been described.

Policies of static redistribution always appear at first sight to offer promising possibilities. The issue of static redistribution has traditionally focused on questions of taxation, especially direct taxes, but this is a case of mistaken emphasis since all that taxes can do is to take away, and it is only through the spending side of the budget that the state can positively assist the poor. There is, however, much evidence showing that the tax system is a rather weak redistributive device, and that government spending can have a greater impact. Many studies have shown that tax systems often lead to an incidence which is roughly proportional to income.[18] In order to use the tax system as a redistributive device, the burden should fall largely on high incomes, and to achieve this result, heavy reliance must be placed on personal income taxes. Company taxes are easily passed on to consumers, and dependence on indirect taxes can be a major obstacle towards the construction of a progressive tax structure, because most are regressive, that is, they fall most heavily on the poor, although they are not inevitably so, for example, Tanzania.[19] If they are confined to luxury goods and services, they will bear most heavily on the higher-income groups, leaving the poor largely unaffected. However, if they are to produce much revenue, they cannot be restricted to items of high-income consumption. Therefore, such systems of indirect taxation tend to be regressive.

In the case of personal income taxes, there are always tax loopholes which can be exploited, and the incentive for this rises as the tax system becomes more progressive. Particular groups will also lobby for concessions and certain exemptions will become built into the tax structure, creating what are now called tax expenditures. Income will be shifted into nontaxable forms, or forms taxed at lower rates, such as company cars and housing, entertainment allowances and capital gains. Introducing an apparently highly progressive tax scale can thus be self-defeating. However, it can have disincentive effects on saving and investment, which can retard the growth of the economy and discourage risk taking and provide disincentives to earn additional incomes.[20] Indeed, it is a belief in the disincentive effects of progressive income taxation which lies behind supply-side

---

[18] See J. A. Peckman and B. A. Ockner, *Who bears the tax burden?*, Washington: Brookings Inst., 1975; and A. Westlake, 'Tax evasion, tax incidence and the distribution of income in Kenya', *Eastern African Economic Review*, vol. 5, 1973.

[19] Y. Huang, 'Distribution of tax burdens in Tanzania', *The Economic Journal*, vol. 86, 1976.

[20] G. Break 'The incidence and economic effects of taxation', in A. S. Linde et al., *The economics of public finance*, Washington: Brookings Inst., 1974.

economic policies. Reduced private savings need not reduce aggregate saving if the state uses the extra resources for capital formation, but if they are redistributed through transfer payments to the poor, then they will be reduced with adverse consequences for economic growth. Table 6.2 shows the relative importance of direct taxation in the GDP for a sample of developed and semi-industrialized economies, and this table adds substance to the frequently articulated objections to the high marginal and average rates of taxation which high income earners bear in South Africa. Given the high relative level of personal and corporate taxation in GDP in South Africa, and the inevitably regressive alternative of indirect taxation, there does not appear to be much scope for further redistribution through the tax system for South Africa.

Table 6.2:   Taxes on income and capital gains as % of GDP

Country	Per cent
Sweden	6,6
Brazil	4,9
South Korea	4,6
South Africa	12,0
Australia	5,6
Japan	8,7

Source:
F. Wilson, 'Sharing the pantry', *Indicator South Africa*, vol. 6, Spring 1989, p. 37.

The thrust of these arguments is that the redistributive power of taxation is relatively small and can be potentially destructive of economic growth in the South African case. One tax which is promising, however, and which has not been mentioned, is that on forms of wealth. In principle this can be a potent egalitarian device because the accumulation and inheritance of wealth is one of the major mechanisms tending to perpetuate inequality. This issue is dealt with later in this chapter.

On the expenditure side of the budget it is useful to distinguish three forms of government spending:

1. the provision of services, such as education and health, which raise living standards in ways which can be measured;

2. cash benefits of transfer payments; and

3. other forms of state spending which confer benefits to the community as a whole, but do so in ways which are not readily identified among income groups.

Transfer payments have significant redistributive potential, for they can be geared to identified poverty groups. Some economists oppose transfers, and argue that, for instance, unemployment benefits act as a disincentive to work. While this might be true for some developed economies, the range of welfare payments available in South Africa does not begin to approach the level at which disincentives might set in. Subsidized or free educational and health services are also important ways of redistributing.

An alternative to static redistribution is the 'redistribution with growth' strategy. Policies must be chosen which will not significantly reduce the growth of gross national product (GNP), for redistribution comes from income gains made by lower groups. As a concomitant part of the policy, resources are also redistributed to target groups using production sector and transfer strategies. Production strategies in urban areas are directed at obtaining correct factor prices and removing discrimination against small producers. This latter policy has the effect of enhancing backward and forward linkages in the urban sector, and can increase the incomes of the poor by increasing employment and the income-earning opportunities of the self-employed. Policies for rural target groups include those to reduce the natural increase of population, reform systems of land tenure, encourage labour-intensive public works projects, improve the terms of trade between agriculture and industry, and reform the cost and availability of credit to small farmers. Transfer strategies in urban areas are focused on improving the supply of health, housing and educational services.[21]

The difficulty arising with this strategy concerns the required assumption that redistribution will not effect the growth rate. This may not be upheld if the growth of demand following from redistribution causes investment to flow into small-scale, low-productivity activities. Political factors may also prevent the policy from working as the restraint on income growth at the upper end of the scale is likely to be resisted.

Stewart and Streeten's assessment of each of these schemes is pessimistic, and they argue that this is the result of ignoring critical links between technology and income distribution, income distribution and decision-makers, and decision-makers and objectives. They argue:

> Once made central it seems difficult to avoid the conclusion that much wasted ingenuity has been put into devising forms of redistribution, when it is not lack of ingenious schemes but a basic political contradiction between the schemes and the real as opposed to nominal objectives of decision makers, that is critical.[22]

Their conclusion is that, after all, trickle down may offer decision-makers a more realistic strategy. Even so, attention should be given to asset redistribution, technical and institutional reform, and wage and price signals,

---

[21] H. Chenery et al., *Redistribution with growth*, Oxford: Oxford Univ. Press, pp. 113–157.

[22] F. Stewart and P. Streeton, 'Past strategies for development: poverty, income distribution and growth', *Oxford Economic Papers*, vol. 28, 1976, p. 396.

which Stewart and Streeten regard as the three legs of 'a steady tripod'. They also stress the importance of the order in which policies are pursued, and this view is supported by Adelman and Robinson's research on non-communist economies which managed to combine successful improvements in the incomes of the poor with accelerated growth in the post-1950 period.[23]

Concluding comments

The preceding review of the literature has shown that there are positive and negative prospects for a successful redistribution of incomes in South Africa. Redistribution policies need not lower average incomes or depress the rate of economic growth; indeed, under certain conditions they might enhance income and employment growth for the poor. The negative side is that income inequalities are remarkably persistent and require a high level of political commitment to eliminate the economic scars of the apartheid policies of earlier years. There are, however, instances of policies which could have beneficial effects on economic growth and redistribution, and these policies should be implemented as quickly as possible; for example, South African competition policy is weaker than that in most Western democracies, and there is scope for giving the Competition Board more teeth. This would be supported by many in the private sector who are critical of policies which favour concentration and militate against competition. In agriculture, the activities of control boards are controversial; for example, the milling industry should be competitive but is not because of restrictive licensing. Other factors which favour large businesses against small are the availability of capital, the imposition of unduly high building and health regulations, and the harassment of small African businesspersons. Small businesses absorb proportionately more labour than do the large ones, and because these distortions favour capital intensity, they militate against employment creation.

The ownership of land is crucial in the unequal distribution of wealth by race group, and the inequality must be redressed. White-owned farms where the owner is absent could be expropriated and redistributed, or individuals could be restricted to owning one farm, and the land thus released could be distributed. The possibility of redistributing land is greater in intensive than in extensive farming areas. Second, any farms offered for sale could be purchased by government and redistributed. However, if redistribution is accompanied by falling levels of output, society will not gain. Agricultural output (especially food) must be maintained and expanded, and therefore

---

23 Adelman and Robinson, *Income distribution policies*, p. 1–48.

it is vital that the land be farmed efficiently and productively.[24] Notwithstanding the difficulties, a more just land dispensation, coupled with access to agricultural markets and credit, and measures designed to increase the productivity of small farms, could substantially improve rural incomes and reduce the pressures for job creation in industry and is a key issue which has to be confronted to eliminate income inequality.

Areas which will be of importance in determining whether economic growth will reduce inequalities relate to wage policies and the ability of the state to promote competitive conditions. The closed shops which still protect white workers cannot be justified on economic grounds, and the time has come for their dissolution. Another related issue is whether attempts should now be made to lower the real wage of the urban labour force to levels more consistent with a labour surplus economy, as occurred in Brazil between 1965 and 1967. Lower real wages in the modern sector would have the advantage of increasing profits, and perhaps the domestic propensity to save and invest, and would provide a stimulus towards less capital-intensive production methods and would increase the competitiveness of manufactured exports.

Freedom of entry to particular markets is central to the operation of the market economy. Thus a fundamental reform designed to improve the distribution of incomes is the removal of restrictive practices and other impediments to competitive conditions. In the South African case, despite progress with deregulation, substantial barriers to competition still remain with agricultural marketing boards, unrealistic health and housing standards, and the wage policies and closed shops, followed by trade unions. An active and consistent policy of encouraging the informal sector can also be significant in generating income and jobs.

Earlier it was noted that static redistribution was of limited effectiveness if underdevelopment and a lack of human and physical capital were the major causes of low income. In the South African case, however, the wide income disparities between white and African do provide some additional scope for static redistribution. For example, a 50 per cent increase in transfer payments to Africans in 1975/6 would have required only a 0,5 per cent increase in the level of per capita taxes on whites, and this would have been sufficient to pay social pensions to all members of the African population who were eligible.

Irrespective of the development strategy which is adopted to speed the process of redistribution, the historical effects of discriminatory practices

---

[24] In the 1980s many white farmers are not making a profit, and incomes earned vary immensely, depending on activity, market prices and climate. The number of full-time farmers has fallen from 116 000 to 65 000 in the last thirty years, and 30 per cent of the farmers produce 80 per cent of gross agricultural output.

will have to be reversed, and in order to do this, higher levels of expenditure on health, housing and education are vital. The low growth rate of the GDP, however, imposes a severe constraint on the ability of government to finance such schemes, which would drive government expenditure as high as 40 per cent of the GDP if equality of services was to be attained at white standards. Even financing less dramatic increases in expenditure by increasing the rate of personal income taxation might have adverse effects on incentives, which could depress the growth rate of the economy (a result which appears likely since South Africa already has one of the severest progressive tax systems in the world[25]), while any increased taxation of the lower-income groups would tend to offset any tendency towards redistribution occurring in the labour market. The expansion of education, housing and health services to black communities will thus have to come about through a redistribution of expenditures within the government budget, and white taxpayers will have to accept significantly lowered standards of services.

Future increases in the rate of sales taxation will also be contrary to the goal of redistribution. Increases in the rate of company taxation will lower both the rate at which companies can plough back profits and the rate of return on capital, which could in turn lower the level of investment and lower the rate of employment growth. It seems inevitable that the state will have to seek new resources of revenue. An important possibility is to expand the taxation of personal wealth. Estate and gift duties in America yield approximately 2,3 per cent of the federal government's revenue, and if South African estate duty were adjusted to attain the same yield, it would have generated in 1978/9 an amount equal to one-third of the total grant from the central government to the homeland administrations. Thus, the taxation of deceased estates is a potentially valuable source of finance which has the advantage of requiring no increases in the tax rates on either current income or consumption. Furthermore, an increase in the rate of taxation of wealth would contribute directly to a reduction in inequalities in the distribution of wealth, and to the process of income redistribution.

In what appears to be an attempt to ease its fiscal difficulties, the South African government has embarked on a programme of privatization, which potentially affects state enterprises employing over 500 000 workers. The potential revenues from such privatization could far exceed R20 billion, or at least 30 per cent of the national debt. The application of such a large capital sum should be of great concern to all South Africans. If the state uses the proceeds of privatization in such a way that personal tax rates are lowered, its capital sources will be dissipated in consumption, with a loss to

---

25 L. Louw and F. Kendall, *South Africa: the solution*, Bisho: Amagi Publications, 1986, p. 96.

society as a whole. As an alternative, some of the proceeds of privatizations could be applied to necessary development projects, while the remainder could be most creatively used in joint ventures with the private sector in establishing new avenues for industrial growth and exports.

This chapter has shown that the high levels of income inequality in the South African economy will persist into the future on the low growth path which the economy is experiencing. The chapter has not attempted to deal with trade and industrialization policy issues, which are discussed in Chapters 17 and 18. They will clearly be important in influencing economy growth. What may be lacking most at this time in South Africa is a comprehensive government strategy for economic growth. This should contain a clearly specified set of goals for the economy, relating to its feasible growth and income distribution, and carefully integrated strategies for achieving these goals. Such an overview should establish target rates of growth of expenditure by government on urban informal settlements and rural areas, certain sectors of manufacturing should be targeted for export growth, essential levels of domestic industrial protection should be established, and target growth rates of the provision of education and training should be identified. The necessary policy should then be implemented to achieve the goals.

This chapter argued that a substantial redistribution of incomes in South Africa is a necessary condition for the long run survival of capitalism. For such a redistribution to take place, there is need for greater economic freedoms through the creation of genuinely free labour and goods market. However, there is also a simultaneous need for the state to provide a consistent policy framework for economic growth and redistribution.

7 Affirmitave action in the public service

Pierre Hugo

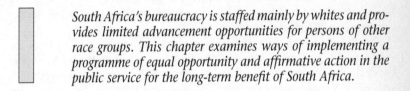

South Africa's bureaucracy is staffed mainly by whites and provides limited advancement opportunities for persons of other race groups. This chapter examines ways of implementing a programme of equal opportunity and affirmative action in the public service for the long-term benefit of South Africa.

Introduction

It is the policy of the government of South Africa to provide equal opportunity in government service to all qualified applicants and employees; to prohibit discrimination in employment because of race, colour, sex or creed and to promote the full realisation of equal employment opportunity through a continuing affirmative action programme in each government department. This policy will govern every aspect of personnel policy and practice in employment, development, advancement and treatment of all employees.

(Suggested government policy statement on employment opportunities in the South African public service — Pierre Hugo.)

Apartheid ideology and practice in South Africa has been at its most unyielding on African participation in state institutions. Their exclusion from the legislative arm of government continues to attract intense national and international attention. The equivalent exclusion of Africans and other blacks from the major public service executive organs of the state which intimately affect their interests has largely been ignored.

This chapter examines some of the historical and contemporary dimensions of this situation and advances a number of possible remedial strategies through affirmative action.

The demise of apartheid in South Africa will be measured in terms of the success achieved in investing the country's major institutions with a real and perceived sense of legitimacy in the eyes of its citizens. Moreover, change in this direction will need to occur at a depth and pace to instil public confidence that the goal is not chimerical or merely more reform rhetoric — a shadow without hope of substance.

Too much time may be lost in waiting for an apartheid-free nirvana; time during which black South Africans should be afforded access to job opportunities in the public service and in this capacity obtain the training and experience to contribute towards the South Africa of the future in which, as in all the developing countries, the public service will play a pivotal role.

Historical legacy

Given the alacrity and consistency with which successive South African governments have passed racially exclusive legislation encompassing most facets of societal activity, legislation on employment in the public service presents a curious anomaly.

In the field of industrial employment for example, laws such as the Industrial Conciliation Act of 1924, the Wage Act of 1925 and the Mines and Works Act of 1926 explicitly disadvantaged Africans to protect white interests. Yet not one of the Public Services and Pensions Act of 1912, the Public Services and Pensions Act of 1923 or the currently applicable Public Services Act of 1957 incorporates any formal racial disbarment. In fact, Section 11 (3) of the latter act stipulates a number of non-racial attributes based on qualifications, merit and efficiency which should be applied in making appointments and promotions.

In practice, however, the apparent anomaly has belied a reality every bit as racially exclusive as in the field of industrial employment; in point of fact, more so.

Public sector employment policy, especially since 1948, has been based on the ideological reasoning that the political destiny of Africans lay 'in their own areas'. Any departure from this principle, particularly in regard to African participation in organs of state, would be tantamount to creating unacceptable black expectations of a political future alongside white South Africans.

The pristine application of this principle in the case of the public service is amply demonstrated by the costs which its proponents have been willing to inflict on the body politic in order to exclude blacks. Nowhere is this more glaring than in officialdom's approach to the critical shortages of staff in all ranks which has always plagued South Africa's public service.

As early as 1946 the Social and Economic Planning Council of the Union of South Africa pointed out that understaffing had seriously jeopardized the ability of the public service to perform its existing tasks as well as ruled out any prospect of its undertaking essential additional functions. By 1950 nearly 15 per cent of a total of 106 956 public service posts were vacant and the situation continued to deteriorate. According to the SABC, the public service reported a shortfall of 33 000 unfilled posts in its approved establishment in 1988.

The government response to the recurrent staff shortages has been premised consistently on the politically motivated assumption that the problem was one of a white public service whose requirements were to be met exclusively by whites. To this end, a host of racially exclusive stopgap, and ultimately ineffectual, remedial stratagems were attempted.

These included: more vigorous recruiting and widespread advertising; short intensive training courses; relaxing entry-grade and promotion requirements; employing (white) women part time; enhanced salary and fringe-benefit incentives; the employment of pensioners; mechanization; the introduction and extension of study bursaries; intensified overseas personnel recruitment; and, as a final surrender to the dictates of racial policy, the curtailment of the functions of the public service to accord with the dwindling pool of available white manpower.[1]

Official pronouncements continued to emphasize that the government was committed to the concept of a 'white' public service where integration would not be tolerated and in which 'non-whites' would accordingly not be trained for employment. In so far as their participation in administration and in public service activities was concerned, coloureds[2] and Indians were to devote their energies to the service of their own people in their own areas,[3] a principle which was to be reaffirmed in the wake of the creation of the 'own affairs' dispensation introduced in the 1980s.

Of course, blacks have been employed as nurses, teachers, soldiers, policemen and as labourers in white areas. In sheer numbers they constitute the majority of civil servants. However, for Africans the only outlets for managerial positions have been limited to the homeland territories.

Coloureds and Indians, although entitled to apply for employment in 'general affairs' departments[4] are in practice employed in their own affairs departments — an avenue seen by some[5] as constituting a *de facto* form of affirmative action in that these two groups are given preferential access to posts at all levels without as strict a test of their credentials as would apply when competing against whites in 'general affairs' departments.

For the present, however, there is no gainsaying the frank admission by the Chairman of the Commission for Administration that the 'whole

---

[1] Information supplied to author in interview with Dr A. L. Sharpe, Department of Foreign Affairs, April 1989.

[2] Terminology is a minefield when applied to the South African population. Terms such as white and 'coloured' in this chapter refer solely to the legal categories established by the Population Registration Act (1950). As Schire (in *South African public policy perspectives*, Cape Town: Juta, 1982, p. viii) remarks, they often simply have to be employed if very real social forces and groupings are to be discussed intelligibly.

[3] House of Assembly Debates, 1969, cols. 7233, 7234, 7254.)

[4] J. De Beer, interview in *Leadership*, vol. 5, no. 2, 1986, p. 49.

[5] Opinion expressed by senior member of the Public Service in interview with author, April 1989.

structure (of the public service) is imbued with the apartheid policy — it has become a way of life'.[6]

Political constraints and imperatives

Only the die-hard proponents of the Verwoerdian vision of the homeland policy would dispute the inequity of black exclusion from the public service of South Africa. The government has recently conceded that its power-sharing programme envisages the access of Africans to the highest levels of political office. Logically, the same dispensation should hold true for the executive organs of state. Certainly, an untenably anomalous situation would ensue were this not to be the case.

When pressed in an interview on this point in 1986, the Chairman of the Commission for Administration stated that as far as 'general' affairs departments were concerned, employment and promotion were open to all, though '. . . not as yet for the African population, because the question of the future governmental structure for Africans has yet to be resolved'.[7]

The most recent (1988) annual report of the Commission for Administration refers to a special project designed to look into the 'more representative utilisation of all population groups in the public service with special reference to the management echelon and the introduction of special training programmes for selected candidates of all population groups with the purpose of also making up circumstantially linked backlogs'.[8] This new initiative will be accompanied by a concerted advertising campaign in which the Public Service will proclaim itself as an 'equal opportunity employer'.[9]

While these are hopeful signals of official recognition of the historical legacy of discriminatory public service employment, it remains to be seen whether any investigation will have the necessary sense of urgency and be followed by a results-orientated policy. Political will on the part of the government is crucial.

The South African bureaucracy harbours a significant segment of white South Africans who are ideologically most antipathetic to political change. The resurgence of white opposition to the right of the government over the last decade, which can be expected to strenuously oppose any black advancement in the traditional white preserve of public service employment, is a further stumbling block.

---

[6] De Beer, *Leadership*, p. 48.

[7] De Beer, *Leadership*, p. 49.

[8] Annual Report of the Commission for Administration, 1987 and 1988; and J. U. Badenhorst, 'Setting black advancement strategy', *South African Journal of Business Management*, vol. 4, no. 12, 1982, pp. 9–10.

[9] Information supplied to author in interview with member of the Commission for Administration, April 1989.

Even if the government commits itself to a goal approximately the policy statement suggested at the beginning of this chapter, its resolve in translating commitment into meaningful practice will be severely tested. The nettle will, however, have to be grasped if accusations of the general hollowness of the government's reform policy are not to be borne out.

Black advancement

Aside from the inability of the public service to fulfil its requirements from the ranks of whites, black advancement in the public service becomes feasible when one considers that the civil service in South Africa is a growth industry.

Despite protestations to the contrary and good intentions to deregulate, privatize, rationalize and improve its function accountability, the civil service is likely to employ even more people in the future. Where there is a growing and urbanizing population in need of development at all levels — as in South Africa — the demands on service and staff increase and must be met largely by the state.

The only way to cut spending and staffing levels in the civil service is to integrate the multiplicity of parallel institutions characteristic of apartheid society.[10] This would be a step towards rationalization and in itself would lead to integration.

Many positions in the civil service would be filled more appropriately by blacks than by whites. A large sector of the population that does and will make use of the services of the public sector would be better served by having a black person in the position of bureaucrat precisely because that incumbent is black.[11] Language dexterity, cultural empathy and an understanding of the impact of apartheid are some relevant factors here.

'Blackness' in and of itself is not, of course, as many a homeland citizen would, no doubt, testify, any guarantee of empathetic treatment. However, given an environment in which appropriate training and the bureaucratic norms of efficiency, accountability and anti-corruption are enforced, the inherent advantages of being black assume a more persuasive relevance.

The question of institutional legitimacy must loom large in any consideration of black advancement in the public sector or in any field of activity in which blacks are consumers of services rendered.

The effectiveness of the many rent boycotts illustrate the importance of developing public service institutions that are legitimate and credible.

---

10 H. Adam and K. Moodley, *South Africa without apartheid*, Cape Town: Maskew Miller, 1986, p. 230.

11 P. Hugo, 'Sins of the fathers: affirmative action and the redressing of racial inequality in the United States. Towards the South African debate', *Politikon*, vol. 13, no. 1, 1986.

Lovell[12] has noted that a public employee group that is representative of the total society is essential to public accountability and organizational effectiveness.

Legitimacy involves the degree to which people feel themselves assured of a reasonable and sympathetic response to their interests on the part of the executive organs of government. Given the ubiquitous role of white public servants in enforcing the panoply of punitive apartheid measures over long years, the corrective effect of an intervention of this kind in the South African public service can hardly be disputed.

There are lessons to be learnt from those countries that did not make a determined effort to advance blacks into positions of responsibility in their public services in the pre-independence period. The Commission of Inquiry into Racial Discrimination conducted by the Rhodesian government in 1976 recorded many of the misgivings made in memoranda submitted by government departments, frequently in justification of the lack of advancement of blacks into senior positions.

Today in Zimbabwe there is regret among former holders of power for not having introduced more blacks to bureaucratic norms and values earlier.[13] The homeland set-up also produces evidence of the consequences of a lack of trained bureaucrats.[14] As has been the case generally in Africa, this lack of training and opportunity will surely return to haunt the South Africa of the future.

Manpower shortages and increasing demands will place an even greater strain on organizational structures already overburdened and seen by some as inefficient. The placement of blacks in the public service will not only benefit blacks themselves — by providing a source of much needed employment and, in some instances, more suitable staff — but will benefit whites as well by permitting the development of an adequately staffed public sector that can meet the needs of society.

Rather than addressing a moral need (a complex issue in itself that is not directly examined here), the advancement of blacks in the civil service should be seen as meeting a social need.

Lessons from history

The history of white advancement in the public service of South Africa illustrates the theory of social closure propounded by Parkin,[15] who argues that

---

[12] In B. S. Steel and N. P. Lovrich, 'Equality and efficiency trade-offs in affirmative action — real or imagined? The case of women in policing', *The Social Science Journal*, vol. 24 no. 1, 1987, pp. 53–70.

[13] P. Hugo, 'Black advancement in the civil service in Rhodesia — a record of missed opportunities (in progress).

[14] R. J. Haines, 'Retarded capitalism in South Africa's independent homelands', unpublished paper, 1988.

[15] F. Parkin, *Marxism and class theory*, London: Tavistock, 1979.

this constitutes a mechanism by which groups seek to maximize rewards by restricting access to resources and opportunities to a limited circle of eligibles. They justify this exclusion on the basis of certain social or physical attributes.

In turn, a class of outsiders is created which, because vertical mobility is denied to them, may use their collective strength to usurp the privileges of the upper class. Exclusionary social closure makes use of the rights of property and credentialism or the inflated use of educational certificates to monitor entry to key positions. In South Africa, race was and is also used as an exclusionary device.

The Afrikaner first entered public service in substantial numbers at the lower-grade levels under the Pact government's 'civilized labour' policies in the 1920s, and continued with the National Party victory in 1948 when the state sector further expanded. Preference for jobs was accorded to the dominant Afrikaner segment of white society. The process merits brief elaboration here as a backdrop to the introduction in the next section of the concept of affirmative action.

The Pact government formed under General Hertzog's leadership in 1924 consisted of both the then Nationalist party and Col. Cresswell's Labour Party. Its policy was explicitly focused on catering for the needs of the poor whites in the cities.

A new Department of Labour was created in 1924 to establish areas of employment in which whites would be protected from black competition. Inducements included tariff concessions to firms whose labour policies entailed demonstrable efforts to employ whites, even at the expense of existing black workers.[16] Local government and other public bodies were also encouraged to employ more whites.

Statistics attest to the success of these 'civilized labour' policies. In 1921 there were 4 705 white unskilled employees in the state railway system, by 1928 the number had expanded to 15 878.[17]

A major effort was also devoted to educating and training whites to participate in a society which was undergoing rapid transformation away from a rural-based economy. This effort at mass upliftment was not extended to blacks. Thus, in 1937 some £8 147 211 were spent on white education and £677 518 on African education.[18] As a result, the whites as a group were launched on the road to universal literacy, giving them a big headstart over blacks for whom such educational support was delayed for many years. In

---

[16] R. Davenport, *South Africa: a modern history*, London: MacMillan, 1985, p. 361.

[17] C. W. De Kiewiet, *A history of South Africa*, London: Oxford Univ. Press, 1957, p. 234.

[18] De Kiewiet, *A history of South Africa*.

addition, whites were able to support their claims on the state by their voting power.

Race, educational qualifications and political clout were then the exclusionary measures exploited to ensure the social closure of the white sector of the population. The lessons to be drawn from this are, firstly, that educational upliftment will be indispensable in the advancement of blacks in the public service or any other sphere, and, secondly, that any black advancement programme must have teeth, preferably legislative, if it is to be effective.

Affirmative action perspectives and the public service

Affirmative action policies vary among countries. In some, legislation is designed to afford disadvantaged groups access to jobs and resources corresponding to their percentage of the total population. In others, a 'softer' procedure is encouraged in terms of which such groups enjoy special compensatory education and training to be able to compete more effectively for employment opportunities. In all cases affirmative action policies are intended to assist those who in the past have been systematically oppressed, denied equal access to resources, skills and opportunities and, more often than not, branded as racially or socially inferior.

In South Africa, which has yet to extricate itself from the historical mire of outright discrimination before moving into an era of equal opportunities for all, the notion of any form of preferential or compensatory treatment for blacks is designer-made to raise adrenaline levels among many, if not most, whites. Nevertheless, the issue of affirmative action will inevitably feature prominently in the emerging debate on change across the spectrum of the nation's business, including its public service.

As Murphree has aptly commented in reference to the then Rhodesia:

> (The) dilemmas and contradictions (of affirmative action) will pose grave questions for the health of both the economy and the national ethos . . . but to ignore its current imperatives either by futile denial or by covert *ad hoc* responses would be to, once again, substitute wishful thinking for the requirements of our survival, both national and sectional.[19]

The debate on the role of affirmative action in black advancement programmes has, in fact, already been under way in the South African private sector for some years. There are any number of lessons to draw on from the experience of this sector, and from comparable experience in the United States:

⊳ There must be a clear and unambiguous commitment, in the form of a

---

19 M. Murphree, *Africanising employment in Zimbabwe: the socio-political constraints*, IPMSA Convention, Harare, Oct. 1979.

statement of policy, to affirmative action by the chief executive officer and senior staff, and frequent reaffirmation of that commitment.

▷ This commitment must be communicated down the hierarchy to all staff members. The City of Atlanta communicated its Affirmative Action Plan through publicity in its in-house magazine, policy inclusion in employee handbooks and departmental annual reports, notices on pay slips, a poster in areas accessible to employees and applicants for employment, and presentation and discussion of the plan as part of the employee orientation and training programmes.[20]

▷ Firm action must be taken against those employees who, through malicious non-compliance or other means, become road-blocks to the implementation of the programme. Hofmeyr[21] and Human and Icely[22] report research results that show considerable resistance to black advancement at the lower and supervisory levels of private sector organizations. These are the people (lacking educational qualifications and prospects for advancement) who feel most threatened by the advent of affirmative action programmes.

▷ Staff in supervisory positions must be made accountable for their performance in the field of black advancement. Progress should be monitored as part of their performance-evaluation and should be part of the determination of merit pay increases, bonuses and promotions.

The City of Atlanta appointed an affirmative action officer to conduct seminars for supervisory and managerial staff to increase their understanding of the scope of the programme and to brief them on the employment of minority group persons.[23]

This point was underscored in the city's Executive Order in which it was stressed that 'affirmative action and equal employment opportunity shall become a more integral part of the day-to-day operations and human resource planning of all city departments, agencies, bureaus and offices and shall not be considered as an isolated area of concern, separate and apart from line management responsibility'.[24] On a more general level, entire departments and organizations can likewise be rewarded or penalized for progress or lack thereof in this area.

---

20 Affirmative Action Office, *City of Atlanta: affirmative action plan for equal employment opportunity*, City of Atlanta: Dept. of Mayor, Oct. 1978.

21 K. Hofmeyr, 'South African business: in search of relevance', *South African Journal of labour Relations*, vol. 4, no. 11, Dec. 1987.

22 L. Human and N. Icely, 'Trends in the attitudes of white workers to the upward occupational mobility of blacks: findings from two companies', *South African Journal of Labour relations*, vol. 2, no. 11, June 1987.

23 Affirmative Action Office, *City of Atlanta*, p. 7.

24 Affirmative Action Office, *City of Atlanta*, p. i.

▷ The task of an affirmative action officer is to assist departments, provide guidelines, review progress, identify problem areas, liaise between the organization and concerned outside groups, and maintain a complaint system to ensure that allegations of discrimination receive immediate and fair treatment. The Citizen's Commission on Civil Rights[25] reports that internal complaint procedures have contributed to a constructive attitude on the part of minority employees.

▷ Written goals and timetables are necessary if this programme is to remain on course. Numerical goals highlight the areas needing remedial action and help evaluate progress toward the ideal of equal opportunity.

▷ Monitoring progress is also considered necessary, as are sanctions for not complying with the programme.

▷ Focus on individuals rather than groups is desirable as this avoids group stereotyping. All programmes should therefore be multiracial and open to all employees.[26]

▷ Tokenism is detrimental to blacks, whites and the programme itself. No one should be advanced beyond his or her capabilities. If this does occur, it can taint legitimate achievements. The achievements of blacks in previously white positions must be real and indisputable.

▷ Programmes will be needed to help bridge the culture from which the individuals come to that of the organization. Hofmeyr[27] has also pointed to the need for attitude change programmes to unfreeze the beliefs and perceptions of employees and to sensitize them to the need for change. In addition, more opportunities for social mixing would improve the communication across the colour line.

▷ The importance of special training for disadvantaged groups is emphasized as this will improve the prospect for equality of opportunity. Affirmative action claims that anti-discriminatory principles alone are insufficient to redress the disadvantages suffered by racial minorities because of historic and systematic discrimination.[28]

▷ Mentorship is an effective way of enhancing the potential in previously discriminatory organizations.

▷ The experience of affirmative action in the United States has shown that it is only when the programmes are accompanied by rewards and

---

25 The Citizens' Commission on Civil Rights, *Affirmative action to open the doors of job opportunity: a policy of fairness and compassion that has worked*, Washington, DC: Center for National Policy Review, June 1984, p. 133.

26 E. Mercer, *Freedom to learn: the development of disadvantaged people in the business environment.* (No publication details.)

27 Hofmeyr, 'South African business', pp. 11–12.

28 Hugo, 'Sins of the fathers' pp. 1–2.

sanctions that meaningful progress will be made. It is felt by some that legislative sanctions against non-compliance are the most effective.

The following six indicators suggest the dimensions of affirmative action programmes in the South African private sector.[29]

▷ Hard quotas or numerical goals are not yet part of these programmes (First National Bank appears to be the notable exception).

▷ White managers perceive it to be good corporate politics to accept black trainees and 'turn them into success stories'.

▷ More time is spent on recruitment on black campuses than the numbers (and often the calibre of education on offer there) of their graduates would seem to justify.

▷ Black matriculant and graduate cadet schemes operate to put talented individuals through specially designed (and expensive) training programmes with the objective of enabling as many of them as possible to compete successfully and on an equal basis with whites for specific jobs. This is usually referred to as pre-employment training.

▷ Targets are set for blacks to fill positions such as apprentices or trainee technicians. Entry standards are not necessarily lowered, but a more exhaustive recruiting effort is usually undertaken among blacks than whites.

▷ Blacks with good track records are specially recruited with a view to rapid promotion into earmarked positions. When such a position becomes vacant, the black candidate who has proved himself or herself is appointed without necessarily being the best candidate available.

Few South African companies run programmes that incorporate all of these affirmative action components. Perhaps half-a-dozen would score four out of six. Others advance blacks mainly because they expect a growing shortage of white skills. This is a large and growing category; understandably so, because it is fuelled by unvarnished self-interest.

There are also indications that a new impetus which looks beyond the traditional concept of training blacks for own needs has entered the lists. This involves the perception by medium to large companies that the survival of the free enterprise system may be at stake. Employers must therefore do their bit to win hearts and minds for a policy of orderly reform and support for free enterprise. As expressed to the author by one senior industrial relations manager: 'In the past we have built houses and schools but this is not enough. More dramatic signs of the benefits of the free enterprise system are required.'

---

[29] Information based on interviews with a number of South African industrial relations' officers in the private sector, April 1989.

It would be wrong, however, to imply that South African business has made great strides in the field of black advancement. Gavin Relly[30] recently admitted:

> We all thought it would be much easier to develop managerial and directorial skills among African, coloured and Indian people than has, in fact been the case. Not in any way because of incompetence but more because our environment in-house and socially has been hostile. Much of this can be traced to apartheid but a good deal to our own shortcomings.

As Welsh[31] points out, projections indicate that from a present base-line of 4 per cent black managers, within ten years 62 per cent of executive and professional jobs and 85 per cent of office jobs will have to be filled by black people.

Implementing affirmative action in the public service: problems and possibilities

Hammerman[32] has stated that in principle there should be no incompatibility between affirmative action and the public sector. In practice, conflict does exist, largely because of discrimination in a number of areas. He links the areas in which discrimination is likely to arise:

▷ selection and promotion through written tests unrelated to job performance,

▷ arbitrarily chosen educational and experiential requirements,

▷ irrelevant requirements,

▷ restricted opportunities, and

▷ selective announcement of opportunities for employment and promotion.

In addition, there are the practices of seniority-based promotion, nepotism and the buddy-system, all of which can effectively block black advancement in the bureaucracy. In the discussion that follows these areas of potential discrimination will be examined.

The need to expand the public service and to improve its function accountability raises the more fundamental question of revamping the service in terms of newly defined social needs. In doing this, the qualifications required of candidates for entry-level positions should be reconsidered. In many instances these could be lowered and provision made for promotion based on success achieved in studies undertaken later.

---

30 D. Welsh, 'Politics and business in South Africa', *Optima*, vol. 36, no. 3, 1988, pp. 168.

31 Welsh, 'Politics and business'.

32 H. Hammerman, *A decade of new opportunity: affirmative action in the 1970s*, Washington: The Potomac Inst., Oct. 1984, p. 65.

A reassessment of selection criteria could in fact lead to better management practices and utilization of human resources, for the criteria should accurately predict likely future job performance. The routine nature of the work required of many entry-level positions in the civil service implies that the selection criteria should not, in any case, be too demanding, even for those products of the inferior educational system. In-house training programmes are essential in this regard.

Where would one find suitable candidates to fill positions in the civil service and where would one locate them within the organization?

For entry-level positions there is a ready supply of candidates in the form of the many thousands of coloured, Indian and African matriculants annually. Many would be qualified to compete with a great number of white candidates for positions in the public service and parastatals.

Reform at this level might well be justified on the grounds of economic efficiency alone. Public service positions would have to be advertised in those areas with large audiences of appropriately qualified blacks. However, according to one respondent for the Citizen's Commission for Civil Rights[33] the best recruitment incentive is the presence of blacks in responsible, visible positions within the organization.

Three problems emerge with introducing a policy aimed at introducing significant numbers of blacks into general affairs departments.

First, there are political consequences at stake. Traditionally, the white working class has wielded a degree of political power quite disproportionate to its numbers. This segment, moreover, has provided a substantial component of the governing party's electoral constituency. However, the emergence in recent years of the extreme right-wing parties has seen most of this class of voter going over to these parties. Their shift is probably irreversible and they should therefore be discounted in any calculation of the electoral cost of giving them 'further offence' by employing significant numbers of blacks in their traditional enclaves.

The second problem concerns the marked politicization of the South African bureaucracy, especially in those arms more directly concerned with matters affecting race relations. This will have obvious consequences, not only on the judgement of those directly concerned with recruiting blacks at lower levels, but also with those white civil servants who may object to working with them.

Research on the attitudes of lower-level employees in the private sector points to considerable resistance to the upward mobility of blacks.[34]

---

33 Citizens' Commission on Civil Rights, *Affirmative action*, p. 134.

34 Hofmeyr, 'South African business'; and Human and Icely, 'Trends in the attitudes of white workers'.

However, research conducted by Rainey, Rajah and Human[35] suggests that resistance may be short-lived and that people come to accept the presence of blacks in the workplace fairly rapidly.

The third problem is that the lower levels referred to are less 'visible' than the high-profile senior positions. Granted that changes at the lower levels will gradually percolate through to the upper, but this is an extremely slow process in a climate in which time has become critical.

A possible solution to problems of reform at the lowest levels of the bureaucracy may lie in the intention to privatize some of the arms of the public service. Changes in staffing policy of a newly privatized operation could more easily be justified on the grounds of economic efficiency. The fact that such an operation would then no longer be state-owned would permit the government to distance itself politically from what transpired.

However, the greater and more urgent demand is for staff with high- and middle-level qualifications who will fill the important function of acting as role models for candidates at all levels. Where does one find candidates with the potential for success in senior public service positions?

Firstly, there is the possibility of recruitment from the private sector. However, given the disparity in remuneration levels, this would probably require a social commitment by the individuals involved. The prospect of advancement to positions of national influence might be a stronger drawcard than appreciated, especially if the persons were convinced that they would be setting an example as well as being in a position to influence appointments. The experience in the United States has been that white officials reporting to a black superior have been much more conscientious in locating suitable blacks for their respective sections than when reporting to a white superior.

The educational system is a second potential source of suitable candidates. Some of the managerial skills accumulated by senior black educationalists could be transferred with success to a civil service environment.

The third option, which should be seen more accurately as an adjunct to the previous two, is a well-organized system of in-house training.

Turning to the potential for reform in the middle and upper levels of the civil service, one is again confronted with political hurdles within the bureaucracy. Prime among these are the practice of seniority-based promotion, nepotism and old-boy networking. The answer may lie in incentive schemes.

The principle of accountability has been instituted in private sector firms

---

[35] P. Rainey, M. Rajah and L. Human, *Occupational mobility and wage differentiation: a qualitative study*, Pretoria: School of Business Leadership, UNISA, April 1985.

which have adopted black advancement programmes. Managers are evaluated for bonus and promotion purposes in terms of their commitment to and success in recruiting and promoting blacks. A manager who over a period of time made no progress in this direction would have to account for his failure to do so. In the private sector this is considered normal management practice. While it would elicit protest if transplanted to the public service, privatization could provide the means to introduce these new practices.

The problem of the old-boy network would have to be overcome by instituting a rigid code at key levels in the recruitment and appointment process. Needless to add, the officials involved would have to be sensitive to the need for reform. This need not entail a shake-up in the personnel sections of the civil service, but only the replacement or transfer of obstructionist officials in key positions, or the exercise would be doomed to failure via outright rejection or subtle sabotage.

In making appointments, the basic skills and level of training required for a post should be carefully respected and there should be flexibility in considering experience and length of service. Indeed, were length of service to be an important criterion for promotion, blacks would in many cases be ruled out of contention because of this past discriminatory system.

There would also have to be a relatively competitive employment package, missionaries being thin on the ground! Moreover, given the general hardening of black attitudes[36] and the expectation of much more comprehensive reform, any top private sector candidate would have to be convinced that his/her future advancement in the public service would not be blocked by recalcitrant remnants of racist behaviour. Any spectacular failures caused by either an unsuitable appointment or on account of frustration and resignation in the face of racism would severely damage the prospects for additional recruitment. In particular, those persons chosen as role models for other talented candidates would have to be seen to be making career progress at a reasonable pace.

The problem of attracting top people from other professions into the public service is complicated by the potential accusations of being 'sell-outs'. This would apply particularly to politically sensitive areas of the public service such as the police, army and constitutional development and planning. This difficulty could best be met by concentrating on the less controversial segments of the bureaucracy, such as transport and communications.

In the long term, any comprehensive employment policy initiative along the lines suggested would fail unless it became part of a process of fundamental reform on a much wider front. The competition for available talent

---

[36] Hofmeyr, 'South African business'.

in black ranks indicates the need for a fundamental reassessment of the educational system in South Africa which will contribute towards repairing the problem on a long-term basis. In the process it is to be hoped that it will be possible to move away from the present system which, aside from its critical problem of legitimacy, will avoid the glut of people who have a Standard 8 to 10 qualification when what is needed is highly skilled people with a high educational base, and also persons with adequate technical and vocational skills. These are areas which, as the African experience has shown, are understaffed while the hordes of academic certificate-holders are unemployable.

Until the whole educational system is restructured to allow it to produce the needed products, the public sector would be advised to follow the example of the private sector, which has seen to its own needs through its own in-house training schemes. Part of the more innovative approach to on-the-job training in the private sector has involved mentoring.

In American affirmative action programmes and in certain South African cases the mentorship concept is combined with the notion that the mentor should have a vested interest in the success of the employee who is in her/his care. This is accomplished by incorporating the mentor's record of commitment and success into an evaluation of own job performance and bonuses. Suitably adapted, there is no reason why such a programme should not be instituted in the public service.

The successful introduction of any such initiative will depend on the co-operation of key members of the civil service. A useful starting point would be the South African Public Servants Association, which in 1987 removed a colour bar from its constitution.[37] The following point should be stressed in any attempt to elicit the support of such a body: 'The need to seek a South Africa in which all segments of the community would feel they had a share and could thus defend.' While vested interests might well temper enthusiasm for such a statement, it is so phrased that few reasonably-minded people could reject it out of hand.

A further tactic would entail, as far as possible, making key segments of the public service leadership believe that the basic idea of equality of opportunity for all persons was their own. Those involved in negotiating acceptance of a programme of black entry and advancement would have to diplomatically steer these key personnel into a position where the need for such a programme was seen as self-evident by them.

If we are to accept that the politics of change in South Africa is to extend to the public service bureaucracy, it is probably as well to admit that the accelerated incorporation of blacks may well be accompanied by a strain

---

[37] Personal information from an employee of the South African Public Servants Association.

on standards of efficient service-delivery to the public — at least in the short term. Partly this will stem from inadequate administrative skills and experience, and partly from the simple fact of opening up a white and largely Afrikaans bureaucracy to reflect a more inclusive representation.

This new representativeness will probably bring in its wake a degree of politicization and tensions between individuals uncertain of each other. If this occurs, the advantages which adhere in a single ethnic/racial unit bureaucracy (organizational coherence stemming from unanimity of values, outlook and established ways of doing things) are at risk. Schrire's assessment of the implications of ending an Afrikaner monopoly of the bureaucracy and the creation of a representative set of institutions is realistic. (See Chapter 5.)

Conclusion

Much the same problems of new adjustments and transitional untidiness are likely to be encountered in coming to grips with reform in the area of political representation. Those who would baulk at these risks need to measure them against the costs of the current conflict in South Africa — a conflict which is largely the result of the unequal access of blacks to the major institutions of power. A determined policy of government-sponsored equal opportunity and special opportunity through affirmative action readily recommends itself. From a *realpolitik* point of view, the risks to the government and the white establishment of such a policy are not to be compared with the real and perceived problems of embarking on the road of whites and blacks competing for political power at a national level.

A more positive and appropriate approach is to visualize the policy of redressing historical racial backlogs in the public service as a relatively low risk opportunity of demonstrating the good faith of the official reform policy. In the process whites and blacks will learn a lot about each other. More importantly, blacks will build up the experience which is necessary to appreciate the value of a sound bureaucracy in a developing state like South Africa.

Whatever the future may hold in store for South Africa, an enlarged cadre of experienced black public servants will be a sound investment. They should be considered as constituting part of the building blocks of interracial co-operation on which a future South Africa must be built. This should be a welcome prospect in the present situation in which racial polarization is escalating at an unprecedented rate.

Acknowledgement

I would like to thank Pat Rainey for helpful discussion of this topic.

8

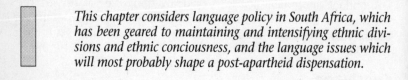

The language question

Neville Alexander

*This chapter considers language policy in South Africa, which
has been geared to maintaining and intensifying ethnic divisions and ethnic conciousness, and the language issues which
will most probably shape a post-apartheid dispensation.*

Introduction

In South Africa today the National Party (NP) government's language policy
is being reconsidered. According to Karel Prinsloo of the Human Sciences
Research Council (HSRC):

> South Africa is currently experiencing severe pressures for change in many
> spheres. In order to accommodate our linguistic diversity better and simultan-
> eously to ensure a dynamic, broad-minded and realistic language dispensation
> in a changing country, an all-embracing language plan could be a useful guide
> for decision makers from different groups.[1]

It is clear, then, that recent political and economic developments have
rendered this particular arena of social policy fluid so that even the Establishment recognizes that language policy reform has become unavoidable.

There is another side to this constellation, however. Since the historic
events of June 1976, the anti-apartheid movement has changed from the
politics of protest to the politics of challenge. Among many other things,
this has meant that the movement has had to formulate alternatives to
those policies which discriminate on grounds of colour, class or gender.

Language policy, whether systematically formulated or not, derives from
and influences decisively economic, political and socio-cultural developments. In South African society as constituted at present, racial, class and
gender aspects of language policy sustain and reinforce inherited social
inequalities and national divisions. In order, for instance, to acquire well-
remunerated employment in any sphere, it is essential that the prospective
employee should be fluent in English and/or Afrikaans. This means that

---

[1] K. Prinsloo, 'Language policy and planning', introductory paper delivered at the Conference of the English
Academy of Southern Africa, 5 Sep. 1986, Johannesburg, unpublished mimeo., 1986, pp. 24–5

for the vast majority of people officially classified black, such employment is simply unattainable because their home language is neither English nor Afrikaans and, in most cases, their schooling does not help them to acquire the necessary proficiency in either or both of these languages. Conversely, it means that official language policy favours those people classified white, coloured and Indian because most of the people so classified are either English and/or Afrikaans speakers.

However, even in the case of coloureds and Indians, inherited racial inequalities are sustained by means of mechanisms that tend in other capitalist societies to rigidify class cleavages. One such mechanism, which is, incidentally, not always articulated, is the requirement that prospective employees for most highly-paid jobs should be able to understand, speak, read and write standard English and Afrikaans. Whether or not candidates meet this requirement is usually gauged by whether or not the individual concerned has a certain certificate obtained through the formal educational institutions or in non-formal industrial training and vocational courses. Often, and perhaps even usually, an *en face* interview will decide whether or not the candidate is up to standard. Besides the (now) eroded instrument of legislative prohibitions on the employment of individuals from certain population registration groups in designated categories of employment and the tenacious legacy of racial prejudice where such prohibitions have been abolished, it is clear that this organic requirement of the system as it is disadvantages many, and perhaps even most, of those classified Indian or coloured when it comes to the upper rungs of the employment ladder.

In short, race, class and language largely reinforce one another in contemporary South Africa. Although I shall not develop the point further in this chapter, the same applies to the complex interaction of language and gender discrimination. The racial capitalist order spawns caste-like practices and is in turn sustained by them. At the socio-cultural and broadly ideological level, this means, among other things, that historically-evolved ethnic divisions and ethnic consciousness are maintained and intensified. Language planning and other elements of language policy have been geared to doing just that for the best part of three centuries of South African history. National unity, instead of becoming an attainable goal, became instead a more or less utopian vision cherished by progressive elements in the intelligentsia and increasingly in the ranks of the national liberation movement since 1945. It took the lightning flash of the 1976 Soweto Uprising to show that the old order was fast becoming a thing of the past and that a new order had been forming in the darkness of the 1963–73 years of silence.

Heritage or mortgage?

During the seventeenth and eighteenth centuries in the period of Company rule, Dutch was the language of government and of all formal occasions. Perfunctory attempts were made to teach Dutch and the Reformed religion to slaves and their children, but these were singularly unsuccessful because of the reluctance of the mercantilist (Dutch East India) Company to waste valuable resources in a land that was, in Acton's celebrated phrase, no more than an obstruction on the way to the East! Malayo-Portuguese vied with pidgin Dutch to become the lingua franca of the Cape of Good Hope. Because of the cutthroat mercantilist rivalry between Holland and Portugal, the Company did everything possible to suppress Malayo-Portuguese, the lingua franca of the East Indies, although there is some evidence that at one time it was allowed to be taught to slave children as a matter of economic necessity.

Once the free burghers inaugurated the process of reluctant colonization, pidgin Dutch (Kaaps-Hollands or Afrikaans-Hollands) in various guises rapidly became the language of commerce, of production and of most informal intercourse. Eventually, by the end of the first half of the eighteenth century, this pidgin had been creolized, having become the home language of the slave population, of most people of Khoisan descent who had not sought refuge in the arid interior from the twin colonial processes of dispossession and proletarianization, and of most of the *trekboers* and of the settled farmers of the Western Cape. Among this last group, of course, a knowledge of High Dutch was prized as a badge of spurious aristocracy for many decades to come! The final displacement of Dutch by Afrikaans as the recognized language of the non-English-speaking whites of South Africa was promoted and consummated in the fifty years between 1875 and 1925 when the Afrikaner nationalist movement entered into the inheritance of Dutch colonialism and British imperialism in southern Africa.

During the century of direct British rule between 1806 and 1910, colonial language policy was clearly defined but, none the less pragmatic. As far as the colonists of European descent were concerned, British policy was one of consistent Anglicization.

That the British authorities saw the importance of language is apparent from the steps periodically taken to compel the public use of English. They applied pressure first in the schools, they extended it by proclamation to the courts from the late 1820's onwards; in 1853 they made English the exclusive language of parliament; and by (1870) they appeared to be triumphing on all fronts. Chief Justice, J.H. de Villiers, could tell an audience in the mid-1870's that 'although the time is still far distant when the inhabitants of this colony will speak and acknowledge one common mother-tongue, it would come at last, and when it does come, the language of Great Britain will also be the language of South Africa'.[2]

---

[2] M. Wilson and L. Thompson, *The Oxford history of South Africa*, London: Oxford Univ. Press, 1978, p. 283.

It was only in the wake of the mineral discoveries and the struggles around the Kimberley diamond fields and, later, around control of the Transvaal gold mines that the unassailable position of English in the Anglo-Afrikaner Establishment came to be questioned. The rise of an agrarian bourgeoisie in the Western Cape winelands and among wool farmers elsewhere in South Africa provided a sufficient basis for primitive accumulation of capital such that eventually this class of people could use their material resources to mobilize a sectionalist (nationalist) movement which took as one of its mobilizing planks the rights of the Afrikaans language. The rise of Afrikaner nationalism demonstrated how ethnic consciousness was generated through class struggles over the control of material resources and eventually systematically mobilized by the rising Afrikaans-speaking bourgeoisie and the petty bourgeoisie to control the political kingdom and thereby control the levers of ultimate economic power.[3]

The rise to power of the Afrikaner National Party in 1948 gave the Broederbond the opportunity to use the constitutionally entrenched binary equality of Afrikaans and English to promote their class and sectionalist interests based on an increasingly mythologized Afrikanerdom. The subsequent Afrikanerization of all aspects of South African life not only served to reinforce the control of the Afrikaner bureaucracy but, more significantly, played midwife to the birth and development of giant Afrikaner-controlled corporations and business empires. The systematic promotion of Afrikaans, especially through the formal education system, had important economic motives and consequences while simultaneously healing the pathological feelings of inferiority which most Afrikaans-speaking whites had *vis-à-vis* the English, caused by the ruthless exploitation of British imperialism.

Control through language policy

This can be seen very clearly from the fact that some Afrikaner theorists and ideologues postulated the same kind of trajectory for the indigenous African people as that which the Afrikaners had traversed. For example, G. Cronje in *'n Tuiste vir die Nageslag* (published in 1945) maintained that:

> the Boer people have themselves gone through the crucible of imperialist and capitalist domination and exploitation . . . The Boer nation can therefore fully understand the sufferings of the Bantu. It is that same imperialism and capitalism, having them believe that the foreign is better than what is their own, which seeks to destroy their tribal life.[4]

Here, in an ironic twist, the dialectic of Verwoerdian language policies

---

3 D. O'Meara, *Volkskapitalisme: class, capital and ideology in the development of Afrikaner nationalism 1934–1948*, Johannesburg: Ravan Press, 1983.

4 W. de Klerk, *The puritans in Africa. A story of Afrikanerdom*, Harmondsworth: Penguin Books, 1975, p. 216.

is manifest. On the one hand, the (probably genuinely held) belief that the different peoples could only develop to full maturity if, among other things, their languages were assisted to acquire full dignity; on the other hand, this did not necessarily mean a transformation from the primitive state of the tribe. Retribalization and intensification — even invention — of ethnic identities as intricate steps in a choreography of separate freedoms, is in essence, the point of departure of Afrikaner nationalist language policy towards those they first called Bantu and now classify Black.

Paradoxically, they based this policy on the work of British and other European missionaries who, during the nineteenth and twentieth centuries nurtured a small mission élite who could understand English while spending much time translating the Bible into indigenous languages. It was on this foundation that the ideologues of Afrikanerdom based themselves. Indeed, W. M. Eiselen, one of the main progenitors of Bantu education, was born to missionary parents.

As I have said elsewhere:

> what had begun among the missionaries as attempts to come to grips with the problem of reducing to writing the indigenous languages they were in contact with, was now used to define and confine groups of people in the prison of social anthropological theory. In other words, whereas the missionaries had inadvertently and unintentionally helped to invent ethnicity, to use Ranger's apt phrase, by drawing usually arbitrary lines through language continuums because of the need, as they saw it, to demarcate their sectarian territorial boundaries, their work was now used to justify pernicious social, cultural and political practices, consciously geared towards the fragmentation and subjugation of the black people.[5]

Apartheid language policy not only entrenched the Cartesian language grid which missionary transliteration and evangelization practices, among other things, had initiated,[6] but also consciously poured increasingly artificial ethnic or tribal content into the vocabularies and even into the syntax and morphology of the indigenous varieties. The insistence on a 'colonial trilingualism' in the sphere of formal education,[7] was calculated to put one more hurdle on the hopeless track on which African school students were expected to compete on a basis of national equality with their English- and Afrikaans-speaking peers. The Afrikanerizing bureaucrats accepted the legacy of the indigenous languages handed down by the missionaries but were implacably opposed to the Anglicizing and Anglocentric

---

[5] N. Alexander, *Language policy and national unity in South Africa/Azania*, Cape Town: Buchu Books, 1989, p. 22.

[6] P. Harries, 'The roots of ethnicity: discourse and the politics of language construction in South-East Africa', *African Affairs* (346), Jan., 1988.

[7] D. Brown, 'Speaking in tongues: apartheid and language in South Africa', *Perspectives in Education*, vol. 10, no. 2, pp. 40–1.

educational ethos and praxis in which it was embedded. With transparent disingenuousness, the theories of the superiority of mother-tongue instruction emanating from UNESCO educationists and linguists in the early 1950s were used to whitewash the pernicious racist aims of Bantu education. Language policy as an instrument of political control came to be used deliberately and recklessly by the children and grandchildren of the Boers who had rejected Milner's Anglicization schemes by establishing their own Christian National Schools!

This reckless policy rushed headlong into disaster on 16 June 1976 when the chilling slogan: 'Kill Afrikaans!' stopped the Afrikaner nationalists in their tracks. African school students in Soweto on that fateful day gave voice in a completely unplanned, spectacular and bloody manner to the resistance to Afrikaner cultural imperialism and national oppression which had been gathering force for decades. Their peaceful demonstration against the imposition of Afrikaans-medium instruction in certain subjects[8] was the concretization at street level of many years of courteous and scholarly protest against an unjust and unjustifiable educational and language policy in a multilingual country.

Resistance to language oppression

For, resistance to oppressive language policies — not surprisingly — dates back to the very foundations of the Cape Colony.[9] With the exception of a handful of (mostly coloured) middle-class interest-groups who regarded Afrikaans as their preferred national language, all middle-class blacks supported the supremacy of English both as lingua franca and (often) as the language of the future which would displace all others. Their economic and class interests were best served by adherence to the unassailable position of English and, of course, their mission education moulded them to become black Englishmen. Dr Abdurahman's statement at the beginning of this century was typical:

> The question naturally arises which is to be the national language. Shall it be the degraded forms of a literary language, a vulgar patois; or shall it be that language which Macaulay says is 'In force, in richness, in aptitude for all the highest purposes of the poet, the philosopher and the orator inferior to the tongue of Greece alone?' Shall it be the language of the 'Kombuis' (kitchen) or the language of Tennyson? That is, shall it be the Taal (Afrikaans) or English?[10]

---

8 K. Hartshorne, 'Language policy in African education in South Africa 1910–1985 with particular reference to the issue of medium of instruction', in D. Young, ed., *Bridging the gap between theory and practice in English second language teaching,* Cape Town: Maskew Miller-Longman, 1987.

9 Alexander, *Language policy and national unity*, p. 22 and B. Hirson, 'Language in control and resistance in South Africa', *Journal of African Affairs*, no. 80, 1981, pp. 219–37.

10 Alexander, *Language policy and national unity*, p. 29.

The other main approach to the language question from those who were fundamentally opposed to the system of racial and class domination was influenced by the interests of black working people. Unlike those who were blinkered by their narrow middle-class concerns, these men and women — mostly humanitarian liberals and communists or radical socialists — realized that an English-only or English-mainly solution was no more than a golden illusion. They knew that the indigenous African languages were overwhelmingly part of the solution. Though few, if any, of them knew Leon Trotsky's writings on South Africa, they accepted intuitively his view that:

> Three-quarters of the population of South Africa . . . is composed of non-Europeans . . . Under these conditions the South African Republic will emerge first of all as a black republic; this does not exclude, of course, either full equality for the whites, or brotherly relations between the two races — depending mainly on the conduct of the whites. *But it is entirely obvious that the predominant majority of the population, liberated from slavish dependence, will put a certain imprint on the state* (my emphasis).[11]

For this reason, educationists in the Communist Party and some of the more liberal-minded members and sympathizers of the United Party emphasized the development of the indigenous African languages. Some of them[12] were also influenced by Soviet nationality (that is, ethnic) theories, which they used to substantiate their views on language policy in South Africa. All of them, of course, opposed the colonial policy of English–Afrikaans supremacy and the *de facto* neglect of the indigenous languages which, even by the time of the 1980 census, were the languages actually spoken by the vast majority of the black working class. Men such as Moses Kotane, for example, visualized a federation of autonomous southern African states based on language groups more or less along the lines of the USSR. This vision was diametrically opposed to the kind of South Africa which inspired the Anglo-Afrikaner ruling class.

However, it was recognized that in the transitional period before fundamental social change had come about, black people would have to acquire knowledge of either English or Afrikaans as part of a survival kit.[13] They chose to promote English, which was closely related to the politicization of the newly-urbanized African workers on the Rand and, to a lesser degree, in the Western Cape. Both Liberals and Communists conducted night schools

---

11 L. Trotsky, *Leon Trotsky on black nationalism and self-determination*, (ed. G. Breitman), New York: Pathfinder Press, 1970, p. 59.

12 B. Hirson, 'Language in control and resistance in South Africa', *Journal of African Affairs*, no. 80, 1981, pp. 219–37.

13 D. Brown, 'The basement of Babylon: language and literacy on the South African gold mines', *Social Dynamics*, vol. 14, no. 1, pp. 46–56.

for (mainly) African workers in which a large part of the syllabus was devoted to learning English through the use of texts that also challenged and stimulated the participants' perception of social reality. One of the better known attempts was called 'Easy English'[14] which was inspired and edited by Edward Roux who, like most progressives, understood that English was destined to become the lingua franca of southern Africa but insisted that it should become such for all the people and not merely for the middle classes and the intelligentsia.

World War II and the subsequent rise to power of the National Party shifted the parameters within which socio-political strategies could be engendered and realized. One of the most determined language-planning exercises ever carried out in the modern world was initiated by the Broederbond through every agency at the disposal of the state, the main one being, naturally, the formal educational system, almost fully controlled by the state. The role of the English language was downgraded and that of Afrikaans enhanced while the indigenous African languages were to be systematically developed in order to imprison their speakers in their ethnic cultures and thus, coincidentally, to curb the rapid growth of African and, more generally, black nationalism. Prime Minister J. G. Strydom stated that: 'Every Afrikaner who is worthy of the name cherishes the ideal that South Africa will ultimately only have one language and that language must be Afrikaans.'[15]

It was this set of language policies — most prominently in the form of *moedertaalonderwys* (mother-tongue instruction) — which united anti-apartheid forces and large segments of the white liberal Establishment against the Afrikaner National Party. A. C. Jordan, a senior lecturer in African languages at the University of Cape Town, in the course of a polemic on the language question in the pages of the *Educational Journal* of the Teachers' League of South Africa, captured the content and the spirit of the entire opposition in a few felicitous sentences:

> In order to achieve their purpose, the rulers must exploit the universally accepted educational principle that the best way to impart knowledge is to use the pupil's own mother-tongue. As educationists, we cannot reject this principle. But as democrats we reject the idea of a Bantu community or Coloured community, and if the given mother-tongue is in such a state that it cannot take the child beyond the confines of the supposed own community, then we must insist that while the child continues to receive training in the use of his own mother-tongue, he should as early as possible receive instruction through

---

14 Based on Ogden's idea of Basic English.

15 K. Chick and M. Seneque, 'The role of the applied linguist in language planning: the medium of instruction problem in KwaZulu/Natal', in D. Young, ed., *Language: planning and medium in education*, Cape Town: UCT and SAALA, 1987.

a language that will ensure him a place in a world community.[16]

This critique of *moedertaalonderwys* together with the general black opposition to Afrikanerization exploded in 1976. That cataclysmic event inaugurated one of the most creative periods in the history of South Africa. In every sphere of life, people (men, women and children) were compelled to wrestle with alternatives to the superannuated practices of a racist society. In the sphere of language, countless smaller and larger projects were initiated by community and religious groups, service organizations, trades unions and private businesses. Yet, it was not until about 1985, when the National Language Project (NLP) was launched, that systematic, all-embracing strategizing and action on the language question began to be undertaken.

The elements of a new language policy

We have examined briefly some aspects of language policy which continue to structure our present situation. The exposition of the NLP in the text that follows will lead us into the heart of language policy for the future.

English as the lingua franca

It is clear that for economic reasons, knowledge of English and to a lesser degree, Afrikaans, will be integral to the expansion of the South African economy regardless of the particular forms in which economic development occurs. In a post-apartheid South Africa, Afrikaans will rapidly lose its most favoured language status and for economic reasons, the promotion of English as the lingua franca will become the most rational policy option. Since considerations of national unity, cultural access and international communication now already reinforce these economic imperatives, little opposition to this component of a new national language policy will be forthcoming, except from the inevitable band of irredentist Afrikaner *bittereinders* (those who will not accept defeat). It is, incidentally, one of the most fascinating twists of fate that through their forty-year sojourn in the wilderness of Afrikaner nationalist rule, most black people have come to associate notions of freedom and democracy with the English language and tend to stereotype Afrikaans as 'the language of the oppressor!'.[17] In a free South Africa/Azania, it can be anticipated that the English that will become the spoken norm will be very different from the standard South African English which today in effect discriminates against the vast majority of the population.[18]

---

[16] A. Jordan, 'The language question', *The Educational Journal*, vol. 29, Jan.–Feb. 1958, pp. 10–12.

[17] K. Heugh, Trends in language-medium policy for a post-apartheid South Africa', in Young, *Language: planning and medium*.

[18] N. Ndebele, 'The English language and social change in South Africa', keynote address delivered at the Jubilee

The political and cultural dimensions of the question of English as the lingua franca of a free South Africa/Azania are of great importance. Few, if any, people in the anti-apartheid movement are motivated by Anglocentric sentiment such as that which could still make a Dr Abdurahman wax lyrical some seventy-five years ago. Pragmatic, instrumental considerations are explicitly acknowledged by the few people who have written on this important subject. In this regard, if we accept the advice of the American social scientist, Kelman, we appear to be on the right track. More than a decade ago he stressed that:

> In terms of general principles, I would argue, very simply, that language policies ought to be based entirely on functional considerations. That is, in selecting languages for various purposes, in influencing the population's language behaviour, and in planning the educational system, central authorities ought to be concerned primarily with two issues: (1) How to establish and facilitate patterns of communication (both internally and internationally) that would enable its socio-economic institutions to function most effectively and equitably in meeting the needs and interests of the population; and (2) how to assure that different groups within the society, varying in their linguistic repertoires (for either ethnic or social-class reasons), have equal access to the system and opportunities to participate in it. Out of these processes, a national language, evoking sentimental attachments, may gradually emerge. I would seriously question, however, any policy designed to promote such a language on a sentimental basis and to suppress other languages in the hope of establishing the national one in their stead.[19]

To promote national unity in a multilingual society, a lingua franca (which becomes such usually for precisely instrumental, economic reasons) plays a pivotal role. There is no doubt that English will increasingly play such a role in a South Africa released from the mortgage of apartheid language policy. On the other hand, however, we should not underestimate the magnitude of the task ahead. As Prinsloo has pointed out, it is an incontrovertible fact that in 1980 under 50 per cent of the entire population of South Africa understood English.[20] However, the increased access to formal education for black children together with the fact that in the schools of the Department of Education and Training, as well as the homelands, less than 2 per cent of all instruction takes place through the medium of Afrikaans where there is a choice between English and Afrikaans-medium

---

Conference of the English Academy of Southern Africa, Johannesburg, Sept. 4–6, 1986 and S. Sepamla, *The role of culture in the struggle, 12 years to the 21st century,* (ed. by the Information Research Unit of Umtapo Centre), Durban: Umtapo Centre, 1988.

19 H. Kelman, 'Language as an aid and barrier to involvement in the national system', in J. Rubin and B. Jernudd, eds., *Can language be planned? Sociolinguistic theory and practice for developing nations,* Hawaii: The Univ. Press of Hawaii, East–West Center, 1975.

20 Prinsloo, 'Language policy and planning'.

instruction[21] means that this situation is changing rapidly.

Encouraging all languages

The second component of a new national language policy is to encourage the growth of all the languages spoken. Here the cultural-political, rather than the economic, dimensions of language policy are paramount. If it is accepted that one of the explicit and implicit goals of the anti-apartheid or national liberation movement is to build a nation, then the conventional Eurocentric theory takes it as axiomatic that only one language ought to be selected as the national language, the means of verbal communication which weaves together all the disparate elements and groups of the nation-to-be. However, this Risorgimento definition of the nation where every nation has its particular language so that the language group and the nation are co-extensive, has been exploded in many recent studies.[22] Today, it is no longer in dispute that multilingual nations are not merely possible but are, in fact, the norm. In post-colonial Africa, according to Smith: 'National identity is rarely associated with language *per se* since this could lead to balkanisation . . .(and) in general, the linguistic criterion has been of sociological importance only in Europe and the Middle East (to some extent)'.[23]

Our future as a nation is indisputably a multilingual one. All proposals for a monolingual future not only go against the global trends, but contain the dangerous seeds of future ethnic conflicts. A consistently democratic approach to the language question has to be based on the sound linguistic premise that all languages are equal in their capacity to serve as means of communication, thought, and bearers of culture. Any attempt to suppress the rights of languages will inevitably give rise to the most bitter resistance, as the recent history of all language-based political movements, including Afrikaners in British-ruled South Africa, proves again and again. We have the task of transforming the languages of our country from instruments of division into instruments of national unification. It is perhaps also necessary to scotch the racist-ethnic assumptions of apartheid language and national theory in terms of which each language group should have the right to form it's own nation-state (Bantustan). The National Party itself has abandoned this chimera of Verwoerdianism but it is still important to insist that the Risorgimento conceptualization of the national question is

---

21 Hartshorne, 'Language policy'.

22 Nosizwe, *One Azania one nation. The national question in South Africa*, London: Zed Press, 1979; and B. Anderson, *Imagined communities: reflections on the origin and spread of nationalism*, London: Verso, 1985.

23 J. Edwards, *Language, society and identity*, Oxford: Basil Blackwell, 1985, p. 11.

quite false as a general theory in the modern world. Should such a partition-ing of South Africa take place eventually, it will certainly not be primarily or fundamentally because of the unfolding of some logic inherent in the evolution of language-groups.

All the languages in South Africa, including Afrikaans, should be encouraged to flourish. While the implementation of this principle will undoubtedly be limited by the availability of material and human resources in the short-to-medium term, it is necessary to enunciate it and to initiate the processes and the patterns that will eventually make possible its realization. Because the economic imperative for learning indigenous African languages by English- and Afrikaans-speakers does not exist, an act of political will is required to encourage them to do so. The fact that many politically conscious people from these groups are beginning to learn these languages indicates that this trend will inevitably accompany the liberatory process in South Africa. Official encouragement from the government's own reform programme as well as the formal relations with the independent and self-governing homelands gives an added impetus in more status-quo-orientated circles. Employment opportunities in homeland bureaucracies, and even in their private sector, are enhanced for those who are able to speak the relevant African language.

We would do well to observe what is happening in other southern African countries. A recent study of the language question in Mozambique, for example, criticizes the fact that not enough practical attention is given by the ruling party to the promotion of the indigenous languages in spite of the rhetorical commitment to this. It was stated at the First National Seminar on Portuguese Language Education held in Maputo in 1979 that:

> If the party and the government confirm this option (of declaring Portuguese to be the official language) they do not intend to relegate Mozambique's Bantu languages into the background by so doing. They are simply wanting to utilise a linguistic resource which has fewer risks and more certain guarantees of success as far as facilitating communication among all the people.

Similarly, the First Conference of the Department of Information and Propaganda of the Party, held in Macomia in 1975, stated clearly that: 'The promotion of the Portuguese language should under no circumstances be interpreted to mean that it is our aim to do away with the languages of Mozambique' (my translation).[24]

According to this study, the Secretary of State for Culture, Luis Bernardo Honwana, in a document entitled 'Contribution to the definition of a language policy for the People's Republic of Mozambique' demanded research

---

24 E. Fuchs, *Alphabetisierung und entwicklung. Die wichtigkeit der sprachproblematik am beispiel Mocambiques*, Frankfurt an Main, Verlag fur Interkulturele Kommunikation, 1988, p. 30.

on and development of the local Mozambican languages without challenging the official status of Portuguese. He maintained that the promotion of the local languages would make possible wider social, cultural and political participation by the people of Mozambique and would begin to put in question the privileged position of Portuguese. If this were not done, through bureaucratic or political inertia, there would be no real difference between colonial and post-colonial language policy.[25]

This illustrates the tendency which has emerged in all post-colonial states that after an initial period of promoting the colonizers' language for pragmatic rather than sentimental reasons, indigenous languages come into their own once again, A post-apartheid South Africa will probably move along similar lines. Those South Africans who are not of English or Afrikaans background are compelled, by the spur of economic necessity, to broaden their language skills, whereas those who try to learn one or other indigenous language are hampered by the Berlin walls of the Group Areas Act and separate schooling. Clearly, a major campaign to encourage the learning of the different languages at all levels will have to be undertaken.

It ought to be clear that one of the main spin-offs of this proposal is that its realization will facilitate communication among the different language groups in our country. The ideal solution is a trifocal one in which each person will know a mother tongue or home language, English, and another (regionally important) language. Another important aspect of this proposal is that Nguni-speakers should be encouraged to learn a Sotho language and vice versa. Theoretically, in this constellation, every individual in South Africa will be able to find a language in which to converse with any other South African.

Language status

There is general agreement that English should and will remain an official language in a post-apartheid South Africa/Azania. The official status of other languages, however, is a matter of debate. One proposal is that all the other languages be given official status at the appropriate regional level. In reaction to this policy option from the NLP in 1986, Karel Prinsloo of the HSRC has recently suggested that:

> If one considers the clearly distinguishable areas of concentration in which the eleven dominant home languages occur, it is immediately obvious that one should ask whether language policy in South Africa should not also make provision for the recognition of languages on a regional basis. We are concerned here specifically with the nine African languages which are dominant home languages. Besides English and Afrikaans as official languages, we ought now to

---

[25] Fuchs, *Alphabetisierung und Entwicklung*, pp. 30–1.

give recognition on a regional basis to the dominant African language in each region (my translation).[26]

As a transitional measure which would raise the status of the African languages in a rapidly changing South Africa, this is an important proposal, which we should certainly support. Of course, we would like to guard against any tendency to interpret this kind of proposal along the lines of moulding in reinforced concrete all the ethnic divisions which colonialism, segregation and apartheid policies have so assiduously promoted in the past. For this reason, amongst others, I have revived a controversial proposal concerning the standardization of the varieties of Nguni and of Sotho respectively.[27] In accordance with this proposal, I would suggest that another possibility would be to accord official status to English, Nguni, Sotho and (possibly) Afrikaans throughout South Africa, but on a reasonably flexible basis so that, for example, official documents and other language-related services would be available in English and Nguni, English and Sotho, English and Afrikaans, depending on the preponderance of speakers of the particular languages. In polyglot areas such as the Witwatersrand, all such services would have to be available at all times.

The status of the genuine minority languages such as Venda, Tsonga, Telegu, Tamil, Gujerati, Urdu, as well as other Indo-Germanic languages, including Portuguese, would be dealt with pragmatically but on the basis of the democratic principle that people ought to be served in the language of their choice wherever possible. The complexity of the language situation emerges very clearly from Table 8.1, derived from the 1980 census data.

The question of national languages is in my view a premature and even a spurious one in the South African context. The fact that in the political and cultural sense there is no nation in South Africa, that indeed all the ruling groups and governments since 1910 have systematically aborted the birth of one South African nation, explains to some extent why no national language and no national culture has emerged. For this reason, too, it is my contention that all the major languages in South Africa are in fact national languages since all of them will have to become instrumental in uniting the people of our country into one united nation. The correctness of this view can be gauged by referring to a convenient definition:

> (T)here is a significant difference between an official medium and a national language. An official language is one that is employed for government administration. So, in Nigeria, Uganda, Singapore, the Philippines and the Southern African region English is an official language, although it is used by a small

---

26 K. Prinsloo, 'n Taalplan vir Suid-Afrika', *Insig*, Sept. 1987, p. 24.

27 Prinsloo, 'n Taalplan', pp. 33–7.

Table 8.1:   Census data (1980) on home language in the RSA
(excluding independent homelands)

Language	Whites	Coloureds	Asians	Africans	Total
Official languages					
Afrikaans	2 581 080	2 251 860	15 500	77 320	4 925 760
English	1 763 220	324 360	698 940	29 120	2 815 640
				Sub-total	7 741 400
Other					
European languages					
Dutch	11 740	0	0	0	11 740
German	40 240	0	0	0	40 240
Greek	16 780	0	0	0	16 780
Italian	16 600	0	0	0	16 600
Potuguese	57 080	0	0	0	57 080
French	6 340	0	0	0	6 340
				Sub-total	148 780
Oriental languages					
Tamil	0	0	24 720	0	24 720
Hindi	0	0	25 900	0	25 900
Telegu	0	0	4 000	0	4 000
Gudjarati	0	0	25 120	0	25 120
Urdu	0	0	13 280	0	13 280
Chinese	0	0	2 700	0	2 700
				Sub-total	95 720
African languages				Grand total	16 777 322
Nguni-languages					
Xhosa	0	8 440	0	2 870 920	2 879 360
Zulu	0	5 580	0	6 058 900	6 064 480
siSwati	0	1 060	0	649 540	650 600
South-Ndebele	0	440	0	289 220	289 660
North-Ndebele	0	100	0	170 120	170 220
				Sub-total	10 054 322
Sotho/Tswana					
North Sotho	0	2 440	0	2 429 180	2 431 620
South Sotho	0	5 320	0	1 872 520	1 877 840
Tswana	0	9 300	0	1 346 360	1 355 660
				Sub-total	5 665 120
Tsonga	0	1 180	0	886 960	888 140
Venda	0	40	0	169 700	169 740
Other	35 020	2 660	11 160	73 900	122 740
Totals	4 528 100	2 612 780	821 320	16 923 760	24 886 020

proportion of the population in each and all of these countries. A national language, on the other hand, is the common medium of daily intercourse between the majority of citizens of a given country. In most Anglophone third world countries, therefore, English is not a national language.[28]

In terms of these definitions, English and Afrikaans are official but not national languages in what is now the Republic of South Africa. They can only be elevated to that status once they become part and parcel of a new national language policy, one of the goals of which would be to build a nation out of all the different language groups in South Africa.

Language medium

As a means of socialization of the individual, schools are to modern industrial societies what the Church was to medieval Europe. For this reason, among others, the language medium in which school students are taught is of exceptional economic, political and cultural importance in any modern state. The predominant medium of instruction inevitably is or becomes the most important language of the state simply because — in the context of compulsory schooling in a multilingual society — it means that every individual in the up-and-coming generation(s) has a relatively good understanding of the language(s) concerned. It is precisely for this reason that this particular question has always been at the centre of language-related controversies in South African history but, of course, particularly so in the era of Bantu education.

The question of the medium of instruction in the formal educational system is complex.[29]

The policy which, in the light of available evidence appears to do justice to all the interests involved — given the availability of adequate material and human resources — would seem to be one which would promote mother-tongue instruction, unless parents specifically determine otherwise in given cases. At the same time, the language which will become the medium of instruction in most, or all subjects (English in our case) should be introduced in the second year of schooling.

In order to meet other requirements of the political economy of a democratic, post-apartheid South Africa/Azania, this policy would have to be implemented in multi-medium schools and be accompanied by a network of non-formal language projects and courses to assist those who might exit

---

28 T. Luzuka, 'English language assimilation and expression in Uganda, Southeast Asia and Southern Africa: a comparative study', in Young, *Language: planning and medium*, p. 145.

29 K. Hartshorne, 'Language policy in African education'; and K. Heugh, 'Underlying ideology of language medium policies in multilingual societies with particular reference to Southern Africa, M. Phil. Dissertation, Univ. of Cape Town, July 1987 and Tiffen, 'English versus African languages as the medium of education in African primary schools', in G. Brown and M. Miskett, eds., *Conflict and harmony in education in Tropical Africa*, London: Allen and Unwin, 1975, pp. 319–35.

from the formal system before they had acquired proficiency in English. Single-medium schools would entrench ethnic consciousness and ethnic identities, hamper multilingualism and undermine the promotion of national unity.

Language planning

Earlier in this chapter, I referred to the need for language planning. It is clear that the realization of the two basic principles of the NLP will necessitate intervention in the ways in which languages are used to influence the attitudes which people have to the country's languages.

Language planning has been defined by Brian Weinstein as a government-authorized, long-term sustained and conscious effort to alter a language itself or to change a language's functions in a society for the purpose of solving communication problems.[30]

According to this definition, the NLP principles are concerned essentially with changing the functions of the languages spoken in South Africa. However, the definition does raise a thorny problem in the South African context in so far as it is based on what has been called 'the Canonical Model of Language Planning'.[31] One of the main objections to this model is precisely that 'it is too much government-orientated' so that: 'Instances of language decisions taken by non-governmental agencies such as private companies, media houses, societies and individual authors are excluded from the realm of language planning'.[32]

It raises the question, therefore, whether what I call language planning from below is possible and, incidentally, whether the work of so many language projects now operating in South Africa, including that of the NLP, can in some sense be said to be planned. Bamgbose goes to the heart of the matter when he charges that:

> Actual experience with language development efforts shows that much significant, and sometimes much more effective, work is done by non-governmental bodies such as language societies, teachers' associations, broadcasters, etc., yet proponents of the canonical model of language planning insist that such activities do not amount to planning, since they do not amount to the 'planning ideal'.[33]

Anyone who has studied the history of the *Genootskap van Regte Afrikaners* and the subsequent history of the Afrikaans language movement knows

---

[30] W. Beer and J. Jacob, *Language policy and national unity*, Totowa NJ: Rowman and Allanheld, 1985, p. 2.

[31] A. Bamgbose, 'When is language planning not language planning?', *Journal of West African Language*, vol. 17, no. 1, p. 7.

[32] Bamgbose, 'When is language planning not language planning?', p. 8.

[33] Bamgbose, 'When is language planning not language planning?', p. 10.

that Bamgbose's point is correct and that language planning from below is possible.

A similar position is taken by Kelman who maintains that he has a general bias against:

> deliberate attempts by central political authorities to create a sense of national identity, whether by a policy of establishing a national language or by any other means . . . What I am arguing is that a sense of national identity ideally ought to — and, in fact, is most likely to — emerge out of a well-functioning national system that meets the needs and interests of the entire population, rather than out of deliberate attempts to create it directly. *Let me qualify my statement further by saying that I refer to the central political authorities, not to various agencies within the society — public or private — that have a special interest in promoting one or another type of cultural or linguistic development* . . . (my emphasis).[34]

I have recently raised the possibility of standardizing the varieties of Nguni and Sotho respectively, a proposal first made more than forty years ago by Jacob Nhlapo, the headmaster of Wilberforce Institute.[35] In addition to its economic and educational implications, its political implications for the promotion of national unity are equally important. Dalby argued that Nguni and Sotho could be developed as alternative official languages:

> He maintains that, if the dialectal differences in Sotho/Tswana and Nguni (Zulu, Xhosa and siSwati) could be eradicated by the development of only two harmonised written languages, it would be a significant movement away from the emphasis of apartheid on small differences between black groups.[36]

Prinsloo says that: 'It would be interesting to discover how the large, closely-associated language groups — such as Zulu and Xhosa, North and South Sotho and Tswana — react to this suggestion. *This is naturally a decision that the black groups will have to make for themselves*' (my emphasis).

This is indeed correct. Nhlapo's proposal was rejected in the 1940s while my own advocacy has fared no better. Sidney Zotwana of the University of Cape Town argues that we are dealing not with dialects but with languages. He also stresses that too many important vested interests have clustered around these language varieties.[37]

It is a complex matter and it is impossible to canvass completely the issue here. Is Zotwana correct in asserting that the difference between the varieties of Shona on the one hand and of Nguni/Sotho on the other hand is the difference between languages and dialects? The definition of languages

---

34 H. Kelman, 'Language as an aid and barrier', pp. 37–8.

35 Alexander, *Language and national unity*, pp. 32–3.

36 K. Prinsloo and C. Malan, 'Cultures in contact: languages and the arts in South Africa', in H. C. Marais, ed., *South Africa: perspectives on the future*, Owen Burgess Publishers, 1988.

37 Alexander, *Language and national unity*.

is notoriously difficult. There are four attributes or criteria which are relevant, namely, standardization, autonomy, historicity and vitality. Stewart describes the kind of situation which, I think, characterizes the language situation in South Africa as follows:

> Under most conditions, a linguistic system will be autonomous in terms of any other linguistic system with which it is not historically related (cf. Khoisan-Bantu NEA). Where two historically related linguistic systems exist, but where structural differences are fairly marked and there is no socio-linguistic interdependence, each will be autonomous in terms of the other (cf. Sotho-Nguni NEA). Even in cases where, within a series of historically related forms of speech, there is no true linguistic boundary evident (i.e., where, over a geographic expanse, dialect change is gradual rather than abrupt), the standardization of two fairly different dialects is likely to produce two centres of autonomy, with the remaining dialects becoming heteronomous in terms of either one or the other standardized form. Because of this, the total linguistic area may come to be regarded as one neatly divided between two different languages (cf. Zulu-Xhosa, etc. NEA). Accordingly, in situations where two or more historically related linguistic systems are involved, the presence vs. absence of autonomy can serve as a useful criterion for distinguishing between *Language* and *dialect*.[38]

In terms of this view, I am pleading for the converging of the different centres of autonomy created/invented by missionary and administrative fiat in a bygone colonial era. Perhaps I should stress that the development of a written Standard Nguni and a Standard Sotho, as an initial phase of a very long-term process of uniformation, need not and will not lead to the disappearance of Zulu, Xhosa, Ndebele and siSwati and their local varieties. These will continue to be spoken, much as German dialects retain their vitality, despite the virtual universality of Standard German in the German-speaking world. Indeed, subject to the availability of resources, they will be encouraged in print and in literature of all kinds. The main difference will be that in all formal situations, including the crucial area of education, the Standard Nguni or Standard Sotho forms will be promoted.

It is to be expected that, over time, the spoken standard — used in both formal and informal situations — will begin to approximate to the written standard even though individuals will inevitably betray their regional or social origins via their accent and intonation as they do in all similar situations!

The process, if it ever begins, will be slow. As Ngara explained:

> Shona has been unified and standardized but no real attempt has been made to develop the language into a vehicle of education and technical development. People still use their regional dialects, and some intellectuals may have objections to aspects of present-day Standard Shona which was, after all, imposed on

---

38　W. Stewart, 'A sociolinguistic typology for describing national multilingualism', in J. Fishman, ed., *Readings in the sociology of language*, The Hague/Paris: Mouton, p. 535.

them by White authorities, but there is no doubt that the standard language is now a reality. It is the officially recognised language with a standardized orthography which has been revised a couple of times . . .[39]

Conclusion

Other questions directly relevant to language policy such as translation and interpreting services, media policies, especially in regard to printing, publishing, newspapers, magazines, radio and television can only be mentioned here. One important question, that of pre-schooling, cannot be marginalized in the same way though. This is in every sense of the term a fundamental question. It is also an exceptionally sensitive one. However, pre-schools and primary schools will play a decisive role in the future in determining whether or not a national culture evolves in South Africa/Azania. If one accepts the notion that an Azanian/South African culture will inevitably result from the flowing together of the four main currents out of which South Africa has been constituted, then one cannot avoid looking at what is happening in pre-schools and in primary schools. The cultural content of these currents — the African, the European, the Asian and (to a lesser extent) the modern American — has got to be accessible to all the children of the nation-to-be. There is no need to go into further detail here, but I believe that such an outcome would be best served by the establishment of non-racial, multilingual pre-schools. In apartheid South Africa, this means — against most writings and theories on the matter — that the children have to be brought out of their communities, that the pre-schools have to be located in industrial (not residential group) areas and in central business districts. Many of the other implications of this suggestion are obvious and also difficult to resolve, but the importance from a cultural point of view of bilingual preschools in multilingual societies is now widely accepted.[40]

Another important theoretical issue that ought to be dealt with is the semiotic aspects of language. In a country where racism and sexism disfigure our social reality, every practitioner in the field of language education should be sensitized to this aspect of language.

It is not enough, of course, to postulate alternative policies without at least some indications of how they are to be realized. There are two decisive considerations. The first is not always within the control of the organizers or co-ordinators of language projects, that is, the desirability of linking the learning of languages with immediate or eventual enhancement of life

---

39 E. Ngara, *Bilingualism, language contact and language planning. Proposals for language use and language teaching in Zimbabwe*, Gwelo: Mambo Press, 1982, p. 17.

40 Van Leer Foundation, 'Bilingualism', *Newsletter*, no. 53, Jan. 1989, pp. 2–10.

chances, specifically the improvement of the learners' chances of obtaining (better) employment. There is no doubt that this economic motive is important and often decisive in sustaining learners' perseverance.

The other important consideration is that of democratic consultation. There are hundreds of language- and literacy-related projects in all provinces of South Africa. They have been initiated for many different, and often conflicting reasons. In so far as all or most of them are susceptible to planning from below, they have to be promoted and executed in constant consultation with their immediate constituency (the learners) and with all other relevant constituencies and organizations. This is a highly political matter and one which can easily be made into a bone of contention if irresponsible and petty power games begin to motivate the participants. The fundamental principle is that all those affected directly and those interested in the matter ought to be consulted. At no stage should anyone or any group be given the right of veto. Should apparently irreconcilable contradictions arise, they have to be debated in public and decided in accordance with the tried and tested democratic procedures.

9 An analysis of health and health services

Michael Savage and Solomon R. Benatar

This chapter looks at how the health care system has failed to meet the needs of the oppressed and disadvantaged, and considers the differing opinions on the changes needed in the current organization of medical services.

Introduction

The health care system in South Africa is coming under increasing scrutiny. Its adequacy is in question because of:

▷ the persistence of high levels of infant mortality among large sections of the population;

▷ the widespread nature of preventable disease;

▷ the continued unequal provision of health services to different sections of the population;

▷ the increasing fragmentation of services; and

▷ apartheid policies that exclude the majority of the population from participation in control over the health care system.

Health care in South Africa reflects many of the problems associated internationally with modern medicine: its technological ineffectiveness in improving the overall health status of large populations, its rising economic costs, and the maldistribution of its resources.

South Africa is not alone in facing these problems, but they are intensified by inappropriate development strategies, resulting in the poor provision of basic services to much of the population, and are exacerbated by current political policies which impede their effective organization. The development of a Western model of health care in an initially colonial and subsequently apartheid South Africa has, in meeting the needs of the most advantaged section of the population, failed to be creative in meeting many of the needs of the oppressed and disadvantaged and has contributed to entrenching disparities in health and access to health care facilities.

There are starkly differing positions on the changes needed in the current organization of medical services. Some argue for increasing privatization of medicine; others propose the creation of a national health service. Similarly, arguments proposing better co-ordination of health services contrast with recent government decisions to fragment responsibility for health services to a variety of homeland governments, own affairs ministries and a general affairs ministry. Critical choices need to be confronted urgently about the form of organization that will best meet the needs of the whole South African population.

Health and society

Despite popular belief, there is a relatively poor direct correlation between medical care and national measures of mortality or disease prevalence. Modern, individual-oriented medicine has been shown to be technically ineffective in improving the overall health status of large populations. The specific medical treatment of individuals is only marginally responsible for reducing the compound disease burden or raising the life expectancy of a population.

The measure of a nation's health is more a direct reflection of the environment created by its economic and political structures. Access to clean water and adequate food, housing, employment and good sanitation play the decisive roles in determining the overall health status of a population. Many illnesses and diseases causing early death or unnecessary morbidity are best combated not by medical technology, but by changing the environment and by altering personal behaviour patterns that are individually open to change.

Mortality and morbidity

In South Africa, disease and death rates are clearly related to the social and economic structure. Although the World Bank ranks South Africa eighth in a group of twenty-four upper middle-income countries (that include Algeria, Brazil and Poland), in 1988 only three countries in this group had life expectancies lower than South Africa's.[1] When contrasted with countries of similar average income, South Africa falls behind them in terms of health indicators, as a direct consequence of the skewed distribution of its economic resources. This emphasizes the often ignored fact that a critical determinant of the health status of the South African population is the manner in which basic resources are distributed.

The burden of disease and ill-health in South Africa is found among the African and coloured population (Tables 9.1, 9.2 and 9.3). This reflects the

---

[1] World Bank, *World Development Report 1988*, New York: Oxford Univ. Press, for World Bank, 1988.

Table 9.1: A profile of the population of South Africa

	Asian	African	Coloured	White
Population in 1987*				
Millions	0,91	26,3	3,07	4,91
Per cent	2,6 %	74,7%	0,87%	14,0%
Birth rate				
1940s	±38	±45	±45	±25
1980	24	40	28	16
Projected population growth rates 1985–90				
Per cent	1,56%	2,72%	1,64%	0,95%
Mortality				
Total (per 1 000 population)				
1940s	±17	±25	±25	±17
1980	5,9	±11	9,2	8,3
Infant (per 1 000 live births)				
1945	82,5	190	151	40,3
1987	15,6	80**	40,4	9,7
Life expectancy (years)				
1950	56	44	45	65
1980 Males	62	±55	56	66,8
Females	67,5	±60	61	73,0
Household income (Rands per year)[†]				
1985	R13 308	R4 224	R8 160	R23 496
Private medical insurance[‡]				
Per cent population, 1985 .	29%	3,6%	29,9%	81,3%
Per cent population over 6 years without schooling	5,5%	20,9%	11,6%	2,6%

Sources:
Statistics from various sources, including *Health trends in South Africa*, Dept. of National Health and Population Development; *Report of the Scientific Committee of the President's Council on demographic trends in South Africa*, Cape Town: Govt. Printer, 1983; and see also references for Table 9. 4.
Notes:
* Includes TBVC countries (Cooper, *Race Relations Survey 1987/8*, p. 11).
** Ranges between 130:1 000 in Transkei in 1980 and 25:1 000 in Soweto in 1983.
[†] The top 10% of the population earn 52% of generated income, the bottom 50% earn 7,2%.
[‡] Zwarstein, 'Expenditure on medical care in South Africa 1978–1982'.

continuing legacy of discriminatory policies which have entrenched the unequal distribution of resources and access to health care.

Disease profiles and mortality patterns among whites closely resemble

Table 9.2: Distribution of causes of death in South Africa,*1984

	Asian	African**	Coloured	White	Total
Cardiovascular disease	[1]37,4%	[3]11,8%	[1]22,2%	[1]40,4%	17,7%
Respiratory disease	[3]8,5%	[4]9,6%	[4]11,3%	[4]10,9%	9,9%
Infectious diseases[†]	3,1%	[2]15,5%+	13,0%	1,8%	12,9%+
Malignant disease	[4]8,4%	7,4%	[3]11,4%	[2]17,2%	9,2%
Peri-natal conditions	4,2%	6,0%	6,6%	1,3%	5,3%+
Non-natural causes	[2]14,2%	[1]17,1%	[2]17,6%	[3]12,6%	16,4%
Ill-defined/other	24,2%	32,6%−	17,9%	15,8%	28,6%−

Source:
C. Simkins, 'Mortality rates compared', *Energos*, 1988, vol. 15, pp. 39–42.
Notes:
Numbers 1 to 4 in square brackets indicate the top 4 causes of death.
* Excluding TBVC areas.
** Immunization — full coverage: measles 39%, polio 45%, diptheria/pertusses/tetanus 44%, tuberculosis (BCG) 63%. The majority of deaths from immunizible diseases occur among the African population (Yach, 'Infant mortality rates').
[†] Data for Africans is the least accurate.

Table 9.3: Infectious disease notifications in South Africa, 1987

	Total number	African	Coloured	White	Deaths
Tuberculosis	62 654	75%	23,0%	<2,0%	4,0%
Measles	24 460	92%	4,8%		1,9%
Malaria	10 599	98%			0,1%
Typhoid	5 014	98%			0,9%
All	105 492	81%	15,7%	2,2%	4,0%
Population		74%	8,6%	14,6%	

Source:
Epidemiciological comments, vol. 13, 1986, pp. 1–50.

the patterns in industrialized countries, whereas those among the African and coloured populations approximate the status of industrialized countries at the beginning of the twentieth century.

The lack of accurate health statistics for Africans (for example those relating to birth, death and causes of death) is another indication of the inadequate health services available to them, especially in rural areas. About 14 million of South Africa's population of an estimated 33 million live in the ten states designated homelands, four of which are considered by the South

African government to be 'independent'. The health status and health services in the homelands reflect their inadequate socio-economic and inferior political status.

As life expectancy improves, there is a progressive change in the distribution of causes of death (Tables 9.1 and 9.2). In general, rising incomes are accompanied by lower mortality rates from perinatal causes, infections and parasitic diseases (especially in childhood), and higher death rates in older subjects from cardiovascular and neoplastic diseases. The proportion of deaths in South Africa from non-natural causes (motor vehicle accidents, other accidents, suicide, homicide and other violence) is notable higher than in other countries of similar economic status.

The infant mortality rate (IMR = number of deaths under one year old per 1 000 live births in a specific year) is regarded as both an indication of infant health and of the health status of, and health services for, a population and its socio-economic status. Although IMRs have dropped for all population groups over recent years, the IMR remains highest among blacks and there is a wide range from one area to another in the country. For the period 1981–5 it has been estimated that the IMR for Africans was 9 to 10 times greater than that for whites.[2]

Morbidity information is meagre except for notifiable diseases, and here again the burden of disease is among the black population (Table 9.3). Data from the Department of Medicine at Groote Schuur Hospital shows that disease morbidity in the different population groups closely parallels reported national mortality rates.[3]

South Africa is the most technologically advanced country in Africa. The economically active population (including the homelands) is about 10 million, of whom about 10 per cent belong to the growing independent trade union movement. Despite recent advances, legislation to protect health in the working environment remains inadequate. On average, 300 000 work-related accidents are reported annually, with 2 000 fatalities occurring in industry and agriculture, and a further 500 on the mines.

The balance of power between the conflicting interests of the employers (predominantly concerned with maximizing profits) and of workers (concerned about their safety) is changing as the unions' strength and their bargaining power increases. Health and safety in the workplace will inevitably become a more prominent industrial relations issue as the union

---

[2] D. Yach, 'Infant mortality rates in urban areas in South Africa 1981–1985', *South African Medical Journal*, vol. 73, 1988, pp. 232–4.

[3] S. R. Benatar and A. Saven, 'Morbidity trends in the medical wards at Groote Schuur', *South African Medical Journal*, vol. 67, 1985, pp. 968–74.

movement consolidates itself.[4]

Structure and function of health services

Current medical services are concentrated in urban areas and tend to favour capital-intensive technology for dealing with degenerative diseases in tertiary care hospitals. Primary health care and community hospital services are poorly developed and only 4,7 per cent of the total health services' budgets are officially allocated to preventative medicine, although the government's stated intention is to increase this to 15 per cent by the year 2000.[5]

More than 75 per cent of doctors work in metropolitan areas and 18 per cent in small towns. About half the population live in rural areas where only 5,5 per cent of doctors practise.[6] This maldistribution has been aggravated by forced shifts in population to the rural homelands and by the rapid growth of the black population. In 1950, an estimated 40 per cent of the population lived in the homelands; by 1980 the figure had increased to an estimated 53 per cent. Access to health services is extremely poor in rural areas, particularly for blacks. Ancillary medical services — inadequately developed even in the cities — are often skeletal in rural areas.

Faced with an enormous backlog in health services as a result of inadequate planning and investment in a national medical service, and with an expanding demand for health care by a burgeoning and increasingly urban population, the South African government is attempting to follow the example set by the American medical system and reduce its own responsibility for health services through privatization.

A broad approach to the provision of health services is outlined in the National Health Services Facilities Plan of 1980. This classifies services into six levels and stresses the provision of four basic requirements — safe drinking water, adequate food, satisfactory sewage and waste disposal, and adequate housing — for minimum levels of health care. The 1980 plan, however, excludes health services in the homelands and does not address how these services are to be integrated, nor how resources and staff are to be distributed to meet its objectives.

The plan is premised on the continuing fragmentation of health services, with each homeland having its own health authorities, regional service

[4] J. E. Myers and I. Macun, 'The sociologic context of occupational health in South Africa', *American Journal of Public Health*, vol. 79, 1989, pp. 216–24; and Anthony Zwi, S. Fonn and M. Steinberg, 'Occupational health and safety in South Africa', *Social Science Medicine*, vol. 27, no. 7, 1988, pp. 691–701.

[5] Republic of South Africa, *Final Report of the Commission of Inquiry into Health Services* (Browne Report), Pretoria: Govt. Printer RP67/86, 1986.

[6] P. Pillay, 'The distribution of medical manpower and health care facilities in South Africa', *Carnegie Conference Paper no. 167*, Saldru: Univ. of Cape Town, 1987.

councils, and central government departments of own and general affairs adding to what has been described as a 'confused jumble' of differing health authorities that provide duplicated and overlapping services.

The current organization of health services — with fourteen Ministers of Health — is patently irrational and damaging to the economy and health care. This flaw in the existing structure of health care is recognized in the 1986 Browne Report of the Commision of Inquiry into Health Services which found that 'there is an excessive fragmentation of control over health services and a lack of central policy direction. This has led to a misallocation of resources and a wasteful duplication of services'.[7]

Official action to address this has been minimal. The government White Paper on the Browne Report ascribes this fragmentation and lack of direction 'to the way in which health services are financed' and indicates that in future 'all budgets of health authorities will be channelled through the Health Matters Advisory Committee to the National Health Policy Council for consideration'.[8]

Health expenditure and finance

There is no single comprehensive, reliable source of data on health care expenditure in South Africa. Existing data sources are fragmented and incomplete, making it difficult to monitor spending in critical areas such as rural and urban health, or preventive versus curative medical expenditure, or to relate health spending to the Consumer Price Index or population growth.

The lack of adequate data 'casts great doubt on the quality of existing health care planning' and points to a clear need for reliable information on health expenditure if rational allocation of resources and adequate health planning is to take place in future.[9] Total expenditure on health in South Africa is estimated to have risen from 4 per cent of gross national product (GNP) in 1970 to 5,3 per cent in 1985, when total health expenditure in both the public and private sectors amounted to R6 000 million.

This growth in the proportion of GNP expenditure on health is more a function of the fall in GNP per person since 1980 than an indication of sharp increases in health care expenditure. The increase in spending per person on health in South Africa over this period (from R23 in 1970 to R180 in 1985) is unimpressive when it is recognized that the 1985 expenditure

---

7   Browne Report, para. 4.2.

8   Browne Report, para. 10.2.1.

9   M. Zwarenstein et al., 'Expenditure on medical care in South Africa 1978–1982' in C. P. Owen, ed., *Towards a national health service*, Cape Town: NAMDA Publications, 1988, p. 33.

amounted to R34 in 1970 prices, or that the rise is the equivalent of R11 per person over a fifteen-year period.[10]

South Africa's health spending in 1985 amounted to 4,9 per cent of its gross domestic product (GDP), compared to the United Kingdom's 5,9 per cent, Australia's 7,8 per cent and the United States' 10,7 per cent (1984 figures). More striking in terms of international comparisons is the low proportion of the GDP spent by the state on health services, which amounted to 2,5 per cent in 1985, in contrast with 5,3 per cent in the UK, 6,6 per cent in Australia and 4,4 per cent in the US.[11]

Several features of South Africa's expenditure on health care are masked by citing national figures. First, relatively little is spent on preventive health. Comprehensive figures on preventive health expenditure are not available, but it is estimated at 4,5 per cent of total health care spending in 1982.

There is a marked dominance of spending on curative medicine over preventive medicine. This means insufficient resources are being injected into a badly planned health care system that places little emphasis on primary and community health services. One consequence is that the resources and facilities in even the best hospitals are under pressure when, with better planning, demands for health care at the tertiary level could have been met more effectively and less expensively at primary and secondary health care levels.

Second, racial bias exists in overall expenditure patterns. A conservative estimate indicates that 1985 spending per person on health care for whites amounted to R451 in contrast with R115 for Africans, R245 for coloured persons and R249 for Asians.[12] Thus, whites have about four times as much spent per person on their medical care as Africans, and more than twice as much as coloured and Indian South Africans.

Focusing only on public expenditure on health care, these inequalities remain pronounced with white spending per person by the state amounting to R248 in 1985 in contrast with that on Africans of R82.

A third notable feature in national figures is the ratio of public to private health expenditure. In 1985 public spending accounted for 51 per cent of all expenditure on health, and private spending, 49 per cent — a ratio that has scarcely changed over the 15-year period since 1970.[13] These figures point to the importance of public finance in health care, particularly for disadvantaged groups unable to afford health services.

---

10 S. R. Benatar, 'Privatization and medicine', *South African Medical Journal*, vol. 72, 1987, pp. 655–6.

11 N. Timmins, 'Reforming the NHS', *Independent*, 27 January 1988.

12 R. E. Dorrington and M. Zwarenstein, 'Some trends in health care expenditure 1970–1985' in Owen, *Towards a national health service*, p. 48.

13 Zwarenstein, 'Expenditure on medical care', p. 33.

Private medical care is expensive and can generally only be afforded by people with medical insurance. In 1985 only 18 per cent of the total population were covered by some form of medical insurance scheme, and this comprised 81 per cent of the white population and less than 4 per cent of the African population, whose coverage tended to be much more limited.[14]

Most of the population relied on public expenditure for provision of medical care and services — financed by their tax revenues and some fee-for-service payments. Less than half of the country's doctors work in the public sector, which houses 87 per cent of all hospital beds, provides care for the sickest patients and is responsible for medical, nursing and paramedical education as well as research and development in medicine!

While more resources are needed to finance adequate health services, levels of spending on whites cannot be taken as a norm to be duplicated throughout the country, for this would involve an expenditure of over R15 billion on health care, or 13,3 per cent of GNP in 1985 (a figure greater than the US expenditure on health of 10,5 per cent of GNP in the same year).[15]

Privatization of health care

There is a discernable shift in government policy toward promoting health service privatization. This shift is taking place against a background of a stagnant economy, declining foreign investment, rising government spending, together with pressures from private interest groups favouring privatization and disquiet among whites facing rising tax levels. While the government has signalled its approval of privatization in the health sector, it has not specified which activities should be privatized nor to what extent, or how this should be implemented.[16]

Arguments in favour of privatization have been challenged by Naylor[17] who points out that the proposals used to propagate the market-place method for delivery of health care are seriously flawed on the grounds that:

▷ market forces are markedly distorted by the nature of medicine;

▷ there are serious public health consequences of free trading in health;

▷ health care is a public good and therefore requires equitable distribution; and

---

14 Zwarenstein, 'Expenditure on medical care', pp. 24–34.

15 Dorrington and Zwarenstein, 'Some trends in health care expenditure', p. 48.

16 Benatar, 'Privatization and medicine', pp. 655–6.

17 C. D. Naylor, 'Privatisation of South African health services', *South African Medical Journal*, vol. 72, 1987, pp. 673–8.

▷ private fee-for-service care creates perverse incentives that lead to the oversupply of services by health care providers and therefore contribute to increasing costs.

The impossibility of applying privatization in poor areas is obvious; this would further aggravate existing disparities in health. The claim that imposing direct charge and user fees can reduce abuse of medicine is only superficially correct. Such schemes predominantly act as deterrents for the poor and elderly, and result in increasing medical fees to recoup losses, and ultimately only redistribute costs rather than effect savings. Naylor also exposes the flawed rationale of the concepts that it is more efficient to subsidize private persons than institutions and that privatization will diminish the load on the taxpayer and de-politicize health care.

Privatization is not the way forward for it will, as Naylor points out, replace overt racial discrimination with economic discrimination to almost the same effect. At the same time, privatization is likely to seriously damage the structure of health care services, particularly public health services, to the detriment of those most in need of them and ultimately to the detriment of the whole health care system.[18]

Medical education

South African medical schools have a proud record of training competent, compassionate and dedicated doctors, many of whom practise their profession in the finest medical tradition in the public and private sectors. Training medical staff in the Western tradition, however, encourages specialization and private practice and sends doctors in directions that deprive many of care. Black South Africans demand access to more primary and community-based health care services than are being provided by Western trained doctors.

Medical schools provide training increasingly considered by some to be inappropriate to the needs of Africa. However, they can never graduate enough medical practitioners for all the needs of a rapidly expanding population. At present, there are seven medical schools in South Africa, approximately one per 4,5 million people, and these graduate about 1 000 medical practitioners each year. At the current rate of population growth, one new medical school will be required every three to four years to maintain the current medical school to population and doctor to patient ratios. Clearly this can never materialize in the current economic, social and political climate.

Philpot has drawn attention to the fact that South Africa's medical schools

---

18 Benatar, 'Privatization and medicine', pp. 655–6; and S. R. Benatar, 'Economics of health in South Africa; past, present and future', *Medicine and Law*, vol. 8, 1989, pp. 111–17.

have catered for the privileged élite; that they have succeeded in keeping people apart and isolating medical students from the community they should serve.[19] There can be no doubt that while the current system of medical education in South Africa provides a vital component of the training and expertise required in this country, there remains an equally vital need to develop medical education in additional directions to ensure that our rapidly expanding population can have their basic health care needs met through access to affordable primary health care clinics and community hospitals.

Suggested solutions to the shortage of medical staff include opening medical schools in rural areas, with entry criteria and curricula designed to produce doctors oriented to family practice, and developing health care teams with auxiliary health workers of various types under medical or nursing leadership. The number of nurses and medical practitioners in South Africa at present are listed in Table 9.4.

The existing context of health services

The current organization of South African health care services, comprehensively described by Kirsch and Benatar,[20] is deficient in several critical respects. These include providing services which are curative rather than preventive, the emphasis on urban-based services, and poor ancillary services. The lack of adequate financing for health services and their continued administrative fragmentation exacerbate these inadequacies.

The South African economy is characterized by deep structural inequalities, low growth rates and rising unemployment (see Chapter 14), which have a marked negative impact on the living conditions and thus the health status of the population.

A recent report indicates that half of the total South African population in 1980 lived below the subsistence level; for Africans this figure was nearly two-thirds (60,5 per cent), while for those living in the reserves, 81 per cent of households were in dire poverty.[21] The absolute number of people living in poverty is estimated to have risen from 13 million to 15 million between 1960 and 1980.[22]

These structural inequalities occur within an economy that since 1972 has been on a downward trend and has experienced a sharp decrease in its capacity to provide jobs. By 1981 it was estimated that over 21 per cent

---

[19] H. Philpot, 'Medical education in changing South Africa', *Energos*, vol. 15, 1988, pp. 34–8.

[20] R. E. Kirsch and S. R. Benatar, 'Medicine in a South African context', *Acta Juridica*, 1988, pp. 1–39

[21] C. Simkins, 'What has been happening to income distribution and poverty in the homelands?', *Carnegie Conference Paper no. 7*, Saldru: Univ. of Cape Town, 1984, p. 18.

[22] F. Wilson and M. Ramphele, *Uprooting poverty: the South African challenge*, Cape Town: David Philip, 1989, p. 18.

Table 9.4:   Selected medical statistics in South Africa

Public and private health care compared:

	Public sector	Private sector
Hospitals	495 (68%)	234 (32%)
Hospital beds*	141 104 (87,5%)	20 158 (12,5%)
Doctors	54%	46%
Nurses	75%	25%
Health expenditure 1984/5**		
Rand x 10^6(GNP)	3318,2 (3,32%)	2647,0 (2,65%)

People in the medical profession:

1986 statistics for doctors		20 229 registered
		93% white
		85% male
		±14 000 in practice
Doctor/patient ratios[†]	1960	1:2 157
	1980	1:1 800
		(urban1:875;
		rural 1:12 700)
Dentist/patient ratios[‡]	1960	1:13 000
	1980	1:10,870
Registered nurses	1980	55 002
Total no. of nurses	1987	129 363
Physiotherapists	1980	2 250
Medical technologists		3 000
Radiographers		3 000
Psychologists		1 775
Optomotrists		800
Occupational therapists		1 000
Speech therapists and audiologists		750

Medical schools	7 = ±1:4 x 10^6 population
	±1 000 graduates per year

Sources:
Statistics from various sources, including S. R. Benatar, 'Special report: medicine and health care in South Africa', *New England Journal of Medicine*, vol. 315, 1986; Race relations Survey 1988; and Kirsch and Benatar, 'Medicine in a South African context'.

Notes:
* Total bed:population ratio is 2,2:1000. Excluding homelands, the ratio is 5,5:1000. (USA ratio is 8,3:1000.)
** Includes homelands (12,3% of public expenditure).
[†]1982 — UK 1:650, USA 1:520, Kenya 1:10 500.
[‡]1977 — USA 1:1 926.

of the population of working age were unemployed, with this figure rising to over 50 per cent in rural areas. Projections by De Lange indicate that, if present low growth rates continue, by the year 2000 only half of the economically active population will be formally employed, some 13 per cent will be employed in the informal sector and over 36 per cent will be unemployed.[23]

Against the background of mass poverty, low economic growth and rising unemployment, the task of providing adequate health care for all becomes a scarcely achievable goal. Such a goal can only be reached by a society which has developed the political will to uproot poverty and promote healthy living and working conditions for all its citizens.

Allied with negative economic patterns, health services occur within the context of a growing population. The South African population is projected to increase by 40 per cent over the period 1980–2000, with an average of 800 000 persons a year being added to the present population.[24] Although South Africa is experiencing declines in its birth rates, its transition to low fertility remains slow and pressures from population growth place further considerable demands on the task of providing adequate health services. (See Chapter 12.)

The geographic distribution of the population also presents particular difficulties. Urban growth will be rapid in the future: the proportion of the population urbanized in 1980 amounted to an estimated 47 per cent and by 2000 it is estimated that an additional 10 million persons will be added to the urban population, when about 58 per cent of the total population will be urbanized.

Health services, already inadequate in rural areas and undersupplied in urban areas, are coming under increasing pressure to meet the needs of a growing and more urban population, while having to contend with the health consequences of deep rural poverty.

Influencing major determinants of basic health

Health services play only one part, albeit an important one, in promoting and improving a nation's health. The challenge facing South Africa lies essentially in improving those economic, social and political conditions that play the major part in determining morbidity and mortality levels.

Dismantling the institutions of apartheid and dealing with their consequences cannot be achieved in a short period. Continuous action will be required to promote what can be termed the socio-economic health of the

---

[23] C. Cooper et al., *Race Relations Survey 1984*, Johannesburg: South African Institute of Race Relations, 1985.

[24] P. Spies, 'South Africa in the year 2000', *Energos*, vol. 10, no. 2, 1984, pp. 153–67.

society. However, four areas of basic needs — adequate nutrition, clean water, satisfactory sewerage, and proper housing — can be identified as being
of prime importance for individual physical health.

In drawing attention to the need for intervention in these areas no
implication is made that a range of other important actions are not also
urgently required to improve the socio-economic health of South Africa.

Nutrition

Turning first to the area of basic needs, urgent attention to the nutritional
status of the population is required. Hansen[25] has reported that approximately one-third of African, coloured and Asian children below the age of
fourteen are underweight and stunted for their age. Fincham[26] estimates
that 10 per cent of the African population, 13 per cent of the coloured
population, 5 per cent of the Indian and 2 per cent of the white population
are currently undernourished. Other research findings indicate that 56,5 per
cent of the rural black population suffer from 'chronic malnutrition'.[27]

Such a pattern of malnutrition has many roots — inadequate wages, deficient food distribution mechanisms, poor nutritional education — which
are aggravated in the South African environment by migrant labour, unemployment and discriminatory land ownership patterns. The web of factors
producing such widespread malnutrition points to the existence of no one
easy solution to this grave situation. However, a variety of effective strategies
have been identified that markedly improve nutritional status and which
are technically feasible.

A recent evaluation of nutrition intervention projects by the World Bank
— ranging from consumer food subsidies, child feeding through institutions, food coupons and food supplementation — demonstrates that nutrition programmes can be implemented at low cost. They can be effectively
targeted at those in need and produce dramatic nutritional improvements
over short periods.[28]

Much can be learned from the successes and failures of other countries
that have mounted programmes attacking malnutrition; yet scant recognition of such experience takes place. Among the first steps in formulating adequate nutrition policies would be a careful sifting of international
evidence on intervention strategies together with a close examination of
previous South African efforts to combat malnutrition.

---

25 J. Hansen, 'Food and nutrition policy in relation to poverty', *Carnegie Conference Paper no. 205*, Saldru: Univ.
of Cape Town, 1984.

26 R. Fincham, 'Positive health and food supply', *Energos*, vol. 15, 1988, pp. 48–52.

27 Cooper, *Race Relations Survey 1984*, p. 807.

28 A. Berg, *Malnutrition: What can be done?*, Baltimore: John Hopkins, for World Bank, 1987.

Two past South African interventions aimed at children of school-going age provide significant pointers toward possible future actions in this area. In 1944 it was reported by the Gluckman Commission that of white school-boys, 47,6 per cent in the Transvaal, 31,5 per cent in the Cape and 43,6 per cent in the Free State were malnourished. National resources were deployed to combat the physical effects of this malnutrition and the whole complex of underlying causes.

It was recognized that malnutrition was only one dimension of the so-called 'poor white problem' — and that it was also necessary to create employment opportunities, ease the transition of poor whites into the towns, provide effective channels of political participation and improve the economic circumstances of this community.

In 1943 a severely limited version of nutritional intervention led to the institutionalization of school feeding schemes in all South African schools;[29] however, these schemes were abolished with the introduction of Bantu Education policies without their impact being assessed.

A recent proposal to establish a food stamp programme in South Africa, aimed at benefiting all households below a minimum living level and not targeted solely at the school-going population, would double the amount of food available to some 18 million persons at a cost of 50 cents per person per day, or about 6 per cent of the national budget.[30] If implemented, this scheme would both improve national nutritional levels and have a multiplier effect of increasing demand for food production and so help to create employment.

Water and sewerage

Outbreaks of cholera, typhoid and dysentry during the past decade, and the endemic nature of diarrhoeal diseases among children living in poverty, emphasize the importance of adequate water and sewerage facilities.

Both more water — to provide for better washing and cleaning — and cleaner water is needed. In areas such as the Mhala district of the eastern Transvaal there is, on average, one water tap for every 760 people; in an area of the Ciskei, daily water consumption per person averages 9 litres, in contrast with the World Health Organization's (WHO) goal of providing 50 litres daily per person.[31]

Also needed are better sewerage facilities, in both urban and rural areas. In Alexandra township, Johannesburg, a recent report recorded 'sewage

[29] N. Bromberger, 'Government policies affecting the distribution of income 1940–1980' in R. Schrire, ed., *South Africa: public policy perspectives*, Cape Town: Juta, 1982, p. 174.

[30] Wilson and Ramphele, *Uprooting poverty*, p. 339.

[31] Wilson and Ramphele, *Uprooting poverty*, p. 324.

flowing in the streets' because of the overloading of the bucket system.[32] In Gazankulu, only half of schools and 20 per cent of households are equipped with toilets.[33] Adequate water and sewerage form basic public health needs that for the large majority of the population have still to be met.

In meeting these needs both state and community initiatives will be required. The effective combination of such dual initiatives is well demonstrated in Epworth, Zimbabwe, where a peri-urban community of 30 000 persons, until recently, had inadequate sewerage and relied on a large number of contaminated open wells for its domestic water supplies.

The Zimbabwean government financed the installation of protected water points and upgradeable ventilated pit latrines, with installation of both these being undertaken by local residents. At an installation cost of four Zimbabwian dollars per head the community is now supplied with 600 thousand litres of potable water daily and has 3 000 odourless, fly-free latrines.[34]

Housing

The existing housing shortage and the extensive overcrowding of present housing stock has a considerable impact on the health status of the population. At the end of 1987 the total housing shortage in South Africa (including the homelands) amounted to between 700 000 and 1 400 000 units.[35]

The housing shortage has worsened since 1982, when the government decided it would no longer take primary responsibility for housing and placed emphasis instead on site-and-service schemes and private housing construction.

Overcrowding of existing housing stock is severe, particularly in urban African townships where national averages indicate that between 12 and 16 persons occupy each four-room dwelling.[36] According to international standards, it is considered that an average of more than 1,5 persons to a room constitutes overcrowding; South African figures for urban black housing indicate average occupancy rates double this figure.

More and better quality housing is required if the prevalance of preventable diseases such as tuberculosis is to be overcome.

---

[32] C. N. Ntoane and K. E. Mokoetle, 'Major problems as perceived by the community', *Carnegie Conference Paper no. 2*, Saldru: Univ. of Cape Town, 1984, p. 9.

[33] P. Harries, 'Aspects of poverty in Gazankulu: three case studies', *Carnegie Conference Paper no. 67*, Saldru: Univ. of Cape Town, 1984, p. 8.

[34] P. Morgan, 'Low cost water and sanitation: a Case study in Epworth, Zimbabwe' in John Pickford, ed., *Developing world water*, London: Grosvenor Press, 1987, pp. 56–8.

[35] C. Cooper et al., *Race Relations Survey 1987/8*, Johannesburg: South African Institute of Race Relations, 1988, p. 198.

[36] M. Kentridge, 'Housing in South Africa', *Carnegie Post-Conference Paper*, Saldru: Univ. of Cape Town, 1986; and National Building Research Institute, *Housing Research Review*, no. 8, Pretoria: NBRI, 1986.

Providing health services

The profiles of health and disease found in different social and population groups in contemporary South Africa are as disparate as the comparison between those which prevailed in developed societies at the start of this century, and those found in developed societies now. The health care needs of the people of South Africa span the spectrum of those relevant to the social and medical aspects of prevention of diseases and premature death (especially in children), to the application of modern science, to the postponement of death from previously rapidly fatal malignant disease and organ failure in later life.

The biomedical model of scientific medicine in the Western world has focused increasingly on super-specialized aspects of disease in a reductionist fashion to try and find the 'magic bullet' with which to cure 'disease'. It is increasingly acknowledged that the adverse side effects of such modern trends have been to lose sight of the patient as a whole, to expend vast human and financial resources on the diagnosis and management of disease among a small percentage of the population, and to fail to develop adequate community services.

Such side effects are most obvious in health services which tend to be privatized (as in the USA) as opposed to those that function on a national and socialized basis (for example, in the UK). Combinations of these structures may be more successful, whether found in Canada with its national insurance system or in those countries providing health facilities nationally, associated with limited forms of user charges.[37]

The choice of an appropriate model of health care and health care delivery leads any society to decisions on the basic structure of its health services, how they should be financed and controlled, and the spectrum and intensity of training for its personnel.

More than forty years ago there was a clear recognition that health care could not be provided for a growing and diverse South African population merely by allowing the haphazard development of entrepreneurial medical services in an uncoordinated and unplanned fashion.

In 1942 a Commission of Inquiry into the National Health Services under the chairmanship of Henry Gluckman, later Minister of Health, was appointed to evaluate the need for the 'provision of an organised national health service for all sections of the people of the Union of South Africa'. It noted that three sets of public health authorities had spawned a 'crazy patchwork of health services' emphasizing curative medicine over primary

---

37 J. Akin and N. Birdsall, 'Financing of health services in LDCs', *Finance and Development*, vol. 24, June, 1987, pp. 40–3; and C. H. W. Paine and F. Siem Tjam, *Hospitals and the health care revolution*, Geneva: World Health Organization, 1987.

and preventive health care and concluded that there was a 'desperate need' for a fully planned national health service.

The Commission proposed creating a service in which all personal health care would be supplied free; also a network of community health centres with one centre for every 10 000 to 30 000 people and staffed by a team of health workers that would include health visitors, dentists, nurses and doctors. Linked to these centres would be a network of general practice specialists and teaching hospitals.

The Commission recommended training several thousand health visitors, to be concerned with basic health education and preventive medical work in the community, and that the proposed national health service be financed by means of a national health tax.

The recommendations of the Commission were ignored and medicine was allowed to develop piecemeal. However, its blueprint for a national health service remains, and has stimulated creative thinking about the future of South Africa's health services. It is increasingly realized that a health care system is needed which:

▷ provides essential health care of adequate quality on a universally accessible basis;

▷ gives priority to those most in need; and

▷ sustains primary health care that is integrated within a supportive referral system.[38]

The identification of these goals emerges from a growing consensus about the need to develop a unitary national health system for the whole country, without excluding a place for private medicine.[39]

Conclusion

Health care services in South Africa are in decline. Inadequate resources, fragmentation and the encouragement of privatization all seriously threaten to undermine the situation.

Solutions will need to focus on the development of a more unified rather than a more fragmented health care service, and the training of staff for all components of a health care system which must be characterized by being well planned, well co-ordinated and adequately funded.

A satisfactory health system must include primary, secondary and tertiary facilities and a considerable degree of unification in their functions and future development, at least at regional levels and, preferably, nationally.

---

[38] C. De Beer, E. Buch and J. Mavrandorius, *A national health service for South Africa (part one)*, Johannesburg: Centre for the Study of Health Policy, 1988.

[39] S. R. Benatar, 'Medicine and health care in South Africa', *Energos*, vol. 15, 1988, pp. 21–8; and Benatar, 'Economics of health in South Africa, pp. 111–17.

Mechanisms for equitable and efficient access to these services must be developed.

A series of critical decisions about the organization of health care needs to be made to enable health services to meet the challenge of fully contributing to the construction of a healthy society. Chief areas in which policy decisions are required include the four in the text that follows.

1. Privatization versus unification

The debate on this issue continues to rage[40] and it can only be hoped that vision and community spirit will prevail to allow the growth of efficient and effective primary and community health services, appropriately supported by tertiary facilities and a small private sector within a unitary health care system. Audit, accountability and control mechanisms also need to be debated, and negotiated decisions taken regarding their position at regional or national levels.

2. Finance and allocation of resources

Allocation of adequate resources for a reasonable health service will require a strong and growing economy, capable of providing the basic requirements for healthy living as well as a range of medical services.

How much South Africa should spend on health care, how these resources should be raised, by what processes decisions should be made in allocating them, whether user fees should be charged to those able to pay them, and many other pertinent issues will depend on the mechanisms and pace of progress towards a more democratic society, sensitive to social justice and in which true consensus negotiations can be conducted.

Resource allocation questions raise three fundamental issues that are faced by most countries: the problem of allocation (of spending too little on cost-effective services in comparison to costly services); the problem of internal efficiency (of funding higher level tertiary health facilities when more effective expenditure can be made at the primary health level); and, finally, the problem of equity (of using funds in such a way that the disadvantaged benefit less than the advantaged).[41]

3. Appropriate distribution and training of medical personnel

The present concentration of health personnel, particularly doctors, in urban and white areas requires attention at a policy level in order to stimulate better distribution into areas of acute need. Possible ways to achieve this include proposals that selection for training should be biased toward those

---

40 C. P. Owen, ed., *The case for a national health service*, Cape Town: UCT Dept. of Adult Education and Extra Mural Studies, 1989.

41 Akin and Birdsall, 'Financing of health services, pp. 40–3.

wishing to practise in areas of greatest need, that training be linked to a period of national professional service, and that registration be conditional on service in a needy area.

These suggestions are riddled with problems concerning their potential impact on the nature of professional training and their impact on the autonomy and needs of the medical professions. They would be difficult to implement in any political framework that values individual freedoms.

Rational and equitable distribution of appropriately trained health personnel is needed, but it is more likely that this may be achieved by increasing the number of primary health care workers at a lower level of training than doctors. Gear has suggested that a ratio of primary health care worker to general practitioner to specialist of 36:6:1 be aimed at.

Successful implementation of this would require recognition by medical authorities that the functions of diagnosis and screening, traditionally undertaken by doctors, be undertaken also by primary health care workers.[42] The formulation of policies that focus on providing appropriately trained staff, empowered to serve the needs of those requiring primary medical care, provides a challenge to policy-makers that is more far-reaching in its implications than would be efforts to redistribute some of the existing pool of trained medical personnel.

Without denying the value and desirability of modern medical education and practices, it is only realistic to acknowledge that a middle-income country with a rapidly growing population must face critical questions on selection of staff, content of training, training of auxiliaries and the use of health care teams, particularly at the primary health care level.

4. Control of medical services

The existing pattern of control of South African medical services occurs within the framework of a tricameral parliamentary system and a homeland system of government. This has led to fragmentation of the control of health services, on both a colour and geographical basis.

Participation by all communities in central decision-making at a national level is not possible within the existing political framework. As participation in central government is limited to select groups and communities, not all South Africans are able to participate in determining the structure and functions of South Africa's health care system. In addition, the ability of communities to express their needs in an informed way to health policy-makers, or to participate in local decision-making on health services, has been severely limited by state suppression of political and community organizations. This has become more pronounced under the current State of

---

[42] J. L. Botha et al., 'The distribution of health needs and services in South Africa', *Social Science Medicine*, vol. 26, no. 8, 1985, pp. 845–51.

Emergency, which has stimulated an increased resistance to collaborating with any state structure.

The challenge facing South Africa in the political sphere is to create and foster a democratic political system that allows all communities to participate in the choice of government and thus in decisions about the structure and policy of South African health services. The degree and extent of community involvement in the control of health services can then be democratically decided.[43]

Conclusion

These issues, some of which have already been addressed in South Africa,[44] need further urgent attention. There is a great need for the public, the medical profession and governing bodies to put aside some of their self interest and desires and to have a vision in planning and implementing a relevant health service which is affordable and which will retain the best features of the divergent health care systems currently in operation.

Full potential for positive change in the organization of health services can only be realized when a more democratic society is achieved which has the political will to commit itself to achieving health for all.

43 R. Crawshaw, M. J. Garland, B. Hines and C. Lobitz, 'Oregon health decision: an experiment in informed community consent', *Journal of the American Medical Association*, vol. 254, 1985, pp. 3213–16.

44 Department of Health, *Report and recommendations of the Committee of Enquiry on possible further facilities for medical and dental training*, 1984.

10 Post-apartheid education: A concept in process (Opportunities within the process)

Ken Hartshorne

As South Africa moves towards a post-apartheid society, can the education dispensation that will evolve respond to the new social, economic and political goals without continuing to be political? It is relatively easy to break down the old; to build up the new demands active common purpose and more besides. This chapter examines the process by which South Africans of all colours and beliefs might prepare themselves for that future education and contribute to its shaping.

Introduction

The Western ideal of a liberal education is being seriously questioned in many quarters in South Africa. It is being challenged on two main counts: for its tendency to élitism, and on its relevance to the present needs of society.

To put it bluntly: what is the use of a liberal education if people are poor, starving and oppressed?

Perhaps an even more important question, as the country moves inevitably towards a post-apartheid society, is whether a new education dispensation can respond to broad social, economic and political goals without continuing to be political — that is, controlled by a particular ideology not necessarily supported by all the members of the society the education system serves, which is our past and present experience.

In a country where education has been used so blatantly as an instrument of control to protect power and privilege, it will not be easy to reach agreement on the shape of education in a future non-racial, democratic South Africa.

It is relatively easy to break down the old — that process of disintegration is well on its way in black urban schools. To build up the new demands common purpose, imagination, energy and commitment.

This chapter is a contribution to the search for that common purpose by considering the process by which we in South Africa might prepare ourselves for that future education and contribute to it, in a way that is consistent with its long-term goals.

The education crisis

Where is education at present? Some indicators are:

> its environment, which is an untidy maze of interactions, volatile and often unpredictable, which differ radically from place to place and from situation to situation, often at the whim of the local security apparatus's officials or youth activists; and

> the participants in these interactions, which are the state and its security apparatus, the education departments, black political forces, education leaders, community groupings, teachers' associations and local groupings of teachers, students and pupils in both organized and spontaneous action, young people outside the schools, the street-children, parents, churches, the trade unions, the business community, and international forces, both political and economic.

In the face of these complexities a neat analysis of the position of education is not possible; nevertheless, it is possible to identify some clear indicators of broad tendencies and of the stances of some of the main actors in the drama that is being played out.

Government

In the first place, it is clear that the government shows no signs of giving way on the principle of segregated education systems: this is a basic tenet that has been reiterated at the highest levels. It will be more difficult for the government to change on this than to free Nelson Mandela, negotiate with the African National Congress (ANC) or repeal the Group Areas Act, because it lies at the heart of the ideology of separate development. Meanwhile, the fact is that the present education system is rejected totally by a wide range of community organizations, both conservative and radical.

In recent years, the full force of the security apparatus has been brought to bear on buttressing the crumbling edifice of black education in the urban areas. In a system in which 'compulsory education' has not been achieved, ironically, children are too often being forced to attend school by the application of the security sjambok.

In the first twelve months of the State of Emergency (first declared on 12 June 1985) more than 700 persons involved in education were detained.[1]

---

1 *Weekly Mail*, 29 August 1986, p. 2.

Of these, 147 were teachers in the service of the Department of Education and Training (DET) (79 from the Cape alone), including the Secretary-General of the national black teachers' organization — the African Teachers' Association of South Africa (ATASA).[2]

From 1986 to 1988 a determined attempt was made to cut off the head of the National Education Crisis Committee (NECC): almost all its leaders have been detained at one stage or another. While most had been released by early 1989, many live under legal restrictions which prevent them from carrying out their work openly. Moreover, of the 17 organizations which were restricted by government in February 1988, 7 were in the field of education, and included student and youth organizations, the NECC and the National Education Union of South Africa (NEUSA).[3]

There has been no genuine attempt on the part of government to resolve the education crisis through negotiation with the community or educational organizations.

As far as the provision and financing of education is concerned, repeated requests in parliament for the government to reveal the details of its ten-year plan and the formula being applied in allocating funds to education departments have failed. Little is known of either. Any discussion or consultation seems to be taking place within closed governmental structures.

However, certain things are clear. The blueprint is based on the principle of 'equal but separate' education.[4] When it was formulated, it assumed a real increase in total education expenditure of at least 4,1 per cent per annum and a projected annual expenditure by 1996 of R10 000 million (in 1986 rand terms). Priority was to be given to those departments with the biggest backlogs, and most of the extra funds were to be spent on 'increasing the qualification level of teachers, on improving the pupil-teacher ratio and on accommodating the increase in pupil numbers'[5] in these departments, including those of the homelands.

Although the ten-year plan has achieved considerable improvements in the material resources and facilities available to black education, as well as in the salaries of black teachers, the fundamental issues of segregation, isolation, relevance and quality have not been addressed. Furthermore, in the 1988/9 budgets the government has not been able to keep to its own limited targets set in the plan.

---

[2] *Hansard*, 1987, no. 5, cols. 207–8.

[3] *SA Barometer*, 11 March 1988, pp. 51–2.

[4] Federated Chambers of Industries (FCI), Meeting of Education Group, address by Director-General, Dept. of National Education, 27 June 1986.

[5] *Hansard*, 1986, no. 10, cols. 3423–5.

The reasons are not far to seek: the economy, because of the cumulative effects of years of apartheid policies, cannot support the cost of wastefully duplicated education systems at the same time as high defence and security costs. The results are already evident: in 1989 the DET began retrenching teachers, cutting back on their study leave and falling behind in the provision of schools and classrooms.

Per capita spending on white pupils is still more than five times higher than that for Africans, the quality of black education is low, and there must also be serious doubts about the ability of the system to cope with the yearly increase in pupil numbers in black education.

In looking at the short term, it is absolutely clear that no fundamental changes within the system can be expected: segregated, divisive education is to remain. However, while the state will not give up control of the formal education system, it has decided within its broad strategies of privatization to provide a social safety valve, particularly for the economically privileged.

It has adopted a more flexible attitude towards private schooling, illustrated by the subsidies now available. However, it has thus also abdicated from its responsibility to provide parents with the non-racial, open school option within the state system, for example in the so-called 'free settlement areas'.

It has also decided to apply privatization to pre-school and university education. While this may create more room to manoeuvre, there is the danger that without proper funding, those with the lowest incomes will suffer; white education could be supported by local levies to add to the funds made available under the 'separate but equal' formula.

In practice, privatization will not help eliminate inequalities but will tend to benefit those already privileged.

Schools

Turning to the schools, in particular those of the DET, the picture is one of continuing deterioration in the relationships between the department and its teachers and pupils.

This has been exacerbated by the introduction of additional school security controls in July 1986, without consultation with parent, teacher or student bodies. Over the last three years student organizations have been subjected to continuing harassment, banning and restrictions but have re-emerged with new names and pursued their protest and resistance.

The serious disruptions and ups-and-downs in attendance at black urban schools have been amply documented. Even more disturbing, certainly for the longer term well-being of education, is the breakdown of the learning environment in the schools. An official record of 80 per cent attendance at an urban school is no guarantee that learning is taking place: teachers are dispirited, pupils are restless and disturbed by what is going on around them, and the general environment is not conducive to learning.

Regular learning habits are breaking down, and discipline is loose or non-existent. There is little respect for teachers, even where it is warranted, and sometimes it is not warranted because many teachers have given up trying to survive in the classroom. Departmental professional supervision is meagre, and some schools are 'no-go areas' for departmental officials unless they have security escorts.

In the urban areas overall, there was no significant improvement in the 1988 senior certificate results in comparison with those of the previous five years: nearly half of all Standard 10 pupils failed (which has been the pattern since 1980), and only 13,6 per cent gained matriculation exemption.[6]

There can be no guarantees and it is improbable that even a radical change in the political dispensation in South Africa would restore a positive learning environment in which post-apartheid education could develop. As Sebidi has so rightly said: 'There are no educational *coups d'états*.'[7]

A further disturbing factor is the influence in education of the young people not in school. They number not only the active boycotters but also those who have dropped out, failed and in one way or another been rejected by the system. Included in this group would be roughly a third of a million pupils who completed a full secondary education between 1980 and 1988, and then failed the final senior certificate examination. Recent market research surveys indicate that, at best, only about 25 per cent of urban black youths between the ages of 16 and 24 are in full-time employment. The educational and social implications are very significant.

This group, disillusioned by failure and lack of work opportunities, exercises considerable pressure on those who are at school or who are using other educational alternatives, using a variety of methods, including straightforward, organized intimidation. One has to ask whether the schools can succeed, under any dispensation, unless something is done to help these youngsters through second-chance alternative forms of education and training.

Teachers

In the middle of the ground contested by the state on the one hand and by pupils, parents and communities on the other, stand the teachers, at the same time members of these communities and employees of the state, and therefore perceived to be part of its policy apparatus.

---

6 *Hansard*, 1989, no. 5, col. 309; and *Hansard*, 1989, no. 10, cols. 650–2.

7 L. Sebidi, 'A brick in the process of "alternative education"', in *Funda Forum*, March 1986, p. 1.

The generally negative image of the teacher, held even among teachers themselves, contributes to the breakdown of the learning environment. Under pressure and criticized from all sides for inadequacies for which they are often not to blame, and treated by departments not as professionals but as instruments of policy, it is not surprising that the morale, confidence and self-image of many is at a low ebb.

They are in an unenviable position. That so many, in spite of all the personal and external constraints, still care about their pupils speaks well of the teachers and the profession to which they belong.

The state, following its usual strategy of combining co-option and repression, is making an all-out attempt to win the support of the black teaching profession. Salaries and conditions of service have been brought into line with those of white teachers; a limited number of promotion posts at deputy regional level have been created in the inspectorate; there is a continual flow of documents, principals' meetings, top-down management programmes — all directed at co-opting teachers and principals into the system, with, it has to be said, some limited success.

On the other hand, restrictive controls are also being increased: attempts are being made to govern every aspect of the teacher's life — political beliefs, activities in and out of school, and membership of societies and associations. Individual teachers and their professional organizations are restricted in what they can say publicly, not only about the DET, but about any other state department. Those teachers' associations not recognized by the DET, such as the non-racial NEUSA, have been restricted in order to silence alternative voices.

Professional associations such as ATASA and the Cape Teachers Professional Association (CTPA) are under pressure, particularly from their younger members, to take a more militant stance of the kind adopted by the newer associations such as NEUSA. Involvement in the NECC and Mass Democratic Movement (MDM) has also brought about a review of relationships with state departments. During 1986 both ATASA and the coloured teachers' association — the Union of Teachers' Association of South Africa (UTASA) — withdrew their representatives from the South African Council of Education (SACE) and from all departmental committees.

The associations are clearly moving away from the departments who employ them and closer to the communities they serve, in the process taking a much firmer stand on the social and political issues that are bedevilling education.

It is not in the interests of the state to permit the mobilization of the teaching profession and therefore part of its strategy is to try to contain the profession within the 'own affairs' segregation model of education. It will tolerate limited negotiations on a 'group' basis only, and so meaningful participation in negotiating the fundamental issues is not possible.

In the short term it is probable that attitudes will harden on both sides, with the position of the teacher in the urban school becoming increasingly vulnerable and untenable.

Community responses

Community responses to the continuing education crisis first crystallized mainly around the NECC movement, which developed out of the conference called by the Soweto Parents Crisis Committee (SPCC) at the University of the Witwatersrand in December 1985.[8]

The NECC movement is easily the strongest initiative to emerge in the educational arena since the crisis in education came to a head in 1976. It is of positive significance for two major reasons:

1. First, in bringing together community, political and educational leaders, trade unions, parents, teachers, students and pupils it has created a powerful negotiating force that government, in spite of its attempt to remove its leadership through detentions, will have to acknowledge and listen to. For as the DET progressively loses control of the urban schools, the NECC movement offers communities a possible alternative mechanism for running schools and continuing with some form of education.

2. In the second place, the NECC is examining not only present alternatives, but also the form and character of a longer-term post-apartheid education system. This thinking has emerged under the banner of People's Education.

The NECC itself is not without its problems and constraints (in addition to those imposed by government). To the extent that it has links with particular political groupings of a broadly United Democratic Front (UDF) nature, its authority and influence will be challenged. It is not yet clear whether NECC leadership is fully accepted by certain student groupings, who feel the initiative has been taken away from them and who are often impatient for more radical action. However, what is clear is that People's Education is no longer solely dependent on the NECC as an organization, but has gained wide support as a major strategy of the MDM.

The future of education in post-apartheid society

People's Education can be regarded as the working out of the educational consequences of the Freedom Charter.

---

8 South African Institute of Race Relations, 'People's Education for people's power', in *Topical Briefing*, PD 3/86 of 3 March 1986, reproducing the full text of the resolution adopted at the Conference of Dec. 1985 at the Univ. of the Witwatersrand, convened by the Soweto Parents Crisis Committee (SPCC).

It is inextricably bound up with the concept of 'people's power', representing an important shift from the politics of refusal towards community involvement in transforming the education system. Indeed, one of its aims has been 'to challenge the militancy of unorganised youth into disciplined action, accountable to the whole community'.[9]

Its broad goals are the setting up of a 'free, compulsory, unitary, non-racial and democratic system of education' relevant to the establishment of a unitary, non-racial, democratic South Africa.

It is intended for 'all sections of our people', allowing students, parents, teachers and workers to participate actively in the initiation and management of People's Education in all its forms. Student representative councils and parent-teacher-student organizations would be key structures in this process.

It promotes the values of 'democracy, non-racialism, collective work and active participation'. Its educational objectives, to be reached through the stimulation of critical and creative thinking, analysis and working methods, are:[10]

> to eliminate illiteracy, ignorance, capitalist norms of competition, individualism, stunted intellectual development and exploitation;

> to enable 'the oppressed to understand the evils of the apartheid system' and to prepare them 'for participation in a non-racial democratic system'; and

> to equip and train 'all sectors of our people to participate actively and creatively in the struggle to attain people's power in order to establish a non-racial, democratic South Africa'.

It is important to pick up the many references in People's Education statements to 'all sectors of our people', and to argue that apartheid education, damaging and destructive as it has been for black South Africans, has also, except in the strictest sense of material benefits, failed the white community.

It has been fundamentally divisive in nature: not only has it separated white children from black children, it has also divided white children into separate camps. It has generally been authoritarian, influenced strongly by Christian National ideology and fundamental pedagogics, and marked by strong, often arrogant, bureaucratic control with little freedom for parents, teachers or pupils to exercise much influence.

It is therefore crucial that the phrase 'our people' in People's Education documents should not be interpreted in the sense of 'die volk' of Afrikaner

9 Z. Sisulu (Editor of *New Nation*), as quoted in *The Star*, 31 March 1986.

10 SAIRR, 'People's Education'.

nationalism, but as all South Africans moving into post-apartheid society. If it has, or develops, a closed sectional meaning and practice, the dangers for education will be manifold.

Broad agreement has to be sought and negotiated in South Africa, and a commitment found to a common purpose in education and society. Without this, questions of control, power and excess ideological baggage will continue to dominate education, to its detriment and that of its users.

It is to this search for broad agreement and common purpose that the proponents of People's Education are beginning to make such an important, positive contribution. There is a growing realization that there is no certainty that democratic changes in government and political structures would necessarily lead to democracy in education; as Franz Auerbach said in discussion: authoritarianism in the schools 'reflects ancient and deep-seated authoritarian child-rearing patterns in the homes of all sectors of South African society'.

Future learning styles in our schools will have to change from passive, rote learning, single-textbook, examination-oriented approaches, to creative learning and problem solving through the active participation and involvement of pupils in the learning process. This must include hands-on experience in the laboratory and workshops, self-study in the library, and questioning, discussion and working together in groups.

Significantly, People's Education statements emphasize 'critical and creative thinking, analysis and working methods', 'active participation', 'collective work', and 'democratic practices', both in generating and developing knowledge and in its implementation.

People's Education has a rightful concern, not only for the kind of people who emerge from the education system (and therefore for the nature of that system), but also for the kind of society in which people have to live and work, in which education systems and processes have to operate and for which education should prepare young people. These are also the concerns of many others, not all of whom would agree with everything in People's Education. Those who have stood for the liberal spirit in education have a hard-earned, experiential understanding of the severe problems that arise for questioning, creative thinking and the education of the critical intellect when heavy ideological pressures are exerted.

This would be their main concern with the position of People's Education as it is articulated at present — the clear presence of an underlying tension between the statements on critical and creative thinking, active participation and democratic practices on the one hand, and implied alternative ideological pressures, educational controls and power issues on the other.

However, given a commitment to a unitary, non-racial, democratic and just society, the common ground is so considerable that there is no reason why debate and action in the immediate future could not be co-operative, positive and productive.

The immediate future: opportunities and options

There are problems with the use of the term 'alternative education' as a working concept to embrace movement and development towards post-apartheid education. There are likely to be various forms of alternative education, ranging from those that are so defined because they are provided by a non-governmental agency and are not part of the formal system, to those programmes and educational practices 'conceived and executed within the struggle for national liberation'. The kind of options include alternative schools within the orbit of the private school system, alternative education programmes, and non-formal educational options.

Alternative schools

Some are existing schools, such as Woodmead or Sacred Heart in Johannesburg, which have radically changed their ethos and character and belong to the new South African Association of Independent Schools (SAAIS) rather than to the older private schools' association.

Some are new institutions, such as those of the New Era Schools Trust (Nest) and of the Leadership Education and Advancement Foundation (Leaf), which are founded on a non-racial basis.

Some, such as the Accelerated Christian Education (ACE) schools, were established in reaction to the secularism of state education. Others owe their origins to the initiatives of individuals or groups attempting to provide alternative education facilities for urban black pupils. They are to be found in offices or industrial buildings in the city, and range from straight profit-making ventures, through conventional schools registered with the DET, to genuine community private schools in which some innovations are to be found and in which parents and students have a say in the nature and programme of the school.

All provide a refuge for parents and students in stormy times. They have limited impact on the general education situation, and tend to be regarded by political organizations in black communities as enabling students from wealthier backgrounds to opt out of the struggle (which is not necessarily true). Nevertheless, they have much to teach South Africa about what happens when children from different backgrounds are brought together in the classroom. These are lessons that need to be learnt.

Alternative education programmes

On the periphery of the formal school system, the relationships of alternative education programmes with education departments range from close co-operation and involvement, through guarded neutrality on both sides, to the maintenance of strict independence on the part of the programme. Their objectives vary from supporting, improving, influencing or changing the education system, to providing remedial or supplementary activities for either pupils or teachers, or both.

Most are funded by the private sector, both South African and overseas, church organizations or foreign governments. In many programmes there is a strong involvement of one or more universities; others are entirely independent agencies set up for a specific educational objective such as literacy, pre-schooling, teacher training, science education, English or adult education.

A 1986 survey[11] lists about 55 non-governmental programmes involved in one way or another with Inset (the in-service education and training of teachers) in South Africa, to take only one facet of these alternative programmes.

Formal alternative educational opportunities for the most part have to be sought outside South Africa and exist mainly at tertiary level in the universities and other higher education institutions of the United States, Britain and Western Europe.

Each year, for example, at least 120 black students (about 80 postgraduate and 40 undergraduate) leave for up to four years of study in the USA. In the first year of this programme, the cost to USAID alone was given as R12,5 million. Most of these students are selected by the Educational Opportunities Council (EOC) and some by the South African Institute of Race Relations. About 400 students are presently in the USA.[12]

Within South Africa, Khanya College, the higher education institution set up by Sached (the South African Committee for Higher Education), is probably the only formal structure offering a true alternative to state controlled higher education, although other projects are planned.

Alternative non-formal education

Arising from community initiatives, these include a wide range of activities established by churches, women's groups and trade unions (for example, as well as 'counter-education' in and around the schools) to conscientize pupils, discuss alternative economic and political models, interpret the processes of exploitation and oppression, and prepare them for 'the liberation struggle'.

---

[11] M. Bot, 'An overview of teacher in-service education and training (Inset) programmes in South Africa', *SA Indicator Project*, Durban: Univ. of Natal, for the Urban Foundation, June 1986.

[12] M. Sinclair, *Community development in South Africa*, Washington, DC: Investor Responsibility Research Center Inc., 1986, pp. 40–1.

What can be done in the short term? Where will there be opportunities for the process of educational change to take place? There are no neat answers. However, there are a number of points of entry to the future which deserve consideration.

Points of entry to the future

The range of 'alternatives' is considerable. They vary from *ad hoc*, transitory reactions against the existing system, to those that are forward-looking, related more directly to the process of social change, and linked in some way to ideas of the nature of the longer-term replacement system.

Support in terms of resources and effort should be given to those programmes and activities that:

▷ are guided by a philosophy and goals which contribute towards education in a non-racial, democratic and just society, and are part of the process by which this will come about; and

▷ are innovative, show a concern for the learner, are educationally soundly based, aim at both quality and relevance, are open to evaluation and subsequent adjustment, effective in their outcomes and accountable primarily to the participants.

Central education systems

The first area to consider is that of the central education systems, and in particular the triangular relationship of government (including the security system), the DET and the broad, democratic People's Education movement. The central issue — as the DET increasingly loses control of its urban schools — seems to be whether the government will allow them to disintegrate further or will it be forced to negotiate a new kind of local management (based on parent-teacher-pupil bodies) and a new curriculum, accommodating to some extent the specifically educational aspects of People's Education?

This will depend on the strength of the MDM as a national negotiating body (which in turn depends upon its ability to survive the Emergency, to maintain its credibility, and to be recognized as a positive factor by the government), and the strength of the more progressive elements in the DET in withstanding pressures from the government's security apparatus.

Until the Emergency is lifted and strong security controls removed, however, the likelihood of significant negotiation remains doubtful.

The continuing breakdown of the learning environment in the schools seems inevitable, certainly as far as the central system (DET) is concerned, and in many areas alternatives will have to be sought outside the formal school system.

At the formal organized level, the role of the private school should be considered. There are historical precedents for the *community-based private school* movement as distinct from the expensive boarding school.

Many school buildings in urban areas were built by community effort, and should rightfully be made available to communities. As the free settlement areas envisaged by government are legalized in suburbs such as Mayfair and Hillbrow-Berea in Johannesburg, and in parts of Cape Town, the arguments for non-racial schools in these areas will strengthen.

The state is unlikely to provide them, but may well under continued pressure agree to lease or sell unused white school buildings for private non-racial day schools, and to provide subsidies.

Peripheral systems

The peripheral systems of education are those of the six non-independent homelands and the four independent territories, where 70 per cent of African pupils are at school.

The issues at stake in the urban areas are spilling over into areas such as Bophuthatswana, Ciskei, Lebowa, KaNgwane and KwaZulu. While having to accept a probable deterioration in the education environment in these areas over the next five years, there is still considerable room to manoeuvre. Because there is a greater readiness to allow outside agencies to experiment with alternative methods and approaches involving both teachers and communities, the homelands offer a potential for innovative programmes in change-directed education which, as yet, has not been fully exploited.[13]

Tertiary education

In the process of moving towards post-apartheid education, the universities and other institutions of tertiary education can play a crucial role. The time has come for a radical change of attitude on the part of sponsors, overseas people providing funds, white universities, and community and political organizations towards the black state universities and those of the TBVC territories.

Many people do not seem to appreciate the significance of the history and development of the University of the Western Cape, from 'a creature of apartheid' to an institution of relevance and meaning to the community it serves.

There is a lesson to be learnt from this. Universities can be transformed by the development of academic leadership and research capability as well

---

[13] K. B. Hartshorne, 'Education in the homelands — in a cul de sac or at the crossroads?' Etheredge Commemoration Lecture, 17 March 1989, Centre for Continuing Education, Univ. of the Witwatersrand, which provides a detailed argument in this case.

as by structural changes in control and composition. There is a potential in both the students and staff of the 'black' universities that has not yet been fully utilized. With support and recognition, both from other universities and from the MDM, many of whose youth have to attend them, they could play a much greater and more positive role in the process of educational change.

For English-medium 'open universities' the issues are somewhat different and are reflected strikingly in a report of the University Witwatersrand.[14] They have to do in the main with the perceptions of the various constituencies of the university, in particular those of the wider black community which saw Wits as:

▷ dominated by big business, government and the white community;

▷ isolated from the experience of black people; and

▷ opposing apartheid but discriminating against blacks within the university.

In the immediate future the university will clearly continue to be contested terrain, but it also has the potential, in the words of the Wits report, 'to create the space that would allow it to restructure meaningfully its role in a changing society'[15] and participate positively in the process leading to post-apartheid education.

In the field of tertiary education one of the most problematic areas, especially for the black community, is teacher education and training. The state has demonstrated forcibly that 'own affairs' colleges of education are at the heart of education non-negotiables. Nevertheless, the possibility of universities building up networks of relationships with black teachers' colleges should not be discounted in spite of the structural constraints. Informal co-operation and mutual support, for example, in the form of staff development programmes, could do much to link the colleges with change-oriented movements in education.

Another opportunity that needs to be explored in the immediate future is alternative higher education within South Africa on the lines of Sached's Khanya College, but not at traditional university level. Resources put into a community college-type of institution and into a private teachers' college to test these models would open up effective options in a future educational dispensation.

---

14 Univ. of the Witwatersrand, *Perceptions of Wits: the role of the university in a changing South Africa*, Johannesburg: Univ. of the Witwatersrand, 1986.

15 K. B. Hartshorne, *INSET in South Africa — the HSRC report of 1985*, Bloemfontein: the Urban Foundation, 1986, pp. 40–0, 43–4.

Non-formal sectors

There is a considerable area of educational ground not occupied by the state or only partially controlled by it. This is the area outside the formal schooling system, in the informal and non-formal sectors of education. The opportunities for innovation, freer action, greater choice, community involvement and private initiative are all much wider than within the schooling system, which governments all over the world tend to regard as their preserve. There are three specific areas of non-formal education of a more organized nature that are important factors in any consideration of the future of education:

▷ Pre-school education is an area that holds considerable promise because of the creative learning opportunities it can offer young children and its opportunities for parental education. The possibilities of positive and effective co-operation between parental and community bodies, private sponsors and professional service agencies are real and already established.

What happens in pre-school education now can have considerable impact on the kind of formal schooling system South Africa has by the end of the century.

▷ There are many broader community needs — personal, social and economic — that will have to be met by strong and effective adult education networks. Here again the potential for community involvement and management is considerable. The need for second-chance programmes, particularly for young adults who have dropped out of, failed or rejected the formal system, is critical. It is doubtful whether any education system, no matter how transformed, can survive unless these young people are rescued within new and innovative learning environments so different from the schools they knew that the bad memories recede into the background of consciousness.

▷ As a distinct part of adult education, both adult literacy and worker education will become of increasing importance over the next few years. In the light of the wide-ranging debate on questions of relevance in schooling and education, and the issues surrounding education and work, the attitudes and contributions of trade unions to People's Education could be of major significance in setting future patterns of educational development.

Teachers

In the highly contested area of the formal state schooling system where the prospects of fundamental change appear to be the most limited, it is vital that in the short term every opportunity should be taken to strengthen the independent, authentic professional position of teachers. Change in the control of education will inevitably come about by political means. New policies, instructions, curricula and syllabuses can be introduced by political fiat. But, in the end, teachers remain the most potentially powerful group of change agents, particularly if they can be freed from present constraints.

This is clearly appreciated by the MDM and the People's Education movement. Yet, more than ever, the state is making it clear that it regards them as employees, not as professionals, and is claiming total ownership of their thoughts, actions and behaviour.

Major structural changes are needed to rescue teachers from the untenable position in which they find themselves, notably:

▷ The education and training of teachers must be removed from the control of the employers, the education departments, to a more independent situation in which colleges and universities could work together and in which the rightful say of the employing departments could be balanced by the interests of the teaching profession and the teacher educators. There are numerous models in many parts of the world, including Africa, for this kind of arrangement.

▷ The appointment and employment of teachers must be removed from the ambit of the civil service to a separate and independent teaching service commission of the kind working successfully in many English-speaking African countries.[16]

Apart from structural issues, however, teachers themselves, particularly in their professional associations, will have to continue to wrestle with such fundamental questions as:

▷ What does it mean to be a professional?

▷ To whom is the teaching profession accountable?

▷ How do teachers show a broad commitment to the idea of a non-racial democratic future for South Africa, and yet remain non-aligned to a particular political ideology or party cause?

The influence of the teaching profession on future developments in education will depend on the extent to which it can combine a commitment to non-racial, unitary education in a transformed society with a positive, professional, non-aligned spirit and position. This can be achieved only if the profession, through the development of teacher leadership at all levels, energetically negotiates its status in relation to the system on the one hand and to the community it serves — leaders, parents and teachers — on the other.

---

16 R. J. Smyke, 'Teacher organisations in international perspective' in *Teachers in a divided society*, M. J. Ashley, ed., Cape Town: Univ. of Cape Town, 1985, pp. 15, 26.

There are clear indications that this is being done, and that the black teaching profession is adopting a much less accommodating and more independent stance towards the state.

However, greater independence of the system also implies that teachers will have to accept increased responsibility for their own professional development, for example, in-service education programmes concerned with the needs of the teacher rather than with those of the department.

It will be even more important for teachers' associations to negotiate an acceptance of an authentic professional stance as educators with community organizations within the broad liberation movement, a process which has already started. It would be a tragedy if teachers could not contribute to the development of People's Education in terms of content, approaches, style, standards and quality.

Community organizations, in return, have already made it clear that they expect the teaching profession to reject existing divisions and to work with purpose towards a unified profession, at least of those teachers committed to a democratic, non-racial South Africa.

Private funding

Finally, it is necessary to look at the implications of this analysis for sponsors, trusts and foundations, private sector corporate responsibility programmes, and all those here and abroad who have control of the allocation of resources in their hands.

In the short and medium terms, as community and teacher initiatives strengthen and as concepts of alternative education are clarified and are expressed in programme proposals, one of the major limiting factors could be the availability of funds to implement these proposals. Funding should be channelled towards those projects and programmes that are part of the process leading to post-apartheid education.

Conclusion

The upsurge of People's Education has provided a new opportunity to debate the realities, the relevance, the quality and style of education in South Africa and to negotiate its future for all its people.

The common ground, now and in the future, must be a commitment to a non-racial, democratic, equitable and just society, in both the political and economic sense, by the parties to the debate and negotiation.

In education, many of the main actors, pupils and teachers, have seen the learning environment collapse around them and the education system disintegrate. The hurts are deep, emotions run high and the obstacles to understanding and shared debate are massive, But there is also hope, because in spite of the slogans and the rejection of much of what at present is *schooling*, there is a common appreciation of the fundamental importance of *education* and what it could contribute in a regenerated society.

Acknowledgement

An earlier version of this paper was presented at the African Studies Centre, Michigan State University in November 1986.

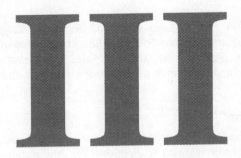

III

Managing resources in a context of relative scarcity

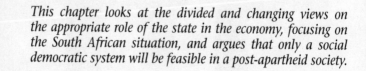

11 The role of the state in the economy

Gavin Maasdorp

This chapter looks at the divided and changing views on the appropriate role of the state in the economy, focusing on the South African situation, and argues that only a social democratic system will be feasible in a post-apartheid society.

Introduction

There are two basic types of economic systems: centrally planned and market. In the centrally planned economies (CPEs) the state is virtually all-embracing, characterized by a command system with decisions percolating down the hierarchy. In the market system, the role of the state today varies widely and this has given rise to the mixed economy where both market and non-market mechanisms exist to allocate scarce resources.

The provision of physical infrastructure and social security — education, health, welfare, housing and social insurance — has become a common economic function of governments in mixed economies. However, governments have also entered some fields previously the domain of the private sector by establishing public corporations to provide transport as well as by nationalizing key sectors such as steel production, coal mining and banking. As a consequence, public expenditure has increased and correspondingly so has taxation.

There are divided views on the appropriate role of the state in the economy on three main issues: (i) the functions which should be performed by government; (ii) whether higher taxation to fund increased public expenditure reduces individual incentives and so lowers efficiency; and (iii) which groups in society are made better or worse off by government action.

The debate involves normative and ethical judgments. Thus, what should the state do and not do? How can the desired ends be attained most efficiently? What distribution of income is socially just?[1]

---

[1] Well-known treatments of this issue are those of J. Rawls, *A theory of justice*, Cambridge, Massachusetts: Harvard Univ. Press, 1971; and R. Nozick, *Anarchy, state and Utopia*, New York: Basic Books, 1974. For an application of their theories to South Africa, see C. Simkins, *Reconstructing South African liberalism*, Johannesburg: South African Institute of Race Relations, 1986.

This chapter will argue that only a social democratic system will be politically feasible in a post-apartheid society, and that anything more maximalist than social democracy will be economically costly.

Changing views on the role of the state

The Western economies

The economic role of the state in the industrialized Western economies arises mainly from 'market failure', that is, markets fail to provide a Pareto-optimal solution (a position in which it is not possible to make one person better off without making another worse off) because of factors such as monopolies and incomplete information and uncertainty.

Market failure gives rise to two principal functions of government. The allocative role is designed to correct inefficiencies in the market solution, for example, by protecting the public from air pollution or providing public goods such as defence, while the distributive role involves intervention to reduce inequities in income and welfare produced by the market.

A third role — stabilization — derives from economic fluctuations and involves intervention through monetary and fiscal policy to reduce inflation and unemployment, stimulate economic growth, and overcome balance-of-payments problems. Finally, the regulatory role entails the regulation of individual behaviour in the general system of law and justice.

In the Western industrial societies, a political consensus emerged after World War II on the responsibility of government to intervene in the economy. Giersch has called the third quarter of the century the 'age of Keynes',[2] referring to the social democratic consensus characterized by short-term demand management on the part of government, which appeared to work well in the 1950s and 1960s. These were decades of high economic growth rates, growing prosperity, low rates of unemployment, and improved social security benefits. Conflicts between growth and welfare payments, or between efficiency and equity, were not matters of prime concern, and the only trade-off which received serious consideration was that between full employment and price-level stability.

The 1970s, however, saw a vastly different economic climate: economic growth rates declined, inflation and unemployment increased, and there was growing competition from the newly industrialized countries (NICs). The oil price increases played a part in the sluggishness of the industrialized economies, but there was a fundamental transition underway in the production of industrial goods world-wide: the rise of Japan and the NICs, and the decline of heavy industry and textiles in many industrialized countries.

[2] H. Giersch, 'Economic policies in the age of Schumpeter', *European Economic Review*, vol. 31, 1987, p. 35.

This economic malaise gave rise to a widespread view that governments had failed in their macroeconomic management, and from the late 1970s onwards conservative parties in the US and Western Europe tended to make gains. In Europe it was argued that the extensive welfare state element in the mixed economy had weakened economic growth, and there was talk of 'Eurosclerosis'.[3] The ideas of the 'New Right' among economists provided the foundations for the policies followed by political leaders such as Thatcher and Reagan.

The Keynesian consensus thus disintegrated during the 1970s. Economists disagreed amongst themselves on such issues as whether tax rates were too high, the desirable ratio between government expenditure and private expenditure, ways of controlling inflation, deregulation and privatization, ways of accelerating growth rates, how much social security should be provided, and, in general, the desirable relationship between markets and governments.

Strong arguments have been made that government intervention, undertaken in order to overcome market failure, itself fails, mainly by stimulating the excessive growth of public-sector activity, for example, the growth and use of political power to benefit politicians and bureaucrats who misdirect the use of economic resources. Social losses from rent-seeking are contrasted with social gains from profit-seeking in the market where entrepreneurs are rewarded for providing more and higher quality goods through their efficient use of new technology.

The main market alternative to the 'New Right' is represented by social democracy, the Nordic countries being good examples. But Swedish social democracy, for example, contains many features advocated by the New Right, combining an efficient private sector with a well-developed welfare system. There is little government interference with business and corporate tax rates are low.

The centrally planned economies[4]

The theoretical basis for the role of the state in the centrally planned economies (CPEs) was provided by Marx and Lenin. In the immediate post-World War II period, fairly strict Stalinist-type central planning was extended beyond the borders of the Soviet Union to embrace Eastern Europe and parts of Asia. In the 1960s and 1970s there were some cautious reforms, but the 1980s have seen far-reaching changes in economic policies in the CPEs, especially in Hungary, Poland and China. Since the advent of

---

[3] Giersch, 'Economic policies', p. 39.

[4] Summarized from G. Maasdorp, 'Perestroika and post-apartheid lessons for South Africa from the centrally planned economies', *International Affairs Bulletin*, vol. 13, no. 1, 1989.

Gorbachev, perestroika (economic restructuring) has become a household word.

Why has central planning failed as an economic system? Most critics have concentrated their attention on the lack of motivation inherent in the system, but the main problem is a technical one, namely, lack of information on the scale required to make planning feasible.

In the traditional Soviet-type model, mandatory directives are handed down from planners to enterprises: planners set targets for each enterprise, quantifying outputs and inputs in physical units in as much detail as is feasible. Here, however, lies the rub: the data requirements of the model are such that the economy 'cannot effectively be steered by detailed administrative directives from the centre, not even with the help of computers'[5].

Lack of managerial motivation stems from the preoccupation with meeting production goals which constitute the measure of an enterprise's success. In attempting to meet their targets, enterprises tend to disregard costs and this leads them into financial difficulties. They are then bailed out by the state, a phenomenon which Kornai has dubbed the 'soft budget constraint'.[6] This overriding concern to meet output targets also leads to a disregard for quality.

For CPEs generally, the 1970s and 1980s have been decades of falling economic growth rates and growing inefficiency, as well as a widening technological gap in relation to the West. It is widely recognized by economists in the CPEs that systemic structures and economic policy need to be changed to incorporate the advantages of the market mechanism. Reforms in most CPEs involve the modification of the system of state ownership and control; thus certain countries are endeavouring to enlarge the field of co-operative and private activity in industry and agriculture. Yet, investment autonomy for enterprises is dependent upon the existence of a capital market for, without this, they will continue to rely on the state for funds.

Another important shift in thinking concerns equality. In Eastern Europe disparities in wages between different occupations have been narrowed considerably, but this 'wage levelling' has acted as a disincentive to individuals to undertake further studies or to accept positions of responsibility. The position has now been reached where equality *per se* is no longer regarded as a positive factor and CPEs are trying to increase wage differentials in order to provide sufficient incentives to encourage efficiency and higher productivity.

---

5 A. von Borcke, 'Gorbachev's perestroika: can the Soviet system be reformed?', *Biost Report no. 1*, Cologne: Federal Inst. for East European and International Studies, 1988, p. 18.

6 See, *inter alia*, J. Kornai, *Economics of shortage*, Amsterdam: North Holland Press, 1980.

Observers agree that economic reform may well fail. There are many obstacles — political, social and economic — to be surmounted. Should economic reform fail, the implications are clear. The CPEs will fall further and further behind the West technologically, become even less able to compete in international markets, and face deteriorating long-term standards of living. As an official Soviet document acknowledges: 'The growing consumer requirements can only be met by proceeding with radical reform'[7].

The Third World

Perceptions about the economic role of the state in the Third World have been influenced by the success of the NICs and the simultaneous failures of radical and populist socialist regimes.

In 1968 Myrdal[8] predicted a dire future for South-East Asia, yet exactly the opposite has occurred.[9] While several countries in the region have transformed themselves from less-developed countries (LDCs) to NICs, continued economic difficulties or stagnation plague Latin America and economic retrogression continues in Africa. In brief, South-East Asia has a philosophy of growth, Latin America and Africa are obsessed with dependency or colonialism; South-East Asia is profit-seeking, Latin America and Africa are rent-seeking.

In the NICs government intervention was limited, pragmatic and competent, and aimed to encourage companies to become internationally competitive as rapidly as possible. The governments took the market seriously, and their macroeconomic policies, which successfully promoted economic growth and efficiency, included realistic exchange rates, positive real interest rates, market-determined prices, and direct as opposed to indirect subsidies.

In Africa, most governments pinned their faith on public enterprises (the parastatals), whose record, as Knight points out, is dismal. Their net effect has been to increase the budget deficits of governments substantially from an average of 1,6 per cent of GDP to 5,4 per cent.[10]

The failure of public enterprises in Africa bears out Arendt's contention that, while there might be a case for government action to supplement private initiatives in LDCs, the state actions may also be imperfect. He concludes that, in practice, government failures often outweigh market

---

7 *The 19th CPSU Conference: a new way of looking at things and making decisions*, Moscow: Novosti Press Agency Publishing House, 1988, p. 36.

8 G. Myrdal, *Asian drama*, Harmondsworth: Penguin, 1968.

9 H. Hughes, ed., *Achieving industrialization in East Asia*, Cambridge: Cambridge Univ. Press, 1988.

10 See J. B. Knight, *Public enterprises and industrialization in Africa*, Oxford: Unit for the Study of African Economies, Inst. of Economic and Statistics, Oxford Univ., p. 3.

failure.[11]

The creation of these parastatals is today criticized both by radicals and conservatives, and experiments with various types of African socialism are more and more being revealed as failures.[12]

Summary

A common trend throughout the world is the growing influence of the market and the collapse of confidence in central planning and state controls.

How long this trend will last is uncertain, but socialist parties which might regain power in, for example, the United Kingdom, are likely to do so from a platform markedly less hostile to market forces and the private sector than a decade ago. The precise nature of the mix in the Western market economies will continue to be debated, and it is significant that the European Commission appears determined not to forego the gains made by social democrats over the years in establishing a social security system. How to blend a free market with democracy and a sense of social justice is the challenge, and this is particularly so in the case of South Africa.

The state in the South African economy

The state has increased its economic activities in the years of unbroken National Party rule since 1948, and notable among these has been the extension of public corporations. However, this trading role of the state was preceded by the pursuit of a policy aimed at eradicating the 'poor white' problem.

The rise of the assertive state

Towards the end of the nineteenth century, many rural white families were in a parlous economic position as a result of drought, rinderpest and the continued fragmentation of farms into uneconomic units. The Anglo-Boer War of 1899–1902 deepened their plight, a substantial proportion of Afrikaner families having lost their possessions, including land. The resultant 'poor white' problem became a major political and social issue after Union and was exacerbated by the Great Depression of 1929–32. The Carnegie Commission of Inquiry estimated that there were 300 000 poor whites in 1929–30 and that almost 50 per cent of white children were inadequately clothed and fed.[13]

---

11 H. W. Arendt, 'Market failure and underdevelopment', *World Development*, vol. 2, no. 16, Feb. 1988, pp. 219–29.

12 In H. B. Hansen and M. Twaddle, *Uganda now*, London: James Curry, 1988.

13 F. J. von Biljon, *State interference in South Africa*, London: P. S. King and Son Ltd., 1939, p. 70.

The general response was the so-called 'civilized labour policy' formulated in 1924, whereby the public sector fulfilled the role of employer of last resort: any unemployed white who could not find a job in the private sector could obtain one in the public sector, especially on the railways. The lowest public-sector wages paid were in effect minimum wages for whites which would enable them to maintain 'civilized' standards of life.[14]

In the public sector, many Africans and Indians were dismissed and substituted by unskilled whites at higher rates of pay. The preferential treatment accorded to whites in employment was further entrenched by the fact that they were allowed to engage in trade union activity while Africans were denied this facility, and also by the fact that the minimum educational qualifications laid down under the Apprenticeship Act meant that Africans, in effect, were excluded from competing in skilled artisanal posts.

The state and public enterprises

In 1924 a coalition government of Afrikaner Nationalists and the predominantly English-led Labour Party came to power. White agricultural and labour interests were powerful in the government, which embarked on a policy of economic nationalism. Active steps were taken to encourage industrialization, and in 1925 the first customs tariffs of a protective nature were imposed. From now on, South Africa would develop a manufacturing industry behind high tariff walls. The embryonic Afrikaner business sector worked closely with, and benefited from, the new state policy, and the overall share of the public sector in the economy began to increase substantially, not least as a consequence of the establishment of public corporations in manufacturing industry.

The first such enterprise was the South African Iron and Steel Corporation (Iscor) established in 1927 after the shares offered for public subscription were not taken up.[15]

The Smuts government created the Industrial Development Corporation (IDC) in 1940 to promote industrial development, establish new ventures in partnership with local and foreign capital, and launch new projects of strategic importance.[16] The IDC established an oil-from-coal plant (Sasol) for strategic reasons in 1950, a phosphate plant (Foskor) in 1955, and an aluminium plant (Alusaf) in 1967, while the government also took the lead in armaments production (later expanded into Armscor) in 1964. It is

---

[14] B. Kantor, 'Racial income differences and the South African labour market', in B. Kantor and D. Rees, eds., *South African Economic Issues*, Cape Town: Juta, 1982, p. 58.

[15] von Biljon, *State interference*, p. 58.

[16] S. P. Viljoen, 'The industrial achievement of South Africa', *South African Journal of Economics*, vol. 1, no. 51, 1983, p. 50.

clear that after 1948, state-owned corporations were fostered as an Afrikaner answer to non-Afrikaner interests in mining and industry,[17] the IDC being used to increase Afrikaner participation in the management of industry.

The implementation of the homelands development policy, formulated and introduced from the late-1950s onwards, led to the establishment of parastatal homeland development corporations to promote industrial and commercial enterprises in these areas. These corporations entered into joint ventures with private capital, thereby further expanding the participation of the state in the production of non-essential goods. Similarly, the separate corporations established for coloured people and Indians in the 1960s were later absorbed by the IDC.

Other state initiatives

In agriculture, assistance to white commercial farmers through subsidies, re-bates and tariffs, and the establishment under the Marketing Act of 1937 of producer-dominated control boards with monopoly powers over marketing[18] have long been controversial issues. Commercial farmers have always been a powerful political lobby, and government has responded to continuing problems in agriculture by greater intervention. The role of the state in agriculture is a 'steadily increasing one'[19] and Rees believes that 'there is little to suggest that the boards have solved any real problems'.[20]

Transport has been a highly regulated sector with the state owning ports, railways and the national airline, as well as providing roads. Goods trans-port by private road hauliers has been carefully regulated to control com-petition with the road and rail services operated by the South African Trans-port Services (Sats). There has been a strong element of cross-subsidization in the road and rail tariff structure with respect both to commodities and routes, while road-users have not been charged the true user costs. It is only in the 1980s that policy has been thoroughly re-examined, and the industry is now being deregulated.

The state in South Africa has, by international standards, played an unusually active role in attempting to influence the location of manufactur-ing industry. After a few sporadic attempts by the IDC between 1945 and 1948, the government in 1960 commenced a policy of industrial decen-tralization. This was intimately tied up with the policy of separate ethnic

---

17 A. D. Wassenaar, *Assault on private enterprise*, Cape Town: Tafelberg, 1977, p. 123.

18 See S. J. J. de Swart, 'Agricultural marketing problems in the nineteen thirties', *South African Journal of Economics*, vol. 1, no. 51, 1983, pp. 1–28.

19 D. Rees, 'Agricultural policy in South Africa — an evaluation', in Kantor and Rees, *South African economic issues*, p. 186.

20 Rees, 'Agricultural policy', p. 189.

homelands for the African population.[21] At first directed at border areas, that is, non-homeland areas on the borders of homelands, the focus later shifted to growth points inside the homelands as well. The policy has been through a number of revisions,[22] but the granting of generous incentives to industrialists by the state has been enormously costly.

A related field of state interference is the market for land. Separate reserves for Africans form the basis of today's homelands and were established prior to Union and subsequently enshrined in legislation. These laws — the Land Act, the Native Trust and Land Act, and the Group Areas Act — form the cornerstone of spatial apartheid. There is thus no single market for land, but a set of segregated markets, one for each race group.[23]

In fact, the state has interfered to an extraordinary degree with the functioning of the market for all four factors of production — land, labour, capital and entrepreneurship. In the case of labour, a panoply of legislation (see Chapter 15) including the now defunct policy of job reservation — has limited interracial competition for jobs, and it was only in 1979 that African membership of trade unions was legalized. The mobility of capital has been inhibited by restrictions on investment by other race groups. As Horwood and Burrows put it:

> the position of the state in the South African economy is anomalous in that, while participation in and direct control over private enterprise appears to be less marked than in some other Western countries, a number of indirect controls, operating mainly against the freedom of the individual, must be viewed as a very severe departure from *laissez-faire* principles.[24]

The growth of the state sector

With the state playing an increasingly active role in the economy over the years, the public sector has expanded not only in absolute terms, but also relative to the rest of the economy.

Defining state expenditure as current and capital outlays by central, provincial, local and homeland administrations, and state and public corporations, Abedian and Standish find that state expenditure grew as a proportion of national expenditure from 29 per cent in 1920 to 63 per cent

---

[21] See, for example, G. Maasdorp, 'Industrial decentralization and the economic development of the homelands', in R. Schrire, ed., *South Africa: public policy perspectives*, Cape Town: Juta, 1982.

[22] G. Maasdorp, 'Hope for the Good Hope proposals', in H. Giliomee and L. Schlemmer, *Up against the fences*, Cape Town: David Philip, 1985.

[23] G. Maasdorp and N. Pillay, *Urban relocation and racial segregation: the case of Indian South Africans*, Durban: Dept. of Economics, Univ. of Natal, 1977.

[24] O. P. F. Horwood and J. R. Burrows, 'The South African economy: the relevance of the competitive *laissez-faire* model', in C. B. Hoover, ed., *Economic systems of the Commonwealth*, Durham, N.C.: Duke Univ. Press, 1962, p. 500.

in 1982[25] — an increase in real terms of 6,2 per cent per annum. Initially government intervention in the economy after 1948 was designed to contain English economic power and promote Afrikaner entrepreneurship and economic interests, and since 1960 the costs of homeland development and other apartheid policies have further increased the state's share of total expenditure.[26] According to Browne, between 1946 and 1981 there was a steady increase in final expenditure by public authorities in relation to gross domestic product (GDP), and also of current government revenue and expenditure relative to GDP.[27] Gouws illustrates that total public sector expenditure as a proportion of GDP increased from 21,9 per cent in 1962 to 37,8 per cent in 1985 before falling again to 35,1 per cent in 1987.[28] General government current spending similarly increased: consumption expenditure by government, for example, rose from 10,4 to 19,2 per cent of GDP between 1962 and 1987.[29]

The increasing state share of total GDP is paralleled in employment statistics: the numbers of civil servants increased by 61 per cent between 1973 and 1988 as against only 17 per cent in private non-agricultural employment.[30] Between 1980 and 1987, partly as a result of the new tricameral parliamentary system, employment in the government sector (excluding the TBVC states — Transkei, Bophuthatswana, Venda and Ciskei) increased by 304 000. This represented 82 per cent of all additional employment in this period.[31] During the same period, the manufacturing sector — the main engine of growth in the economy — shed 67 000 jobs.

Thus, the non-goods-producing public sector has been expanding much more rapidly than the productive sectors of the economy. Rising government spending has led to high rates of taxation and a 'growing appropriation of capital resources by the public sector'.[32] The rent-seeking society has gained at the expense of the profit-seeking.[33]

Guidelines for policy

Under National Party rule, the growth of the public sector has been influ-

---

25 I. Abedian and B. Standish, 'An analysis of the sources of growth in state expenditure in South Africa 1920–82', *South African Journal of Economics*, vol. 4, no. 52, 1984, p. 392.

26 Abedian and Standish, 'An analysis of the sources of growth', pp. 392–3.

27 G. W. G. Browne, 'Fifty years of public finance', *South African Journal of Economics*, vol. 1, no. 51, 1983, pp. 166–7.

28 R. P. Gouws, *The growth of the public sector and use of privatisation proceeds in South Africa*, Johannesburg: Rand Merchant Bank, 1989, p. 2.

29 Gouws, *The growth of the public sector*, p. 3.

30 Gouws, *The growth of the public sector*.

31 *Daily News* (Durban), 26 April 1989.

32 Gouws, *The growth of the public sector*, p. 3.

enced by the existence of inequality — first by income differentials between Afrikaner and English; second, and more recently, by the need to improve the economic position of blacks.

Inequality has been an important factor leading to the establishment of (i) public corporations in fields normally left to private enterprise, and (ii) a bureaucracy which is large by international standards. These steps, in turn, coupled with the policy of separate development, have led to a highly regulated economy with legislative impediments to the mobility of all factors of production.

The legacy of apartheid

The basic reason for the continuing disparities in economic and social conditions between whites and blacks is that whites reinforced the initial inequality in technological endowment with customary discrimination and legislative measures which prevented equal access to social services and employment, and hence to the accumulation of wealth.

Three centuries of racial discrimination, followed by over forty years of institutionalized apartheid, have led to the creation of a highly unequal society. For our purposes the following are the main features:

1. Whites control most of the land, only some 13,4 per cent being reserved for African use, mostly on a communal basis of tenure.

2. Whites fill most of the skilled, well-paid positions in the economy, enjoying per capita incomes on average some 12,9 times that of Africans in 1980.[34]

3. Whites own and manage almost the entire spectrum of large businesses in the economy.

4. Whites enjoy far higher standards of education and other services such as health, and receive a disproportionately high share of state expenditure on these items.[35]

As a corollary, inequality has resulted in the emergence of an African labour force and intelligentsia deeply resentful of their past treatment and

---

[33] C. Lingle, 'A public choice: perspective on apartheid and the post-apartheid political economy', *Occasional Paper no. 21*, Durban: Economic Research Unit, Univ. of Natal, 1989.

[34] M. McGrath and G. Maasdorp, 'Limits to redistribution', Paper delivered at Conference on The Post-Apartheid Economy in Southern Africa, Univ. of York, Oct. 1986.

[35] Despite reductions in the white–African per capita expenditure gap, between 1975 and 1985, expenditure on African school education increased at an average annual rate of 130 per cent as against 18 per cent for whites, and the white–African per pupil expenditure ration fell from 14,9 to 7,6 — in absolute terms the interracial gaps were still considerable. Average expenditure per pupil at school in 1985 was R2 370 for whites, R1 204 for Indians, R828 for coloureds and R311 for Africans. These figures include the independent homelands. See G. J. Trotter (assisted by A. J. Shave), *The social costs of South African education*, Durban, Economic Research Unit, Univ. of Natal, 1988, pp. 22–3. Since 1984 the minimum requirement for new teachers is M + 3, but in 1988, 52 per cent of African teachers had no more than a Standard 8, compared with 29 per cent for coloureds and 0 per cent for whites and Indians (*Social and Economic Update*, no. 6, June/Oct. 1988, p. 12).

present lot, and often with little sympathy for an economic system based on markets. The market system ('capitalism') is regarded by many as co-terminous with apartheid — an equal villain which ought to be eradicated.

The nature of the economy

The following features of the economy are of special importance for this chapter:

1. South Africa has a highly open economy. In 1986 it was the fifteenth largest trading nation in the world, and international economic conditions therefore significantly affect the health of the economy.

2. Foreign capital inflows have traditionally been extremely important for domestic investment. These inflows virtually ended in 1985, and domestic savings subsequently have had to finance domestic investment as well as substantial capital outflows.

3. The domestic propensity to save has fallen rapidly in the last few years as real personal disposable incomes (PDI) per capita have declined at a mean annual rate of –0,5 per cent between 1980 and 1988.[36] Total personal savings fell from 11,7 per cent of PDI in 1962 to only 1,6 per cent in 1988.[37] PDI has been adversely affected by the increase in personal taxation rates — the ratio of direct personal income tax to current personal income increased from 4,6 in 1962 to 11,8 in 1987.[38]

4. The overall population growth rate is approximately 2,5 per cent per annum, and a real economic growth rate of about 4 per cent per annum is required for significant improvement in real per capita incomes. However, because of the absence of foreign capital inflows, high growth rates are impossible without leading to even higher inflation.

5. The economic growth rate is vulnerable to shocks in domestic investor confidence caused by periodic waves of political unrest and repression.

6. Internal instability coupled with foreign pressures (trade and investment sanctions and boycotts) have led to very slow growth in the 1980s, GDP in real terms having risen by only 0,6 per cent per annum between 1980 and 1988.[39] Employment creation has lagged behind the growth of the labour supply, and real incomes of whites have fallen.

---

[36] A study by the Bureau of Economic Research, Univ. of Stellenbosch, quoted in the *Natal Mercury*, (Durban), 25 May 1989.

[37] Study by the Bureau of Economic Research, Univ. of Stellenbosch, quoted in the *Natal Mercury*, 25 May 1989; and Gouws, *The growth of the public sector*, p. 4.

[38] Gouws, *The growth of the public sector*, p. 4.

[39] Study by the Bureau of Economic Research, Univ. of Stellenbosch, quoted in the *Natal Mercury*, 25 May 1989.

The position at the end of the 1980s is a far cry from the high economic growth rate necessary to speed the narrowing of the income gap between whites and blacks.

7. In the last ten years there has been a considerable reduction in economic (and social) apartheid, and this has contributed to the declining interracial income gap. Africans have been granted trade union rights, wage discrimination in the public sector has been ended, large firms have introduced 'social responsibility' programmes, and there has been considerable vertical occupational mobility for all black groups.

8. The establishment of the African homelands and the tricameral parliamentary system has led to a spectacular growth in the bureaucracy and in the number of well-paid jobs available to blacks.

9. The repeal of influx control legislation has boosted an already high rate of African rural-to-urban migration. As a corollary, agriculture is declining in importance for Africans, who are becoming an increasingly urbanized and sophisticated consumer society. Black economic empowerment is being proposed as an alternative strategy to the politics of boycott and non-cooperation.

10. Certain structural economic problems — shortages of key entrepreneurial, managerial and technical manpower and the high cost/low productivity of labour — have been exacerbated by the growing power of (confrontationist) trade unions, which has led to relative wage increases for Africans. This, in turn, may have stimulated capital intensity and slowed job creation, thereby contributing to an already serious unemployment problem.

11. Unemployment would be higher were it not for the growth of the urban informal sector where, however, incomes are in general very low. Significant income inequalities exist within the African population, between urban and rural households and between urban insiders (in the wage economy) and urban outsiders (in the informal sector).

12. South Africa continues to draw migrant labour from neighbouring countries (approximately 300 000 persons at any one time), especially for work on the mines.

13. The sanctions and disinvestment campaigns may have significant deleterious long-term effects on the economy. The loss of export markets may be difficult to regain, and plant may become obsolescent because of the lack of access to certain types of technology. With the depreciation of the rand, it will be extremely expensive to retool.

14. Disinvestment has stimulated the purchase (mainly by conglomerates) of large firms from multinational corporations, and this has led to increasing concentration of ownership in the economy.

15. There are two distinct labour markets — for skilled and unskilled workers. The market for skilled labour is a First World market, and accountants, computer operators and medical doctors, for example, have internationally portable skills and therefore receive remuneration roughly comparable to the international rate. The supply of skills is artificially low because of legislative impediments and differential government expenditure on education and training, and hence there is inadequate competition. The market for unskilled labour, however, possesses all the characteristics of a Third World labour market with supply exceeding demand, and the shadow price of unskilled labour is therefore extremely low. The effect of trade unions is to bid up wages to artificially high levels.

It is with these features in mind that the economic role of the post-apartheid state will have to be formulated.

What should the state do and not do?

An African nationalist government in office today would be in a not dissimilar position to that faced by its Afrikaner nationalist predecessors, namely, group-based inequalities of income and economic power.

A new government would wish to redress the inequalities of the past but would lack the financial resources to do so. A new set of demands would face the government — from returning exiles (for good jobs either in the public service or private sector), workers (for higher wages and more economic power), unemployed and rural-to-urban migrants (for wage employment), students (for educational equality), squatters (for improved housing and urban services) and rural families (for land).

Many of these demands have faced governments of newly-independent countries in Africa and some of their responses have had serious economic implications. For example, employment in the public sector and government expenditure on social services have been expanded beyond the state's taxable capacity; loss-making parastatals have been established; state marketing monopolies have been set up to control food prices; political rhetoric to placate followers has scared off foreign investors; and government interference with the employment practices of firms has reduced investor confidence. These have been attractive short-term responses, but in the long term have resulted in the extension of political patronage so typical of a rent-seeking society rather than in the development of an efficient profit-seeking one.

Policy-makers may either nationalize the 'commanding heights' of the economy, or promote black economic empowerment and improve black social welfare. The second alternative will be more difficult now than it was for Afrikaners because of the difference in relative population size, the rapid rate of population growth and the run-down state of the economy, but the experiences of other countries suggest that it is the preferable option. South Africa cannot afford to repeat their mistakes. The mere possession of mineral wealth does not make a country rich, but South Africa has certain skills (entrepreneurial and technical) and a relatively efficient business and public sector, and should harness these in its new economic policies.

It is clear that conflicts over the role of the state will revolve around three broad issues — redistribution of wealth, ownership of the means of production, and the economic upliftment of blacks. Specific matters which will need to be addressed are those of land ownership and wage policy.

Redistribution

The specific private/public sector mix in any economy will be determined by the special characteristics of that country. In South Africa the special feature is the strong feeling of political, social and economic injustice and deprivation among blacks. Redistribution of incomes and wealth to rectify a historical legacy of extreme inequality will be a major driving force in post-apartheid politics.

An important issue relates to the economy's capacity for redistribution. South Africa is a middle-income developing country which has recorded a relatively poor economic performance in the 1970s and 1980s. The amount of wealth available for redistribution is limited, the proportion of wealthy individuals being small relative to the poor. Nor would there seem to be great scope for increasing personal and corporate taxation rates, which are already high by world standards. In fact, there is evidence that a lowering of tax rates would stimulate economic growth and hence raise the amount of tax revenue accruing to the state.

There are several reasons why economic growth in post-apartheid South Africa in itself would facilitate redistribution. The major reason is demographic and has been operating since the late 1960s: the growth rate of the white population is stagnating and this means that during rapid economic growth, whites will not be able to provide all the skilled labour required. Thus, black groups will find that their vertical occupational mobility will be facilitated, and with it a more equitable interracial distribution of income will emerge.

To illustrate this, figures show that the African share of personal income increased from approximately 20 per cent in 1970 to 25 per cent in 1975 and 29 per cent in 1980; the white share of total disposable income declined from 66,7 per cent in 1972 to 55,5 per cent in 1985; the poorest 40 per cent of the population increased their share of total income from 3,9 per cent in 1970 to 7,6 per cent in 1980; mean annual real earnings for Africans increased from R410 to R763 between 1971 and 1979 compared with a fall for whites over this period; and African real per capita incomes rose from R64 in 1970 to R108 in 1980. More recent figures show that the personal disposable incomes of the three black groups increased far more rapidly in real terms than did that of whites between 1972 and 1985; in fact, in the 1980s white real incomes have fallen.[40]

It should be noted that these trends occurred during a period of slow economic growth and that they would accelerate if growth rates increased. Indeed, Knight[41] argues that the share in national income of the poorest 40 per cent could be doubled by just two years of pre-1970 growth rates.

Yet, the degree of impatience among blacks is such that there are pressures for immediate redistribution. However, not only are the resources lacking for this, but the priority which ought to be attached to income redistribution *per se* is debatable.

In terms of resources, the state is unable to provide education, health and other services for all race groups at the level at present offered to whites. Thus, as Hartshorne shows in Chapter 10, the government has acknowledged that its programme for providing universal free and compulsory education to matriculation level cannot be achieved within the planned ten-year period. A new government would find a misfit between its egalitarian goals and its revenue resources, but some expenditure currently incurred because of apartheid could be channelled to these fields and other sources of finance could be found.

The cost of implementing apartheid is incalculable; clearly, the bloated bureaucracy could be cut substantially but, as alluded to above, a new government would be under pressure to reward its followers with jobs, as has happened in other countries. The defence budget could be cut — the opportunity costs of the Angola-Namibia operation have been immense — although obsolete equipment will have to be replaced once the arms embargo is lifted, and this will be costly. Nonetheless, expenditure could be diverted to education, health, pensions and housing. More rapid results, albeit of a limited nature, could also be achieved by the optimal utilization of currently underutilized white educational and health facilities.

Clearly, the efficient use of existing facilities and qualified personnel would contribute to the reduction of interracial gaps in educational and health standards. In education, too, the use of modern electronic aids should be explored as a means of rapid improvement of black standards.

Additional sources of revenue, however, will need to be found. Some

---

40 These figures are drawn from S. Devereaux, 'South African income distribution 1900–1980', *Working Paper no. 51*, South African Labour and Development Research Unit, Univ. of Cape Town, 1983; and a study by the Bureau of Market Research, Univ. of South Africa, quoted in *South African Digest*, 17 Oct. 1986.

41 J. B. Knight, *A comparative analysis of South Africa as a semi-industrialised developing country*, Unit for the Study of the African Economies, Inst. of Economics and Statistics, Oxford Univ., p. 31.

policy leads could be drawn from World Bank experience in Third World countries: the Bank found an 'untapped willingness of households to pay for education'.[42] The Bank recommends free education at primary level — something which is probably affordable in South Africa — with a combination of cost recovery, that is, fees, and selective scholarships at secondary and tertiary levels. Studies show that the state in Third World countries can sustain a substantial number of scholarships for needy secondary school pupils even if pupil numbers are large. The Bank also recommends the development of a credit market for education, that is, loans from financial institutions (guaranteed by the state because of high collection costs and default rates) where recipients would finance their current studies against future incomes. Another recommendation of the Bank is the encouragement of private and community schools.[43] A variant in South Africa would be for the government to encourage firms above a certain size to engage in the sort of corporate social responsibility programmes already followed by some of the larger companies. These are intended to upgrade the educational, housing and other welfare requirements of black employees and their families, and sometimes also of black communities.

National schemes which are essential are those for pensions and medical aid. Management could be provided by several different financial institutions but the clear advantage of a national pension scheme is that it would allow individuals to change employment without adversely affecting their pensions or becoming locked into the scheme of any particular employer, as is the case at present.

Given the existing financial constraints, some symbolic gesture by government might be necessary as at least a partial solution to the politics of redistribution. Of course, the repeal of all racial legislation would in itself be of tremendous symbolic value, but this would have to be backed by further action. A considerable amount of affirmative action is required in both the public and private sectors to ensure that blacks are able to participate in equal-opportunity policies, as is explained by Hugo in Chapter 7.

Although income inequalities must be tackled in the longer term, it is the eradication of the present high level of absolute poverty (based on some notion of a minimum subsistence level or similar measure) which should enjoy the highest priority. A type of basic-needs approach could be framed around the public provision of serviced sites in urban informal settlements and of water points in rural areas, coupled with a system of vouchers for access to basic goods and services or a negative income tax, that is, an

---

42 Knight, *A comparative analysis.*

43 G. Psacharopoulos, J. P. Ten and E. Jimenez, 'Financing education in developing countries', *IDS Bulletin*, vol. 1, no. 20, 1989, p. 55.

income subsidy. However, the ability of the economy to finance such a policy would require investigation. As mentioned earlier, a few years of rapid economic growth would lead to a swift increase in the income shares of the poorest 40 per cent while, in the short run, a redirection of public expenditure in fields such as housing, health and education could facilitate redistribution. In the long run, however, the greatest potential for reducing inequality would seem to lie in policies which equalize access to education and training facilities.

For any government the choice is between immediate redistribution and the maintenance and subsequent increase of production. Experience in other countries suggests that attempts at immediate redistribution not only reduce economic growth, but also tend to benefit the middle-income groups rather than the poor.[44] Economic growth, however, is critical both for future well-being and for redistribution. Continuous structural changes in socio-economic life are more important in promoting equality than are attempts at immediate redistribution; nationalization of enterprises, in particular, does little to benefit the poor.

Ownership of resources

There is little doubt that the question of ownership of enterprises and land will be a major issue in post-apartheid South Africa. The Freedom Charter of 1955 advocates the nationalization of mines, banks and 'monopoly' industry, but no specific commitment to such action is contained in the 1988 Constitutional Guidelines of the African National Congress, which make provision for public, private, co-operative and small-scale family sectors of the economy.[45] Nevertheless, state control of the so-called 'commanding heights of the economy' is often mentioned as a desirable goal in the literature,[46] reference being made in particular to the largest half-dozen conglomerates which are alleged to represent 'monopoly capital'.

The accuracy of this view requires careful consideration, since many of the operations of these conglomerates occur in highly competitive industrial sectors, for example, mining, automobile production, insurance, etc., and, moreover, it is difficult to establish ownership patterns with any precision. It is well known that the largest conglomerates together account for an overwhelming proportion of shares on the Johannesburg Stock Exchange, but the question is, who owns the conglomerates? Apart from large individual investors, shares are owned by public bodies, institutions (such as pension funds) and small investors. In the life assurance sector the firms

44 Knight, *A comparative analysis*, p. 32.

45 T. Lodge, 'The Lusaka amendments', *Leadership*, vol. 4, no. 7, 1988, p. 17.

46 A. Erwin, 'Towards a planned economy', *South African Labour Bulletin*, vol. 1, no. 14, 1989.

are owned by millions of policy-holders, the fastest growing market being among blacks. Thus, the nature of and alternatives to nationalization should be thoroughly investigated.

Nationalization could be accomplished in several ways, ranging from minority shareholding by the state, to majority or complete ownership without taking managerial control, to total ownership and management.[47] One alternative to nationalization would be to enforce the provisions of the Maintenance and Promotion of Competition Act and break up any operations of the conglomerates which do, in fact, constitute monopolies. More important, the costs and benefits of state as opposed to private ownership require close examination. The main interest of the government in a post-apartheid economic system, given the long period of poor economic growth which is likely to precede substantial political change, should be to create a climate favourable for the efficient operation of enterprises, to ensure that enterprises are profitable and that they contribute to public coffers by way of corporate taxes. Judging by the record elsewhere,[48] nationalization need not necessarily have beneficial effects on government revenue; indeed, it is likely to have a negative impact via adverse effects on efficiency, investor confidence and economic activity.

There are other good reasons why a post-apartheid government should proceed with caution. First, in order to encourage economic growth and create jobs, it is essential that investment be maintained at a high level. Thus business confidence is crucial, and is easily lost if nationalization features prominently in a political programme.

It is important to retain the confidence of foreign investors and the experience of Zimbabwe is instructive — links severed during UDI have not been restored since independence. Many multinational corporations (MNCs) have already disinvested from South Africa and will not return unless they gauge the investment climate to be favourable. If business confidence is sacrificed on the altar of political rhetoric, the post-apartheid government would have great difficulty in maintaining political stability because of growing unemployment and poverty.

Second, the large conglomerates and MNCs have instituted considerable programmes of equal opportunity employment and social responsibility, investing funds in fields usually outside the scope of company activities such as education, staff housing and community projects. It could well be preferable for government to persuade companies to step up these programmes,

---

[47] R. Davies, 'Nationalisation, socialisation and the Freedom Charter', Paper delivered at Conference on the Post-Apartheid economy in Southern Africa, Univ. of York, 1986.

[48] For example, the abysmal record of public enterprise in Africa is 'difficult to justify in terms of any objectives of a responsible government', quoted from Knight *Public enterprises*, p. 5.

as has been suggested above, rather than itself to take control.

Third, government might find the existence of six large conglomerates, in which so much economic power is concentrated, convenient.[49] An alliance with them through government representation on their boards, would enable the state to exercise enormous economic muscle in influencing capital accumulation and investment. Moreover, taxes paid by efficient private-sector conglomerates could well contribute more to government revenue than inefficient state ownership. For the post-apartheid state there would seem to be more urgent priorities than to seek to secure the 'commanding heights'; participation in equity or representation on major company boards, together with its macroeconomic policy instruments, would appear to provide government with sufficient power to influence private-sector behaviour and investment decisions.

Fourth, nationalization could operate against the weaker elements in society by having an adverse effect on the incomes of small investors and institutional investors such as pension funds. Workers would thus be financially disadvantaged.

From a redistribution point of view, workers might well gain more through having genuinely independent trade unions bargaining with the private sector than through state ownership. Another more beneficial system for workers would be through membership of producer co-operatives or participation in equity of companies.

The co-operative movement, of course, is well entrenched in South Africa, especially in the field of agricultural marketing, and this form of economic organization could play a larger role. However, the performance of co-operatives (at least at producer level) is patchy and generally less efficient than private firms.

For workers, participation in company equity could be a more promising alternative. Several employee share-ownership schemes are already in operation in South Africa, and what is now known as the 'share economy' deserves further attention. A variant of company-specific share-ownership schemes is for trade unions to adopt the Swedish model whereby they invest in a wider range of shares on behalf of members. This could be enforced by representation on company boards; again, Sweden might provide a model, workers there being entitled to elect two members to the boards of all companies employing more than twenty-five persons.

It is consistent with trends in both the CPEs and in Western democracies to consider co-operative and share-economy schemes as preferable to state ownership. Nevertheless, there are precedents, even in Western countries, for the nationalization of banks, financial institutions and mines. Some

---

49 McGrath and Maasdorp, 'Limits to redistribution'; and Davies, 'Nationalisation'.

degree of state ownership of enterprises might well be a political necessity, but it should be confined to existing public corporations and enterprises still to be established, for example, the beneficiation of minerals would add value and increase export earnings, and the state could play an active role (perhaps with 51 per cent holdings) in such schemes.

With regard to existing public corporations, a problem arises in that the present government has committed itself to a policy of privatization of public undertakings and state activities. Shares in Sasol and Iscor were offered to the public in 1979 and 1989 respectively, and other possibilities for privatization are Escom, Alusaf, Foskor, Sats and the Department of Posts and Telecommunications, while parts of the road network have been contracted out as toll roads. Public housing for Africans is being transferred to occupants under title. These steps have not been popular among trade unions and various black-dominated organizations, and it is necessary to examine the desirability of privatization in the South African context.

In the West the state has been accepted as the provider of pure public goods, but these do not include merit goods, that is, housing, health, education, welfare and pensions. The debate on the economic role of the state has gathered new impetus with the advent of privatization, and several empirical studies have compared the efficiency of private versus public production, especially of merit goods.

If a government sells the ownership rights of public or regulated goods and services, it will have to protect consumers (especially the poor) from higher prices and poor service. The best guarantee of consumer interests is that the privatized enterprise should operate in a competitive sector, although it is possible for the government to control prices in cases of monopoly. Some element of regulation is feasible, either through a delivery contract or regulatory law, while restrictions might also be placed on the rate of return accruing to such enterprises. In South Africa it is important for the state to retain its tradition of providing basic infrastructure and essential services to disadvantaged individuals. Some control over privatized enterprises is therefore necessary. The public has some legitimate concerns about privatization, for example, will people pay more for services and will the standard of services decline? If efficiency increases, prices can be kept down, but enterprises have to make profits, and consequently unprofitable services may be cut. The solution in such cases is for government to give direct subsidies to the company to maintain the services.

Blankart[50] finds limits to the contracting of government services especially in the case of 'sunk-cost goods', that is, services such as water and electricity which can be produced only with relatively large amounts of

---

[50] C. B. Blankart, 'Limits to privatisation', *European Economic Review*, no. 31, 1987, p. 349.

contract-specific, sunk-cost capital. Here the government has to maintain the right to interfere in the operations of the contractor who is then placed in much the same position as the previous public operator. Studies thus show no significant cost differences between public and private production in electricity, water distribution and railways.

However, there are significant cost differences in favour of private production in services using less sunk-cost capital, for example, bus transport, airways, public works and waste collection. Blankart[51] distinguishes between 'inspection goods', 'experience goods' and 'trust goods'. In the case of inspection goods, for example, raw materials, fuel and stationery, contracting out is relatively easy and this category should be privatized. Experience goods, such as consulting and auditing services, are also possible candidates for privatization based on customers' experience of previous contracts. In the case of trust goods, that is, intangible services such as justice, defence and public welfare, privatization is not suitable as output is evaluated by rule adherence and not by the development of new markets or technology. Blankart concludes that opportunities for privatization lie in the field of inspection and experience goods rather than in sunk-cost and trust goods.[52]

This has clear implications for South Africa. The political benefits of continued state ownership of key public corporations, particularly Escom and the railways, might well outweigh the doubtful economic benefits of privatization. Moreover, in order to promote income equality in a share-earning democracy, it is important to ensure that staff or worker organizations have preferential access to share purchasing. It is, of course, also possible for the state or other public bodies themselves to remain important shareholders.

In any country as unequal as South Africa, it is essential that privatization not be seen as a deflection of a commitment by the state to parity in the provision of physical and social infrastructure. Gouws[53] raises the valid question whether many of the services currently provided by the state need to be provided by the state alone. What seems to be required is a creative policy in which both the public and private sectors provide the goods or services, with the state guaranteeing the provision of essential services at certain standards and prices to all communities and areas.

The private sector itself could also play an important role in spreading ownership. Bethlehem, for instance, makes a strong case for firms,

51 Blankart, 'Limits to privatisation', p. 350.

52 Blankart, 'Limits to privatisation', p. 351.

53 Gouws, *The growth of the public sector*, p. 7.

acting in their own self-interest, to enter into a 'social accord' with African-dominated institutions (such as trade unions) to correct the power imbalance in the economy.[54] He sees this as a serious short-term problem and argues that a social accord would provide for a rearrangement of corporate ownership whilst leaving the functional economy as undisturbed as possible. The Anglo American sale of General Mining to Afrikaner interests in the 1960s and the partnership schemes pioneered by Rupert are possible models. He also mentions other possibilities, including consumer and producer co-operatives, kibbutz-type farms, and the establishment of interracial partnerships. He acknowledges, however, that this would be a short-term programme of redistribution and that long-term redistribution would be best accomplished by high rates of economic growth.

In some countries which appear most successfully to have followed a redistribution-with-growth policy, substantial land reform played an important role. This was the case with both Taiwan and South Korea. The question of land ownership is an emotional issue in South Africa and clearly will have to be addressed. Statistics on land use are poor, but it appears that about 60 per cent of the total area of the country is in the hands of private white owners. This could be redressed in several ways without the formation of state farms which, judging from their record in the CPEs, would be a serious error.

First, tax laws which encourage individuals to own several farms and laws which restrict the breaking up of farms into smaller units could be amended. Second, any farms offered for sale could be purchased by government at market prices and redistributed, or the government could follow a limited programme of land purchase. Kassier believes that liquidations are likely to increase and that land prices consequently should fall to a point where market values equal productive values; it is at this point that the state should purchase.[55] Third, an element of compulsion could be applied, for example, absentee white-owned farms could be expropriated (with compensation) and redistributed, or the number or properties per individual owner could be restricted (in Yugoslavia it is three) and the land thus released could be redistributed to blacks at a price.

Funds for the purchase of land for redistribution could perhaps be obtained from multilateral and bilateral aid agencies. Such aid could also be directed towards achieving parity in education, health and urban services, and in black economic empowerment. A Marshall Aid-type programme for post-apartheid South Africa is sometimes mentioned; this could be viewed

---

54 R. Bethlehem, 'Social accord', *Leadership*, vol. 3, no. 8, 1989, p. 69.

55 E. Kassier, 'A richer yield', *Leadership*, vol. 3, no. 6, 1987, p. 51.

as a form of reparation from the West for the damaging economic effects of sanctions and disinvestment, but whether South Africa would be considered sufficiently attractive for such a programme is doubtful. The minimum condition necessary would be the adoption of liberal-cum-social democratic policies.

If land redistribution is accompanied by falling levels of output, society will not gain. Agricultural output (especially of food) must be maintained and expanded. This is an essential requirement for the future economic well-being of South Africa because of balance of payments considerations. With shrinking ore reserves, gold mining cannot remain the prime earner of foreign exchange in the long term. At the same time, demographers project that the population will grow to between 58 and 68 million by 2020, and any shortfall in food supply would necessitate imports. The combined effect on the balance of payments of declining gold exports and increased food imports would be severe, especially if manufacturing exports were not competitive on world markets. It is vital, therefore, that the land be farmed efficiently and productively. Kassier argues that, with only modest increases in productivity, the demand for food could be met with less land than is at present farmed.

However, this would require greatly improved extension services for African farmers.[56] To be avoided is the experience of farms purchased for the homelands; hitherto productive land there has often deteriorated rapidly.

The factors which together have made farming less financially attractive than in the past also require examination. Many white farmers today are not making profits, and incomes vary immensely depending on crop, market prices and climate.[57] The climatic factor would have a significant bearing on land redistribution, the possibilities being greater in intensive than in extensive farming areas. For example, the carrying capacity (in livestock units per hectare) of land in Gordonia is lower than in the Cape Midlands which, in turn, is lower than in the Natal Midlands. The potential for dividing farms in the more arid districts into smaller units is clearly less than in regions of higher rainfall.

The major demand by Africans for land may, however, be in urban rather than rural areas, that is, for residential, not agricultural, purposes. The majority of Africans will soon be urbanized and the proportion of households committed to serious, full-time, commercial farming could be lower than anticipated. Thus the granting of freehold tenure in urban areas and the

---

56 Kassier, 'A richer yield'.

57 Wealth in the farming community is highly skewed. Of the total gross income from farming, 15 per cent is produced by the top one per cent, 35 per cent by the top 5 per cent, and 75 per cent by the top 30 per cent. The number of commercial farmers peaked in the 1950s and is now less than half of that figure; during the same period, in contrast, the mean size of farms has more than doubled, Kassier, 'A richer yield', pp. 45, 47.

provision of normal mortgage bond financing would be key aspects of asset redistribution.

Rural policy, however, will have to play an extremely important role, not only in ensuring continued food surpluses but in absorbing the labour force. Agriculture will remain a key sector, and sound government policy would include the redirection of marketing, credit and other inputs, as well as extension services to small African farmers. The lack of these services at present constitutes a severe structural obstacle in the way of Africans running their own farms successfully, and special financial institutions might have to be established to serve the small-scale farming and business sectors. The land-tenure system in the 'homelands' also constitutes a barrier to efficient commercial farming, and a market in land should be created. On the periphery of the major metropolitan centres and towns, it might be possible to develop small private gardens (allotments or kleinegarten) as in Britain and West Germany; indeed, land near the airport in Durban has been made available to market gardeners.

Wage policy

Continued economic growth would of itself reduce interracial income disparities in the long run since, as explained earlier, it would necessitate greater vertical mobility and hence higher-income positions for blacks. The skilled/unskilled wage gap, however, might be difficult to bridge. Skilled wages might well be artificially high because of the scarcity rent enjoyed by whites as a result of past discrimination in employment and education, but even in a post-apartheid economy the question of international mobility for certain skills (especially in high-technology fields) would remain. As Knight[58] points out, it will be very important to retain the high-level manpower which manages the economy, and this cannot be done if their real incomes are squeezed.

On the unskilled market, supply greatly exceeds demand; this is not surprising given the Third World demographic profile. Labour is the abundant factor of production, and consequently labour-intensive methods are desirable. It might be politically difficult for a post-apartheid government to resist worker demands for at least some degree of 'wage levelling', but several important consequences would occur. First, dysfunctions operating in the CPEs could manifest themselves. Second, 'wage levelling' could lead to greater unemployment. This would occur if the state set minimum wages for unskilled labour above market-clearing levels, and this encouraged firms to use capital-intensive techniques. Experience has shown that high minimum wages lead to the creation of an urban élite in paid employment,

---

58 Knight, *A comparative analysis'*, p. 30.

protected through unionization from competition from the mass of out-siders (urban and rural unemployed) who would be prepared to sell their labour for lower wages but who are frozen out of the labour market. Another effect of high minimum wages could be to reduce international competit-iveness. However, if unskilled wages are left only to market forces, they may well be below poverty levels, and one would not wish to advocate a 'dark Satanic mills' syndrome in South African industry. The negative income tax is theoretically preferable to a national minimum wage.

Growing unemployment will be a major problem, and conflicting pres-sures will exist between policies to increase wages and policies to increase employment. In many Third World countries governments have found it politically expedient to expand employment in the public sector, but this is unproductive, misallocates resources and ultimately reduces economic growth and employment. Employment-creation policies could be framed, which would include the stimulation (by deregulation) of small business and the informal sector. The latter could grow if it is able to compete with goods and services produced in the formal sector. The policy could also include a public works programme (PWP). Indeed, the PWP which was implemented in the 1930s to solve the poor white problem could be rep-licated on a larger scale, and perhaps represents the best way of creating employment and alleviating poverty. Such a programme can have both short-term results and substantial medium- and long-term benefits in the form of acquisition of skills and provision of infrastructure, both of which are among the pre-conditions for renewed economic growth. A PWP could be introduced both in urban and rural areas and could be widely dispersed geographically, but it would require good organization, planning and man-agement, as well as the adoption of realistic techniques and a sustained political commitment. A PWP should be capable of being phased out rapidly as economic recovery occurs and unemployment falls to acceptable levels. An unpublished study shows that if 10 per cent of the capital budget is al-located to a PWP, between 1,8 and 3,3 million jobs could be created, which would mop up current unemployment.[59]

Conclusion

It is clear that any preoccupation on the part of a post-apartheid govern-ment with issues such as nationalization would run counter to economic reforms instituted in the West, the CPEs and the Third World in the 1980s. The economy already has a considerable state sector — the public sector accounts for some 35 per cent of GDP — and this, together with monetary,

---

[59] An unpublished study by I. Abedian and B. Standish for the Urban Foundation, 1986.

fiscal and other policy instruments, gives the state an enormous amount of economic power. How that power is used, is critical. This chapter argues that the welfare goals of a new social contract would be most effectively met if the state were to concern itself with black economic empowerment by raising the share of the black majority in asset ownership and in managerial positions, and in promoting equality of access in employment, social services and physical infrastructure. The market must be nurtured as the engine of growth in an efficient, mixed economy.

This would be in accordance with social democratic practices in Western Europe, and nothing less than this would encourage social harmony in a deeply divided country. That this is a realistic assessment is supported by the statements of scholars from divergent philosophical schools. For example, Lombard acknowledges that 'an unadulterated libertarian ideology or political philosophy would not be fully in accord with many fundamental realities of South Africa'[60] and that the role of the state in the economy will be greater than libertarians would wish, while Innes argues that the future of South Africa is dependent upon finding that accommodation between the demands of radical workers and conservative businessmen which a social democratic system offers.[61] The state has a major responsibility to redress the inequities of the present economic framework, but should do so in a manner which takes heed of the experiences of economic systems and policies in other countries so that the mistakes made there are not repeated: there is always a delicate balance between equity and efficiency goals, and the framers of economic policy in a reformist South Africa will have to perform a particularly nimble egg-dance.

---

[60] J. A. Lombard, 'The evolution of the theory of economic policy', *South African Journal of economics*, vol. 4, no. 52, p. 330.

[61] D. Innes, 'Social contract', *The high road*, Cape Town: Leadership Publications, 1988, p. 36.

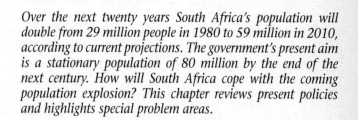

12 Population policy

Charles Simkins

> *Over the next twenty years South Africa's population will double from 29 million people in 1980 to 59 million in 2010, according to current projections. The government's present aim is a stationary population of 80 million by the end of the next century. How will South Africa cope with the coming population explosion? This chapter reviews present policies and highlights special problem areas.*

Introduction

Population policy in its broadest meaning refers to government action affecting the three main demographic variables — fertility, mortality and migration. A great deal of what the government does in these areas can be considered part of population policy. Its entire health effort is obviously relevant, as is state intervention designed to influence the spatial distribution of the population. Also important are urban and rural development policy and education.

More narrowly, population policy refers to a specific package of government policies assembled to achieve defined demographic goals. Until recently, population policy in South Africa in this narrow sense has been fairly limited, confined largely to local adaptation of programmes adopted in Europe and the United States. It has also been directed exclusively towards fertility. In 1974, World Population Year, the government adopted an official countrywide family planning programme.[1]

Fertility policy options fall into two categories:

1. supply-side measures, which emphasize the supply of the means to fertility control (contraception, sterilization and abortion), focusing on costs, availability and distribution; and
2. demand-side measures, which concentrate on the determinants of demand for fertility control. Here socio-economic developmental variables are important (the organization of production, education, the

---

[1] Science Committee of the President's Council, *Report of the Science Committee of the President's Council on demographic trends in South Africa*, PC 1/1983, Cape Town: The Govt. Printer, 1983.

status of women and so forth) as well as fiscal incentives and more direct controls, such as prohibition of marriage for people under a certain
age.

Until the early 1980s the South African programme was predominantly
supply-side oriented. There was a modest advertising component designed
to stimulate effective demand.

The framework for a radical revision of population policy was created by
the President's Council report on demographic trends in South Africa. This
introduced three major innovations:

1. It brought mortality and migration within the scope of an explicit
   population policy for the first time.

2. It shifted the emphasis in the analysis of fertility from the supply side
   to the demand side, recognizing that improvements in the quality of
   life are necessary to lower black fertility.

3. As a result of this shift in emphasis, there was a shift from the narrow
   to the broad conception of population policy. The report indicated that
   such a policy has to concern itself with health, education, economic
   development, urbanization, housing and community development.

Reorganization within the civil service followed the publication of the
report. The Department of Health and Welfare became the Department of
National Health and Population Development, with a mandate to implement a Population Development Programme (PDP). A Chief Directorate
of Population Development was created, supervising Directorates of Development Strategy, Demographic and Population Analysis, and Information,
Education and Communication.[2] At the level of policy debate, an important
initiative of the PDP was to convene a conference on population development in southern Africa in October 1988. This chapter is based on the
papers delivered to that conference, relating them to the wider demographic
literature.

The shape of the current policy debate

An analysis of the 106 papers delivered to the Population Development
Conference by subject indicates the distribution of concerns of the population policy establishment. (See Table 12.1.)

The conference was conceived partly as an extension exercise. Particular
groups — the urban, rural and community development communities, the
private sector and women's organizations — were clearly targeted, hence
the large number of papers in these fields. This is clear testimony to the

---

[2] Dept. of National Health and Population Development, *Annual Report of the Department of National Health and Population Development*, Cape Town: The Govt. Printer, 1987, 1988.

Table 12.1:   Analysis of the 106 papers delivered to the
Population Development Conference (Oct.1988) by subject

A	Fertility	7
	Contraception	1
B	Mortality	7
	Health	2
C	Migration	3
	Urban/rural nexus	1
	Urbanization and housing	12
	Rural development	14
D	Economic development	3
	Regional development	3
	Employment	1
E	Education	6
	Community development	17
	Women	21
	Private sector	8
F	Monitoring and indicators	6

development/demand-side orientation of current policy. This chapter will argue that the PDP may be paying insufficient attention to the supply side and technical demographic issues. Consequently, it risks losing a demographic perspective on development issues.

To make this case in detail and to understand more precisely the gaps and deficiencies in the present approach, it is necessary to consider separately each main area: fertility, mortality, migration, population growth and economic development and monitoring.

Fertility

The objectives of the PDP on fertility are clear. They are:

▷ to achieve a stationary population of 80 million by the end of the next century; and

▷ to achieve a total fertility rate of two for the population as a whole by the year 2010.[3]

Why these should be desirable goals depends on a view about the relationship between population growth and economic development, itself requiring critical analysis. The direction of policy, however, if not the quantifiable goals, is in line with demographic orthodoxy which holds that there are benefits in reducing fertility from very high levels.

---

[3] B. Schoeman (Dept. of National Health and Population Development), 'The necessity of monitoring a population development programme', Population Development Conference, Johannesburg, Oct. 1988.

What are the facts of fertility at present? Two leading South African demographers, Sadie and Mostert, have produced the estimates of total fertility rates between 1980 and 1985 shown in Table 12.2.

Table 12.2: Estimates of total fertility rates (1980–5)

	Sadie	Mostert
Whites	2,08	2,06
Coloureds	3,24	3,07
Asians	2,78	2,65
Africans	5,38	5,60

Sources:
W. P. Mostert (HSRC), 'Levels and trends in fertility in South Africa'; and J. L. Sadie (Bureau of Market Research, Univ. of Pretoria), 'A reconstruction and projection of demographic movements in the RSA and TBVC countries', Population Development Conference, Johannesburg, Oct. 1988.

Even for the coloured and Asian groups, for whom there are reasonably reliable statistics, the discrepancy in the estimates is noticeable. It is greater in the case of African people, where many births are not registered.

The African average conceals considerable spatial variations. Mostert and Hofmeyr[4] put the total fertility rate for African people outside the homelands at approximately four and the Department of National Health and Population Development reported a total fertility rate of 2,8 for African people in the PWV region in 1985.[5] This implies total fertility rates of close to or exceeding six in the remoter rural homeland areas.

Even with rather shaky information on aggregate levels of fertility, it is possible to survey the socio-economic determinants of fertility. The Human Sciences Research Council (HSRC) conducted a World Fertility Survey type of investigation outside the homelands in 1981–2.[6] Statistical analysis led to the following conclusions about African marital fertility in these areas:

▷ The average desired family size was 4,3 children, close to the actual total fertility rate (TFR) outside the homelands. (It is not reported whose desires are reflected. In the course of a fertility transition, the average family size desired by women is usually lower than that wanted by men.) Of currently married women between the ages of fifteen and forty-nine, 57 per cent reported current use of contraception. (The corresponding figure for coloured people was 73 per cent, Asians, 78 per

---

[4] W. P. Mostert and B. E. Hofmeyr (HSRC), 'Socio-economic factors affecting fertility in the developing countries and of the developing population groups in South Africa', Population Development Conference, Johannesburg, Oct. 1988.

[5] Dept. of National Health and Population Development, *Annual Report*, 1987, 1988.

[6] Mostert and Hofmeyr, 'Socio-economic factors affecting fertility'.

cent and whites, 84 per cent).

▷ Education, occupation and urban/rural residence can be expected to affect fertility. Mostert and Hofmeyr[7] conclude from survey evidence that a negative relationship between a wife's education and marital fertility exists if she has received post-primary education. The effect of a husband's education is in the same direction, but stronger. Long-standing urban residents have lower fertility, but migration to urban areas from rural areas in itself does not reduce marital fertility significantly. Finally, slightly more women who work use contraceptives than those who do not.

A more detailed picture of contraceptive use among African women in the PWV area is provided by Du Plessis.[8] Here never-married (rather than currently married) women aged between fifteen and forty-nine were surveyed. Knowledge of contraceptive methods was found to be virtually universal, though many respondents did not know of sterilization — particularly vasectomies — as a contraceptive method. Forty-six per cent of the sample was currently using contraception. This is close to the Mostert and Hofmeyr[9] estimate for non-homeland areas as a whole.

More surprisingly, the rate of contraceptive use among women not wanting more children was only 60 per cent, pointing to a substantial unmet need. (To a lesser extent, this can be found among other groups. The figures for coloureds, Asians and whites in 1983 — all non-homeland areas — were 73 per cent, 82 per cent and 89 per cent, respectively.) Use of contraceptives declines with age, rises with education and up to four living children, and also correlates, as expected, with employment status and childhood place of residence.

An important issue is the persistence of attitudes favouring fecundity among African people. Preston-Whyte et al.[10] discuss the issue in relation to Zulu-speaking people in and around Durban. They conclude that traditional ideas persist even among the most sophisticated townspeople, though they may be modified to cope with new circumstances.

An important factor is the traditional approach to marriage, with its unhurried negotiations between families and often slow accumulation of bridewealth. With far from complete contraceptive cover among the young,

---

[7] Mostert and Hofmeyr, 'Socio-economic factors affecting fertility'.

[8] G. Du Plessis (HSRC), 'Contraceptive trends in South Africa', Population Development Conference, Johannesburg, Oct. 1988.

[9] Mostert and Hofmeyr, 'Socio-economic factors affecting fertility'.

[10] E. Preston-Whyte, M. Zondi, G. Mavundla and H. Gumede (Univ. of Natal), 'Teenage pregnancy, whose problem? Realities and prospects for action in KwaZulu/Natal', Population Development Conference, Johannesburg, Oct. 1988.

a high pre-marital fertility rate is inevitable. Among many groups, this is the occasion for formal condemnation, but practical acceptance, especially since fertility continues to be culturally valued.

A second important issue is the impact of nationalist sentiment on fertility decisions. Here it will be important to distinguish between superficial political rhetoric and the real determinants of fertility decisions. (In the case of white people, nationalist sentiment can have had very little real impact on fertility decisions.) Analysis of the effects on African people should take account of the real interests at stake. Sadie's[11] population estimates imply that 75 per cent of the population was African in mid-1989. Even if African fertility were to fall instantly to the average level of whites, coloureds and Asians (a TFR of 2,5), this proportion would continue to grow because of the greater momentum within the African population. Nothing will change this situation except massive and racially-selective increases in mortality. In terms of demographic dominance, therefore, the position of the African population is assured. No further advantage can be gained by increasing the proportion slightly and there are likely to be substantial advantages to a lower fertility rate from the point of view of African incomes. A rational African nationalist would therefore seek to reduce the African fertility rate rather than to maintain or increase it.

On both these issues, more detailed work remains to be done.

Existing literature lacks information on the supply of the means of fertility control through the public and private sectors and an assessment of the efficiency of the pattern of supply. While supply should not be allowed to run ahead of demand, this does not remove the need for careful monitoring of the pattern of supply, especially in the light of Du Plessis's[12] findings about the high incidence of unmet need.

A useful account of the highly organized Taiwanese approach to this issue is contained in Chang.[13] Taiwan has experienced one of the quickest fertility transitions ever. In twenty years, the net reproduction rate fell from 2,27 to less than one.

Mortality

Estimates of mortality rates between 1980 and 1985 have been made as shown in Table 12.3.

Mortality analysis is not well developed in South Africa, despite the fact

---

[11] Sadie, 'A reconstruction and projection of demographic movements'.

[12] Du Plessis, 'Contraceptive trends'.

[13] Ming-Chen Chang (Taiwan Provincial Inst. of Family Planning), 'The attainment of family planning targets: the example of Taiwan', Population Development Conference, Johannesburg, Oct. 1988.

Table 12.3:   Estimates of mortality rates (1980–5)

	Sadie	Mostert
Life expectancy at birth		
Male		
Whites	66,8	67,3
Coloureds	55,4	56,5
Asians	63,1	62,8
Africans	55,1	58,7
Female		
Whites	74,3	74,7
Coloureds	63,5	64,0
Asians	69,8	69,3
Africans	62,5	62,7
Infant mortality rate (per 1 000)		
Whites	13	13
Coloureds	56	60
Asians	19	20
Africans	82	68

Sources:
W. P. Mostert (HSRC), 'Levels and trends in fertility in South Africa'; and J. L. Sadie (Bureau of Market Research, Univ. of Pretoria), 'A reconstruction and projection of demographic movements in the RSA and TBVC countries', Population Development Conference, Johannesburg, Oct. 1988.

that our mortality rates are high for our level of development.[14] The only useful study presented to the Population and Development Conference was that which investigated the relationship between infant and child mortality (the latter referring to children over the age of one and under the age of five) and fertility and socio-economic factors.[15] Data collected from coloured, Asian and African women under the age of thirty-five showed the following:

▷ For African women, infant and child mortality is significantly higher for children born to mothers under the age of seventeen. For older women, there is a trend towards higher infant mortality as the age of the mother at the time of birth and as parity (beyond three) increases.

▷ In accordance with international findings, infant mortality rises when the average birth interval is less than two years.

▷ There is a large difference in child mortality between educated and uneducated coloured and African women.

14 C. E. W. Simkins, 'Mortality rates compared', *Energos 15*, Cape Town: Mobil Southern Africa, 1988.

15 J. P. H. Rossouw and B. E. Hofmeyr (HSRC), 'Relationships between child deaths, fertility and related socio-economic factors among the black, coloured and Indian population groups in South Africa', Population Development Conference, Johannesburg, Oct. 1988.

▷ Rural residence increases infant and child mortality for African and coloured people, though the effect in the case of coloured people is marginal.

Rossouw and Hofmeyr[16] rather incautiously conclude that unless lower fertility and better socio-economic conditions are achieved, health services are unlikely to succeed in reducing either fertility or mortality to low levels. This goes beyond the evidence they cite; there is no reason to suppose that, even if nothing else changes, an improvement in rural health services will not reduce infant and child mortality. It is clear that the great divide in infant mortality experience is between African people in rural areas and all other people. To take but one example of the evidence which has recently come to light, Donaldson,[17] on the basis of the 1985 Transkei sample census, estimates the infant mortality rate at 31 per thousand in the urban and peri-urban areas and 94 per thousand in the rural areas.

The urban figure is close to estimates of urban infant mortality in other urban areas in South Africa. Much higher rural infant mortality is a consequence, not so much of the general level of development, as of considerable social disorganization and low levels of health services in the rural areas. These are circumstances which will not necessarily improve if real income per capita rises or even if apartheid comes to an end. They will have to be addressed by specific programmes.

Some theorists have supposed that high levels of infant and child mortality keep fertility levels high, as households seek to be certain of raising a certain number of children to maturity. As experience of low infant mortality levels accumulates in the urban areas, this effect can be expected to disappear. But one may expect its persistence in rural areas for some time to come.

In mortality analysis, as well as in fertility analysis, studies of health delivery with an analysis of their achievements and limitations are lacking. Too exclusive a focus on the broad developmental picture can result in neglect of the serious task of improving the health system. Here again, studies of health facilities with an analysis of their achievements and limitations are lacking. Too exclusive a focus on the broad developmental picture can result in neglect of the important task of improving the health system, a subject which is analysed in Chapter 9.

Migration, urbanization and urban and rural development

If the quantitative analysis of fertility and mortality and their determinants

---

[16] Rossouw and Hofmeyr, 'Relationships between child deaths'.

[17] A. Donaldson, 'Fertility and mortality estimates for the Republic of Transkei based on the 1985 Sample Census', *Report 2.5*, Umtata: Dept. of Commerce and Industry, Govt. of Transkei, 1988.

is underdeveloped, a serious study of migration has yet to begin. The only data set from which gross migration flows can be estimated is contained in the answers to the question in the 1980 Population Census: 'Where did you live five years ago?' Central Statistical Services has not published tabulations of the answers, but Zietsman[18] has analysed the data tapes, producing a picture of a rather complex process of circular migration by African people.

The importance of understanding these movements is pointed out by Prothero[19] in his study of population mobility in sub-Saharan Africa. He argues that policy measures should not be concerned so much with long-term population redistribution as with stable mobility systems based on long-term circulation and its effects on the rural economy and investment in agriculture. In this process, the role of small and intermediate towns and their interaction with the rural economies of their immediate hinterlands have to be considered. Circulatory systems still exist and have important economic effects which need study.

It is possible to obtain net migration estimates from successive population censuses. Given the substantial, but uncertain, underenumeration, particularly of the African population, these estimates are at best only a rough indication of the balance of inmigration and outmigration to the regions studied. They can be used to provide a context for other studies — for example, population removals — but no further quantitative analysis can be based on them.

For this reason, attention has been concentrated on studies of population distribution between urban and rural areas and between particular metropolitan areas. Spies has produced estimates and projections of urbanization, which can be compared with mine. (See Table 12.4.)

The estimates and projections are not greatly different for whites, Asians and coloureds and can be put down to differences in the adjustments made to the 1980 population census counts. In the case of African people, the annual rate of growth of the urban population projected by Spies is 4,8 per cent; my projected rate is 4,3 per cent. I expect slower population growth in the PWV area than Spies. Our estimates for the three smaller metropolitan areas are much closer.

Under these circumstances, how are we to conceptualize the context and tasks of urban and rural development and to assess their demographic

18 L. Zietsman, 'Regional patterns of migration', *South African Geographical Journal*, vol. 17, no. 2, 1988, pp. 85–99.

19 R. M. Prothero (Dept. of National Health and Population Development), 'The evolution of population mobility in Africa south of the Sahara', Population Development Conference, Johannesburg, Oct. 1988.

Table 12.4: Estimates and projections of urbanization

| | Urban dwellers (thousands) | | | |
| | Spies | | Simkins | |
Population group	1980	2010	1980	2010
Whites	3 965	5 111	4 096	5 136
Coloureds	1 983	3 467	2 139	3 832
Asians	725	1 130	764	1 196
Africans	8 500	35 028	9 150	32 703
Area				
PWV	5 908	23 556	6 072	16 277
Durban	1 956	8 056	2 074	8 036
Cape Town	1 790	5 097	1 986	4 589
Port Elizabeth	697	2 035	687	1 762

Sources:
P. H. Spies (Univ. of Stellenbosch), 'Rural–urban interaction in South Africa', Population Development Conference, Johannesburg, Oct. 1988; and C. E. W. Simkins, 'An Urban Foundation demographic model: phase three' (Unpublished report), Johannesburg: Urban Foundation, 1989.

context? Let us first look at the rural side. The most interesting paper presented to the Population Development Conference[20] makes the following important points:

▷ South African agriculture is divided into a relatively efficient, capital-intensive and commercially-oriented white sector and a subsistence-oriented African sector. White commercial farming produced an output of R1 298 per worker (R119 per hectare) compared with African earnings of R65 per worker (R34 per hectare) in the mid-1980s.

▷ Despite this dualism, evidence is emerging both from Zimbabwe and South Africa that high levels of productivity are generally related to areas of favourable environmental conditions and support systems, irrespective of the farming mode (for example, large-scale commercial farming versus farming on communal land). It shows that the smallholder farmer can successfully grow a wide range of crops, and that smallholder support programmes yield viable returns.

▷ The position of commercial farmers has deteriorated in recent years. The ratios of gross farm income to total costs and investment to total debt have declined. A return to more labour-intensive methods can be expected.

---

[20] J. van Rooyen (Development Bank of Southern Africa), 'Thoughts on the role and contribution of Southern Africa's agriculture to rural and economic development: conditions for growth', Population Development Conference, Johannesburg, Oct. 1988.

▷ Agricultural policy should aim at unifying the existing dual structure, based on a range of programmes designed to support both subsistence and commercial farmers. Restrictions on access to land need to be removed, entailing substantial amendments to the Land Acts.

Van Rooyen's approach to politically sensitive issues is cautious and the following additional points need to be made:

▷ African outmigration from the rural areas outside the homelands was greater between 1980 and 1985 than during any other five-year period since 1920. About a million and half more people moved out of these areas than moved into them. The parts of the country from which the largest movements took place were the Orange Free State, Natal, Eastern Transvaal and Northern Transvaal, areas in which labour tenancy has been concentrated.[21]

▷ Unlike the 1960s and 1970s, when a smaller net outmigration from the farms showed up mainly as inmigration into homeland rural areas and dense settlements, inmigration in the 1980s has been heavily concentrated in the homeland parts of the metropolitan areas: the Durban periphery, the northern PWV (Pretoria, Witwatersrand, Vereeniging), and Botshabelo near Bloemfontein in particular. There was also substantial net inmigration to the Cape Town metropolitan region.

▷ How much of these movements was the result of rural push factors is debatable, but it is likely that a reform and stabilization of tenancy relationships rather than a reduction in their number would have lowered the rate of rural outmigration considerably.

It is unlikely that any rural development programme can restore the former labour absorptive capacity of farms outside the homelands. The cost of restoring even some of it will be much higher than if the policies of the last thirty years had been replaced by the non-racial access rules and reform of the tenancy system. We shall bear much of the cost of our history of rural apartheid in the urban areas in years to come.

▷ Even given the projected rise in the African urban population, the African rural population is projected to continue to increase. The population on farms outside the homelands was estimated at 3,2 million in 1985, while the homeland population outside the metropolitan fringe and formally proclaimed urban areas (the homeland 'rural' population) was estimated at 9,3 million, of whom at least 2,1 million lived in dense settlements. Projecting the population on farms outside the homelands to stabilize and then decline slightly to 3 million by 2010 means that

---

[21] Simkins, 'An Urban Foundation demographic model'.

the homeland rural population must rise to 12,5 million, of whom at least 4,3 million will live in dense settlements.

These projections reproduce the underlying imbalance in the rural populations between the homeland and non-homeland areas. What actually happens at this level will depend on rural policy taken as a whole. It is sometimes assumed that urbanization will render the rural development issue less pressing, but the projections show clearly that this supposition is false.

In many ways the urban issues are more obvious and better researched. Government policies from the time of Union have aimed at stemming African urbanization.[22] Publication of the President's Council report on urbanization and the abolition of the pass laws in 1986 merely confirms and implements the recommendations made by the Fagan Commission forty years earlier. Now the issue is how to cope with a rate of inmigration which should have occurred some time ago.

A major concern must be the breaking of existing constraints on productive activities and the provision of services. Strelitz and Morkel[23] identify as constraints on housing delivery the timeous identification of land for township development, a suitable public financial framework for the delivery of bulk infrastructure, the provision of home loan finance, and a revision of local authority attitudes towards housing standards. Progress is needed on all four fronts to create an efficient supply of housing with which effective demand — determined by demographic and income factors — can interact to produce a rapid increase in urban housing stock.

Missing almost entirely from the Population Development Conference papers on urbanization are demographic projections. Kok and Gelderblom[24] consider the prediction of migration and urbanization only to dismiss attempts at it as futile. But no one can work without expectations. It is true that the longer the prediction period, the more uncertainty there must be in the predictions. Nonetheless, the establishment of a range of possible futures serves to orient present policy discussions. And predictive models can always be constructed so that they can be revised as new data become available.

The incorporation of new information into an existing set of expectations yields new insights which can never be extracted from an agnostic

---

[22] A. Wessels (Univ. of the Orange Free State), 'Die rol van politiese faktore in die formulering van die Suid-Afrikaanse verstedelikingsbeleid: 'n historiese perspektief', Population Development Conference, Johannesburg, Oct. 1988.

[23] J. Strelitz and M. Morkel (The Urban Foundation), 'Urbanisation and low income housing in South Africa', Population Development Conference, Johannesburg, Oct. 1988.

[24] P. C. Kok and D. Gelderblom (HSRC/Univ. of South Africa), 'Perspectives on the patterns of urbanisation and metropolisation in South Africa', Population Development Conference, Johannesburg, Oct. 1988.

approach. Moreover, purely demographic work (including more creative use of data on urban fertility and mortality and new survey material on migration) can be integrated with work on income distribution within and across regions to achieve a more refined understanding of the determinants of population distribution. All this is needed both to gain a better understanding of what might be achieved by way of increased private sector production, and of more creative responses by local authorities to the provision of amenities and services. The debate needs to move on from the broad direction of policies to a more detailed discussion of public policy adjustments and the improvements which can be expected from them.

Given the introduction of a more liberal policy framework for urbanization in 1986, it can be expected that the proportion of African households split by the migrant labour system will decline. What will be the effect of this on African fertility? Probably very little on marital fertility, since the historical evidence suggests that the rise of the migrant labour system did little to lower marital fertility. But a decreasing role for the migrant labour system may mean that the average age at marriage among African people, which has risen sharply since the turn of the century, will start to drop again, exerting upward pressure on fertility levels. Even so, the effect is likely to be small since, firstly, African extra-marital fertility is high in relation to marital fertility, and, secondly, only about a quarter of African married couples live apart at present because of the migrant labour system and this proportion is likely to drop rather slowly.

One therefore expects a possible small rise in fertility associated with a decline in the migrant labour system.

Population and economic development

Having considered separately the key individual demographic magnitudes — fertility, mortality and migration — we can now return to the central issue underlying the debate on population policy. What is the relationship between population growth and economic development?

We are a considerable way from constructing models for the South African economy. Two papers delivered at the Population Development Conference considered the matter from the government's point of view only. Gouws[25] contrasted the implications of the HSRC's high and low population projections with the PDP's target projections. He considered the difference that would be made to government expenditure on education,

---

[25] N. B. Gouws (Dept. of National Health and Population Development), 'The implications of too rapid population growth on the economy of a country, with special reference to the position of South Africa', Population Development Conference, Johannesburg, Oct. 1988.

manpower training, health (including family planning), economic development, housing, development of urban and rural areas, and social welfare
(pensions, allowances, etc.).

He concluded that between 1985 and 2010, the government would save
R189 billion at constant 1987/8 prices if the population growth path were
reduced from the HSRC low projections to the PDP's targets and R272 billion
if the reduction were from the HSRC high projections to the PDP's targets.
In both cases, the savings on education dominated, being above 85 per cent
of the total.

Gouws concluded that these calculations provide ample proof of the
adverse implications of a too rapid population growth on the economy
of a country. But, in themselves they do not, unless there are no returns to
government expenditure.

This criticism can also be applied to the analysis of Mullins and Myburgh,[26]
even though they bring the government revenue side of the equation into
the picture. They argue that if population growth is concentrated among
the poor, this will both increase the average size of claims on social services
and (because the tax system is slightly progressive) decrease the average tax
revenue per capita, leading to higher tax rates.

Both papers implicitly assume that government expenditure augments
consumption standards only and has no impact on the productivity of the
wider economy.

Again, the issues need more careful investigation. A fuller treatment
would have to consider the operation of the economy as a whole, including the constraints on its efficient operation. Any realistic analysis would
also have to depart from the standard full employment models, at least
in the medium term. It would also have to take into account the existing
disjunction between the educational system and the labour market.

At the end of the day, it may well be found that these social constraints
are the most important reasons why South Africa will be unable economically to cope with rapid population growth.

The extension effort

Nearly half the papers at the Population Development Conference were
devoted to the extension effort needed to promote the goals of the PDP. Four
avenues in particular were targeted: education, community development,
women's organizations and the private sector.

---

[26] D. Mullins and A. Myburgh (Central Economic Advisory Service), 'The implication of a high rate of population growth on the South African economy', Population Development Conference, Johannesburg, Oct.
1988.

Garbers et al.[27] propose that population education be introduced in schools. This would aim at informing pupils of the causes, consequences and dynamics of population development and population growth, as well as of the benefits of family planning in terms of a rise in the quality of life. Chang refers to the family planning education programmes for factory workers and for Defence Force recruits and reservists in Taiwan.[28]

Monitoring

The PDP has developed a monitoring system which uses indicators to measure the changes in socio-economic conditions in a community from year to year. The indicators selected are: the total fertility rate, the infant mortality rate, life expectancy at birth, the percentage of births which occur to teenagers, personal per capita income, percentage literacy (taken to require at least a Std 4 qualification), percentage children not attending school, room density (equivalent persons per bedroom) and the economic dependency rate.

These indicators are monitored annually in each of forty-four planning regions.[29] They are then compared with objectives set by the Department. These comparisons form the basis for allocating PDP resources. In some cases, planning regions are subdivided and priority communities (a community being a particular population group in a particular magisterial district) are identified for special attention.

If one or more indicator is adverse in a particular region or community, the regional staff of the PDP gather together knowledgeable persons in the area to try and determine what can be done to improve conditions. A high infant mortality rate, for instance, may be ascribed to a lack of hospitals or clinics, or to inadequate water supplies, or to a lack of competent midwives. This analysis leads on to recommendations for appropriate development expenditure.[30]

The HSRC carries out some of the surveys on behalf of the PDP. Each population group in each development region and metropolitan area is surveyed separately, except where the numbers of particular groups are very small. A round of forty-two surveys is executed in cycles of three years.[31]

---

[27] J. G. Garbers, S. W. H. Engelbrecht, F. J. Nieuwenhuis and G. D. Kamper (HSRC), 'The effect of education on population growth', Population Development Conference, Johannesburg, Oct. 1988.

[28] Chang, 'The attainment of family planning targets'.

[29] Schoeman, 'The necessity of monitoring a population development programme'.

[30] N. B. Gouws (Dept. of National Health and Population Development), 'Practical considerations regarding the monitoring of a population development programme, with special reference to the position in South Africa'

[31] C. F. van der Merwe (HSRC), 'The HSRC's socio-economic surveys to effect monitoring data for the population development programme', Population Development Conference, Johannesburg, Oct. 1988.

This is an ambitious monitoring programme. Unfortunately, the technical details of sample size and standard errors in estimates were not reported to the Population Development Conference. The required sample sizes must be large if year to year movements are to be detected reliably above random errors in the estimates. Life expectancy must be particularly difficult to estimate. One awaits an evaluation of the performance of the monitoring system with interest.

Evaluation and conclusions

The transition from a narrow and supply-side oriented preoccupation with fertility control to a broader developmental approach has been a real advance. In addition to creating a context for a more detailed understanding of the determinants of fertility, it has brought the issues of mortality and migration within the scope of population policy.

In some respects, the orientation of population policy can now be described as broadly liberal, especially at the level of specification of goals. The aim of equalizing demographic and social indicators across regions and groups over a period of time is one example; a more developmental approach to urbanization is another.

Yet there are other aspects of policy which remain profoundly illiberal. Of these, the approach to settlement is the most important. Rural development will always be a losing battle while state pressures remain for black depopulation of rural areas outside the homelands. Equally, urban development is prejudiced by the continuing application of the Group Areas Act and harsh approaches to informal settlement.

At the level of health delivery, the current efforts to segregate the system further in order to rationalize it along 'own affairs' lines must work against efforts to improve our poor mortality record.

A major current challenge is to develop more refined demographic measurement and analysis in order to develop more effective policies. The quality of our basic demographic data as supplied by population censuses and registrations of births and deaths leaves much to be desired, especially in relation to African people. Without improvements at this level, the effectiveness of survey-based research must be subject to question.

At the level of analysis, the most urgent need is to develop a more convincing set of reasons for encouraging a slower rate of population growth. Neither the reasons given in the President's Council report nor the analyses presented to the Population Development Conference are adequate.

More attention needs to be given to the distinction between social and private costs of high population growth and to policies which bring these into alignment. Without them, individual interests will not add up to a socially optimal outcome.

The next most urgent need is to develop ways of assessing the efficiency of public expenditure in meeting defined fertility and mortality goals. A third important issue is the assessment of the impact of migration patterns on development possibilities and economic welfare.

All these issues challenge demographers and economists to find ways of improving the quality of life for the population at large.

13 South Africa's cities — crisis management or courageous leadership?

Ann Bernstein

This chapter reviews the legacy of urbanization in South Africa, its impact on social change and the need to develop a new urbanization strategy. Three phases in developing such a strategy are outlined: establishing freedom of movement for all South Africans, developing policy on where contemporary patterns of African urbanization should take place, and formulating principles on 'who decides' on urbanization policy. The chapter concludes by raising twelve key issues central to the debate on a new national agenda for the cities.

Introduction

The process of urbanization, that is, the transformation of a society from a predominantly rural to a predominantly urban culture, is of great significance for any society. In South Africa, the rapid urbanization of African people will have the most profound consequences for every aspect of the lives of South Africans generally.

Over the past ten years or so, the reality of burgeoning African urbanization has become more visible throughout the country and the inability of present policy, structures and attitudes to deal with this situation increasingly apparent.

Today the process is complicated by four constraints:

1. a history of racially discriminatory legislation;
2. a backlog of deliberate decline of urban conditions;
3. the relatively large numbers of people moving to the urban areas; and
4. most important, that the majority of people urbanizing do not yet have the franchise.

For most of this century, South African society has been structured so as to prevent the large-scale urbanization of African people.

It was officially held that the cities were for white people; that Africans were only 'temporary sojourners' in the urban areas and should live in the predominantly rural reserves.

The implications and consequences for our society have been devastating. Increasingly, apartheid ideology has clashed with the reality of modern South Africa as a single interdependent economy with a growing and irreversible rate of urbanization, and the concomitant interdependence of black and white South Africans on each other.

This conflict between traditional policy and hard reality has led to the long overdue recognition of the permanence of African people in the South African urban economy and the tentative exploration of the legal, practical, social and political ramifications of that recognition.[1] Yet, the implications of changing policy in South Africa as regards accepting black citizenship are immense. Ultimately, a fundamental reassessment is required of how policy is formulated, power allocated and development managed.

After extensive research and policy work, the Urban Foundation and the Private Sector Council on Urbanization concluded that a new urbanization strategy for the country must be based on freedom of movement and full citizenship for all.[2] This means making South Africa a country where race does not determine opportunity; where development — urban and rural — is for all its citizens and not racially based; and where cities are managed in order to facilitate access and opportunity rather than exclusion, denial and restriction.

Formulating and implementing a new, non-racial urbanization strategy will include restructuring some of the major political, legal, social and economic institutions. It will entail fundamental change in the traditional way South Africans do things. We will need to answer such questions as: who owns what land; who lives in what part of town; who has access to resources; who governs; who implements; who has homes; who gets services; and who is employed?

Developing a new urbanization strategy

The development of a new urbanization strategy must be viewed as a process and not a single event. Unfortunately, the reality of South African politics makes it inevitable that the myriad issues involved in managing urbanization will be tackled sequentially, to the detriment of the millions of disenfranchised people. As in other areas of South African life, there is no 'quick fix'. Three phases of development can be identified:

1. The start of the first phase was marked by the post-1976 opening up of the entire debate in the establishment on the irreversibility of African

---

[1] See *The Report of the Committee for Constitutional Affairs of the President's Council on an urbanisation strategy for the Republic of South Africa*, Pretoria: Govt. Printer, 1985.

[2] A. Bernstein, 'Cities and citizens', Bertha Solomon Memorial Lecture, Johannesburg, 28 April 1989; and Private Sector Council on Urbanisation: *A statement by the Private Sector Council on Urbanisation*, Johannesburg: Urban Foundation, 1985.

urbanization and culminated with the abolition of influx control in June 1986 and the partial restoration of citizenship to African people.[3]

2. The second phase is characterized by a multi-faceted debate on where and how African urbanization should occur.[4] Only when this question is satisfactorily, resolved will a number of current disputes (forced removals, shack demolitions, Group Areas Act, etc.) fall away.

3. The third phase concerns decision-making: who formulates policy on urbanization, who implements that policy, and what priority is this allocated in national expenditure?

There is nothing inevitable about movement from one phase to the next in this complicated process of developing a new and effective urbanization strategy. In fact, any assumption of a smooth progression will lead to a misinterpretation of precisely what progress has been made and what battles remain to be fought before the quality of people's lives is improved on a mass scale.

Progress in removing the many discriminatory obstacles to an effective approach will depend on two factors: the inevitable realities of the urbanization process, and strategic co-ordinated intervention in policy-making by a number of key actors.

Phase one: towards freedom of movement for all South Africans

After the events of Soweto and elsewhere in 1976 the rigid Verwoerdian approach to the presence, conditions and future of African people living in urban areas began to disintegrate. In its place emerged a hesitant acceptance of the permanence of African people in the 'white' urban areas. This reversal culminated in the President's Council Report on Urbanization,[5] the White Paper on Urbanization, and, finally, the Abolition of Influx Control Act.[6]

The White Paper paved the way for the abolition of the laws and regulations that comprised the influx control system. It rejected the President's Council's report of 'approved accommodation', recognized that informal settlement is an inevitable part of urban growth, and formally stated government acceptance of the irreversibility of African urbanization.

The Abolition of Influx Control Act gave legislative effect to the intentions of the White Paper. It repealed the formidable array of laws and regulations that governed the movement of Africans in urban and rural

---

[3] See the *Restoration of South African Citizenship Act*, Act no. 73 of 1986, Pretoria: Govt. Printer, 1986.

[4] A. M. Thompson and S. F. Coetzee, *Urbanisation and urban growth in the SATBV states*, Midrand: Development Bank of Southern Africa, 1987.

[5] See the *White Paper on Urbanisation*, Pretoria: Govt. Printer, 1986.

[6] See the *Abolition of Influx Control Act of 1986*, Pretoria: Govt. Printer, 1986.

South Africa, their entry into urban areas, their presence and employment therein and their removal therefrom.

It also amended the Slums Act (to make its provisions applicable in black areas) and the Illegal Squatting Act. The amendments to the Slums Act provide for increased penalties and for the designation of land by the relevant minister for 'controlled squatting'. The thrust of the Squatting Act had been that informal settlement was undesirable and should be prevented. The new section providing for areas to be designated by the minister for controlled informal settlements could be seen either as a mechanism of forced removals or as a positive measure to allow informal settlement.

Citizenship

There is one major caveat to the abolition of influx control. The government has linked freedom of movement to South African citizenship, but when the Transkei, Bophuthatswana, Venda and the Ciskei (the TBVC states) took independence, some 9 million black South Africans lost their South African citizenship.

The 1986 Restoration of South African Citizenship Act enables only those people who can prove permanent residence in South Africa to reclaim their South African citizenship. The authorities estimate that 1,75 million people will qualify for the restoration of citizenship.

The position of TBVC people who cannot regain South African citizenship is uncertain and the actions of the authorities have not clarified the situation. The Urban Foundation's best assessment is that TBVC citizens do not require permission to be in the Republic because of an exemption in terms of Section 7 (*bis*) of the Aliens Act. However, there are still uncertainties as to whether TBVC citizens are legally obliged to obtain work permits to work in the Republic.

What we have here is a typical South African conundrum which is, however, a tragedy for the people involved. Theoretically, all that is required to resolve the matter is the automatic restoration of South African citizenship to all TBVC citizens. Their citizenship was automatically taken away from them and it can automatically be restored. The South African government rejects such a step on the grounds that it would belittle the sovereignty of the four independent homelands. It has chosen instead to negotiate the granting of dual citizenship to TBVC citizens permanently resident within those countries.

This is a very serious matter for millions of people. While some 14 million black South African citizens have acquired a new freedom of movement through the abolition of influx control, some 6 to 8 million TBVC citizens, who cannot prove rights to permanent residence in the RSA, are in a position of considerable legal uncertainty and perhaps greater legal disadvantage than before as regards access to the South African job market.

Phase two: where and how should African urbanization occur?

In 'white' South Africa, African urban growth is found in segregated formal urban townships in the metropolitan areas and small towns; in backyard shacks in these townships; in informal settlements in and around the formal townships; in free-standing informal settlements on vacant urban and peri-urban land; and in illegal residence in the white suburbs of the large metro-politan areas.

In the homelands, urban growth occurs in formal township develop-ments; in large, generally informal settlements on the borders of white urban areas (for example Winterveld, KwaNdebele, Inanda, Botshabelo, etc.); and in settlement areas far removed from formal economic and urban centres, where people live in very dense settlements and do not derive the bulk of their income from agriculture.

Since the publication of the White Paper on Urbanization and the ab-olition of influx control, there have been a number of disquieting events, including:

▷ the demolition of mainly informal settlements (or the threat of such demolition) in cities throughout the country, including Crossroads and KTC in the Cape, and Oukasie near Brits;

▷ the reappearance of the forced-removals policy whereby black commu-nities are forcibly removed from land they have owned or occupied in South Africa for decades and relocated into (or on the border of) a homeland;

▷ the legal inhibition on freedom of movement for TBVC citizens, thus potentially holding millions of people to an urbanization pattern of single migrancy and insecurity in the cities or in informal settlements on the borders of 'white' South Africa; and

▷ the Guide Planning Process where totally inadequate amounts of land are allocated for black settlement in the heart of the country's largest metropolitan areas. (The thrust of these documents confirms the policy of restricting the economic growth of the cities and encouraging future urban and economic growth in places on the periphery of existing urban areas.[7])

The reasons for these developments are to be found in the official atti-tude to urbanization which is still influenced by apartheid principles. The functions of joint policy can be identified as the following:

---

[7] See, for example, *The central Witwatersrand: Draft Guide Plan*, Pretoria: Dept. of Constitutional Development and Planning, 1986; and the Private Sector Council on Urbanisation's response in *Submission on the central Witwatersrand Draft Guide Plan*, Unpublished Paper, Johannesburg: Urban Foundation, 1986.

▷ The existing metropolitan areas are too big and further African urban settlements should be restricted and redirected wherever possible.

▷ Urban development must continue to be racially segregated.

▷ Economic growth is to be induced in uneconomic locations on the peripheries of the cities and in the homeland areas.

▷ The location and pace of African urbanization is to be controlled through restricted access to land and serviced sites in selected areas, through a generally negative response to informal urban settlement, and through the provision of subsidized rental housing in decentralization and deconcentration points.

▷ A large percentage of the African population will continue to be confined to some 13 per cent of the land area — the 'homelands'.

▷ The white rural areas will have little formal role to play in the development needs of the black community.

▷ Homeland development will take precedence over comprehensive national urban and economic development.[8]

Government's traditional policy approach indicates a strong preference for where African urbanization should occur. Viewing the country as a whole, traditional policy encourages urbanization away from the metropolitan areas and towards the homeland borders or fringe settlements. Within the urban areas, the Group Areas Act, the Black Communities Development Act, and the decentralization and deconcentration policies restrict African settlement and growth to segregated, confined townships and then push additional African settlement away from the heart of the city to the periphery of the metropolitan heart of the country. This policy has five consequences:

1. It ignores where most African urbanization is actually taking place, irrespective of the ideological wishes of the policy-makers.

2. It denies the reality of the integrated nature of South African economic growth and the inevitable spatial consequences of that form of growth.

3. It establishes a pattern that has all the bad features of rapid urbanization and few of the positive features (unless urbanization occurs organically in the large urban centres, the society will fail to capitalize on the benefits of increased urban agglomeration and the urban newcomer will be denied access to the opportunities and benefits of city life).

4. It ensures that the impact of rapid urban growth falls most heavily on those public authorities (homeland governments and black local authorities) least able to deal with the necessary economic, technological

---

8 See the *White Paper on Urbanisation*.

and management demands required to create, maintain and improve complex urban environments.

5. It diverts public money in an inefficient allocation of resources through the expensive industrial decentralization policy and homeland development policy.

It is important to note three areas of some change:

1. *Group Areas*: the Free Settlement Areas Act provides for selected areas to become open to non-racial residential settlement. This mechanism, designed to cope with the growing number of inner-city grey areas, is seen by government as a means of dealing with the exceptions to its desired norm of segregated living areas, rather than the forerunner to a normalized society.

2. *Informal settlement*: although there has been justified negative comment on the Prevention of Illegal Squatting Amendment Act of 1988, nevertheless, there have been indications of positive changes in the attitude among officials and politicians towards informal settlement. From the early 1970s to the late 1980s, we have seen a critical change in the nature of this debate. As a generalization, officials are no longer arguing that 'we must demolish the shacks and send these people back to where they came from'. The use by officials of Section 6 and 6A of the new Act to permit transit camps and regulation-free areas for site and service schemes may be one example of this new attitude. Moreover, today the debate concerns how informal settlement should be managed in South Africa's cities. That shift — however much delayed — is a change of fundamental importance.

3. *Land*: finally, there appears to be some momentum developing within selected metropolitan areas concerning the identification of land for African settlement. Preliminary indications are that the identification of land for lower income residential development is actually in advance of effective demand in some metropolitan areas. In certain regions, however, this is not the case (for example, the Eastern and Western Cape). Moreover, in the future, the available 'soft-options', in political terms, in other metropolitan areas will become fewer, and land identification for the poor may become more contentious.

Phase three: who decides on urbanization policy?

This question of the locus of decision-making needs to be looked at at a number of levels.

▷ At the individual level, people are already challenging the dictates of the authorities. This can be seen in the defiance of the pass laws before their repeal; in the creation of shelter in unauthorized locations; in the creation of jobs without official authorization; and in the growing evidence of black occupation of so-called white housing.

▷ At community level there is growing demand for black participation in decisions taken on their future. Examples range from community resistance to forced removals and subsequent initiatives in formulating proposals for on-site upgrading as an alternative; communal occupation of authorized land, and the creation of community-wide informal services and representation.

▷ The next level is that of local government — the key institutional agent for managing urban growth effectively. In this arena the last four years have witnessed the rejection by popular community groups throughout much of the country of the local government system imposed on them.

▷ At national level, the black demand for the franchise and the implications of that demand implicitly raises the question of who decides on South Africa's new urbanization strategy and its place in the nation's priorities.

The development of a new urbanization strategy in South Africa is a complex process. Its success will depend on progress in the following key areas:

▷ Freedom of movement and full citizenship for all South Africans, including people from the TBVC states.

▷ Increased urban concentration in the country as a whole and within the towns and cities themselves. This, in turn, means the reversal of race discrimination in the ownership and occupation of all urban and rural land in South Africa; the reversal of the ideological approach to industrial decentralization and urban deconcentration; and, ultimately, the reversal of the independent homeland policy.

▷ Full, meaningful and equal participation of all South Africans at all levels of decision-making.

Focus on the cities

South Africa faces three major challenges. The first is the economic challenge to increase its rate of growth and development so as to provide millions of new jobs for a large and growing population. Some of the issues involved in employment criteria are discussed in Chapter 14. The second challenge concerns urbanization. Society must capitalize on the dynamics of the African urbanization process so as to make the phenomenon 'an instrument of national development and personal betterment'.[9] The

---

9 O. Stark, 'Research on rural-to-urban migration in LDCs', in *World Development*, vol. 10, no. 1, 1982.

third challenge is political. It is the task of building an inclusive non-racial democracy and with it the institutions necessary to meet the economic development challenge and provide the mechanisms to manage urban growth.

All three demands are highlighted in the challenges facing South Africa's urban areas. The three national demands — increased economic growth and massive job creation, rapid urbanization, and the challenge of building an inclusive democracy — all come together at the fulcrum of the nation, in the cities.

The attention of the national decision-makers should be turned to these cities: their place in the social structure, how they should be managed and governed, and the interrelationship of sound urban growth with healthy rural and regional development.

Failure of the White Paper on urbanization

The government's White Paper on urbanization, published in 1986, is a watershed document. It contained the first official recognition of the irreversibility of urbanization for the African population as a whole. It also provided the case for the legal abolition of influx control.

However, the White Paper did not provide South Africa with a new urbanization strategy, nor an urban policy. The document essentially restated traditional government policy in many areas of importance (for example regional development, the Group Areas Act and local government) and merely hinted at some fluidity and new thinking in certain areas of policy (growth of the cities and informal settlements).

The White Paper is a document caught between South Africa's past and its future. It makes no sense to accept African urbanization and the expansion of the cities and yet simultaneously cling to a set of policies designed to prevent, redirect and disguise African urbanization.

Yet, this is what the White Paper attempts to do. The result is a confusing and contradictory set of policy injunctions that retards urban development rather than leading it into a more prosperous, inclusive future.

The White Paper argues for a differential approach to urbanization in the different areas of the country,[10] yet couples this with a general injunction supporting the creation of artificial shortages of industrial land in the metropolitan core areas.[11] Simultaneously, we are told that the metropolitan areas should continue to be actively extended and promoted.

The White Paper argues for the development of more compact cities, for the optimal use of existing infrastructure, for raising residential densities,

---

[10] See the *White Paper on Urbanisation*, para. 6.3, p. 24.

[11] See the *White Paper on Urbanisation*, para. 6.1.2, p. 25.

and for the more efficient use of land.[12] How can any of these instructions be implemented if the Group Areas Act, the Separate Amenities Act,[13] the racial zoning of land and the creation of new racially-separate towns continue to be policy?

The White Paper argues that new towns should be developed and that one of the objectives should be to create viable communities, able to accept responsibility for administrative and financial independence.[14] A detailed empirical analysis of South Africa's existing black local authorities shows that there is possibly only one such body that is financially sound. How can viable, new towns be created that are racially segregated, composed primarily of poor people and cut off from the core economic centres of South Africa's existing cities and towns?

In essence, the White Paper is inherently an ambiguous document and, as events since 1986 have already shown, a transitory one as well.

It is ambiguous in two fundamental areas: in its attitude to the cities and their role in the urban and national development process; and on the impact of freedom of movement and the restoration of citizenship on South Africa's present package of policies affecting the rural and urban sectors of the country.

In a relatively short time it has been overtaken by events. Since 1986 the government has been forced to change policy, or is considering doing so, on the Group Areas Act, regional development and informal settlement.

The full implications of accepting African urbanization entail far more than a mere shift in the rhetoric of apartheid or a belated acceptance of black population growth and migration to the cities. The practical consequences of accepting African urbanization entail a fundamental reassessment of South Africa's cities and the policies that affect them.

Some demographic realities

▷ By the year 2010 the total population of South Africa will be almost an estimated 60 million people, compared with a 1980 total of an estimated nearly 34 million.[15]

▷ In terms of the government's definition of racial groups, population

---

12 See the *White Paper on Urbanisation*, para. 6.15.7, p. 33 and para. 6.11.4–6, p. 29.

13 Government has now indicated its intention to repeal the Separate Amenities Act, but questions remain concerning the timing of repeal and the so-called 'replacement' legislation that has been mooted by Minister Kriel.

14 See the *White Paper on Urbanisation*, para. 6.11.1, p. 28.

15 The Urban Foundation is completing a computer demographic model of South Africa developed by Dr Charles Simkins. These figures are taken from that model. See 'An Urban Foundation demographic projection model: phase three', Unpublished Paper, Johannesburg: Urban Foundation, 1989.

growth is most rapid among Africans, who by 2010 will comprise approximately 80 per cent of the total South African population, in comparison with an estimated 72 per cent in 1980.

▷ The major anticipated geographic shift in the population is from the rural areas (the platteland) to the metropolitan areas. Metropolitan areas in 1985 (across homeland borders) had a total African population of an estimated 9,3 million. These same areas in 2010 will have a total African population of an estimated 26,8 million. It is important to note the rapid 'blackening' of the metropolital areas between 1980 and 2000 in this period.

▷ By the year 2000 South Africa will have at least four major cities with a population as large as the Witwatersrand today — well over 4 million people. If the PWV (Pretoria, Witwatersrand, Vereeniging) is conceived as a single metropolitan complex — which functionally it will be — the total population of South Africa's largest urban complex by 2000 will be close to 12 million people, and by 2010 will be over 16 million people.

Thinking of the PWV, for example, as a metropolitan area of 12 million people in just over ten year's time, requires a quantum leap in how we think about cities and the future. We should already be planning for a scale of urbanization which makes existing institutions and approaches look parochial.[16]

Ascendant role of cities

Accepting the irreversibility of African urbanization implies an acceptance of the ascendant role of the cities in the development of the country. This is a future characterized by:

▷ unprecedented numbers;

▷ limited financial resources;

▷ new issues (informal housing, informal job creation, large-scale urban poverty, mass service delivery, managing large urban areas);

▷ new relationships (incorporating black citizens, organized community groups, mass trade unions, new roles for private and public sectors); and

▷ new methods (privatization, community involvement in planning, shelter provision, job creation).

In South Africa, as elsewhere, the cities must play their historic role as the vehicle for modernization. The urban areas are the arena in which economic

---

[16] A. Bernstein, 'South Africa's cities — crisis management or courageous leadership', paper presented at the Conference on the Witwatersrand, (Carlton Conference), Johannesburg, 27 June 1989.

growth must take place to increase and maximize job creation; the benefits of urban agglomeration must become available to an expanding population and black and white South Africans must learn to live together on an equal basis.

The international experience is mixed. It shows that some Third World cities have failed to respond to the reality of urbanization and are not functioning efficiently or equitably. The costs of this failure are borne most heavily by the urban poor, but also by the country as a whole since national economic recovery and growth is hindered. Yet, other cities in the developing world have coped remarkably well with an expanding population, and have indeed been able to improve the quality of life for millions of urban dwellers.

Hence, the fundamental question is whether South Africa as a nation is willing and able to change its attitudes to the cities, and radically adapt its policies so that the urban areas can change from *cities of exclusion*, restriction, control and in some instances economic decline; to *cities of opportunity*, expansion and economic growth for all.

Towards a national agenda for the cities

How does South Africa move towards a different urban future? How do we start to build cities of opportunity and growth? Policy-makers will need to deal with a number of complex and interrelated issues which are summarized in the text that follows as twelve core policy questions.

The issues that face the PWV highlight the critical practical policy concerns that face South African cities nationwide. For this reason the first two questions deal specifically with the PWV.

1. Does the policy of deconcentration close to homeland borders still form one of the cornerstones of the long-term development strategy of the PWV complex?

If so, why, as all the South African and international evidence points to its economic cost and failure in development terms?

Has a cost-benefit analysis of this policy and its impact on the PWV been undertaken? Has the policy been tested with the key affected interest groups — the business sector and black community leadership?

Why do we need to create artificial growth points on the PWV when we already have a complex, multi-nodal metropolitan structure with adequate existing points of growth (for examples, East and West Rand, and Vanderbijlpark) where economically justifiable deconcentration is already occurring?

2. What is government's vision of the future of the PWV?

The 1986 Draft Guide Plan for the Central Witwatersrand was heavily criticized; other guide plans for the PWV were prepared before the White Paper on urbanization and the subsequent change in urbanization policy. A consortium of private planners was appointed to look at the land needs of the region; government's recent identification of land for African residential settlement in the PWV is the result of their still confidential report.

The guide plans are based on racially discriminatory planning considerations, racial allocations of land, and racial planning for an urban area that bears little relationship to an economically and increasingly residentially integrated PWV.

The question is: are the guide plans still the official framework for the region's future?

If one looks at the Witwatersrand today, it is apparent that far from over-concentration being the problem, as the authorities assert, one of the key issues is actually how to manage greater concentration at the centre. Despite curbs on industrial development and their policies of deconcentration, by the year 2000 the greatest absolute increase in employment and in population in the PWV region is projected to occur in the Central Witwatersrand.[17]

Two processes are occurring that are of fundamental significance for the future. Both cut right across traditional government thinking on the cities:

1. The one inexorable trend is the expansion of the black population and the continuing growth of informal settlement in backyard shacks and free-standing new communities on a scale beyond any official prediction. Our research indicates that there are at least 2 million people living in informal housing on the PWV.[18]

2. The second inexorable trend is what might be called the greying of the city. In the past decade or so — largely in response to the enormous housing shortages for blacks and the preferential location of white housing opportunities — black families and households have increasingly taken up housing opportunities legally reserved for whites. Our research indicates that the extent of black movement into housing in the white suburbs of the greater Johannesburg area is much more extensive than anyone has suspected and that this trend will continue. We estimate that there are as many blacks living in the Johannesburg municipal area today as there are whites (compound dwellers, domestic servants, coloured and Asian residents, illegals occupying white housing).

The effect of these two processes will be to create a city fundamentally different from anything South Africans have experienced hitherto.

---

17 Bernstein, 'South Africa's cities'; and C. Simkins, 'An Urban Foundation demographic projection model'.

18 A. Bernstein, 'Informal settlers: South Africa's new city builders', in *Optima*, vol. 37, no. 1, March 1989.

What are the government's plans to deal creatively and responsively with the scale, the affordability and the racially-integrated nature of South Africa's new urban realities — today and in the future?

The more general issues to be resolved are encapsulated by the ten questions that follow.

3. Whose city is this? Who governs and in whose interest do they rule?

All South African urban areas have racial rather than functional boundaries. Government and administrative structures flow from that division rather than functional criteria. This has serious implications for each and every urban area and the consequences — economic, political, financial, administrative — are far-ranging.

4. Who is planning for the city as a whole?

How do we plan effectively for cross-checking expanding urban regions which are racially separated and administratively divided? How do we ensure effective representation of community viewpoints? How do we test the planners' understanding of what is best for people as against people's knowledge of what is best for them? How do we plan the effective provision of facilities if officials must ignore the illegal black residents of white suburbs?

5. What is our guiding image for the city?

Is it the old conception of a colonial town combining neat First World suburbs with far-removed migrant accommodation? Or is it a future-oriented image of the city — a city which works as a thriving urban entity, combining its skilled and unskilled components, its formal and informal settlements in a creative and growing synergy?

6. Do we manage our urban areas as environments for economic growth?

Cities are competing with each other (nationally and internationally) for the attraction of investment resources. The cities need to be managed so as to emphasize their comparative advantage as an efficient and desirable environment for economic growth, for that is the necessary base to provide opportunities for an expanding population.

7. Are we geared up to respond to the scale of urban population growth?

Are our cities and their managements sufficiently expansion-oriented? Are we thinking big enough and far enough ahead to meet the growing challenge of rapid urbanization?

8. Do we understand the difference between executing some development projects and the process of managing urban growth?

We need to move away from a few good projects that create islands of privilege in a sea of poverty, and instead pinpoint the essential areas of intervention to ensure that the city performs better. Projects must be conceived within policy frameworks that tackle the development problems of the city as a whole.

9. Is there an increasing disjuncture between the legal city (formal planning rules, regulations, zoning) and the real city (informal jobs and settlements, grey areas)?

How does this affect the structure and economic development of the city and its accessibility for all its citizens?

It is important to be clear about what precisely is at stake for South Africa in managing informal settlements. This involves more than merely how to deal with a few pockets of illegal squatters. The question is rather how society intends to manage the urbanization process.

'Many Third World countries still try to plan and build cities for societies which exist only in the minds of technocrats and politicians.'[19] Willy-nilly, informal settlers are reconstructing South Africa's urban areas.

The new suburbs of Cape Town, for example, are in Khayelitsha and the shacks of the Cape Flats are not problems to be demolished, for they provide prolific and affordable shelter that must be preserved and upgraded. The squatters are, in fact, South Africa's new city builders and we need to think through the implications of that reality.

The wrong response is to ignore this phenomenon and to condemn people to whatever they can provide in the most insecure circumstances imaginable.

10. Do we consider sufficiently how policies will affect the poor?

Unless attention is given specifically to incorporating poor people, they will continue to be excluded and denied opportunities.

As the city grows, the competition for resources of all kinds will increase. We need to look closely at the service provision network to ensure that the poor — by definition those who have least access to everything — are gaining increased access to the opportunities of urban agglomeration.

11. Is it possible to meet the challenge of urbanization if we persist with racial thinking on urban issues?

All urbanizing societies are in a race against time, for every day that passes, more people are being born in or moving to the city. To compound the situation and spend time debating whether a black South African can live next to a white South African is precious time wasted on the wrong issues altogether.

---

19 J. Hardoy and D. Satterthwaite, 'The legal and illegal city' in L. Rodwin, ed., *Shelter, settlement and development*, Boston: Allen and Unwin, 1987.

12. Are we to continue to respond to change in our cities by *ad hoc*, crisis management? Will we accept the demographic and economic realities and face the challenges of the present and the future with vision and leadership?

The question at the core of this chapter can be defined quite simply: is there sufficient leadership on urban issues? The challenges that face the cities are essentially political. National and local leadership must seek to develop popularly accepted, effective processes and, ultimately, institutions that will develop and then communicate a shared vision of the future.

Concluding remarks

The countries where urbanization has been successfully harnessed to ensure development have used this irreversible process as an opportunity to implement national goals that include:

▷ eradicating absolute poverty;

▷ maximizing job creation;

▷ restructuring access to economic opportunity; and

▷ incorporating hitherto excluded sections of the national population.

At its best, a positive urbanization policy can be a vehicle for restructuring a divided society and building a nation.

A new urbanization policy must be national in scope and span both rural and urban sectors of the country's space-economy. Within this balanced and dual approach attention must focus particularly on managing the urban areas. The ascendant role of the cities in the life of the country demands that they play a leading role. The key components of an effective urban policy will include those outlined in the text that follows.

A focus on urban management, which is the key to success

Policies of decentralization and deconcentration should not be adopted or advocated as substitutes for effective urban management. In particular, strategies for managing the large cities are required. The urban management agenda goes beyond physical planning and shelter provision to the heart of many of the economic, geographic and political linkages of the society.

Effective urban management in South Africa requires six core components:

1. New urban government institutions whose boundaries are defined on functional, not racial criteria and in which all inhabitants participate equally.

2. An economic approach to urban development.

3. The 'reconstruction' of South Africa's divided cities and towns where new development is channelled away from a dispersed and racially

divided urban growth pattern, towards more compact, accessible, economically prudent and productive urban systems.

4. 'Opening' the city to all residents so that there is equality of opportunity and access to all the amenities, facilities, services and opportunities of the urban areas.

5. An urban finance strategy that increases the resources available in the urban areas and provides incentives for local government and the private sector to play an increased development role.

6. An effective housing policy incorporating:

   ➤ increased access to land and finance for the poor;

   ➤ appropriate standards;

   ➤ service provision on scale; and

   ➤ a positive attitude to informal settlements, recognition of their contribution to a national housing policy, and mechanisms to promote upgrading.

The cities and towns must compete for new public and private investment

The pre-selection of urban areas where economic growth and population concentration is subsidized and induced has failed. A new policy approach must encourage cities and towns to market their comparative advantages and emphasize locally-based economic growth strategies.

All development activity should be directed by four guidelines:

1. In a capital and skills-hungry country, all existing physical, human, institutional and financial resources must be used to the maximum. We cannot afford unnecessary 'new towns', underutilized schools, and unnecessary duplication of administrative or government structures.

2. The strength of South Africa's highly developed private sector must be capitalized upon in meeting the development challenge. The private sector can play a critical driving role within a state-defined and supportive facilitating environment.

3. A special focus must be on state assistance to raise the living standards of the poor. The manner in which this is achieved must be to bring the poor into the economic system and harness their energies in creating jobs, shelter and services.

4. There must be a recognition that community participation is essential for effective urban and rural development. This will include democratic, representative urban government institutions, involvement in local decision-making, and participation in development projects.

Central government has a pre-eminent lead role to play

In negotiating, defining and communicating the new urbanization policy and promoting an environment in which all the other participants (municipalities, communities, business, trade unions, farmers, etc.) can play their local and sectoral leadership roles, government has a predominant role to play.

The removal of all racially-based legislation and policies is an urgent and essential component of a new urban policy

This will involve a systematic programme to repeal:

▷ the Group Areas Act (and related legislation);

▷ the Separate Amenities Act;[20]

▷ the Land Acts of 1913 and 1936 (and related legislation); and

▷ all racially-based local government legislation.

In conclusion, it must be emphasized that segregation and statutory discrimination is the critical obstacle in the future development of South Africa's cities. However, the removal of racial discrimination alone will not provide a way of managing urbanization. That task requires a fundamentally new urbanization policy for South Africa.

Acknowledgement

This chapter derives from the experience of research, policy and lobby work in the Urbanization Unit of the Urban Foundation.

---

[20] See note no. 13.

14 Unemployment and the job creation challenge

Wolfgang H. Thomas

This chapter considers the size and diversity of types of unemployment and of the relationship between unemployment and (under)development; reviews the known policy options and packages; and, finally, focuses on the crucial issue of policy implementation.

Introduction

The issue of unemployment — its size, nature, manifestations and consequences — has gained increasing attention since the mid-1970s in South Africa.

The subject has figured in annual government reports, addresses by business, trade union and community leaders, and in academic writings. Institutions like the President's Council and the National Manpower Commission have given special attention to unemployment issues.

In view of all this, it would be wrong to suggest that South Africans are not aware of the problem. In fact, after inflation and the deterioration of the exchange rate, unemployment ranks as a major theme in the economic debate.

Despite all this, there is a danger of it being widely talked about but not acted upon. Dramatization of the problem is not being matched by the implementation of effective policy steps to combat it.

As background to the analysis, the following facts are relevant:

▷ High unemployment rates are not a recent phenomenon, but historically have been present amongst all the communities of South Africa.

▷ Despite the seriousness of unemployment, wide discrepancies exist in estimates about its size.

▷ Some critics of the present government blame rising unemployment on apartheid, suggesting that a non-racial society would have produced less unemployment. Opponents of the African National Congresses's (ANC's) socio-economic strategy, however, are equally convinced that alternative policies would lead to increasing unemployment.

▷ Concern for the high — and apparently rising — level of unemployment has led to the search for unique solutions, implying that present policies have failed.

▷ While the current emphasis on market solutions is supposed to be the most effective way of countering unemployment, these policies have often produced increasing short-run unemployment.

▷ Several countries cited as examples for South Africa to emulate, including market-oriented newly industrialized countries (NICs) and socialist model cases, themselves suffer from high unemployment.

▷ With most of the debate about unemployment focusing on the macro level, comparatively little attention is given to detailed micro studies or to the implementation of grassroots job creation policies.

▷ Despite the expressed concern about unemployment, it is striking that no attempt has been made by government to set even modest job creation targets.

Against this background, the thrust of this chapter can be stated as follows: The South African unemployment problem is not unique and has been experienced internationally in other semi-developed countries. It is wrong to conclude that during the past ten to fifteen years no progress has been made in job creation, or that present policies need radical revision. We should thus not expect the job creation challenge of a post-apartheid South Africa to be significantly different from that currently facing the country.

In our quest for a more effective unemployment policy, we will hardly find dramatic new policies. The answer lies in new combinations of existing policies and better policy integration, programming and monitoring.

Unemployment: size and diversity

How high is unemployment in South Africa? In the public debate, figures range between 800 000 and 6 million. Equally confusing is the distinction between the annual increase or decrease in unemployment, given population growth and the increase in the economically active population, and the total stock of unemployment.

To set an empirical framework for the discussion in this chapter, the guesstimats shown in Table 14.1 are put forward without any pretence at 'correctness'.

Section A (Status quo) of Table 14.1 establishes the link between total population, manpower, the labour force or actual labour supply, different types of employment and effective unemployment. Manpower refers to all persons in the economically active age group of sixteen to sixty-four years, the labour force refers to all those in this age group who are able and

Table 14.1: Guesstimates of population, employment and unemployment statistics

A. *Status quo* 1989
1. Total population
   (including the TBVC states)   — 38 million
2. Population in the economically active
   age groups   — 20 million
   (52,6% of total population)

3. Labour force (persons able
   and interested to work)   — 14 million
   (36,8% of total population)
4. Employment in the formal sector   — 7,5 million
   (53,6% of labour force)

5. Persons underemployed and/or sub-
   stantially involved in the informal sector   — 4,2 million
   (30% of labour force)

6. Persons seeking work (stock of unemployed)   — 2,3 million
   (16,4% of labour force)

B. *Annual increase (percentage growth 1989–91)*

1. Total population	2,5%	950 000
2. Manpower	2,6%	520 000
3. Labour force (or labour supply)	2,8%	392 000
4. Formal sector employment	2,0%–2,8%	150 000–210 000
5. Informal sector involvement	2,5%–3,5%	105 000–150 000
6. Unemployed		32 000–140 000

C. *Extrapolations for the year 2000*
1. Total population   50 million
2. Manpower   27 million
   (54% of total population)
3. Labour force or labour supply   19 million
   (38% of total population)
4. Formal sector employment   10,3 million
   (54% of labour force)
5. Informal sector involvement   5,3 million
   (28% of labour force)
6. Stock of unemployment   3,4 million
   (18% of labour force)

D. *Projected changes 1989–2000*

1. Total population	31,6% or 12 million
2. Labour force	35,7% or 5 million
3. Formal sector employment	37,3% or 2,8 million
4. Informal sector involvement	26,2% or 1,1 million
5. Unemployment	47,8% or 1,1 million

willing to work, and unemployed refers to those who receive neither full-time nor part-time earnings as employees or self-employed persons. The distinction between formal and informal employment is derived from the rather nebulous classification of economic activity as being either within the formal or the informal sector, which in this context relates primarily to its inclusion or exclusion from official statistics.

The 1989 unemployment estimate of 2,3 million may not be completely accurate because of factors such as the actual population and the under-numeration of current official employment statistics.

An unemployment rate of about 16,4 per cent for the whole labour force is high, but probably not different from other semi-developed countries.

The figures in Section B of Table 14.1, however, give us an indication of the magnitude of annual flows and the resultant job creation challenge. Almost 400 000 people are added to the labour force each year, that is, in addition to the 2,3 million job-seekers, another 392 000 are added to those 'able, willing and seeking work'.

Depending on the assumption made about the absorptive capacity of the labour markets, unemployment is increasing by 32 000 to 140 000 annually. It can be more during cyclical downswings in the economy, but this is counterbalanced by higher absorptive rates in boom years.

Based on assumptions discussed later, Section C in Table 14.1 presents a medium-level projection for the rest of this century, when the labour force will grow to 20 million and unemployment as defined here may increase by another million. Naturally, different assumptions would produce significantly different employment and unemployment figures. The guesstimates in Sections C and D should be seen as a basis for discussion only.

The roots of South Africa's unemployment

It has become conventional to distinguish between different types of unemployment, linking the various types to major underlying factors. They are:

▷ *frictional unemployment*, that is, joblessness resulting from a time lag between the end of one job and the start of a new one;

▷ *seasonal unemployment*, that is, joblessness resulting from seasonal fluctuations in production and employment in fields such as recreation, tourism and construction;

▷ *cyclical unemployment*, which is the result of cyclical fluctuations in sectors such as construction and raw material exports;

▷ *structural unemployment* refers to a mismatch in the demand and supply of certain jobs because of structural changes in specific economic sectors (for example, a permanent decline in the demand for certain products could result in those with specialized skills no longer in demand becoming unemployed); and

▷ *demographic unemployment* reflects a particularly rapid increase in the labour supply which cannot be absorbed in the short-term by the market. (This is a major problem in Third World countries experiencing a demographic transition).

The level of unemployment in a country at any time is the sum total of these five broadly defined types of unemployment. The significance of each will differ from country to country — depending on economic structure, resource endowment, politico-economic policy framework and labour market institutions, and seasonal, cyclical and structural changes.

In South Africa, all of these factors are important, though special emphasis has to fall on the structural and demographic dimensions, given South Africa's status as a semi-developed, developing or Third World country.

The underlying causes of the present high level and rate of unemployment are greatly influenced by South Africa's demographic transition.

During the last two decades the African birth rate has remained high, whereas mortality rates have declined significantly. (See Chapter 9.) Because of the high drop out rate at school, African youngsters are able and willing to enter the labour market at a relatively early age, and since there are few jobs available for the young and poorly educated, most either remain unemployed for lengthy periods, are drawn into the informal sector, or acquire skills.

For older Africans, changing lifestyles require longer periods of employment. While many migrant workers previously abandoned active employment after about twenty years of migrant involvement, most now have to look for employment up to normal retirement age — thus remaining almost twenty years longer in the labour force.

A third socio-demographic factor is the changing role of women, most of whom are now under pressure to enter or remain in gainful employment. Frequently in poorer households women are the primary breadwinners.

Finally, urbanization, with its associated changing consumption patterns, rising expectations and shift towards core families, places virtually all members of the family (except school-going children) under pressure to earn an income. Thus, over the past three decades the labour force participation rate of Africans has increased substantially.

These changes are far less significant in the coloured and Asian communities where high levels of urbanization had already been achieved by the early 1970s. The extension of secondary and tertiary education has also delayed their entrance into the labour market.

In the white community low fertility rates, emigration, military service and a lengthy preparation for entrance to the skilled labour market all dampen the rate of entry.

Taking all these demographic changes into account, it is obvious that rapidly increasing demands are being made on the labour market. High unemployment among Africans resulting from these pressures cannot be seen as signs of economic policy failures, but should be regarded as logical strains in a medium-term transitional process.

A second fundamental structural factor which has influenced the increasing level of unemployment is rural underdevelopment and the inequality in South Africa's land-use pattern.

All over the world the modernization of agriculture goes hand in hand with the rationalization of labour usage. The effect this process has on employment levels depends on the availability of additional land for those redundant, and the absorptive capacity of other economic sectors.

In South Africa, more than in many other developing countries, socio-political and economic forces have worked against a smooth transition. Apartheid policies have accelerated the rate of labour substitution on the farms, while rigid, racially differentiated controls over land ownership and use have led to the eviction of hundreds of thousands of Africans from the rural sector, with women and children pushed to resettlement areas and men forced to seek migrant labour employment or suffer unemployment.

Virtually no attention was given to alternative employment (or self-employment) in the white controlled farming sector. In fact, efforts at squatter farming or rural self-employment have been harshly suppressed, and income generating links between rural areas and adjoining African settlements have been minimized.

To make matters worse, the deliberate dualism in the country's agricultural development strategy — capital intensive, highly modern farming in the white-owned farming sector and lack of capital and know-how in the high-density rural settlements in the black tribal areas — has systematically undermined rural job creation. The more immediate prospects for change — and a higher rural labour absorption — are not bright as long as effective land reform is politically unacceptable to the white farming community.

This rural dilemma, together with the demographic transition, had a decisive influence on the third major factor raising the unemployment rate — the urbanization tide.

By 1990, it is estimated that between 55 and 58 per cent of Africans in South Africa (including the TBVC states) will be urbanized. The relationship between urbanization and employment is complex and differs over time. While rapid rural-to-urban movements almost always cause serious absorption problems on the labour markets, notably visibly higher unemployment in the towns, the longer-term effect may be just the opposite — stimulation of economic activities in the metropolitan areas and easing of land pressures and facilitation of land reform.

The characteristics of urbanization of the last ten to fifteen years — squatter settlements in overpopulated townships, poverty and high levels of unemployment — are likely to continue for another five to ten years, until an urbanization rate of 65 to 68 per cent has been reached and the task of absorbing new migrants in addition to those already settled becomes increasingly less onerous. (See Chapter 13.) For example, under Third World conditions it may take an urban dweller newly entering the labour market at least two years to find a regular full time job or create self-employment. An uneducated rural newcomer may take much longer — say three to four years. As the proportion of new immigrants decreases, so should this type of unemployment be reduced.

The rapid increase in relatively poorly-educated black youngsters also places a particular burden on a labour market already strained to the utmost. Thus, a two to three year waiting period for a black matriculant to be fully employed — and a three to four year wait for those with Standard 8 and less — seems almost normal at present. To some extent the problem has been aggravated by rising and unrealistic expectations among higher level school-leavers, that is, they wait for a job with acceptable status and remuneration rather than move down the job scale.

Turning to the macro demand for labour, the growth rate of the economy is usually viewed as the pivotal factor on the assumption of a positive correlation between gross domestic product (GDP) growth and employment. However, there may be many reasons why high(er) growth need not result in high(er) employment.

Assuming such a positive relationship, South Africa's GDP growth record over the past fifteen years seems to explain much of the high and rising level of unemployment. In contrast to real rates of growth of about 6 per cent in the 1960s, the average rate dropped to about 3 per cent in the 1970s and less than 2 per cent in the 1980s.

Official statistics on GDP growth and total employment in the formal economy follow similar trends: a decline in real growth is matched by a less expansive — if not negative — formal sector employment trend.

These trends do not take account of informal or statistically unidentified employment and GDP segments. In line with South Africa's rapid urbanization process, this informal sector has diversified and expanded substantially over the last fifteen years, in particular during the 1980s when deregulation gained ground and African urban settlements were tolerated. Today, as much as 30 per cent of the labour force may be involved in the informal sector.

Many reasons have been advanced for South Africa's lower growth in the formal sector, including over-regulation, inefficient government, the apartheid framework, capital flight, disinvestment, emigration of skilled labour, low productivity and high defence spending.

Not all of these are directly linked to the labour intake, but the impact of lower growth is more unemployment.

Other factors closely interact with structural impediments to faster economic growth and/or higher labour absorption at given GDP growth levels. The first relates to technological asymmetries, that is, a shift towards higher capital intensities and labour-saving technologies. The second factor relates to the broader framework of regulations, monopolistic constraints and administrative controls in the economy which have hampered the mobilization of entrepreneurship and the growth of the small business sector.

Unemployment caused by these structural changes has been further aggravated by the absence of effective policies to counter frictional, seasonal and cyclical unemployment. In South Africa's racially compartmentalized labour-market, frictional unemployment is relatively low among whites but much higher among coloured and Asian workers and, especially, African workers. This can be traced to decades of deliberate protection of white workers against competition from other groups. Since steps to dampen frictional employment were largely administered by the Department of Manpower — also responsible for job reservation policies — it is obvious that attitudes and policies changed slowly.

Seasonal unemployment is particularly important in the agricultural sector, where black workers are in a weak bargaining position. White labour in the past has been less sensitive to cyclical unemployment with the result that little emphasis was placed on counter-cyclical employment policies. Even now the state's stabilization policies — aimed at the balance of payments or dampening inflation — seem to accept cyclical unemployment as inevitable, with relatively little compensation provided.

This brings us to the last factor contributing to the relatively high level of unemployment — inequality in the distribution of income and wealth and the virtual absence of redistributive steps to minimize unemployment. This problem can be illustrated with a few examples:

▷ In contrast to several other developing countries, South Africa has no formalized tradition of labour sharing (where two or more persons share one formal sector job).

▷ The lack of wealth ownership among blacks makes it almost impossible for them to live off their assets during times of unemployment; this was possible with the widespread holding of cattle, but urbanization and land scarcity have reduced such opportunities.

▷ The only major unemployment insurance scheme, the Unemployment Insurance Fund, excludes large segments of the labour force and is primarily dependent on funds accumulated from reinvested member contributions. The state seems reluctant to supplement these funds.

▷ Low educational and skill levels, weak trade union leverage and the lack of effective political power make it difficult for black unemployed, low-income workers to re-enter the labour force.

▷ South Africa's racially stratified urban development patterns also discriminate against the unemployed, most of whom can only find accommodation furthest away from the more competitive employment nodes.

Taking into account the full range of these fundamental factors, we should not be surprised by the magnitude of South Africa's unemployment. Indeed, predictions that formal sector unemployment will further increase now seem plausible. That the actual level of unemployment is not even higher is the result of compensatory processes already taking place outside the formal sector.

Unemployment in broader perspective

South Africa is a semi-developed country, structurally comparable to a number of Latin American and Asian NICs, such as Malaysia and Thailand. These countries share with South Africa the following:

▷ a fairly advanced stage of demographic transition,

▷ a relatively advanced urbanization process;

▷ a relatively small and declining, but not insignificant, agricultural sector;

▷ attempts to increase the industrial sector as a base for further expansion;

▷ the rapid growth of informal sector activities, mostly in or around metropolitan areas;

▷ the maintenance of close ties with Western, highly developed economies — especially for investment capital, technology and know-how, the supply of capital goods and the absorption of exports;

▷ attempts to reduce such foreign dependency;

▷ frequent and often sharp cyclical fluctuations, linked to their export sectors, the inflation syndrome and balance of payment instabilities;

▷ relatively high and often increasing levels of unemployment; and

▷ a large, fairly autocratic public sector with increasing pressures to reduce the level and interventionist nature of state involvement in the
economies.

It is conventional in South Africa to judge our economic performance and
policies by comparing ourselves to highly industrialized Western countries,
most of whom experienced fairly high real per capita GDP growth rates,
low inflation and declining unemployment rates over the past decade. By
comparison with such economies, South Africa's performance is poor.

However, comparison with the semi-developed countries shows South
Africa to be remarkably in line with this group.

For example, the unemployment position is probably very similar. While
there are no reliable comparative figures available, even a 20 per cent (open)
unemployment level and 30 per cent informal sector labour absorption in
South Africa would probably be in line with current trends in most of these
countries. We also find similarities in rural poverty and under-employment,
high rates of youth unemployment and lengthy job search periods.

While the educational system seems to be in disarray in many of these
countries, average literacy rates, school-leaving standards and tertiary education accession rates are increasing from year to year — slowly, if measured
in conventional terms, yet significantly if looked at over a decade or a
generation.

While much informal sector involvement in these countries is little more
than a struggle for survival by those unable to get regular employment, the
informal sector also creates significant numbers of entrepreneurs, steady
jobs, and viable enterprises with growth potential.

In South Africa, as in other semi-developed countries, the past ten to
fifteen years of socio-economic transformation have seen the beginning of
many of the changes necessary for a breakthrough towards higher growth,
lower inflation, faster job creation and greater international competitiveness.

In the light of these similarities, what effect have South Africa's apartheid
policies had on our present high unemployment level? Are they likely to
prevent lasting success in the transformation process? As already shown,
there are several areas where socio-political action or institutional structures
linked to racial differentiation undoubtedly dampened economic growth
and black employment. These include:

▷ the abolition of squatter farming, which eliminated opportunities for
farmworkers to generate supplementary employment;

▷ the Physical Planning Act, which reduced employment in urban areas
and stimulated capital-for-labour substitution;

▷ draconian controls over African self-employment and informal sector
activities in the urban areas;

▷ racially-based restrictions on black property-ownership;

▷ racially biased job reservation regulations; and

▷ inadequate black education and training.

From the above, we can draw two seemingly contradictory conclusions: on the one hand, South Africa's unique apartheid system negatively influences overall growth and the absorption of black labour; on the other, the process of structural changes and rising unemployment in South Africa follows a path similar to that in other semi-developed countries.

What has happened is that socio-political restrictions and discriminatory policies have delayed certain adjustment processes, redistributed the pain of unemployment in favour of whites, and lowered the numbers of jobs created, but have not fundamentally changed or stalled the transformation process characteristic of most semi-developed countries.

This complex interaction between political (racial) and economic (structural) forces suggests that critics who try to blame all of our current unemployment and low growth on apartheid are just as one-sided as those who pretend that racial policies play no role in the unemployment dilemma.

We can now integrate the main elements likely to determine future patterns of economic development and employment. Structural changes taking place at present are likely to continue, even if the polity changes fairly drastically; induced changes hitherto not yet generally visible are likely to gain in strength, in particular if these changes are re-enforced through appropriate socio-economic policies.

In South Africa, more than in some other semi-developed countries, evolving majority governments are likely to place increasing emphasis on ameliorative policies benefiting their key support groups — which could dampen or even distort the overall process of transformation.

Within this overall process job creation and maintenance policies play an important role.

Policies to reduce unemployment

In South Africa, as elsewhere, public debate on high and increasing levels of unemployment has led to the formulation of a wide range of policy options. Closer scrutiny of these proposals reveals a host of contradictions and much wishful thinking. In fact, (un)employment levels and trends are really the outcome of the interaction of all economic sectors and the combined effect of all sorts of policies. Since the economy works as an organic system, the scope for direct or autonomous stimulation of employment is limited. This also explains why proponents of certain economic policy paradigms — for example, free marketeers — usually place more emphasis on the implementation of a coherent overall policy framework than on specific (job creation) policies.

Figure 14.1 outlines the interrelationship between fifteen major target areas for policies aimed at reducing unemployment. In Table 14.2 an attempt is made to summarize a range of policies, grouped under each of the fifteen target areas. A summary of the hypothesized relationship underlying each of the fifteen segments of the policy framework is outlined in the text that follows.

Figure 14.1   Target areas for policies to reduce unemployment

Quantitative labour supply ⑴	Quantitative labour supply ⑵	Cost and organization of labour ⑶	Labour market efficiency ⑷
Amelioration & redistribution of the unemployment burden ⒂	Social, political, historical		Capital supply and efficiency ⑸
State employment, subsidization & job creation ⒁	Local	**The economic process** Structure, level and trends of unemployment Inter-national	Supply and efficiency of entrepreneurship ⑹
Economic growth and cyclical stabilization ⒀	Institutional and economic forces		Market efficiency and competition ⑺
Sector development and labour absorption ⑿	Regional development and labour absorption ⑾	Urbanization and labour absorption ⑽	Local development and job creation ⑼	Small business and the informal sector ⑻

Table 14.2:   Countering unemployment: a policy menu

1. LABOUR SUPPLY QUANTITY

Policy instruments
1. Raise compulsory school age*
2. Expand primary, secondary and tertiary educational and training facilities*
3. Institute military and/or alternative community service for all youngsters
4. Expand full-time adult education facilities
5. Lower statutory pensionable age (male/female)
6. Encourage early retirement
7. Stricter control of foreign immigration*
8. Repatriation of foreign workers*

---

* In use or under consideration in South Africa.

9. Encourage family planning*
10. Increase female labour participation

Probable employment impact
1. Delay entry to labour market
2. Delay entry to labour market
3. Delay entry to labour market
4. Temporary exit from labour market
5. Higher exit from labour market, but little effect on overall unemployment
6. Higher exit from labour market, but little effect on overall unemployment
7. Little effect since immigration is mostly restricted to skilled workers
8. Most workers are from neighbouring African states; short-run results could be significant (about 400 000), but implementation politically and socially questionable
9. Only long term dampening effect on unemployment
10. Long-run positive growth effect, but in the short-term it increases unemployment

2. LABOUR SUPPLY QUANTITY

Policy instruments
1. Improve on-the-job training*
2. Deracialize education and training*
3. Improve the regional spread of educational and training facilities*
4. Develop re-training facilities for previously employed/skilled jobless*
5. Stimulate productivity through productivity drives and the reorganization of production

Probable employment impact
1. Increase labour productivity, economic growth and, hopefully, employment
2. Spread the burden more equally
3. Improve employment in neglected regions
4. Facilitate re-employment in neglected regions
5. Improve labour productivity, economic growth and, in the longer run, employment

3. PRODUCTION COST AND THE ORGANIZATION OF LABOUR

Policy instruments
1. Dampen minimum wage levels*
2. Deregulate wage determination machinery*
3. Dampen union wage bargaining or extend it to productivity bargaining*
4. Deregulate other employment controls (e.g. de-control SBDC Hives)*

Probable employment impact
1. Reduce wage costs and possibly stimulate demand for labour
2. Reduce wage costs and possibly stimulate demand for labour
3. Reduce wage costs and possibly stimulate demand for labour
4. Reduce wage costs and possibly stimulate demand for labour

---

* In use or under consideration in South Africa.

4. LABOUR MARKET EFFICIENCY (See also nos. 2 and 4 under Section 3.)

Policy instruments
1. Deracialize all remaining labour market regulations/practices*
2. Expand, streamline and decentralize state labour bureaux*
3. Further expand private recruitment system*
4. Improve inter-regional recruiting*

Probable employment impact
1. Reduce wage costs and possibly stimulate demand for labour
2. Reduce frictional unemployment
3. Reduce frictional unemployment
4. Reduce frictional and regional unemployment

5. CAPITAL SUPPLY AND EFFICIENCY

Policy instruments
1. Stimulate local capital formation (via fiscal, monetary and other means)*
2. Stimulate net foreign capital inflow*
3. Reorientate public as well as private investment priorities towards employment creation/higher labour intensity*
4. Stimulate and apply appropriate, labour intensive technologies (R/D and dissemination)*

Probable employment impact
1. Can increase employment if funds are re-invested in production process
2. Can have positive effect on growth and employment
3. Medium- and long-term stimulation of employment
4. Medium- and long-run stimulation of employment (or dampening of labour replacement)

6. SUPPLY OF ENTREPRENEURSHIP

Policy instrument
1. Improve entrepreneurial training*
2. Adjust tax structure to stimulate entrepreneurship
3. Encourage subcontracting and other types of derived entrepreneurial growth*
4. Strengthen entrepreneurship in the public sector

Probable employment impact
1. Job creation effect could be substantial
2. Net employment effect depends on re-investment policies of firms
3. Positive employment effect depends on techniques and productivity levels
4. More dynamic public sector could stimulate economic growth and longer-run employment.

---

* In use or under consideration in South Africa.

7. MARKET EFFICIENCY AND COMPETITION

Policy instrument

1. Expand the deregulation drive*
2. Counter monopolistic market restrictions*
3. Prevent disruptive competition*

Probable employment impact

1. Improve job creation opportunities — not necessarily total employment
2. Prevent constraints on job creation with possible employment increase
3. Protect existing jobs

8. SMALL BUSINESS AND THE INFORMAL SECTOR

Policy instruments

1. Accept, accommodate and support informal sector activities (public and private sector action required)*
2. Counter obstacles to small business (SB) growth*
3. Mobilize/channel capital for SB growth*
4. Strengthen interaction between SB and larger enterprises*

Probable employment impact

1. Facilitate self employment and reduce open unemployment
2. Stimulate economic growth, self-employment and overall employment
3. Stimulate economic growth, self-employment and overall employment
4. Stimulate economic growth, self-employment and overall employment

9. LOCAL DEVELOPMENT AND JOB CREATION

Policy instruments

1. Establish/encourage or assist community development projects*
2. Establish/encourage or assist local enterprise/industrial hive schemes*
3. Prevent constraints on local job creation and improve the local job creation environment (include no. 1 from Section 7 and nos. 1 and 2 from Section 8 locally)*

Probable employment impact

1. Stimulate local job creation
2. Stimulate local job creation
3. Stimulate local job creation

10. URBANIZATION AND LABOUR ABSORPTION

Policy instruments

1. Phase out migration/influx controls*
2. Encourage self-help settlement and housing*
3. Strengthen links between new and established urban communities*

---

* In use or under consideration in South Africa.

4. Strengthen urban development strategies (based on growth sectors/comparative advantages)*

Probable employment impact

1. Increase short-term unemployment but stimulates economic growth and employment in long-run
2. Facilitates self-employment
3. Increases employment only indirectly
4. Medium-term job creation effects

---

11. REGIONAL DEVELOPMENT (Note links with Sections 9 and 10.)

Policy instruments

1. Identify and propagate regional comparative advantages; develop an appropriate development strategy*
2. Deregulate regional labour in/outflow*
3. Claim proper share of public sector activities for regional economy*
4. Replace decentralization policies with more cost-efficient support (Nkuhlu Report)*

Probable employment impact

1. Create basis for regional growth and medium-run job creation
2. Could increase or decrease short-term unemployment; positive effect in longer run.
3. Could increase regional employment at cost of other region(s) (suitable for neglected/lagging regions)
4. Employment stimulation only indirectly, due to budget savings

---

12. SECTOR (RE)DEVELOPMENT (Linked to Sections 5 to 11.)

Policy instruments

1. Evolve sector (re)development strategies, taking account of structural changes*
2. Set sector employment targets for key sectors
3. Implement structural adjustment policies in each sector (e.g. land reform, export promotion, import replacement, etc.)*
4. Proactive anti-cyclical sector policies (e.g. in mining, agriculture, tourism)

Probable employment impact

1. Create stronger awareness of employment needs and scope; positive medium-run effect
2. Strengthening of job creation commitment could have positive medium-run effect.
3. Higher growth to stimulate employment in the longer run
4. Dampening unemployment during downswing

---

* In use or under consideration in South Africa.

---

13. ECONOMIC GROWTH AND CYCLICAL STABILIZATION (Also see no. 4 of Section 12 and Sections 7 and 14.)

Policy instruments

1. Stabilizatory/expansive monetary policy*
2. Stabilizatory/expansive fiscal policy*
3. 'Liberal' foreign trade policies*
4. 'Flexible' foreign exchange policy*
5. Tax reform (lower taxation and less emphasis on direct taxation)

Probable employment impact

1. Positive employment effect assumed but time lagged
2. Employment effect could be substantial if timed properly (which is difficult due to political factors)
3. Direct employment effect likely to be limited or negative in the short-run (but substantial in the longer-run — Taiwan model)
4. Positive employment effect possible due to dampended imports and expanding exports
5. Could stimulate entrepreneurship, capital formation and self-employment/job creation in the longer-run.

---

14. STATE EMPLOYMENT AND EMPLOYMENT STIMULATION

Policy instruments

1. Increase in public works projects
2. Decrease in state expenditure and taxes
3. Privatization of state enterprises*
4. Nationalization of 'key' enterprises*
5. Subsidization of wage bills*
6. Subsidization of recruitment
7. *Ad hoc* job creation programmes (currently in existence, e.g. through Department of Manpower)*

Probable employment impact

1. Significant short-term employment effect, but costly
2. Supply-side approach to higher medium-term employment creation; net effect uncertain in short-run
3. Net direct employment effect likely to be negative; indirect effect due to growth stimulation could be positive
4. Net employment effect could be positive but at high costs (and in the long-run most probably negative)
5. High cost per job actually created (net)
6. High cost per job actually created (net) but less than no. 5
7. Danger of high cost and low retention rate

---

* In use or under consideration in South Africa.

15. AMELIORATION AND REDISTRIBUTION OF THE BURDEN

Policy instruments

1. Industrial relations policies (retrenchment procedures, severance pay, retraining, re-employment)*

2. Expand the UIF-system to cover more categories and all black areas*

3. Consider introduction of expanded poverty or unemployment relief system (or no. 4)

4. Introduction of 'negative income tax' (minimum household income or food stamp system)

5. Youth employment programmes

6. Shortened work week and/or controlled overtime

7. Job splitting/work sharing

Probable employment impact

1. Better phasing of retrenchment and some compensation of the unemployment; no overall reduction in unemployment

2. Reduction of burden on unemployed worker

3. Reduction of material burden of unemployment

4. Reduction of material burden of unemployment

5. Improvement of labour market entry; reduction in burden of unemployment, but no net job creation

6. If implemented, it will better spread the burden of unemployment

7. If implemented, it will better spread the burden of unemployment

---

* In use or under consideration in South Africa.

1. Quantitative labour supply

If the number of people entering the labour markets at age sixteen can be reduced and/or the exit from the labour force increased, overall labour supply will decrease and the employment task will appear more manageable.

2. Qualitative labour supply

A better educated, trained and experienced labour force should improve productivity levels. It could also dampen cost inflation and might even stimulate consumer demand. It is also generally assumed that well educated and skilled workers find it easier to adapt to unemployment, create their own jobs or generate further job opportunities.

3. Production cost and the organization of labour

Excessive wage inflation and/or obstructionist attitudes of organized labour are likely to lead to the more rapid substitution of capital for labour. Cost increases through wage cost inflation can also dampen consumer demand and exports. The reverse of this reasoning suggests that lower real wage costs and relatively docile labour is good for cost effective production, competitive exports and local sales of cheap products. Underlying this reasoning is the Taiwan/Hong Kong model of successful industrialization. The applicability of this model to South Africa is, however, limited, because other characteristics of these communities do not apply here.

4. Labour market efficiency

A considerable proportion of unemployment (in particular frictional unemployment) is caused by inefficient labour markets: supply and demand are not in balance, either because the actors are not aware of each other or because other obstacles prevent the market from functioning. Such obstacles could include restrictive rules and regulations, racially discriminatory policies, weaknesses in the system of labour bureau and other aspects of the recruitment process.

Again, it is generally assumed that improvements in market efficiency will lower unemployment levels.

5. Capital supply and efficiency

With the exception of parts of the informal sector and some service establishments, virtually all employment-creating economic activities require considerable amounts of capital. The amount depends on the capital:labour ratio in the enterprise. Thus, it is argued that lack of capital or unduly high cost of capital will dampen job creation and so contribute to more unemployment.

6. Supply and efficiency of entrepreneurship

As with capital, entrepreneurship is necessary to initiate production and can therefore be seen as a pre-condition for more employment. Steps that stimulate or mobilize private entrepreneurship are thus seen as benefiting job creation.

7. Market efficiency and competition

More efficient and competitive markets improve productivity and lower costs — consequences which are usually linked to economic growth and higher employment. On the other hand, monopolistic or oligopolistic market restrictions are seen to dampen output and employment.

8. Expansion of the informal sector and small business activities

It is generally assumed that small, informal enterprises are more labour intensive, that they make fewer demands on scarce capital resources and that the mobilization of entrepreneurship and the necessary skilled labour is less problematic than with larger enterprises. However, as much of the informal sector is merely a fall-back position ('survival entrepreneurship') for those unable to find employment in the formal sector, there is a risk of overstating the job creation potential of this sector.

9. Local development and job creation

Because macroeconomic job creation is not effective and regional job creation usually expensive, emphasis among policy planners during the last decade has shifted towards the local or community sphere. It is argued that at such grassroots level different input requirements can be co-ordinated more effectively, leading to significantly higher employment.

10. Urbanization and labour absorption

This relationship is complex, since short- and long-term effects upon the rural and urban areas must be considered. The more painful short-term effects, like overcrowding and unemployment, in peri-urban slum areas are obvious, but they trigger counteraction which is assumed to further stimulate entrepreneurship and self-employment.

About the positive relationship in the medium and longer term between urbanization and employment there is little doubt.

11. Regional development and labour absorption

Given the geographic immobility of much of the labour force, emphasis over the last two decades has shifted from national to regional unemployment. In many countries regional growth and unemployment levels differ sharply: South Africa's long history of separate development and influx control has aggravated this.

Regional development proponents suggest that appropriate policies can spur development to match each region's resources and stimulate employment at reasonable costs. Free market proponents regard such steps as unnecessary as long as labour and other markets are allowed to operate to reduce inequalities.

12. Sector development and labour absorption

Because stagnation or declining growth in specific economic sectors can create unemployment, efforts to stimulate sector growth are generally regarded as beneficial for employment. The interrelationship can, of course, be quite complex. For example, changing technologies could result in expanding sector output and lower employment. Alternatively, a sector may be doomed in the long run because of changing demand, so that short-term stimulatory efforts to save jobs may be more costly than a sectoral redirection of retrenched labour.

13. Economic growth and cyclical stabilization

It is often assumed that steps to stimulate overall economic growth or efforts to counterbalance cyclical downswings will directly stimulate employment and reduce unemployment. A satisfactory growth rate would, accordingly, also guarantee the solution to unemployment problems.

More careful observation of broad economic policies aimed at faster growth indicates a more complex reality. For example, jobs lost during a stabilization phase may not be easily revived in an expansion phase. Also, employment usually follows cyclical upswings with considerable time lags.

14. State employment and the subsidization of job creation

Conventional views about the relationship between public sector employment and direct state subsidization of job creation on the one hand and overall employment on the other are full of contradictions.

The public sector undoubtedly can reduce unemployment through state employment. In sharp contrast, free enterprise proponents argue that less state employment will stimulate the economy so that total employment increases even faster. Between these opposing views lies much of the controversy about the job creation effect of privatization and nationalization strategies and other direct ways of subsidizing job creation.

15. Amelioration and redistribution of the unemployment burden

This target area does not focus on the creation of jobs but rather seeks to reduce the socio-economic burdens of joblessness. It is likely to gain far more attention in future, if the numerically important unemployed increase their political leverage, as seems likely.

This brief overview of key target areas for economic policies aimed at the employment challenge, read with Table 14.2, should make us wary of any simplistic set of policy proposals put forward as the solution to unemployment.

In many of the policy areas the desired stimulation of employment is only a possibility, the realization of which depends on the interaction of various other policy steps and intermediate structural adjustments.

Despite the rhetoric of politicians and policy planners, job creation is frequently only a secondary goal. Thus, fighting unemployment is often advocated in support of policy proposals, if for no other reason than to win support for policies which actually have totally different primary objectives. Furthermore, the analysis in this chapter suggests that the effect may often be quantitatively insignificant, especially in the shorter run. It is worth noting, furthermore, that frequently positive effects can only be expected over the longer term.

In the list of potential policies in Table 14.2, a number of contradictions should also be obvious. Thus, proponents of privatization and nationalization cannot both be correct in motivating their approach with an expected stimulation in job creation. Similarly, the supporters of less state spending and those of public sector job creation programmes hold contradictory views, though each seems logically consistent in terms of its own assumptions.

To overcome these problems, we need to look closely at each of the policy steps. What is more, a number of rather complex policy areas — like support for small business and the informal sector — have not even been discussed in any detail.

Within the constraints of this chapter such discussion of detail is not possible. It seems more appropriate to take a dynamic look at the policy range and priorities currently discernable in South Africa and to stress the need for greater strategic planning in countering unemployment.

Implementing a job creation strategy

In Table 14.2 an attempt is made to identify a wide range of policy areas appropriate for the support of job creation. Of seventy-two such policy areas about twenty are either not pursued in this country or commitment to them is lukewarm. Nevertheless, the actively pursued range of policies is already very broad and expanding.

If we view the policy areas summarized in Figure 14.1 in the context of the fundamental changes that have taken place in South Africa's economic policy stance over the past decade, we can discern a clear shift away from state employment, cyclical stabilization and old-style regional job creation towards greater market efficiency, an improvement in the quality of labour, the stimulation of entrepreneurship and small business, and greater willingness to accept urbanization.

Recently, the emphasis has shifted further towards mobilizing greater capital supply and sector or industry specific structural adjustments which have the potential for more job creation in the longer term.

Three areas with the lowest priority so far are the dampening of the quantitative labour supply, which is essentially a long-term strategy; ameliorative and redistributive policies, which are politically and financially difficult to pursue; and local or community-based job creation efforts, which depend on local rather than state policy initiatives.

Against this background of changing policies and high levels of un(der)-

employment we have to ask what can be done to increase the effectiveness of policies. Six areas suggest themselves:

1. First, we need the political will of policy-makers as opposed to mere lip service to achieve significant results. Given the present structure of power in South Africa, those directly affected by unemployment play, at best, only a subordinate role in decision-making. Dominant interest groups focus mostly on policies which only indirectly support job creation. Those directly concerned with unemployment have little leverage in the decision-making process.

   With the changing balance of political power in South Africa we should, however, expect the thrust of such policies to change.

2. A second pre-condition for more effective policy implementation is the close monitoring of present policies on their success in job creation. The task seems vast, since we do not actually know which policies will succeed in stimulating employment. Besides, more detailed measurement of employment are required with respect to regions, towns, economic sectors, industries and community areas.

3. A third dimension follows directly from the above — the need for explicit quantitative targeting of job creation policies. National employment targets related to the expected growth in the labour force should be set, as well as indicative targets for different regions, sectors, industries and local communities. This does not suggest that job creation policies can be designed to achieve any chosen target, but it forces policy-makers to think carefully about their promises.

4. A fourth dimension concerns the education of the public about feasible and/or effective job creation policies. In a polarized, semi-developed society like South Africa it will often be difficult to mobilize support for specific policies, especially if there is no guaranteed short-term net employment increase. The dilemma becomes even greater if longer-term policies (like wage restraint) are seen to have a detrimental short-term or distributional effect on some interest groups — particularly those more exposed to short-term unemployment.

5. Greater policy efficiency will depend largely on the structuring of particular policies. For example, the Small Business Development Corporation is constantly reviewing the effectiveness of alternative ways of assisting informal sector job creation and job maintenance. Secondly, the debate about practical ways of work-sharing and/or reducing the work week of those employed (to benefit the unemployed), has hardly started in this country.

6. Finally, far more attention must be paid to the employment process at the level of macroeconomic data analysis and the government's

budgets. Most short-term economic forecasts contain virtually no employment projections, while the authoritative Reserve Bank Bulletin pays only marginal attention to employment trends.

These proposals for a more effective job creation strategy also indicate the need for a broad-based job creation movement in South Africa. The need for such a movement does not contradict the undeniable progress that has already been made in job creation so far. It merely suggests that there is enormous scope for improvement.

Who should initiate such a movement? Undoubtedly, central government has a major role to play, as have regional and local authorities, organized business, big business, consumer organizations, organized labour, the small business sector, community groups and voluntary organizations.

The co-ordinating role in such a national employment drive might fall upon the National Manpower Commission or the Department of Manpower, although both are probably too closely tied to government to be able to ensure bi-partisan support. It might thus be necessary to create an umbrella body broad enough in its composition to represent all those interests, yet flexible and streamlined enough to play the role of an efficient co-ordinating secretariat, rather than adding yet another bureaucratic layer.

Such a secretariat, supported by the different bodies mentioned above, would have to draw up a medium-term employment framework with broad, overall targets for job creation. All relevant policy-making bodies would have to co-operate to set annual targets linked to different policy areas. The annual revision of these targets, based on detailed monitoring of the job creation process and ongoing policy adjustments, would be the symbolic focal point of such a movement, where development is measured in employment and job creation.

15 Industrial relations: the emerging choices

Bobby Godsell

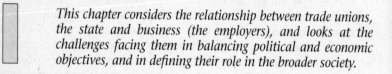

This chapter considers the relationship between trade unions, the state and business (the employers), and looks at the challenges facing them in balancing political and economic objectives, and in defining their role in the broader society.

A brief historical overview

Before the discovery of diamonds and gold a little over a hundred years ago, South Africa was essentially a subsistence farming economy with a small and fragile mercantile sector. These discoveries marked the start of the creation of an industrial society out of this caste-like feudal social order.

Nowhere were the consequences more dramatic than in the labour market. Up to the third quarter of the nineteenth century South Africa's labour market consisted of three categories: most people were engaged in subsistence agriculture, either in a tribal/traditional context or as labour tenants on settler farms; a smaller group were domestic servants; the third, much smaller category was made up of merchants and traditional craftsmen. Large-scale mining of diamonds and gold required two new kinds of workers — industrial tradesmen (fitters, boilermakers, timbermen and miners) and industrial labourers.

Industrial tradesmen were initially imported from metropolitan countries, notably the United Kingdom. They brought not only their skills, but also their trade-union traditions, and indeed their unions themselves. The South African Amalgamated Engineering Workers Union, for example, was a branch of the British mother union of the same name until 1957.

To these imported skilled workers was added a domestic supply drawn from the newly urbanizing Dutch-derived settlers, who were forced out of rural society by a finite and ultimately insufficient supply of farming land. This process of urbanization became significant in the first decades of the twentieth century. The key characteristic shared by those who came to the new mining camps both from across the seas and from the farms was their white skin and its important advantage of political participation.

The creation of new economic classes brought with it new forms of conflict. Skilled white labour soon came into conflict with both employers and the state. A climax was reached in the 1922 'Rand Rebellion' when striking workers transformed themselves into an army of occupation. This alliance between immigrant British socialist and newly-urbanized Afrikaner nationalists was to dominate labour policy until 1948, when the interests of English-speaking socialists were no longer politically relevant.

The state's response to the 1922 rebellion was to start a process of economic and political incorporation of worker interests that was remarkably successful.

Through their unions, workers became politically involved in a process of self-government of industry through collective bargaining with employers in the institution of the industrial council. The council was both a forum for collective bargaining and a structure for representative government, enjoying the same powers of permitted domestic legislation as provincial and municipal councils.

There are about a hundred industrial councils and they have become the structure for an industry-wide pattern of social welfare provision. Most operate retirement funds, medical funds or services, holiday-bonus schemes and, in some industries, 'slack-time' unemployment benefits.

For fifty years the system transformed economic and political conflict into industrial peace and economic partnership. This 'politics of incorporation' was, however, limited to white workers who were also politically enfranchised, and, by historical accident, to coloured and Indian workers.

Knocking on the door

The union concept was evident among African industrial workers from the outset of South Africa's industrial revolution. Throughout this century serious efforts have been made to organize African workers into either general or industrial-style unions. In each decade the recruitment campaigns succeeded, but the unions which resulted met opposition from both employers and the state. They failed to get to the collective bargaining table. These new unions became involved in political campaigning and either were effectively repressed by the state or dissipated themselves knocking on a firmly locked door.

The pattern of mobilization, union formation, recruitment, employee resistance and state repression was broken in the 1970s. A number of reasons can be identified, but the key factor was certainly the changing skills base of African workers. The expanded levels and types of production required by the war effort (on the Namibian border) and the absence of about a quarter of a million white workers in war service drew hundreds of thousands of Africans into new skilled and semi-skilled occupations. In the early

1960s the South African economy had diversified into secondary production of manufactured goods. This required more skilled and semi-skilled workers. The increased base of skilled African workers in turn gave existing and new unions new clout. A skilled and semi-skilled labour force cannot easily be replaced. It has bargaining power.

The new power of African workers was first demonstrated in the Durban area in a spate of strikes in the first three months of 1973. What distinguished these strikers from their predecessors was the different response they produced from both employers and the state. Most employers did not dismiss strikers, and many strikers won significant wage increases. Attitudes to African unions softened. Smith and Nephew became the first large company to start negotiating with African unions.

The state's response was also a break with the past. Prime Minister John Vorster, said that everyone could learn from the 1973 Durban Strikes, and that what they could learn was that African workers were human beings with souls and not just labour units. The government's initial reaction was to pass legislation providing for workplace committees. These committees were clearly intended by the legislature to be an alternative to the trade unions which had served white, coloured and Indian workers effectively for fifty years. The committee system never took root, while the union movement — still unrecognized by the state — went from strength to strength.

In 1977 the government set up a multiracial commission of inquiry into the country's labour laws under the chairmanship of Professor Nic Wiehahn. Two years later the Wiehahn Commission recommended, and the government accepted, that African unions should enjoy the same legal rights as white unions. This commission also successfully recommended the abolition of the statutory colour bar in industry.

Contemporary patterns of labour relationships

The decade since state-recognized union rights were extended to African workers has seen a dramatic growth in union membership. Currently, some 2,5 million workers belong to unions, almost 2 million of whom are Africans.

The pattern of union organization has also changed. In 1979 the union movement was dominated by a national federation, the Trade Union Council of South Africa (Tucsa). Its leadership was made up of craft unionists, and in some respects the body resembled the American Federation of Labour. Its membership was predominantly white, coloured and Indian.

Ten years later the trade union geography is dominated by two (predominantly) African federations. The Congress of South African Trade Unions (Cosatu), with about a million members, is the largest and most powerful federation. Its membership reflects, in the main, single industrial unions in most industrial sectors such as mining, metal, paper and textiles.

Cosatu has strong national and regional structures. It also has important relationships outside the labour movement. Internally it has defined a relationship with the United Democratic Front (UDF) as well as other 'resistance' organizations such as the self-styled Mass Democratic Movement (MDM). Externally, a relationship with the African National Congress (ANC) was defined shortly after Cosatu's formation. Close co-operation, regular contact and joint 'programmes of action' have linked Cosatu to political organizations and issues since inception. This labour/politics relationship is ambiguous and complex.

The second largest federation, The National Council of Trade Unions (Nactu), also comprises predominantly African unions. It has its origins in a merger of unions with the Urban Training Project as their base and those affiliated to the Azanian Congress of Trade Unions (Azactu). These unions, whose membership totals about 250 000, have sought to maintain a greater organizational autonomy in their relationship with political organizations. Judging by their rhetoric, however, the degree of political conviction and commitment is neither less pronounced, nor in any sense moderate. The Nactu unions are often described as standing in either the Africanist or black consciousness political traditions.

White workers continue to constitute a powerful element in the labour movement, particularly evident in the craft unions such as the fitters' (AEU), electricians' and boilermakers' unions. The abolition of the industrial colour bar in 1979 produced a range of responses from these craft unions. Some, such as the AEU, have opted to remain exclusively white organizations, retaining white control, but limiting membership growth. Others created racially parallel unions. However, most of the African parallel unions have exercised their autonomy and ended up in the Cosatu or Nactu camp. A third group has chosen multiracial membership, though some, such as the boilermakers' union, have given some recognition to race within union structures.

White industrial unions, often drawing much of their membership from state-run corporations such as Iscor (South African Iron and Steel Corporation), have declined both in membership and national influence.

The employers have strong and effective associations in most industrial sectors, where bodies such as the metal industry's Seifsa and the Chamber of Mines provide a full range of economic and industrial relations services. At national level, however, no organizational equivalent of Cosatu and Nactu exists. The three national bodies representing commerce (Assocom) industry (FCI)[1] and Afrikaans business (AHI) do combine with sector specific bodies, such as those mentioned above, in the South African Employers Consultative Committee on Labour Affairs (Saccola). This body, though no more than a standing committee served only by a part-time secretary, has represented employers in debate about labour legislation with Cosatu and Nactu. It also acts as a vehicle for presenting consensus views on labour matters to government.

The last decade has seen steady progress in the development of the structures and conventions of collective bargaining. African industrial unions are becoming staunch advocates of multi-employer, industry-wide bargaining. The decade has also seen the development of private mediation and arbitration, with a key role being played by the Independent Mediation Service of South Africa (Imsa). African unions and union federations have been equally active in creating a new and vigorous body of labour law, stimulated by the creation in 1979 of a new-style Industrial Court.

The state, in the form of the re-designated Department of Manpower (formally Labour), has sought to reduce its role in labour relations to that of umpire and bureaucratic facilitator. The actions of security agencies on the one hand and the political programme of the African union federations on the other have often frustrated this desired technocratic role.

Future dilemmas: the challenge to the state

What effect will the industrial actors and their interrelationship have on the broader processes of transforming society now underway? We can try to assess this by looking at some of the key challenges facing the key actors.

The challenges the state faces come both from within the labour relations arena and from outside it.

The challenges from within arise from a fundamental asymmetry. The key state agency, the Department of Manpower, operates between the cabinet and parliament, which sets the agenda for administrative and legislative state action, on the one hand and the unions and employers on the other. From the publication of the first Wiehahn Report, the Department of Manpower has assiduously sought to de-politicize labour issues and its own role. It has adopted a technocratic approach to labour. It has also tried to achieve broad-based support for changes to labour legislation through extensive consultation with unions and employers. However, the department has also had to take its cue from the cabinet and parliament. This is where the asymmetry occurs. The interests of African workers do not find expression in the parliament of South Africa. No African serves in parliament. It is

---

[1] Assocom and the FCI will merge during 1990

therefore to be expected that the two major (predominantly) African union federations, Cosatu and Nactu, dispute the legitimacy of parliament and react to its deliberations with mistrust and hostility. Equally, these federations have refused to serve on the statutory advisory body whose job is to review labour legislation and initiate change where required, the National Manpower Commission (NMC).

The absence of representatives of Cosatu and Nactu from both parliament and the NMC means that there is no structured means for African unions to be drawn into the governance of the labour-relations system. The problems this causes are illustrated by Cosatu/Nactu's opposition to the 1988 Labour Relations Amendment Act, and the form this opposition has taken. In June 1988 the union federations staged a three-day stayaway. Both before and after this event Cosatu and Nactu were engaged in talks with the employer committee, Saccola. These talks occurred in parallel with the parliamentary processing of the Amendment Bill, and the investigations and review activities of the NMC.

The state faces the dilemma of wishing on the one hand to secure the broadest possible support base for labour law (and therefore encouraging the Saccola/Cosatu/Nactu talks) and on the other hand wishing not to undermine the formal structures already in place to deal with these issues (therefore discouraging them).

A challenge from outside the labour relations system arises from the political role the African union movement is playing in South Africa. African unions in general, and Cosatu in particular, form the largest and most powerful segment of the internal black political organization that currently styles itself as the MDM.

Externally, Cosatu is part of a formal alliance with the ANC, which sees itself as at war with the South African government. This gives Cosatu a sort of Jekyll and Hyde character as viewed by the state.

As a prominent participant in the new labour dispensation, Cosatu and its affiliates constitute an important part of the new social order. As allies of both internal mobilization and external armed challenges, they operate (again in the eyes of the state) on the edge of treason.

During the security crackdowns of the 1985 and 1986 States of Emergency union leaders were detained and restricted. In February 1988 Cosatu was prohibited from engaging in a range of political activities. These restrictions appear to have had little practical effect on the federation: its industrial union affiliates have continued to function and grow, despite the attention they have received from state agencies.

How can the state respond to these challenges?

The challenge from within the disputed legitimacy of state institutions will not be resolved until African access to and involvement in South Africa's political institutions is the same as that of their compatriots. Until this occurs the state can try to find means of accommodating bodies like Cosatu and Nactu in the legislative process, so removing labour issues from the broader struggle for political power.

Such an attempt is not as forlorn as it may seem. Unions require 'fair' rules of the game to recruit, mobilize and bargain. If unions place their wage-setting, workplace conflict resolution role at risk through political campaigns, they will lose both economic and political capacity.

As regards the 'revolutionary' or treasonable aspect of this political role, the same challenge faces both security agencies and the cabinet. Can government distinguish between peaceful democratic mobilization and the advocacy or conduct of armed insurrection? There is a line between the two that needs to be observed by both government and its challenger. It requires an understanding of the nature and robustness of popular politics and an ability to measure revolutionary rhetoric against deeds which are often far from revolutionary but indeed strengthen the present social order.

The challenge to the unions

The union movement in South Africa faces a critical double challenge:

▷ It must define its role in the process of political transformation.

▷ It must establish its role in the processes of economic development.

The first challenge is complex. Trade unions in pluralistic, democratic societies perform a dual role. Alongside their economic purposes they act as an important vehicle for the collective political aspirations of their members. The history of industrializing societies is replete with examples of the tensions between the political and economic roles of unions.

Perhaps this conflict is best described in the nature of collective bargaining itself. To establish their power base, unions mobilize mass support around grievances. In their mobilizing role, they articulate conflict. To maintain their mass membership, they must produce tangible benefits, which they do by resolving the issues in conflict, or at least some of them, through negotiation with management. In their negotiating role, unions resolve conflict.

Whether trade unions successfully reconcile their economic and political objectives seems to be determined by the balance between conflict articulation (if not generation) and conflict resolution on the one hand, and relations between unions and the broader society on the other.

In stable, democratic societies conflict articulation and conflict resolution often achieve an equilibrium which makes the union movement simultaneously an instrument of social order and social change in both economy and polity. Where bargaining fails in the economy, and/or there is no space for unions to develop a role in political negotiation, unions can become a major force for social instability.

Nowhere is this role more clearly illustrated than in Germany between the two world wars, and in West Germany after the World War II. In the first period (1918–33) the union movement played a key role in destroying the Weimar Republic through economic disruption and political violence. From 1951 onwards (and indeed starting from the first winter after the end of the European war) the unions were a pillar of West Germany's reconstruction. Two key variables appear to be:

1. the success or failure of collective bargaining; and

2. the presence or absence of a range of political parties competing for power through elections.

Where bargaining succeeds, it establishes a habit and pattern of conflict resolution through compromise. Where parties must regularly compete for power through the ballot, unions establish their autonomy as free and independent organizations. Their relationship with the political process becomes one of creative tension. Such tension is evident in the relationship between German unions and the Social Democratic Party, between the British TUC and the Labour Party, between American unions and the Democratic Party.

The tension is evident in the institutional relationship between union federation and political organization. It is also evident in the ambivalent capacity of union federations to deliver the votes of their members. Elections this century demonstrate the capacity of loyal union members to ignore the advice of union bosses when voting.

What of South Africa?

The evidence thus far is mixed. In the earliest decades of craft unionism mostly white workers showed both their destabilizing power (in the 1922 Rand Rebellion) and their electoral power (in causing changes of government in 1924 and 1948). Until the 1970s the role of industrial unions (largely African) was one of frustration and futility. Repeated campaigns to mobilize a significant part of the industrial work-force foundered on the rock of employer intransigence. Denied a place at the collective bargaining table, these industrial unions turned their hand to populist politics. Here too they were frustrated both by the repressive actions of the state (for example in the 1930s and again in the 1960s) as well as the absence of franchise rights among their members.

The diversification of South Africa's economic life in the 1950s and 1960s dramatically changed the skills base of the industrial labour force. By the early 1970s the critical mass of African industrial workers were employed in semi-skilled occupations. This enabled the re-emergent African union movement to break into the collective bargaining arena. It also made state repression very costly, if not altogether impossible.

Today South Africa's major African industrial unions exist in political tension between the South African state and the organizations seeking political power in the name of black South Africans.

Relations between unions and the state are ambiguous, to say the least. In recent times the South African government has sought to prosecute key union leaders and, at least by implication, the major union federation Cosatu for treason. At the same time another government department was inviting this same federation (and its rival Nactu) to serve on a statutory advisory body, the National Manpower Commission!

From the union side, most African unions eschew meetings with political representatives of the present government, yet make extensive use of the statutory collective bargaining machinery created by it.

Relations between unions and political movements such as the ANC, UDF and Pan African Congress (PAC) are no less complex. Cosatu has formal alliances with the ANC and with the UDF. To understand Cosatu as a mechanical extension of either the ANC or UDF would be a dangerous simplification. Which is the tail and which is the dog?

The current debate on the need for a workers charter, which would take its place alongside the 1955 Freedom Charter and the recent ANC revised Constitutional Guidelines, illustrates Cosatu's desire to retain autonomy in defining the political agenda of its members, if not the working class as a whole. The debate that has raged for some years within Cosatu, and which commentators have come to label the workerist/populist debate, is a further indication of the ambiguity of Cosatu's political role. This debate is as much tactical as ideological.

Nactu, Cosatu's smaller rival, has eschewed formal political alliances with the ANC and its less prominent political rival, the PAC. Nevertheless, it is viewed as being in broad sympathy with Africanist trends in South African politics.

What will the relationship be between the political and economic agendas of South Africa's mainly African industrial unions? This will turn on the future success of collective bargaining and the political culture dominant in those seeking power in the name of the majority.

On the first score the track record is encouraging. Notwithstanding some spectacular conflicts, such as the three-week mine strike and the ten-week railway conflict of 1987, most negotiations result in agreements. The habit of compromise is well established in the workplaces of South Africa. The union movement has much to lose by resolving its political ambiguity into a position of unqualified hostility and non-cooperation with the present social order.

As regards political culture, the outlook is less encouraging. A response to the failure of popular insurrection over the period 1984–6 has been to cast the union movement as the engine of resistance politics. Instead of being seen as an independent, autonomous element of a post-apartheid society, its identity is being subsumed in that of organizations such as the ANC and popular fronts such as the UDF and MDM. This may encourage the unions to try to play a role inconsistent with the nature of their structure and power.

The key economic choices facing South Africa's unions are those endemic in the economic process. Modernization, through a process of industrialization, urbanization and economic growth, confronts all actors with a set of dilemmas. Unions in particular must often choose between policies and actions which consolidate the interests of the already industrialized at the expense of incorporating those still on the borders of modernity.

High wage policies, restrictive job demarcation policies and a range of benefit demands which have the effect (though not the intention) of discouraging employment creation have characterized the union movement in some industrializing societies, particularly English-speaking countries. Elsewhere, enhanced worker reward and security has been balanced against concerns about national and international competitiveness and an acknowledgement of the need for technological innovation.

In the second half of this century the union movement in Sweden, Japan and West Germany has succeeded in achieving this balance and its members have benefited from the sustained growth in prosperity which these societies have experienced.

In South Africa the issues of wages and technological change are bedevilled by race. African unions can hardly be expected to accept developing society wage levels when white artisans aspire to and receive developed society rates. Equally, decades of racial prejudice and racial exclusion have distorted job structures and are an ever-present source of suspicion in regard to job-restructuring.

Some broader economic policy issues illustrate these dilemmas. Moves to deregulate industry and to privatize state industries have been generally opposed by the African Union movement. In the first case they have detected attempts to create zones of labour exploitation by giving exemptions to minimum standards legislation. With privatization, the unions see the state seeking to evade its responsibilities for welfare and development.

The debate about economic development is in its infancy in South Africa.

A golden opportunity exists to replace theological rhetoric with debate about concrete issues. Many models exist for the positive roles unions can play in the process of economic development.

The challenge to employers

As with the unions, key challenges can be defined in both the political and economic order.

In the polity employers need to critically re-define their relationship to government and to resistance politics. A fundamental symmetry exists for the relationships between business and government and between business and resistance.

Business and government

The relationship between business and government in an industrializing society is, of necessity, an ambivalent one. (See Chapter 11.) Business shares with government (whatever its ideological character) two key goals:

1. the need to preserve, maintain, and even defend elements of the existing order; and

2. the need to maintain, if not expand, economic production.

These goals produce conflict for both government and business, though often in very different ways.

Contemporary examples of such conflicts for business can be seen in the present near universal rejection by business of apartheid policies (which often puts them at odds with government), coupled with their as nearly universal rejection of economic sanctions (where they have common cause with government). On these two issues, of course, business has precisely reversed relations with resistance groupings such as the ANC and UDF.

A second example is provided by widespread business opposition to Emergency powers, detentions and bannings, and the equally forceful opposition of most businesses to the disruption of both the work-process and the workplace by unions as part of generalized, politically-directed defiance campaigns.

In the decades that lie ahead business must define its political values more clearly. The FCI's Charter of Economic, Social and Political Rights was an important step in this direction. Businesses are not constituted to serve political or ideological purposes. They exist to create wealth, or to put this in different terms, to add value. The track record of business as a direct political actor is not encouraging. However, business has a set of systemic interests and values essential to its survival. It will need to become both more focused and more forceful in both defining and defending these interests, as discussed in Chapter 11.

Business and resistance

A second political challenge exists in the relations business has with political organizations, including both present and would-be governments.

Business in South Africa shares the dilemma of business in other market-oriented economies. Should business fund political organizations? (Most businesses world-wide do). If it does fund such organizations, what type of influence or benefit, if any, should it expect in return? To what extent can business leaders use their business roles to become players on the political stage? Do business organizations have a political personality and can they define a set of political beliefs, policies and interests?

These questions are common to businesses operating in South Africa, West Germany, the UK and USA. However, in addition to these universal challenges, South Africa's partial democracy creates an additional set of complexities in the relationship between business and political organizations. Because of its white employees, it is challenged to define its relationship with the government elected by white South Africans. Business can also define its relationship with white political parties in the light of their policies and electorally demonstrated support.

Africans have no formal political parties. No electoral experience exists to demonstrate the degree of support enjoyed by rival political organizations. Not only are these political movements untested by the polls, but bannings, detentions and the State of Emergency have made other patterns of accountability extremely difficult and have led — at least in part — to the emergence of Front or Alliance organizations such as the UDF or MDM, whose constituencies, policies and authority structures are elusive at best.

In the light of these complexities how is business to chart its course in the 1990s in its relationship with South Africa's political parties and political movements?

Firstly, business needs to understand that it cannot be a political actor of the first order. It cannot transform itself into a social institution whose purpose is primarily defined by political ends. Shareholders do not invest, workers do not take up employment, suppliers do not supply goods and services and customers do not buy from companies on that basis.

Companies — as with all social institutions — do have political interests. Businesses are wealth-creating machines. Certain social and political pre-conditions exist for the sustained creation of wealth. Nowhere are these more apparent than in South Africa. These pre-conditions define the political interests.

Two levels of politically significant action exist for business. The first and primary level is that of action in its own sphere of authority, that is, the realization of its own values and interests within the factory gate. Here a

major agenda exists:
> developing equitable and stable relations with unions;
> abolishing racism in the workplace;
> investing effectively in human resources; and
> helping employees to achieve positive home environments.

The secondary level of political challenge is defined by the corporate citizenship of business. Business must interact with the broader community, on the basis of the political interests inherent in its wealth-creating character. It needs to establish relationships with both government and white political organizations on the one hand and resistance groupings on the other that have integrity. The relationship that business must seek is neither that of unrelenting opposition nor that of ally — but rather that of an advocate of its own agenda.

Economic choices

The essential challenge faced by South African business is that faced by business everywhere: the challenge to create wealth. Right now the challenge produces a set of difficult choices.

Business is committed to a decision-making partnership with trade unions. Unions are here to stay. The choice facing business is whether the industrial democracy which unionization produces will occur with or without growth.

The experience of other societies indicates that this is an open choice in which the actions of management will be decisive. In countries as different as Canada, Australia, the UK, France, Italy and the USA union/management relationships have been a major factor in the decline of key industries such as shipbuilding, car manufacturing, steel production and mining. In other countries, again as different as Japan, Sweden and West Germany, effective union/management co-operation has contributed to those economies growing international competitiveness.

In South Africa, business must ensure that the outcomes of collective bargaining are economically responsible. They must resist the temptation to buy labour peace at the price of future economic growth. Equally, management must ensure that collective bargaining is a two-way street. Enhanced worker reward must be funded from technological innovation and greater workplace flexibility and efficiency. This has been the Swedish, Japanese and West German experience.

A second set of tough choices exist in the question: which road to economic growth? The South African situation is particularly complex. Though a developing economy, some sectors are technologically advanced and have locked into world trading and technology networks. Business must combine the comparative advantages offered by South African circumstances with the need to compete effectively in world commodity markets. Much greater sub-contracting of low technology areas of production and the establishment of a dual-logic relationship between big and small business are of particular importance.

Towards a new social order

The new dynamics of the workplace are eroding apartheid, defining interdependence, creating new forms of authority and new institutions and processes of decision-making.

If in this process of transformation managers and unions can preserve that which is good and transform that which can be made better; if they can enhance worker reward and promote growth; if they can define roles for business and unions in the broader society which are consistent with their nature and main function; if they can define a relationship with each other and with state agencies which respect their ideological interests, yet allow selective co-operation — then they will have earned the appellation which Friedman offers the union movement as 'the builders of tomorrow today'.

16 Reconstruction in post-apartheid South Africa: the potential of the social market economy

Pundy Pillay

Between the two extremes of a free-market society and a centralized planning system based on the Soviet model is a middle-ground alternative based on social democratic, social market, principles. This chapter examines the conditions necessary for it to operate successfully in South Africa and the benefit it offers.

In search of a post-apartheid economic system

The past few years have witnessed a phenomenal increase in the number of publications which try to predict, analyse or provide a rationale for the future economic system in South Africa. The economic scenarios they portray can be categorized broadly as follows: free market capitalism, social democracy, democratic socialism and Marxist-Leninism.

The fundamental proposition of this chapter is that both extreme positions — free markets and Soviet-type centralized planning — are economically untenable. It explores the middle ground which traditionally has encompassed such economic philosophies as market socialism, social democracy, democratic socialism and, more recently, the social market economy.

This chapter represents a preliminary attempt to construct an economic strategy for South Africa based on social democratic, social market principles. The definition of social democracy includes as a minimum a non-racial democratically elected government. The social market economy is based on both markets and planning, yet it goes beyond the conventional mixed economy because of a fundamental prerequisite that it include a variety of economic ownership forms as well as active measures to foster worker initiatives and achieve a more egalitarian society.

There are several forms of social democracy in the industrially advanced societies, the best examples being the Scandinavian countries of Sweden,

Finland and Denmark. Some of the basic principles underlying a social democratic system include the following:[1]

▷ The existence of a parliamentary democracy.

▷ The retention of free enterprise to encourage private initiative, but with the state setting the ground rules within which the economy operates.

▷ Private ownership: the means of production remain in private hands but the state guards against undue concentrations of economic power so as to break up monopolies and ensure free competition.

▷ Market mechanism: the free market remains the basic mechanism regulating the allocation of resources and the distribution of goods and services. However, the state may fix minimum wages for certain job categories. It may also regulate prices of essential commodities such as agricultural produce to eliminate price fluctuations or to aid disadvantaged sectors of the economy.

▷ Equality of opportunity, ensured through such measures as subsidies, free and equal education and training, consumer protection and regional equalization strategies.

▷ Social securities: the less fortunate are protected through unemployment insurance, pension schemes and subsidized health schemes.

There is, however, a major difference between the social democratic economies of such mature societies as Sweden or West Germany, or even the planned capitalist economy of Japan, and the social market economy envisaged for a developing country such as South Africa. They do not face the massive problems of underdevelopment and impoverishment that exists in South Africa. Therefore, the roles of state and the market will be radically different in the South African social democracy.

This chapter is deeply critical of the free marketeers' (sometimes referred to as the New Right) simplistic conception of freedom, their lack of concern for economic democracy and their naïve belief in the ability of the free market to solve all economic problems. However, it also calls for a thorough assessment of the Left's traditional approach to the economy. It argues that the social market economy can foster economic growth, reduce unemployment, raise living standards for all, and engender a more equitable distribution of income.

Social and economic goals in a post-apartheid South Africa

The nature of the economic system desired depends on the objectives of economic policy. A social market economy would be concerned with high

---

[1] J. Leatt, T. Kneifel and K. Nurnberger, *Contending ideologies in South Africa*, Cape Town: David Phillip, 1986.

rates of economic growth, full employment, restoring effective public services and reducing regional, racial, gender and other inequalities. Its most important economic and social goals should be:

▷ the elimination of poverty;

▷ high growth rates, leading to high prospective standards of living;

▷ equitable distribution of income and wealth;

▷ security of standards of living against short-term downward shocks from recession and also against long-term shocks from resource exhaustion and technological change; and

▷ compatibility of economic institutions with personal liberty and civil rights.

The elimination of the market sector clearly would not be a goal. Competitive markets provide socially useful feedback mechanisms, and thus motivation for economically rational decisions. They also stimulate cost reduction and the adaption of production to demand and innovation. On the other hand, there is no reason to suppose that market processes alone will guide an economy along a socially acceptable and economically meaningful path.

An appropriate balance must be struck between planning (the attempt by the state to regulate production and distribution to achieve social objectives) and the market (the determination of production and distribution by independent firms).

Social democratic strategy means developing a mix of institutions which combines market processes with collective strategy formulation. In practice, all the centrally planned economies have experienced varying combinations of planning and the market, with a tendency for the market proportion to increase over time.

The ideal economy goes beyond the extremism of pure *laissez-faire* and traditional central planning. It must be built on the bedrock of consensual planning and markets. It will be a mixed economy with the roles of planners and markets clearly defined.

The market dimension

Two economic consequences of centrally planned models

The experience of Soviet-type economies shows that most attempts at centralized control of the whole economy through direct command and detailed physical allocation lead to serious consequences with regard to economic efficiency and the growth of bureaucracies.

Economic efficiency

Soviet-type economic and political centralization leads to an over-accumulation bias, which at first yields fast growth but then persists well past the exhaustion of labour reserves, causing falling utilization of plant and excess demand for labour and intermediate inputs.

Commitment to price stability prevents excess demand for labour and goods being translated into higher prices; shortages and queues ensue, disrupting the supply system and aggravating the economic inefficiency of the centralized system; cycles appear, as retrenchment from over-accumulation is forced upon central powers by domestic and external constraints, or as popular dissatisfaction with economic performance is dealt with by alternate bouts of liberalization or further centralization.

Growth of bureaucracies

To execute the centralized planning of output and inputs in a large country with hundreds of thousands of enterprises requires a hierarchical, bureaucratic structure which inevitably tends to dominate society.

The role of markets in the social market economy

In the social market economy, markets would be concerned primarily with the structure of output by sectors and enterprises and the determination of prices. Three issues are relevant here: production of goods and services, externalities and natural monopolies.

Production of goods and services

A large part of production of goods and services would be through the market mechanism. A pre-condition is the existence of competition to avoid the development of undue concentration of economic power, except where substantial economies of scale justify one producer.

For the market to operate requires a price system which is either free to respond to supply and demand, or, if controlled (or taxed or subsidized), controlled with the aim of eliciting the required response — other than by issuing orders.

Another pre-condition is the absence of major external effects (other than those that can be legislated against, such as environmental pollution).

Externally-prone sectors

Particularly the building of infrastructure, especially in rural areas, require a different approach, as do public services. Docks, airports, roads, public transport generally, water supply, posts, telephones and garbage collection must all be operated efficiently and economically. All citizens must be supplied with decent roads, clean water, and other basic needs; letters and telephone calls must reach small communities, and so on. Often the private sector is not keen to provide such services, especially to small, rural communities. The public sector must then ensure an efficient and economic service.

Some large-scale industries and services are either natural monopolies (for example, electricity generation and distribution, telephones and urban transport networks) or have such substantial economies of scale that centralized control and decision-making is the most rational way of handling production. These tend to be sectors which even under capitalism are operated by large corporations and are in varying degrees centralized.

The bottom line is that public sector organizations should and must be efficient, but efficiency criteria cannot depend solely on financial results.

The planning dimension

The case for macroeconomic planning

The failure of the centrally planned economies has put the New Right on the offensive. However, it is just as important to devise an effective strategy to debunk some of the myths of free market capitalism.

The first of these myths is that the market is self-correcting. Markets do not automatically clear, and this is not only because of market imperfections, for example, in the labour market.

Secondly, the public sector can create real, productive jobs, although historically there has not been much evidence of this in South Africa. In several Western European countries the capacity of the public sector for productive job creation is clearly evident.

Thirdly, there is no clear-cut evidence that privatization of public sector companies results in greater efficiency. The evidence from the United Kingdom does show that privatization has brought about greater economic efficiency, but similar studies in the United States, Canada, and Australia show that the public sector can be just as efficient, and in some cases more so, than private companies.[2]

Fourthly, the New Right has a tendency to ignore externalities. In most capitalist economies, airports, urban transport and harbours are in the public sector because they benefit people and organizations in ways that are not reflected in profit and loss accounts.[3]

Finally, the attempts to privatize the provision of public welfare goods

---

[2] P. Pundy, 'The economic and political implications of privatisation', *Working Paper no. 2*, Johannesburg: Centre for the Enrichment of African Political Affairs, 1988.

[3] A. Nove, 'Planning and markets', in P. Nolan and S. Paine, eds., *Rethinking socialist economics: a new agenda for Britian*, New York: St Martins Press, 1988, pp. 72–82.

invariably results in higher prices and should be resisted because a democratically elected government has a duty to provide basic medical care, education and social security services to its citizens.

The weaknesses of the free market capitalist system are well known: unemployment, cyclical fluctuations, unacceptably high income inequalities and growth in monopoly power. At the same time, it is important to be aware of the weaknesses of real-world state systems and the limitations of the state-owned and controlled economy. The state is just as capable as capitalists of extracting the surplus from labour and using it in ways which do not advance the interests of the working class. It is also just as capable of maintaining hierarchical, non-participatory management structures and fostering worker alienation.

Unless there is good reason to act otherwise, the state should be treated essentially like the market — a necessary but imperfect way of achieving socio-economic goals. Each must be reformed (by democratizing their operating institutions); and each should be used to improve the working of the other. For example, the state can act to reduce monopolistic pressures in markets. The market can cut the cost of state errors and indicate the scope for state (not just private) initiative.

Economic planning should go no further than major macroeconomic variables, while markets should be allowed to determine detailed output structure and relative prices by the actions of competing firms unrestricted by central controls. Taxes and subsidies can be used to convey to companies public choices about environmental protection, desirable patterns of income distribution and any other relevant factor neglected by markets.

At the same time, the experience of capitalist economies has shown that the sphere of markets should go no further than output decisions and relative prices; economic planning should control major economic variables to prevent some or all of such macroeconomic evils as unemployment, inflation and imbalances in international trade.

In the macroeconomic sphere markets can make any kind of expectations come true if they are widely held, or they can act perversely (for example, by lowering wages, possibly lowering the level of unemployment) or turbulently through plunging exchange rates. Markets are often much too slow or incur economic and social costs which cannot be tolerated. Increased reliance on markets is a poor response to macroeconomic imbalances.[4]

Macro planning with micro markets is the current model of the Hungarian economy. It is the model towards which the People's Republic of China and Poland are moving. With the addition of workers' self-management

---

4 M. Nuti, 'Economic planning in market economies', in Nolan and Paine, *Rethinking socialist economics*, pp. 83–100.

and group ownership, it is also Yugoslavia's basic model.

There is no doubt that self-management can contribute to economic planning because of the greater economic democracy it achieves. It is still an open question, however, whether self-management can directly affect economic performance. The economic performance of Yugoslavia leaves much to be desired. Labour-managed firms have tended to maximize net income per worker rather than total net income or profit. Emphasis on capital intensive projects has caused high levels of unemployment and emigration. This has been coupled with consistently high rates of inflation.

A feature of many social democratic economies is the extent to which they rely on indicative or consensual planning.

Indicative planning

The rigorous type of planning that occurs in Soviet-type economies is regarded as imperative planning. Imperative planning goes beyond the aggregate economy to include the fine structure of the economy as a whole and also of a country's regions.

Indicative planning or consensual planning, on the other hand, is a milder form of planning. It operates mainly by convincing participants that they will benefit by following the plan, though in some cases they are threatened with the denial of privileges or penalties for not following administrative guidance. Indicative planning is also consensual, meaning that the planning authority includes representatives of various interest groups as well as civil servants and planning technicians. Among groups represented may be some or all of the following: the financial community, the military, organized business, organized labour, organized agriculture, organized taxpayers, organized consumers, and representatives of the different regions of the country.

The most successful examples of capitalist planning have been carried out in Japan, Sweden and France.

With indicative or consensual planning, plan targets must be accepted by representatives of large and small business, labour, agriculture, finance, the public sector, and so on. Such macroeconomic variables as the growth rates of money, credit, employment, labour productivity, and wage and price levels must also be agreed on. The same is true of changes in taxes and spending, as well as the means of financing deficits and surpluses. Even changes in imports, exports, capital movements and the balance of payments position must be approved by consensus.

In developing countries, consensual planning is evident in the successful newly industrializing countries of Asia such as South Korea, Singapore, Taiwan and Thailand. Contrary to the generally perceived notion that these are pure *laissez-faire* economies, their success stems also from the degree of economic planning and the unique consensual relationship between government and business.

South Korea, for instance, has had one of the most successful experiences in economic development over the past thirty years. While there are serious social and political problems there, it is nevertheless a developing country which has achieved a level of equity and material progress that is rare in the developing world, with a Gini coefficient less than any other developing country.[5]

This has been achieved through the establishment of a market economy, but with the development of many institutions that are anathema to free marketeers, namely, a successful state-driven rural development programme, minimum wages, a national pension plan, state-subsidized health insurance schemes, subsidized housing and extensive state-funded education, which ensures that 90 per cent of the population is educated up to the age of eighteen and a third to university level.

Economies based on a mix of indicative planning have shown in both industrially advanced and developing countries that they have the capacity to create consistently high economic growth rates and employment levels and equitable patterns of income distribution.

Setting the rules of the game

In the social market economy the role of planners should extend to management of the economic environment. This would include environmental protection, regional development, the responsibility of management to the labour force and customers and the rules within which foreign trade is carried on. These rules are essential because uncontrolled markets can cause major social and economic distortions.

Democratizing the economic process

The dominant trend in twentieth century socialist thinking has been to regard industrial democracy as simply collective bargaining plus nationalization. This chapter views democratization of the workplace as the foundation for wider political democracy. Fundamental reform of the workplace to ensure that workers are involved in meaningful roles is crucial for the development of a more egalitarian society.

This section sketches the nature and scope of initiatives in workplace democratization and participation that a government committed to a more humane and democratic society might consider introducing. The first part

---

5 *The Economist*, 21 May 1988.

looks at the economic potential of the co-operative sector, the second at how democracy can be effected in the workplace through a series of reforms.

The role of worker co-operatives

Worker co-operatives are not a panacea for the problems of the modern enterprise. However, when introduced in appropriate circumstances and given viable structures, such as individual ownership stakes and strong supporting institutions, co-operatives can yield net social benefits. Preliminary findings from comparative analysis of co-operatives in the UK, France, Italy, the USA and Poland support the theory:[6]

▷ Participation is usually associated with higher productivity.

▷ Co-operatives can perform at least as well as their counterparts in the capitalist or state-owned sectors.

▷ Evidence from many co-operatives shows much less inter-enterprise income inequality than for state-owned organizations. There are important examples of earnings differentials within coops deliberately being kept narrower than those found in comparable capitalist companies.

▷ Investment is not necessarily a major problem. To the extent that underinvestment has been a problem, this probably reflects the particular institutional structures in those companies acting to constrain the supply of funds generated internally as well as discrimination by banks.

▷ Job creation: there are certain sectors in which coops are likely to do well and others in which the outcome is uncertain. Sectors to be avoided are those in which demand fluctuations are pronounced, technical change is rapid and large capital requirements are the rule.

In the long run, it would be possible for a worker co-operative sector to constitute a significant proportion of the economy.

Coops could also emerge in sectors from transformed capitalist concerns and, to some extent, from converted public sector organizations. Legislation to encourage worker buy-outs, with provisions for loan and tax incentives, could be introduced. Such new coops should be structured so as to have broad appeal for all workers and not only for management.

Furthermore, a variety of fiscal incentives should be introduced both for mainly unemployed workers to form new coops and for existing coops to employ additional workers.

The establishment of worker co-operatives on a significant scale should increase employment, income distribution and productivity.

---

6 R. Jackall and H. M. Levin, *Worker co-operatives in America*, Berkeley: Univ. of California Press, 1984; D. C. Jones, 'The scope and nature of feasible initiatives in workplace democratisation and participation', in Nolan and Paine, *Rethinking socialist economics*, pp. 270–83; R. Oakeshott, *The case for worker co-operatives*, London: Routledge and Kegan Paul, 1978; and P. Pillay, 'Worker control of enterprises: some theoretical considerations', *Industrial Relations Journal of South Africa*, vol. 7, no. 1, 1987.

Reforms in the workplace

To bring about democracy in the workplace, a series of workplace reforms is proposed. Following Carnoy and Levin,[7] a series of changes in the organization of work is listed in the text that follows.

Microtechnical changes

At this level the focus is on changes in jobs or job situations within the organization as a response to an individual problem or set of problems.

Job redesign

This can be explained by using a common example. A productivity problem for a specific operation might be traced to boredom or difficulty in staying alert. Technical experts would redesign the job to alleviate these conditions. Job enlargement refers to expanding the numbers of tasks performed by the worker to reduce tediousness of repetition. Similarly, job rotation represents a way of rotating workers periodically among different jobs. Each job is considered to determine whether redesign might improve productivity or alleviate difficulties.

Changes in the physical work environment

This involves removing hazards that might impair health, safety or job performance of employees, changing the physical layout of the workspace, installing ventilation systems and reducing noise levels. Efforts might also be made to make the work environment more pleasant.

Macrotechnical changes

While microtechnical change is localized, macrotechnical change embraces the entire organization.

Organizational development

This represents attempts to improve communications and human relations within the organization and to manage conflict. An attempt is made to find a shared perspective among conflicting groups, whether workers and supervisors or top executives and middle managers, so that the individual role can be more fully integrated. The Japanese model of consultation with workers fits within this framework. Increased opportunities for training and education should also contribute to worker satisfaction.

Representative of organizational development reforms are methods of improving communication among staff, open-door staff policies, sessions

---

7 M. Carnoy and H. M. Levin, *Schooling and work in a democratic society*, California: Stanford Univ. Press, 1985.

among managers and workers emphasizing more productive group processes and dynamics for resolving conflicts, and reduced formality in communication and attire.

Profit sharing

The adoption of profit sharing or other types of work incentive plans is based on the presumption that workers will tend to be more productive if they have a stake in how well the firm does. By bringing the reward structure into line with the objectives of the organization, workers will come to support the organization's goals through self-interest.

Redesign of organization

Macrotechnical change might include new organization and staff configurations as well as modification or replacement of plant, equipment and technology to create a new mode of operation. A notable example of re-design at this level is the case of car manufacturers in Sweden who have moved away from traditional assembly lines in some of their plants. In some cases engines and bodies are produced by teams of workers who organize and schedule production, provide training and rotate particular tasks. Significant improvements in productivity, quality control and work-force stability have been reported.

Flexible work schedules

There are two principal versions: the compressed work week and flexible working hours. The former reduces the normal five-day work week into three or four days of longer duration. The adoption of flexible working hours permits employees to choose their own work schedules within limits set by the firm, boosting motivation. However, there are limits to how extensively flexitime approaches can be adopted without requiring other organizational changes.

Decision-making roles within organizations

Changes at this level should increase the participation of workers in decision-making on matters that affect the nature and organization of their work. Some inherent change in the distribution of power over particular decisions will be included in the reform; some traditional managerial prerogatives are relinquished or shared with workers — limited, however, to specific areas governing the execution of work, such as production schedules, training programmes, work assignments, and work methods. Excluded would be participation in discussions that affect the overall control of the organization, such as choice of products or services, pricing policies, investment plans, distribution of profits or overall organizational structure.

Job enrichment

It is argued that the most important motivating factors in a job are intrinsic rewards such as feelings of achievement, personal recognition, control of the work process and responsibility. The job enrichment approach assumes that workers can be more highly motivated by increasing the vertical (or hierarchical) responsibility for the job — that is, by planning, organizing and evaluating the work themselves in addition to performing it.

Indirect forms of participative management

The most important forms are worker councils or committees which are either elected by workers or appointed jointly by workers and managers and which resolve jointly with management major policy issues. To a large extent this is the approach used in traditional industrial relations, where the shop stewards represent the interests of unionized workers in settling management/worker conflicts and negotiating changes in employment and work practices.

However, there is clearly a difference when worker participation and consultation are established by law, as in West Germany, and when they are established voluntarily by management. In the former case there is a sharing of power in such areas as wages, working conditions, hiring and firing, new work methods, and so on. In the latter, worker participation is limited to those areas that management finds to be in its interest and can be withdrawn or modified unilaterally by management.

Some macro policy areas

In the social market economy, planners should be involved in labour market, social, industrial, investment, regional development and distribution policies.

Labour market policy

Employment creation and unemployment present challenging problems. To reduce unemployment and move towards full employment requires a set of policies that should include demand creation strategies such as public works programmes and labour-intensive social services. The state should also assume the role of employer of last resort.

Employment creation can also be enhanced by promoting a multiplicity of different producers including co-operative, private and public sectors.

In some countries, for example, Sweden, the state acts as employer of the last resort. Agencies of the state provide work (public works, public services, sheltered employment, etc.) for those unable to find work elsewhere.

A democratic government should create institutions and encourage programmes which enable it to fulfil the function of employer of the last resort.

It makes sense to provide income support for those between jobs. For the long-term unemployed, however, it would be more sensible to provide jobs.

Important lessons can be derived from the experience of the Nordic countries. Unemployment has not exceeded 3,5 per cent of the work-force and has usually been well below that rate for the last decade.[8] Sweden has sought to provide jobs for everyone who wants one. Low unemployment can be ascribed to a combination of incentives to capitalists and the active labour market policy of successive governments. Benefiting from low taxes — a nominal rate of 52 per cent is halved by tax breaks — Swedish managers are exceptionally adaptable and cost conscious.

The labour policy begins with a law that bars private employment agencies that operate for profit. On the face of it this seems an outrageous example of public employment service protecting its monopoly. The government's argument is that labour markets, like stock markets, work best when all information is collected in one place and made easily available to all interested parties.

The Swedish system means that workers seeking jobs and employers seeking workers are put in touch with one another through centrally collected information that is available on video terminals in local employment centres. While many jobs are still secured through personal contacts and newspaper advertisements, the government employment service handles up to 60 per cent of all job openings (compared with 10 to 20 per cent in other countries). The government's labour market policy also extends to a youth employment scheme and retraining unemployed workers.

In order to fulfil the employer of last resort function, suitable institutions are necessary. A National Employment Commission, as in Sweden could fulfil a useful role.

Investment

Major investments must clearly be the central planners' responsibility, taking into account regional and employment problems as well as the expected demand for goods and services. Establishing new enterprises is another vital function. Some sort of capital market may be necessary to mobilize retained profits (of those enterprises which do not need to invest in themselves) as well as private savings, these being sources additional to credits from the state banking system.

A national investment bank could finance projects unattractive to the private banks and financial institutions and also compete with them in financing economically and socially attractive projects.

---

8 *The Economist*, 21 November 1987.

Industrial policy

Direct intervention in industry and finance to create additional productive capacity, especially in the underdeveloped homelands, will undoubtedly be necessary. There is a wide range of possibilities, for example the creation of new organizations and co-operative ventures, credits for existing companies, the purposive use of state procurements, creation of and improvements to existing infrastructure, the provision of a trained and qualified labour force, and support for research and development.

Regional policy

Reducing regional inequalities and developing declining regions would be a major objective. This could be done by decentralization, the creation of powerful regional planning bodies, public investment and mobilizing local people and local resources.

Social policy

It should be unnecessary to argue that the welfare state, with free education, medical services, old age pensions, etc. must play an important role in a social democracy. The boundary line between what is free to the citizen and what must be paid for is a matter of democratic decision involving the national economic plan and its priorities.

Distribution policy

Redistribution can be achieved through taxation policies and changes in the organization of enterprises.

Taxation

More progressive tax strategies could ensure a lessening of the indirect tax burden on the poor.

Changes in the organization of enterprises

Changes at this level provide workers with greater input into the enterprise as whole, rather than just within their own work units. Reforms would include changing the governance and direction of the total work organization. In principle, such reforms can increase the participation of workers in virtually all the policies of the firm. In West Germany, worker councils appear to have powers in such areas as job evaluation, employment policies, training, layoffs and wage structure.

Employee ownership

The specific form of any reform made at this level is crucial in determining its results. This is evident in the case of employee ownership, the most far-reaching of the macro-political changes. Employee ownership should vest in workers the right to govern their own work organization and the nature of the work situation; in practice employee ownership may have little to do with employee participation in management.

There are at least two general forms of employee ownership: management initiated, and worker initiated.

Management-initiated employee ownership usually consists of a programme in which part of the remuneration of employees is offered in the form of stock or options to buy stock on the basis of seniority, salary or position. In other cases, the employees, acting as a group buy the firm by obtaining a loan that is repaid out of profits. Best known of this scheme is the Employee Stock Ownership Plan (ESOP).

Typically, management will choose the first of these plans as a means to supplement wage and salary benefits while building a mechanism to increase employee motivation and productivity. The second plan is usually adopted primarily to increase the capital in the firm, which is an intrinsic attribute of the ESOP approach.

It is hardly surprising that management-initiated plans to increase employee ownership do not constitute a mechanism for employees to participate in the management of the firm. Indeed, in most of these cases the employees seem content to leave managerial decisions to traditional hierarchies, probably believing that professional expertise is necessary to obtain maximum growth and return on their stock ownership.

By contrast, employee-initiated ownership plans almost invariably involve workers in direct or representative participation in governing the work enterprise. The most typical approach is the co-operative, in which the members both own and manage the organization. Co-operatives may be created from scratch or by converting conventional firms. In either case, the workers exercise control over the internal organization of work, levels of remuneration, product planning and development, marketing, pricing and other functions. In capitalistic societies, the producer co-operatives represent the most complete form of reform of the traditional capitalist/worker relationship.

Worker representation

A second reform is the inclusion of worker representation on corporate boards. This is especially prevalent in Western Europe. In West Germany a policy of co-determination requires that a third to a half of the places on the governing boards of firms be delegated to workers.

Worker self-management

A third form of work reform is worker self-management when the enterprise is not owned directly by the employees. This mode of control can take many forms: the Yugoslav version, which is the most highly developed, has workers' councils that make the major policy decisions for the firms. Unlike some forms of worker participation where workers and work councils are accountable to management, the Yugoslav arrangement makes the management accountable to the workers.

Versions of worker self-management are also found in China, Cuba and Israel. In both China and Cuba the emphasis has been on direct participation in management and operation, rather than participation through representation. All members of the enterprise are expected to contribute to the formation of the work process.

The Israeli kibbutz, or collective, is another example of macro-political worker control: all decisions about production, distribution and surpluses are made by the membership. The traditional work hierarchy is eliminated in favour of a democratic mechanism for making collective decisions on production and consumption.

Nationalization of industry

The transfer of a firm or industry from the private to the public sector has obvious implications for altering how work is organized and how investment policies are controlled. The exact form of change will depend on the nature of the transfer and the political context in which nationalization takes place.

At one extreme, a traditional corporate management is replaced by a traditional government bureaucracy, with no significant modification in the organization of work. It has been argued that from the viewpoint of the workers, nationalization can reduce the possibilities of change rather than increase them. This has been one of the major criticisms of the Eastern Bloc countries.

Nevertheless, it is possible to construct a scheme of nationalization that integrates worker participation in the decision-making apparatus — as the case of Yugoslavia shows. Again, the exact form and implications for modification of the workplace will depend on both the national and historical context.

In general, organizational reforms represent the most far-reaching possibilities for changing the nature of organizations to increase the participation of workers in deciding on the nature of their jobs and their work relationships. With changes in overall governance, corresponding modifications can take place in internal governance and in the technical arrangements of work organization.

Which types of reform will predominate — management reforms that restore discipline and raise productivity relative to wages, or worker reforms that give labour greater control over the production process — is largely a political issue. It depends on the level of worker consciousness and worker political power relative to the dominant groups, state and/or capital. However, if true economic democracy is to prevail, workplace reforms such as those described in this chapter must be implemented in some form or another.

Conclusion: the political dimension

This chapter has proposed the creation of a social market economy based on the coexistence of markets and some form of indicative planning to achieve the social and economic goals of a democratic South Africa.

The social market economy has to be linked to widespread democratization of and participation in the workplace. The envisaged social democracy would thus reflect greater concern both for participatory forms of ownership and control and for reducing social and regional inequalities in all their manifestations.

Appropriate institutions and policies would have to be developed for the successful implementation of a social market economy. They do not have to be necessarily imported from successful social market economies elsewhere, but important lessons can be derived from their experiences.

The social market economy is an effective counter-attack to the offensive of the New Right because it suggests solutions to market failure which free marketeers either pretend do not exist or, if they do acknowledge its occurrence, attribute to extraneous factors. On the other hand, the real weakness of the Left is its lack of any clearly articulated alternative.

The social market economy can be promoted only by a state committed to gradualist economic transformation. It would not be an appropriate economic strategy for a non-racial, democratic government committed either to free market principles or for one wedded to a Marxist-Leninist centralized planning model. The social market economy, as outlined in this chapter, can only be an effective strategy for a government committed to a mixed economy.

Its successful implementation requires a positive attitude towards market forces, entrepreneurship and profit-making. The government should, while developing institutions to supplement the many areas in which the market fails, recognize the usefulness of market forces. The market mechanism should not be regarded as a temporary phenomenon to be dispensed with when socialism/central planning is introduced. The idea that centralized Soviet-type planning can achieve the economic and social goals desired by the majority should be laid to rest.

Neither markets nor the state are ends in their own right. Each needs to be democratized and used to improve the efficacy of the other in achieving better living standards for all. The social market economy functioning in a democratic environment will foster participation and ensure progress towards an egalitarian society.

References

Bowden, E. V., *Economic evolution: principles, issues, ideas*, Cincinnatti: South Western Publ. Co., 1985.

Caldwell, D., *South Africa; the new revolution*, Johannesburg: Free Market Foundation, 1989.

Ellman, M., 'Images of a socialist economy' in P. Nolan and S. Paine, eds., *Rethinking socialist economics*, New York: St. Martin's Press, 1988.

Innes, D., 'Social democracy or democratic socialism', *Business Alert*, no. 95, Johannesburg: Wits Business School, 1988.

Le Roux, P., 'The economics of conflict and negotiation', in P. L. Berger and B. Godsell, eds., *A future South Africa; visions, strategies, realities*, Cape Town: Human Rousseau Tafelberg, 1988, pp. 200–39.

Louw, L. and Kendall F., *South Africa: the solution*, Ciskei: Amagi Publications, 1986.

Nolan, P. and S. Paine, eds., *Rethinking socialist economics: a new agenda for Britain*, New York: St. Martin's Press, 1988.

Nove, A., *The economics of feasible socialism*, London: George Allen and Unwin, 1983.

Paine, S., 'Notes on late twentieth century socialism for an advanced industrialised mixed economy', in Nolan and Paine, *Rethinking socialist economics*, 1988. pp. 53–68.

Skidelsky, R., *The Social Market Economy*, London: The Social Market Foundation, 1989.

Sunter, C., *The world and South Africa in the 1990s*, Cape Town: Human Rousseau Tafelberg, 1987.

Terreblanche, S. J., 'A new fiscal policy and economic philosophy for South Africa in transition', Paper read at an international conference *South Africa in transition: the process of creating a non-racial, democratic nation of South Africa*, White Plains, New York, 29 Sept to 2 Oct., 1987.

17 Macroeconomic policy: goals and limitations

Iraj Abedian and Barry Standish

This chapter looks at the scope for economic policy in South Africa, focusing on inflation and the conduct of fiscal policy, in particular the management of both foreign debt and the public debt.

Introduction

In May 1989, hardly two months after the Budget speech, the Minister of Finance revamped his fiscal policy structure, introducing a new set of tax and expenditure measures. The Reserve Bank likewise introduced a number of restrictive policy measures, its ninth policy rearrangements in little over a year.

These frequent adjustments to policy raise an important question. Did economic policy changes create the need for these adjustments, or is policy a slave to the circumstances in which South Africa finds itself?

This chapter analyses the scope for macroeconomic policy in South Africa, focusing on the following:

1. the conventional objectives of macroeconomic policy and the process of policy-making;
2. inflation and unemployment in South Africa;
3. the conduct of fiscal policy, including taxes and expenditure, fiscal deficit and public debt; and
4. theories of public choice and rent-seeking as applied to economic policy-making in South Africa.

Macroeconomic policy: aims, means and process

Macroeconomic policy traditionally is concerned with correcting short-term changes in the economy. The economic system is subject to fluctuations caused either by external factors such as droughts, earthquakes, floods and the like, or internal shocks that include a drop in the level of total demand, low levels of investment, and so on. The object of macroeconomic policy is to reduce the impact of such fluctuations through economic stabilization, which means maintaining internal and external economic balance.

Policy aims

In practical terms the internal balance amounts to maintaining high economic growth (and hence low levels of unemployment) and price stability (no or low inflation). The relationship between price stability and unemployment occupies the centre of debate. The external equilibrium objective can be reduced to ensuring a pattern of foreign trade that will minimize the impact of exchange rate fluctuations on the economy.

Policy implementation

In pursuit of these objectives, the means available for implementing macro-economic policy consist mainly of fiscal and monetary measures. Fiscal measures include taxes and government spending as well as fiscal regulations that govern production. Monetary tools, on the other hand, include interest rates, money supply, exchange rates and financial regulations. There is no consensus among economists on the relative effectiveness of each. Controversies abound at the theoretical level, while empirical evidence is indeterminate on many issues.

Balancing internal and external equilibria in today's world of flexible exchange rates is a delicate and, at times, impossible act. Achieving internal equilibrium might prove detrimental to external equilibrium, and vice versa. For example, the interest rate necessary for the appropriate money supply growth could well be inappropriate for maintaining balance of payments stability.

The rent-seeking paradigm

Economic policy is not made in a vacuum. It is influenced by socio-political forces in the country as various groups exert pressure for the identification of issues, policy choices and policy implementation. This behaviour is known as rent-seeking. Successful rent-seeking can result in large gains for specific groups.

The more heterogeneous the society, the more pronounced is the rent-seeking behaviour. In divided societies the ruling group has a clear advantage in allocating rent to its own members. The more such governments use their position to favour their own, the higher are the aspirations and incentives for other groups to govern.

There is almost inevitably a trade-off between pressure group interests and those of the community at large. There is no reason why the rent-seeking effort of any particular group should coincide with the interest of the general community. More often than not the opposite is true.

Since 1948, for instance, the monopoly power of the state has been used to direct the country's macroeconomic policy in the perceived interest of Afrikaners. Of course, in many instances the interests of the English and

Afrikaner have coincided, although not always with the overall interests of the economy.

Today the ethnic differences between English and Afrikaner have been replaced largely by economic class differentiation. As a result, new lobbying groups have emerged. Moreover, with the rise of black groupings, an additional dimension is introduced into policy-making. As a result, trade-offs have become not only more numerous, but politically crucial.

The rent-seeking paradigm explains many of the forces which underlie the process of economic policy-making. At the same time, it points to the institutional limitations and distortions that impinge on the means of achieving the objectives of the policy.

Macroeconomic policy

The overriding goals of macro policy in South Africa are controlling inflation and reducing unemployment.

South Africa has experienced high and rising inflation for the last decade. Economists differ over the source of this phenomenon. Some regard it as a purely monetary phenomenon caused by increases in the money supply. Others consider it exclusively a structural problem stemming from the highly concentrated structure of the economy. We subscribe to the view that inflation in South Africa is caused mainly by the declining value of the rand and is exacerbated by administered price increases.

Exchange rates and inflation

Inflation in South Africa, as measured by the Consumer Price Index (CPI), is affected by and closely linked with the price of imports.

The effective exchange rate of the rand is the most significant determinant of the actual value of import prices. The higher the effective exchange rate, the lower is the price of imported items, and vice versa.

Given that over 75 per cent of our imports are either intermediate or capital goods, a rise in the price of imports will soon impact on consumer prices. This is borne out by the comparison given in Figure 17.1. As can be seen, the CPI and import prices move together and both are negatively correlated with the effective exchange rate.

In addition to raising the price of imports, the declining rand also affects the domestic price of locally produced goods. In the absence of any restrictions, domestic producers will tend to raise their prices in the local market to match what they could receive by exporting their product. Allowing for transportation costs, the higher the rand value of export products, the higher will be their local prices. Other things being equal, any decline in the effective value of the rand results in an equivalent rise in the domestic price of goods.

Figure 17.1: Effective exchange rate, import prices and CPI, South Africa, 1980–8

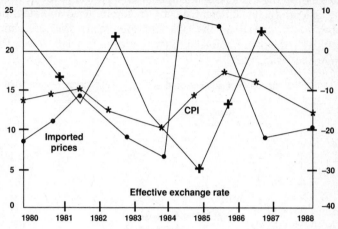

Sources:
Reserve Bank Quarterly Bulletin (various issues); and Budget White Paper (various issues).

It follows that a declining rand generates inflation both through imports and locally made products. The policy implication is obvious: curbing inflation calls for halting the fall in the value of the rand.

Inflation and administered prices

The largest and most important of the administered prices are those set by the Agricultural Control Boards. However, there are many others, such as those of bricks, cement, bus fares, bread, petrol, etc.

Table 17.1: Comparison of average growth rates of CPI and selected administered prices, 1970–1985

Item	Average % rise
Meat	13,9
Grain	13,7
Fuel	12.6
Sugar	12,5
CPI	11,8

Source:
Central Statistical Services, SA Statistics 1986

Table 17.1 shows the trend of administered prices between 1970 and 1985. They rose faster than the average price in the economy (as represented by the CPI). As the CPI already incorporates the growth of the items listed in the table, the actual differential between administered and other prices is substantially larger than the table indicates. When they are removed from the CPI, the rise in non-administered prices is markedly lower. This is illustrated in Figure 17.2.

Figure 17.2:   Comparison of administered and non-administered prices, 1970–85

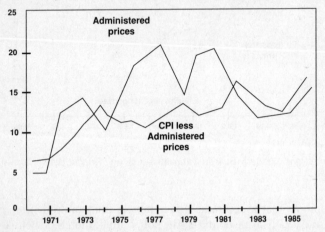

Source:
Calculated from Central Statistical Services, *SA Statistics*, 1986.

These differentials are best explained in terms of the rent-seeking behaviour of economic agents. As long as administered prices continue, there will be specific groups able to exploit these opportunities for their own advantage.

Fighting inflation

South African inflation will be addressed only when the effective value of the rand stops falling and the current system of administered prices is addressed. While the latter is the concern of the domestic political economy, the former is basically a monetary phenomenon which is inextricably linked to the actual and expected capital flight from the country. This in turn is intertwined with international financial sanctions and the debt moratorium.

Foreign debt management

Since it came to a head in August 1985, the foreign debt issue has dominated the domestic macroeconomic scene. The root causes are clearly political, reflecting the international community's abhorrence of apartheid, although economic factors played the major role in precipitating the debt crisis.

Traditionally, South Africa has not been a heavy international borrower. In the decade following the mid-1970s, net foreign capital financed only 1,5 per cent of gross domestic investment. In 1980, total foreign liabilities amounted to 20,3 per cent of the GDP. With the adoption of a new monetary policy in the 1980s, interest rates were increased substantially. This encouraged offshore borrowing, particularly for trade purposes (Table 17.2).

Table 17.2: Interest rates and foreign debt in South Africa, 1980–1984

Year	Interest* Rate (%)	Foreign debt (Rm) Short-term Debt	Total Debt	Percentage Short-term
1980	9,5	3 596	13 695	26,3
1981	17,0	6 587	18 081	36,4
1982	18,0	9 040	23 245	38,9
1983	20,0	11 362	27 531	41,3

Source:
South African Reserve Bank, *Quarterly Bulletin* (various issues).
Note:
* Prime overdraft rate.

Consequently, while the volume of medium-to-long term debt was fairly stable, short-term debt increased sharply, as shown in Table 17.2. Over and above this, debt maturing within twelve months increased from 52 per cent of total debt in 1980 to 65 per cent by the end of 1984. This made the country highly vulnerable to a liquidity crunch.

The refusal of the foreign (mainly American) banks to roll over a hump of $4 000 million (then 2,5 times South Africa's foreign reserves) led to the inception of the debt moratorium, ultimately resolved by the March 1986 Leutwiler Arrangement and the Stals Accord of February 1987. South Africa undertook to repay outstanding debt according to the following schedule:

15 July 1987	3,0 per cent
15 December 1987	2,0 per cent
15 June 1988	2,0 per cent
15 December 1988	1,5 per cent
15 June 1989	1,5 per cent
15 December 1989	' 1,5 per cent
15 June 1990	1,5 per cent

The debt accord was greeted with bullish sentiment in the country. Yet it marked the end of macroeconomic autonomy in South Africa. Obsessed with meeting the schedule, the authorities have subjected the economy to a succession of monetary and fiscal shocks. Huge sums have been sliced from national savings in the form of capital outflows.

In 1985, the net capital outflow was R9,2 billion or 7,7 per cent of the GDP. For 1986 this figure declined to R6,1 billion, constituting 4,3 per cent of the GDP, and for 1987 the net outflows amounted to R3,1 billion, or 1,84 per cent of the country's output. By March 1989, South Africa had redeemed R13 billion of its debt with a further R4,2 billion to be paid during 1989. These are enormous amounts for any developing economy.

The foreign debt influences the economy in three important ways:

1. It drains the economy of keenly needed capital.

2. It constrains economic policy options.

3. It subjects the economy to a vicious cycle of pessimism, undermines the potential for growth, and creates poor future prospects.

There is an ultimate irony in our debt repayment: the more the economy pays, the less it can afford to pay.

Why has this debt repayment schedule been met with such fervour? The rationale behind such policies has been to keep the country's good credit record intact. Yet the only advantage to date is that a small amount of short-term debt has been converted to long-term debt.[1]

Under these circumstances, is there any advantage in accepting such an onerous debt repayment schedule? There is really only one way South Africa will be able once again to borrow from overseas. That way is to bring about political change which is both meaningful and acceptable to the international community. Without political change, South Africa has no chance of reopening any of the closed lines of credit, even by conforming to the terms of the accord.

As long as the spectre of foreign debt hangs over the economy, the results will be a falling rand and lower economic growth, which in turn bring higher inflation and rising unemployment. Given these consequences, there is only one short-term solution to the debt crisis: South Africa must withdraw from the moratorium arrangements and undertake to repay the debt over a time which suits the economy, not the international banking community.

This is clearly not a conventional solution. Yet, it is vastly superior to the alternative which subjects the economy to continuous destabilizing torrents. This option must be given serious consideration, both now and for the renewal of the accord in 1991.

---

1 By May 1989, of the total foreign debt of $22 billion, only $3,5 billion had been converted to long term debt; i.e. debt with maturity of longer than one year.

Unemployment in South Africa

As in most dual-economy developing countries, measuring unemployment in South Africa is fraught with definition and measurement problems, and estimates differ substantially.[2]

Whatever the true size of unemployment, the fact remains that South African society is currently moving from rural to urban areas. This is a change from subsistence agriculture to conditions with substantial division of labour. In such conditions the labour leaving the rural areas has no skills and is largely unemployable in the formal economy.

In the short term, there is nothing that stabilization policy can do to remedy the situation. The labour situation is not caused by short-term fluctuations in output, which might be addressed by macroeconomic policy. Even at its peak, the economy would have limited capacity to absorb unskilled labour.[3]

In a dual economy in a state of transition it is possible for economic growth and unemployment to coexist for a time. Figure 17.3 illustrates the point, with the trend of African urbanized labour not employed in the formal sector estimated and compared with the rate of economic growth in the country from 1970 to 1988.

Figure 17.3 shows that over the entire course of the business cycle there is a constant growth in African labour outside the formal sector. It might be argued that this labour is employed in the informal sector, in which case it should not be classified as unemployed.

This is at best half the truth. South Africa's informal sector is strongly dependent on conditions in the formal economy. As a result, their peaks and troughs correspond.

By implication, Figure 17.3 clarifies an important point in the macro-economic debate. In South Africa the unemployment problem is only partially dependent on stabilization policy. To address it properly, other areas of economic policy should be investigated.

Changes in production and the form of capital being used, the low level of skills, poor economic growth and the maldistribution of income and wealth in the country are the major factors that have a direct bearing on unemployment. While some of these factors fall outside the ambit of stabilization policy, some can be addressed by fiscal policy.

---

[2] For a full account of the theoretical and empirical problems of measuring unemployment in South Africa, see the first four chapters of P. A. Black and B. E. Dollery, *Leading issues in South African macroeconomics: selected readings*, Johannesburg: Southern, 1989.

[3] Theoretical economics has, however, solved this type of problem by allowing wages to fall indefinitely so as to avoid the emergence of unemployment. In reality, there is a floor below which wages will not fall. This is the subsistence level of wages.

Figure 17.3:   Economic growth rates and African urbanized labour
                     not employed in the formal economy, 1970–88

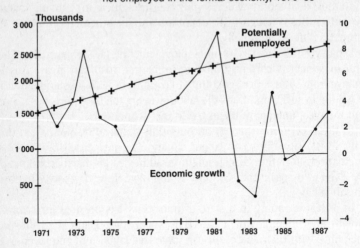

Source:
Abedian and Standish, 'The myths and truths of "the informal sector"'.

The conduct of fiscal policy

Current monetary policy is constrained by the need to repay our foreign debt. Fiscal policy is accordingly the more significant element of macro-economic policy.

Government expenditure

A popular impression conveyed by many observers of the economic scene in South Africa is that government spending is too large for the size of the economy. This might be correct in relation to the public sector, but not if the size of the central government only is addressed.

The public sector is enormous and includes all levels of government, the state enterprises of Sats and Posts and Telecommunications, the various control boards and statutory bodies, and all the public corporations (Escom, Foskor, SABC, IDC, etc.).

Such an intrusion into the economy by the public sector is counter-productive and must be diminished. The ideal means is extensive privat-ization. Although this is on the economic agenda of government, little real progress is evident, although Iscor has now been privatized.

While the relative size of the public sector is too large, the same is not true of central government. Figure 17.4 shows total government expenditure as a percentage of GDP compared with other countries. As a percentage of GDP,

South Africa's budget is among the lowest in the world for both developed countries and comparable developing countries.

Figure 17.4:   Share of government in the economy

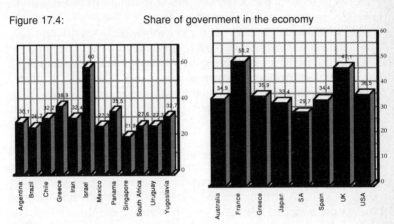

Source:
Abedian and Standish, 'Job creation and economic development'.

The composition of outlays is more important than the size of government spending. Figure 17.5 shows this composition for 1989/90.

Figure 17.5:   Functional expenditure by the central government, 1989/90 (RMl)

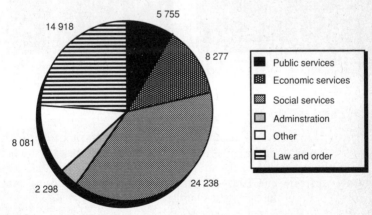

Source:
Calculated from the *Budget White Paper*, 1989/90.

The allocation of government revenue is not conducive to the long-term well-being of the economy. As can be seen from the figure, expenditure on economic services, public services and other administration constitutes the bulk of government spending. These are largely the result of economic controls which are at the centre of the current deregulation debate.

Government's own initiative on deregulation is not wide enough. It focuses only on specific types of deregulation. A large part of expenditure on regulation is incurred in administering the separate development edifice.[4] Any attempt to improve economic efficiency and reduce government expenditure by deregulation must address the policy of separate development.

Sources of revenue

As with levels of government expenditure, it is commonly believed that tax levels are too high in South Africa. An international comparison suggests otherwise. Figure 17.6 shows government receipts (that is, taxes) as a percentage of GDP. As can be seen, the revenue the government draws from the economy is modest relative to many developing countries.

Figure 17.6:   Government receipts as a percentage of GDP

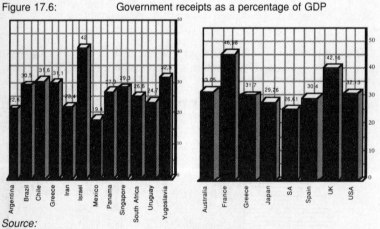

Source:
Abedian and Standish, 'Job creation and economic development'.

Given that South African tax burdens are not high compared to other countries, why does the impression persist that South Africans are overtaxed? The reason lies in the structure of the tax system and the skewed distribution of income. The result is that the middle- to high-income earners bear the brunt of the income tax burden.

---

[4] M. Savage, 'The cost of apartheid', Inaugural lecture, *New series no. 121*, Univ. of Cape Town, 1986, p. 7 calculated that 12 per cent of taxes are spent on maintaining apartheid.

Taxes on income, especially at high marginal rates, can have a significant disincentive effect on the willingness to work of middle- to high-income earners, with a consequent negative effect on productivity. This is a powerful argument for financing increases in government expenditure through increases in public debt.

Deficit financing

Fiscal deficits, when government spending exceeds current revenue, can occur for purely economic reasons, that is, when fluctuations in national income lead to lower than required income; alternatively, because of sociopolitical reasons, government might not be able to match its income. In South Africa, both factors are causes of fiscal deficits. In turn, accumulated deficits become the public debt.

A fiscal deficit can be financed in one of three ways:
1. It can be borrowed from the public or local financial markets.
2. It can be financed by borrowing offshore.
3. It can be financed by what is called monetizing the deficit.[5]

Why debt at all?

Companies borrow largely to finance increases in capital expenditure, believing that the return will allow them to repay the debt and make a profit.

Ideally, governments hold the same view. The objective of capital expenditure by government is to stimulate economic growth; if successful, the economy is able to repay the debt. Capital expenditure by government, which will affect the ability of the economy to produce, can be on physical investment (roads, bridges, dams) and in human capital (education, health, housing).

Fluctuations in economic activity also cause changes in public debt. As the economy enters a recession, a portion of government expenditure automatically increases; for example, unemployment payouts and production subsidies. Private incomes and spending fall, causing a drop in tax revenue. The result is an automatic rise in the fiscal deficit. In the upswing phase of the business cycle this position is reversed. Ideally, the increase in government revenue should offset the previously incurred deficit in a continually evening-out process, which in the long term produces zero deficit.

Public debt, therefore, can be divided into two components: a structural portion used for capital expenditure and a cyclical component brought

---

5 The common notion of 'monetizing the deficit' is where the Treasury borrows from the Reserve Bank. Under current monetary practices in South Africa, Treasury borrowing from the commercial banks amounts to the same thing.

about by the business cycle. There are two situations in which an increase in the public debt can be a burden to the economy.

The first is where the cyclical component of the debt continues to increase, irrespective of the condition of the economy. This is in effect the same as using public debt to fund current expenditure. As this expenditure is not designed to stimulate long-term economic growth, it does not increase the economy's ability to pay increased taxes in the future. It obliges future generations to pay for benefits enjoyed today.

The second is where capital expenditure financed by debt does not add to economic growth. This happens when capital expenditure is used on unproductive projects, thus impairing the long-term ability of the economy to repay the debt.

Size of the public debt

It is important for policy purposes to have a clear perspective on the size of the public debt.

The popular notion of public debt is that it is the total value of all outstanding debt issues, that is, the total par value of all existing public debt, shown in Figure 17.7. As can be seen, the value of the debt has grown consistently over the period under observation.

Figure 17.7:   Par value of public debt, 1966–86

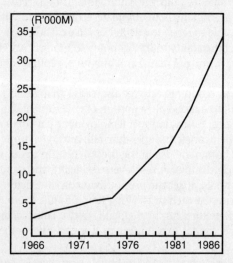

Source:
Standish, 'The measurement and economic effects of fiscal deficit'.

This measure of the public debt has, however, three serious shortcomings.

First, it is an examination of the nominal value of the debt and is not adjusted for inflation. Inflation causes the real value of public debt to be lower than its nominal value. When the debt is finally repaid, its purchasing power is less than when it was first issued. Inflation therefore acts as a kind of invisible tax which is borne by the holders of public debt, and hence contributors to pension funds and life assurance schemes.

Second, this trend is an illustration of the par value of public debt and not its market value. Third, it does not evaluate the size of the debt relative to the size of the economy. These last two problems are discussed further in the text that follows.

From nominal par to real market value

Converting the value of total public debt to a more realistic level requires two changes. The first is to reduce its nominal value to real value by discounting for changes in the price level. The second is to change the par value of debt into its market value. This is an important transformation as it is the market value and not the total par value which the government owes at any point in time.

Calculating the market value requires a net present value discounting of outstanding debt issues as the actual value of the debt at any point in time is the present (market) value of the debt and not its face (par) value.

Public debt and the size of the economy

Public debt figures, whether at par or market value, are meaningless in themselves. To be of any relevance they must be considered in a relative context. This might be relative to the size of the economy, the level of government expenditure or the total value of assets under government control.

The measure chosen here is to contrast public debt with the size of the economy, shown in Figure 17.8. It can be seen that relative to the growth in the economy, the par value of public debt has declined since 1970, while the market value has declined over the entire period from 1966 to 1986.

Use of public debt

The chief criticism against fiscal deficits in South Africa is that they are used to finance current expenditure. This can be seen in Figures 17.9 and 17.10. Figure 17.9 shows the ratio of current to capital expenditure (as defined by official sources) by government between 1950 and 1987. After fluctuating around a fairly constant ratio until 1976, current expenditure increased far faster than capital expenditure. This increase in current expenditure was financed partly by fiscal deficits. This can be seen in Figure 17.10, which shows the level of government savings.

Figure 17.8:   Public debt as a percentage of GDP

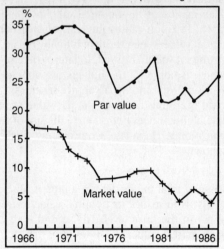

Source:
Standish, 'The measurement and economic effects of fiscal deficit'.

Figure 17.9:   The ratio of current to capital expenditure, 1950–87

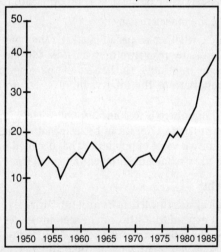

Source:
Calculated from data supplied in Browne, 'Fifty years of public finance'; and updated from *Budget White Paper* (various issues).

Figure 17.10:   Government savings, 1934–87

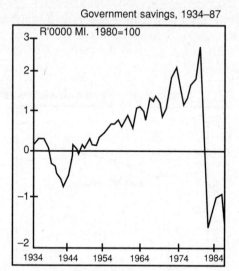

Source:

Calculated from data supplied in Browne, 'Fifty years of public finance'; and updated from *Budget White Paper* (various issues).

Government savings are the difference between current revenue and current expenditure. When savings are positive, they are used to repay debt or, more likely, to incur capital expenditure. When savings are negative, it means that current expenditure is being funded partially by increases in public debt. As can be seen from Figure 17.10, government savings have been negative since the late 1970s.

The conclusion often drawn from such analysis is that increases in the public debt have been used to finance current expenditure and that this trend must be curtailed. We believe this deduction is erroneous, caused by a misunderstanding of the composition of current expenditure as it is presently reported.

In analysing government spending, it is important to distinguish between current expenditure, expenditure on physical capital and expenditure on human capital. Official data on government spending is divided into expenditure on capital goods and recurrent expenditure, which includes all outlays of a non-capital nature.

This conventional composition of recurrent expenditure is not satisfactory. It is important to distinguish between current expenditure and expenditure on human capital. Just as capital expenditure will (if correctly implemented) lead to economic growth in the future, so will expenditure on human capital, albeit with a longer time lag. It is just as important to allow for deficit financing of human capital as it is for that of physical capital. To illustrate the point, we show the result of a simple reclassification of data in Figure 17.11.

Figure 17.11:

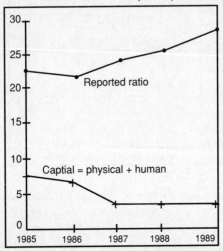

Source:
Calculated from *Budget White Paper* (various issues).

This figure shows two ratios. The first is identical to that of Figure 17.9 and shows the ratio of current to capital expenditure increasing between 1985 and 1988. The second ratio removes all current expenditure on social services[6] and adds it to capital expenditure. This new capital expenditure figure is now a rough proxy for expenditure on physical and human capital. As can be seen, the ratio of current to capital spending is far less than under conventional reporting procedures and the ratio shows a decline for the entire period under observation.

Implications of public debt changes for fiscal policy

Any reasonable measure of public debt shows a decline in debt financing in South Africa over the last twenty years. This is inappropriate fiscal policy.

When a country has a developed, highly industrialized economy, a reduction in public debt is desirable. South Africa is neither developed nor

---

6 Expenditure on social services as reported in the *Budget White Paper*.

highly industrialized. This means government must increase its investment in human and physical capital development,[7] funded not by increasing taxes, but by increasing public debt.

There are two reasons for this. First, increases in taxes, particularly income tax, can dampen enthusiasm for work. Second, because this type of expenditure generates future economic growth, it is more appropriate to use debt financing.

Economic effects of deficit financing

The choice between taxation or deficit-financed government spending must be influenced by whether increases in public debt cause interest rates to rise, so crowding out private investment, and whether they lead to expansion of the money supply and are therefore inflationary. The conventional view holds that deficit financing stimulates growth.

Given that domestic interest rates are determined by the ruling bank rate, it is unlikely that increases in public debt will lead to immediate increases in interest rates and the crowding out of private investment. As interest rates are directly governed by the Reserve Bank, the important question must be whether increases in public debt will cause the Reserve Bank to raise interest rates.[8] This depends on whether there are monetary consequences to the increases sufficient to cause the Reserve Bank to take action.

Monetary effects of financing the fiscal deficit

Different methods of financing the fiscal deficit can have different effects on the money supply. It can be shown that borrowing from the private non-banking sector and the Public Investment Commissioners will have no effect on the monetary aggregates. However, borrowing from the commercial banks and the Reserve Bank will increase the money supply by the amount of the initial deficit. In empirical testing for the monetary effects of fiscal deficits, no relationship could be found on the monetary effects of the different sources of funding the deficit. The one which does appear to have a positive effect on money supply is the growth in the structural component of the public debt, although the actual effect is probably small.[9]

Reserve Bank reaction to fiscal deficits

The related issues of whether changes in the fiscal deficit will induce changes

---

7 See I. Abedian and B. Standish, 'Job creation and economic development in South Africa', *HSRC Manpower Series no. 9*, 1989.

8 For a full account of the determination of interest rates see J. Whittaker and A. J. Theunissen, 'Why does the Reserve Bank set the interest rate?', *South African Journal of Economics*, vol. 54, no. 4, 1987.

9 For a detailed analysis of the subject see B. Standish, 'The measurement and economic effects of fiscal deficits in South Africa', Report submitted to the HSRC, 1989.

in interest rates depends largely on how deficits are viewed in the Reserve Bank 'reaction funding'. The Reserve Bank sets the re-discount rate according to conditions in the economy and 'reacts' as conditions in the economy change.

Under normal conditions fiscal deficits will not induce the Reserve Bank to change interest rates as changes in the deficit are usually contra-cyclical. The deficit decreases automatically in the boom phase of the business cycle and increases in the recessionary phase. Simultaneously, interest rates tend to increase during a boom and decrease during the recession. As a result, increases in the fiscal deficit might actually be associated with decreases in interest rates.

However, attempting to predict what impact large increases in public debt will have on the bank rate is more difficult. There is certainly some degree of co-operation between the Reserve Bank and the Treasury. This in turn might serve to limit either interest rate increases as a result of public borrowing or inhibit increases in public debt in times of tight money. In the event that the fiscal deficit becomes both pro-cyclical and has a significant impact on money supply, then the Reserve Bank might react by raising interest rates.

Policy implications of public debt

Despite the rise in the actual level of public debt in South Africa, when relevant adjustments are made, its level has been falling for the last twenty years. In addition, in recent years some of the expenditure on the development of human capital has been funded from current revenue. As a result, the development of human capital has been constrained by an inability to increase taxes.

These developments are not desirable in a semi-industrialized, developing country. In South Africa there is every reason to increase expenditure on the development of human capital by resorting to public debt. Such expenditure, if carefully chosen, will not have an adverse effect on the current account of the balance of payments. As such, they are unlikely to bring about increases in the interest rates and the subsequent crowding out of private investment.

Summary

1. The politicization of the South African economy at the international level makes a mockery of conventional macroeconomic strategy. Given the authorities' mismanagement of policy, it simply does not work. Economic (mainly monetary) policy helped precipitate South Africa's debt crisis and there is little this policy can do to overcome the problem.

If anything, monetary policy is currently based on meeting this debt repayment schedule. It has little autonomy to address domestic needs.

Fiscal policy has also become constrained by the repayment arrangement of the debt. Neither monetary nor fiscal policy is free from the limiting impacts of the foreign debt repayment schedule. It is vital that the debt repayment is re-scheduled so that it is more appropriate to the ability of the economy to repay.

2. As regards the specific fiscal policy and issues of taxes and spending, in view of the outcry over the high burden of taxation and the undisputed resource requirements to upgrade the socio-economic infrastructure, we favour debt financing by the central government.

18 Policy and economic development

Iraj Abedian and Barry Standish

In an overview of economic development in South Africa, this chapter focuses on an analysis of economic policy and policy-making, and proposals for the establishment of a comprehensive and internally coherent policy package.

Introduction

Many factors contribute to the general quality of life in a country. One of the most important is the success of official economic policy. For many years now various aspects of economic policy in South Africa have been under criticism. The issues range from the underlying economic philosophy, to specific aspects of general economic policy and the conduct of macroeconomic policy.

At a fundamental level, the underlying philosophy of the economic order has been called into question. Here some critics argue that a distrust for market forces has led to excessive government intervention in the economy. Yet there are others who argue the reverse and call for more intervention in the economy. Specific aspects of policy have also been under criticism. At one level, development economists object to the inefficiency of the country's development policy. In turn, the strategy of separate development has come under attack for both ideological and economic reasons.

Irrespective of how it is considered, both economic development and growth have been lagging. The combination of inadequate economic development and low economic growth is clearly untenable, especially in a country with a rising population.

It is against this background that we discuss economic policy and policy-making in South Africa. The chapter is divided into three sections. The first section gives a brief résumé of economic development in South Africa. The second section examines the important theoretical prerequisites for economic development. In the last section, the policy implications of the analysis are discussed.

Economic development

In order to give context to the analysis and proposals which follow, some of the salient features of South African economic development are given. As the earlier years are well documented, only the briefest details are mentioned here. However, recent changes are reported in more detail.

Up to the formation of the Union in 1910, economic development was confined to the location of resources and, sometimes, people. Over the following fifteen years, legislation was introduced which still dominates aspects of current economic policy. The Land Act of 1913, the Apprenticeship Act of 1922, and the Native (Urban Areas) Act of 1923 are but a few examples. These policies, while ostensibly racialistic, were inherently redistributive.

This period was the heyday of white poverty eradication.[1] With the help of a nation-wide public works programme, the state effected a massive redistribution of income in favour of the poor whites. This redistribution process was reinforced and sustained by the economic growth caused by South Africa leaving the Gold Standard in 1932.

The end of the 1940s saw the introduction of the policy of separate development and its many concomitant problems.

During the 1950s, as a result of widespread theoretical and political support, interventionist economic policies became the order of the day. South Africa, in line with many developing countries, opted for this policy. South Africa's economic policy in the 1950s and 1960s, supported by extraneous factors, brought about impressive economic growth. However, the process of economic development left a lot to be desired. The vigorous pursuit of separate development, facilitated by the rising fortunes of the economy, created tremendous bottlenecks for subsequent growth and development. Of these numerous disastrous consequences three are still binding on current policy.

The most important implication for policy today is the result of previous attempts to keep Africans out of the major urban areas.[2] The demographic consequences of this policy are so fundamental to economic development that the later inability of the economy to finance adequate socio-economic utilities can be blamed largely on this policy. The policy prevented people from improving their relative standard of living by urbanizing. Confined to the rural areas, the bulk of the population faced the prospect of life-long poverty.

---

[1] I. Adedian and B. Standish, 'An economic inquiry into the poor white saga', *Working paper no. 64*, SALDRU, Univ. of Cape Town, 1985.

[2] For a fuller account of the implications of these policies see I. Abedian, 'Economic obstacles to black advancement', in R. Smollan, *Black advancement in the South African economy*, Johannesburg: Macmillan, 1986.

Second in importance is the damage inflicted by the training and education policy. Both the nature of current education and the constraints imposed on the acquisition of skills have far-reaching consequences for the economy. These policies have resulted in a national labour force which is largely unskilled. This, in turn, has set the pattern of income distribution and the composition of domestic demand.

The third implication for policy is the result of the economic strategies conducted in and on behalf of the homelands. These have undermined growth and development and are reflected in over-population, land erosion and abysmal infrastructure. The result has been a gradual weakening of the economic base of the homelands and a growing dependence on the rest of the economy.

South Africa entered the 1970s with one of the most skewed distributions of income, measured by a Gini coefficient of 0,71.[3] The homelands, with 33 per cent of the population, produced only 2,5 per cent of total GDP. In 1985 per capita urban income was nearly thirty times greater than that of the homelands.[4]

The decade of the 1970s can be seen as watershed years in South African economic development. In spite of fantastic increases in the price of gold, the economy registered an average annual growth rate of only 2,9 per cent over the decade. Three of the major causes are:

1. The internal and external pressure for change in South Africa led to declining confidence on the part of both foreign and domestic investors and investment time-horizons were shortened.

2. The policy of import substitution reached its limits, yet export promotion, although recommended by the Reynders Commission in 1972, was never seriously pursued. Industrialization slowed and further expansion of manufacturing became dependent on the whims of the gold market.

3. The poor conduct of monetary and exchange rate policies led to substantial inflation and inflationary expectations which further reduced investment.

These events left their impression on official economic policy. Despite modest economic performance, the 1970s is a period in which some redistribution of income occurred in favour of blacks. This happened as a result of both market processes and the redistributive fiscal policy which was pursued by government and is illustrated in Tables 18.1, 18.2 and 18.3.

---

[3] C. W. Simkins, *The distribution of personal income recipients in South Africa 1970 and 1976*, Durban: Univ. of Natal, 1979, p. 9.

[4] S. F. Coetzee, 'Regional development in southern African development area, an assessment of theories, prominent features and the policy framework', *Development Southern Africa*, vol. 3, no. 3, 1986.

Table 18.1:   Income from central government employment, selected years

	1970	1975	1981	1985	1987
Whites					
No. of employees	93 113	106 768	129 858	150 396	238 684
Average income					
(R/per year)	3 262	5 304	9 240	15 684	20 740
Income index	100,00	162,60	283,26	486,33	635,81
Coloureds					
No. of employees	30 745	42 227	60 089	70 477	82 989
Average income					
(R/per year)	1 350	2 335	4 178	8 997	11 905
Income index	100,00	172,96	309,48	666,44	881,85
Indians					
No.of employees	7 304	8 706	13 011	17 426	19 146
Average income					
(R/per year)	1 745	3 885	8 437	14 157	20 901
Income index	100,00	222,69	483,50	811,30	1 197,74
Africans					
No. of employees	135 465	114 686	132 064	141 639	178 235
Average income					
(R/per year)	536	1 280	2 842	5 769	8 953
Income index	100,00	238,81	530,22	1 076,30	1 670,33
*Income to lower income group**					
(R x 10³)	108 779	238 023	626 424	1 440 029	2 546 687
Index	100,0	218,8	575,9	1 328,8	2 341,2
Consumer price index	100,0	156,7	319,0	533,5	736,40

Source:
Central Statistical Services, *SA Statistics*, 1988.
Note:
* In calculating the total benefits it has been assumed that 80 per cent of coloured and Asian and 90 per cent of African employees are part of the lower income groups.

The role of the central government in this process was most noticeable in the employment and wage policy pursued by the public service (see Table 18.1). Over the period, the racial wage gap for government employees diminished substantially. In particular, the ratio of white to African income received in central government employment declined from 6,1 in 1970 to 2,3 in 1987. This was achieved partly as a result of facilitating the upward mobility of labour in the public service and partly by resorting to racially differentiated wage increases.

The homeland governments also contributed to this redistributive process. In this case it was targeted at Africans. Table 18.2 provides an estimate

Table 18.2: Total employment by the governments of the homelands and independent states, and resultant benefits accrued to lower income groups

Year	Total no. African employed	Average earnings p.a.* $(R \times 10^3)$	Wage index salary	Total wages and accrued** $(R \times 10^3)$	Total benefit (CPI)	Price index
1973	93 018	705	100	65 578	55 741	100,0
1975	129 123	1 049	149	135 450	115 133	126,7
1981	202 638	2 550	362	516 727	439 218	257,9
1987†	284 987	8 028	1 139	2 287 876	1 944 694	593,5

Sources:
BENSO, *Statistical Survey of Black Development*, 1978, 1981; Central Statistical Services, *SA Statistics*, 1988; Inst. of Race Relations, *Race Relations Survey*, 1987–8.
Notes:
* Average earnings are calculated on the basis of public service wages in the independent States (R669 p.m.).
** It is estimated, on the basis of Transkei Government employment data, that 85 per cent of the total wages and salaries paid accrues to the lower income groups.
† Employment figures for the self-governing homelands are for 1986.

Table 18.3: Indices of per capita benefits received — selected welfare schemes, 1970–87

Year	CPI	Old age pension				Disability pension			
		W	C	I	A	W	C	I	A
1970	100	100	100	100	100	100	100	100	100
1975	156,7	171,3	172,3	172,8	244,4	169,0	163,8	189,6	246,7
1981	319,0	332,9	404,9	402,5	771,7	332,0	389,7	417,2	783,1
1987	736,4	598,2	837,5	856,7	2 237,1	547,5	779,2	856,6	236,4

Year	Maintenance grant				Total no. of beneficiaries			
	W	C	I	A	W	C	I	A
1970	100	100	100	100	136 551	102 265	25 732	298 760
1975	156,5	158,9	167,3	133,3	170 327	134 523	33 554	227 601
1981	270,2	425,7	409,8	309,6	190 064	197 358	51 520	299 525
1987	429,0	716,1	839,1	428,3	200 010	255 421	61 336	435 799

Source:
Central Statistical Services, *SA Statistics*, 1988.
Note:
W = white, C = coloured, I = Indian, A = African

of these changes.

In addition to these wage and employment policies, government expenditure was also used to affect some redistribution. This was particularly evident in social welfare expenditure. Table 18.3 compares the indices of some social welfare measures over time. Two important points merit attention. One is the fact that old age and disability pensions for all but whites exceeded the rate of inflation. As such there was a real transfer of resources. Second, the differential growth of the indices helped reduce the racial gaps in these benefits. However, it must be noted that while these changes are desirable, they are unfortunately a drop in the ocean for old-age pensioners. The indices shown are calculated from very different bases and in all cases the actual rand amount is very small. For instance, the old-age pension for a coloured person was less than R130 a month in 1987.

Along with the process of direct government redistribution, changes were made to the labour laws. These contributed to the upward mobility and the unionization of African labour and, as a result, to some redistribution of income. These measures, together with substantial increases in the gold price, reduced the private sector wage gap.[5] Table 18.4 shows the extent of the changes.

Table 18.4: Recorded private sector income — rands per month

Year	White		Coloured		Indian		African		
	CPI	Rand	Index	Rand	Index	Rand	Index	Rand	Index
1970	100	270	100	78	100	87	100	40	100
1975	157	450	167	144	185	170	195	91	228
1980	274	765	283	253	324	336	386	190	475
1984*	457	1 404	520	486	623	683	785	365	913

Source:
Central Statistical Services, SA Statistics, 1976 and 1988.
Note:
* At the time of writing, this was the last year for which earnings data were available.

The sum total of all the above changes helped reduce the maldistribution of income in South Africa. The Gini coefficient declined remarkably from 0,71 in 1970 to 0,57 in 1980 and continued to decline, at least during the early years of the 1980s.[6]

In the decade of the 1980s it is probably the lack of economic growth which has dealt the severest blow to economic development. The average growth rate of 1,1 per cent over the decade is far below that experienced over any previous decade. Given a population growth rate of over 2,3 per cent, this growth rate implies a decline in real standard of living and has serious implications for the future well-being of the country.

---

[5] The rise in the price of gold removed the constraint on the ability of mines to pay higher wages. Given the relative significance of the mining sector, the entire economy was affected.

[6] S. Devereux, 'South African income distribution 1900–1980', Working Paper no. 51, SALDRU, Univ. of Cape Town, 1983.

Economic policy: a theoretical perspective

From a policy point of view it is important to know whether the recent poor performance of the economy represent a short-run aberration of a long-run trend or whether it is symptomatic of more fundamental flaws in the structure of economic policy. In order to address this question it is necessary to establish some framework.

Theoretically, three general issues merit close consideration. First, the relationship between development policy and macroeconomic policy. Second, the interaction between economic growth and economic development. And third, the role of the state in the process of economic development. Each of these is discussed in the text that follows.

Development policy and macroeconomic policy

Economic policy may be defined as the combination of the long- and short-term guidelines, laws and regulations that govern the utilization of the resources available to the society. Resources in turn include both the material endowments of the economy, such as human resources, minerals and land, as well as the opportunities available or accessible to the society.

Ideally, economic policy should not only allocate resources as efficiently as possible, but also create economic opportunity. The latter is conventionally regarded as development economics, while the former is more of a macroeconomic nature. However, this distinction is both simplistic and misleading as it underplays the significance of the important links which exist between these two types of policies.

The relationship between the overall strategy and macroeconomic policy can take a number of forms. Theoretically, it is possible to conduct the macroeconomic policy in the absence of any particular development framework. Policy then consists of a series of reactions to socio-economic shocks and influences. Such a phenomenon-driven approach to economic policy has a major shortcoming. It is not uncommon to find macroeconomic policies which are incompatible with the overall development strategy. Such methods almost inevitably lead to inefficient resource allocation and as a result undermine economic growth. Many developing countries conform to this method of economic policy and South Africa is no exception. Over the past fifteen years, economic growth and employment creation have been the overall objectives of economic policy. Yet, when carefully examined, the conduct of macroeconomic policy has been both contractionary, and conducive to capital intensification.[7] The result is less rather than more economic growth and fewer formal sector jobs — a result surely at odds with stated development policy.

---

[7] Abedian, 'Economic obstacles to black advancement'.

A major influence on this type of *ad hoc* policy formation is the economic success of other countries. In many cases items of policy are implemented simply because they have worked elsewhere.

Unfortunately, as conditions in other countries are rarely similar to those in South Africa, the policies might prove not only unsuccessful but damaging. A prime example of this was South Africa's fight against inflation in the mid-1980s. The USA and UK had successfully corrected inflation by allowing their economies to enter severe recessions. When the same policy was instituted in South Africa, the result was social unrest, capital flight and a substantial depreciation of the rand. The consequence was the highest ever levels of domestic inflation. Apart from the failure to combat inflation, massive real economic damage was inflicted needlessly on the economy.

Macroeconomic policy and development strategy are inextricably interrelated. As a result it is this which should underpin economic policy-making. Ideally, the development strategy should set the parameters of the economic framework, the medium- to long-term goals for the economy and the economic philosophy within which resource allocation takes place. Macroeconomic policy is then conducted within the constraints imposed by the development strategy. A set of compatible development strategies and macroeconomic policies is by far the most superior combination.

The overall strategy can take a variety of forms. It can be regional development, import substitution, export promotion, maximum employment, or simply 'free enterprise'. While each of these strategies, given the resource endowment of the society, will have a different growth potential and follow a different development path, each is capable of leading to economic growth if accompanied by suitable and consistent macroeconomic policies.

The experience of many developed and developing countries offers ample evidence to support the viability of each of the above frameworks for effecting economic development. The NICs, for example, followed a very successful strategy of export-promotion, while Brazil and South Africa pursued successful import-substitution policies in the 1960s. The emergence of the economic strategy of supply-side free enterprise over the last ten years suggests that this too can be an effective long term plan, as has been demonstrated in both the British and American economies.

Two aspects of general policy are of importance: the choice of policy itself, and the need for consistency in the policy framework once the policy package is chosen. The choice of any particular policy package must be made given the opportunities and constraints in the economy. Once the policy package is established, all other policies, including macroeconomic policy, must be made within the framework of the package itself.

Growth and development

In economic analysis, growth and development are often used synonymously, even though they relate to two different concepts. Usually, economic growth refers to either a sustained increase in per capita or total income, while economic development implies continuous structural change which encompasses all the complex effects of economic growth. As suggested by Sir John Hicks:

> Underdevelopment economics is a vastly important subject, but it is not a formal or theoretical subject . . . the appearance of a branch of theory called Growth Theory, at a time when the economics of underdevelopment has been a major preoccupation of economists, has made it look as if there must be a real connection.[8]

Hahn and Matthew maintain that in the case of dual economies, 'Growth theory is applicable only to the advanced sector whereas the problems of the backward sector must be regarded as part of the theory of development rather than the theory of growth'.[9]

There is also some confusion over the meaning of development. Rostow's well-known development hypothesis presented in the 'The Stages of Economic Growth' implies that a development path is fairly predictable in any country and is a process of economic unfolding. However, the historic determinism and the inevitability of progress implied by this line of thinking are questionable both theoretically and empirically.

Alternatively, economic development may be viewed as a convoluted process, as postulated by Wilber. In this case, 'the best model of development is the one that any society forges for itself on the anvil of its own specific conditions'.[10] Recently, international development strategy has been moving in this direction. Under this approach each case must be taken on its own merits, depending on opportunities and constraints faced by the individual economy.

However, even given this disparate nature of the development process, there are some aspects which are important for the development strategist. It is our opinion that economic development is the process of interaction over time between economic growth and the distribution of wealth. Through economic growth, society generates surpluses of income over consumption. These, in turn can be distributed in order to effect changes in the social, demographic and economic structure of the country.

---

[8] K. Choi, *Theories of comparative economic growth*, Iowa: Iowa State Univ. Press, 1983, p. 8.

[9] Choi, *Theories of comparative economic growth*.

[10] C. K. Wilber, *The political economy of development and underdevelopment*, New York: Random House, 1984, p. 21.

Under ideal conditions the pattern of economic development will consist of periods of growth followed by periods of redistribution. In the periods of growth, surpluses are generated which allow for subsequent redistribution. This will occur over and above whatever distribution takes place through the market mechanism. Given the inextricable links between redistribution in one period and economic growth in the next, the challenge to policy-making is a technically enormous one. Overshooting the desirable level of redistribution will have negative growth effects while undershooting reduces potential development. As there are no a priori guidelines, it amounts to a process of trial and error.

This distributive process and its resultant structural changes can take three possible forms:

1. They can be growth neutral. In this case the policies neither support nor hamper economic growth. However, if population growth exceeds the rate of growth of the economy, per capita income will fall, diminish the scope for redistribution and retard economic development.

2. Redistribution can be hostile to economic growth. In fact, the experience of many LDCs testify to the case where redistribution has led to a slow-down in economic growth. The end result is increased well-being for some but a rapid deterioration in the standard of living in general. If uncorrected, this marks the inception of economic underdevelopment.

3. Redistribution can be growth supportive in two major areas. It allows for increases in the level of aggregate demand. The result is increased production and further increases in income, the central theme of the literature on redistribution with growth that emerged in the late 1970s. In addition, appropriate redistribution can have positive supply-side effects in the longer term by increasing the productive capacity of the economy. This type of effect requires redistribution which is conducted in order to increase the efficient use of resources. It will include such elements as manpower development, and providing financial and physical infrastructure.

A growth-supportive development policy will ideally fulfil three criteria. First, for development to sustain itself, redistribution must occur, but only to the extent that economic growth is not harmed. Second, in deciding on the correct combination of growth and redistribution, growth should be given priority. Third, the means by which redistribution is actually brought about should be those which increase the ability of the people and the economy to increase production.

Economic development and the role of the state

The state can play a variety of roles in the development process. Broadly speaking, these can be summarized into three possible approaches:

1. *Central planning:* Under this type of planning goals and means are set ideologically and carried out under some direct control. The problem with this approach is that market fundamentals are often ignored — at great cost to the country.
2. *Regulatory state:* In this approach emphasis is placed on:
   the rules and procedures of competition and not substantive outcomes . . . regulatory States do not believe that government should promote the growth of one industry or abandon another. The fate of industries is left to the marketplace on the assumption that the invisible hand is the most effective manager of substantive outcomes.[11]
3. *Developmental state:* In this approach, goals and policies are related in terms of market realities. 'For developmental States, substantive choices are matters of national concern, the rules of competition have lesser priority . . .'[12] Based on this philosophy, economic development, both on the supply and distribution sides, is not a matter of a natural course. Efficient economic management on the part of the state and private sector has substantial bearing on the course of the economy. In a sense this approach to development calls for a widening of the classical notion of comparative advantage in order to encompass economic policy advantage.

Policy implications for South Africa

The forgoing analysis has suggested that policy-making in South Africa has suffered from a number of problems. These can be summarized as follows:

▷ South African economic development has been characterized by the dominance of sectional political interests over general economic well-being. As a result, policy has been short-sighted, caused economic underdevelopment and inhibited economic growth.

▷ Much of the growth and development of the country is due to its rich economic resource base rather than appropriate economic strategy.

▷ The performance of the economy in the 1980s underscores the inability of the existing economic policy to affect sustainable growth in the overall living standard of society.

▷ Until recently the country's redistribution policies have been mainly growth-supportive. There is, however, little scope for any further expansion of this process in the absence of any sustained economic growth.[13]

---

[11] B. R. Scott, as quoted in P. E. Kotze, 'Aspects in devising an industrial strategy', in van de Walt and van Pletsen, eds., *Modern trends in industrialization with reference to South Africa*, 1987, p. 190.

[12] Scott, as quoted in Kotze, 'Aspects in devising an industrial strategy.

[13] It might be argued that a change in government expenditure priorities might lead to substantial redistribution. One item often cited is the Defence Budget. Defence expenditure constitutes about 15 per cent of the

▷ South Africa has long had contradictory development and macro policies. Its existing policy package may be best defined as a set of accumulated *ad hoc* measures. An analysis of contemporary policy-making points to the failure of this strategy. This is evidenced by the current low, sometimes negative, growth rates, limited scope for redistribution, and the lack of any policy direction on the part of the state.

Given these conclusions, it is important that serious consideration be given to establishing a comprehensive and internally coherent policy package. Some of the principles of such a policy package are outlined below.

Clarify development strategy

Any sustainable economic development in the country necessitates a well conceived and clearly articulated policy approach which will constitute the bedrock of a medium- to long-term development framework. Given the country's resource endowment, it appears that an export promotion strategy is the only logical choice.[14]

Remove constraints to growth

Whatever policy paradigm is chosen, the constraints to economic growth, and hence development, must be faced. The most important of these constraints are:

▷ *Investment issue:* While the problem is epitomized by disinvestment, the causes go back a lot further. As early as the 1970s foreign and domestic investors faced diminishing expected return on their capital, due largely to increasing political tensions. Socio-economic factors such as low labour productivity, inconsistent economic policy, and a small domestic market compounded the problem. It is obviously important that these investment constraints be addressed. Soothing statements or authoritative promises by government are poor substitutes for positive action.

▷ *The manpower issue:* This is perhaps the most intractable obstacle to South Africa's economic progress. The fact that South African labour is so poorly skilled is the result of sixty years of political myopia. The rise in unemployment, relatively lower wages, and the rising level of poverty in particular sections of the population are some of the manifestations of the same phenomenon. The solution to the problem calls for a two-prong policy approach. On the one hand, a dramatic

---

government budget, even if it is cut by a half, the resultant resources are too meagre in comparison with the required amount for meaningful redistribution.

14 See C. L. McCarthy, 'Structural development of South African manufacturing', *SA Journal of Economics*, vol. 56, no. 1, 1988.

restructuring of the education system is needed. On the other, a comprehensive policy of on-the-job-training must be implemented. The importance of appropriate upgrading of the skill structure of labour can hardly be overemphasized.

Address the distribution issue

Ultimately, it is the skewed distribution of income and wealth which is the major impediment to political change in South Africa. The various dimensions of the problem can be examined in a number of ways. The three which are presented here are the racial distribution of income, the regional discrepancy in economic activity and the differences in the standard of living between urban and rural areas.

While there has been some improvement in racial income distribution, whites still have the lion's share. Estimates of this are shown in Table 18.5.

Table 18.5:   Racial distribution of personal income, 1980 and 1988

Population group	1980* %	1988** %
White	61,5	53,9
Coloured	6,5	6,6
Asian	3,0	3,2
African	29,0	36,3
Total	100,0	100,0

Notes:
* From Devereux 'South African income distribution'.
** Projected on the basis of the 1970s trend.

The regional disparities of economic activity are given in Table 18.6. It can be seen that there are quite large disparities in the distribution of economic activity and, as a result, in standards of living. Under normal circumstances such regional disparities would not have mattered as resources are not located evenly around the country. As the concentration of industry depends on the availability of resources, there is no a priori reason to expect industry to be evenly located either. However, what makes this problematic for South Africa is that a large part of the population is confined to specific regions. Consequently, discrepancies in per capita income of up to seven times that of other regions is in fact a proxy for the distortions that successive governments have imposed on the economy.

Even more stark than regional differences are the enormous differences in production capacity and standards of living between urban and rural South Africa. This is shown in the Table 18.7.

In addition to its political implications, this pattern of income distribution, given that whites constitute a small part of the total population, has

Table 18.6:   Regional distribution of the SA GDP, 1987

Region	% Share of GDP	Population (million)	GDP/capita (rand)
A: Western Cape	12,6	3,24	5 765
B: Northern Cape	2,8	1,02	4 085
C: OFS	5,8	2,44	3 516
D: Eastern Cape	7,2	4,52	2 353
E: KwaNatal	14,3	8,73	2 421
F: Eastern Transvaal	8,4	2,07	5 974
G: Northern Transvaal	3,8	4,24	1 314
H: Witwatersrand	39,9	7,47	7 892
I: Western Transvaal	5,2	1,71	4 525

Source:
Calculated from data received from DBSA

Table 18.7:   Rural–urban distribution of economic activity in South Africa, 1985

Area	GDP %	GDP (Rm)	Population (1 000)	GDP per capita (R)
Metropolitan area	62	67 817	10 179	6 662
Non-metropolitan area	33	36 517	9 298	3 927
Homelands	5	5 266	14 221	370
Total	100	109 600	33 698	3 252

Source:
Coetzee, 'Regional development in southern Africa'.

serious implications for the composition of aggregate demand and other macroeconomic variables.

It is beyond the scope of this chapter to suggest a detailed solution to the phenomenon. Certainly there is no real short-term solution. A longer view of the issue suggests that a three-prong approach is required. The first calls for the removal of the entire maze of discriminatory policies which prevent the free accumulation of capital. The second is the need for expedient use of fiscal measures to support the market mechanisms. Finally, a coherent growth strategy is needed. For this latter component to succeed, South Africa must regain access to world capital markets, which will only happen if fundamental political changes are brought about.

Specify the role of the state

It is our contention that the state's role in the development process should be clearly spelled out. This chapter has suggested that government should play a critical role in establishing a policy framework which is both in-ternally consistent and conducive to socio-economic development. The overriding objective of the government should be the maximization of the general standard of living. Details cannot be spelled out here. However, two principles can be stated. The first is that the allocation of public resources must be in terms of the stated development objectives. The second is that frequent meddling with the policy, once established, must be avoided at all cost.

Conclusion

Attention must be given to three areas if economic growth and development are to continue. First, South Africa needs access to offshore capital. As a result, a prerequisite for rapid economic change is political change. Second, an economic policy is needed which is both internally consistent and conducive to growth and development. In particular the need for harmonization between development policy and macroeconomic policy has been stressed. What is called for is a bold, consistent, and clear policy package that will marry the existing potentials of the economy with the realities in the market place. Finally, government must be proactive in addressing those structural conditions which constrain economic growth and development.

19 Agriculture: its problems and its prospects

David Cooper

This chapter argues for a change in agricultural policy that will increase the standard of living of sections of the rural population, as well as agricultural productivity. It proposes a land distribution programme that brings about a change of control of the core productive farms, presently comprising a third of white farming units. It argues that if white dominance of agriculture is allowed to continue without check, the post-apartheid state faces continually being held to ransom by this group, and thus unable to fulfil its reform development objectives for the rural poor.

Introduction

Some 15 million people, about half of South Africa's population, live in the countryside, either in homelands or on farms in 'white' areas. For decades, influx control laws maintained an artificially large rural population. Though the controls which block urbanization are now being relaxed and the number of people moving to towns is increasing fast, rural poverty will not be eased by an exodus from the land. Indeed, natural population increase is so rapid that, despite urbanization, the number of people living in rural areas will probably remain the same, though it will drop as a percentage of the population of South Africa.

Racist land policy

South African agriculture is based on a highly inequitable racial division of agricultural resources. A small élite of white farmers owns most of the farmland, including the best and most productive areas, while some 9 million black people are crowded into the fraction of the country's total land area set aside for homelands.

This racial division of land was first laid down in the 1913 Native Land Act. Along with the Population Registration Act, the Group Areas Act and the Bantu Authorities Act, this law is a pillar of the apartheid system. The Land Act set aside a mere 7 per cent of the land for occupation by 'Natives'.

Before its enactment, Africans could buy freehold land in the Cape and Transvaal, and had done so to a limited extent. In 1936, the Native Land and Trust Act extended the area set aside for African occupation to 13,6 per cent of the total land area of South Africa, and in addition gave white farm-owners almost absolute control over the black people living on white-owned farms, whether as tenants or labourers.[1]

Today, white-owned farms total 77 million hectares; coloureds and Indians together — who were legally prevented from buying much farmland — occupy half a million hectares; and the homelands make up 17 million hectares.[2]

A minority of white, settler farmers developed a highly mechanized, sophisticated form of agriculture, but most were not as successful and their farming remained more marginal. They relied on non-wage labour, did not invest in machinery, buildings, soil conservation, fencing or water supply, and often misused the land by overgrazing and poor cultivation.

White farms and the homelands make up an interdependent system of land use. The link is cheap labour: as the industrial, mining and farming economy developed, the homelands created a cheap migrant-labour system in which workers' families had some land to produce food and to live on. It meant that mine, factory and farm-owners did not have to provide for the families of workers. Later, the homelands became a means for the government to control a reservoir of surplus labour, once the economy had developed to the point where its use of cheap labour was decreasing.

Influx control laws were also essential to the system. By refusing farmworkers the right to seek work in towns, the influx control laws created a tied labour force. By the 1960s the only way farm people could legally leave farms for town was by first moving with their family to the homelands. Though never entirely successful, influx control laws did allow farmers to employ workers very cheaply.[3]

As mechanization increased in the 1960s, the homelands were forced to absorb over a million redundant farm-workers and their families. During the same period, the government campaign against black people dominating the countryside — the so-called 'verswarting van die platteland' — resulted in restrictions on the number of Africans allowed on any one farm.

White agriculture's support system

The state provides an impressive support system for white farmers. This

---

[1] F. Wilson, 'Farming, 1866–1966', in *Oxford history of South Africa*, Oxford: Oxford Univ. Press, 1971.

[2] RSA Dept. of Agricultural Economics and Marketing, *Abstract of agricultural statistics*, Pretoria: Govt Printer, 1987.

[3] M. Lipton, *Capitalism and apartheid South Africa, 1910–1986*, London: Wildwood House, 1987.

includes financial aid and credit, research institutes, educational facilities in high schools, technical colleges and universities, and extension services and marketing systems.

However, the extremely cheap credit provided by government until the mid-1970s had an important effect on the structure of agriculture: it helped to maintain South Africa's unusually high level of individual, as opposed to corporate, farm ownership. Cheap credit and other subsidies designed to win farmers' political support made investing in agriculture cheaper for individual farmers than for corporations.

At the same time, agricultural profits were lower than in the mining and industrial sectors, and corporate investors were not attracted to farming in any numbers until relatively recently. Even then, they invested in types of farming — like poultry, frozen vegetables, fruit farming, sugar and forestry — which are profitable, if capital intensive, or which produce raw materials for subsidiaries.

Today, the importance of corporate ownership in agriculture is rising. It produces a significant proportion of agricultural product, and can be influential in dictating the nature of farming and labour relations on the farm.[4]

South African agriculture's private sector support system is also extensive. It is dominated by multinational corporations, which supply the necessary machinery, materials, chemicals, feed and services, and a highly centralized food industry, which buys farmers' products, then processes and retails them. Private sector banks, too, supply a good deal of agricultural credit.

South African agriculture is very much part of an international system. It relies on imported machinery, chemicals, seeds and technology; and it sells its most profitable produce on markets abroad.

Low farm productivity and high inflation

But, with all this support, farm productivity in South Africa is low compared with that in other countries with a similar level of investment and facilities. International technology has improved productivity — the amount of produce obtained from a fixed area of land — but only on the most fertile land.

Generally, South African natural resources of soil and rainfall are more meagre than in most other countries. Despite this, high technology is applied in less fertile areas, where it does not increase productivity sufficiently to justify its cost. Heavily subsidized white farmers have been able to invest more capital in poor quality land than would be economic without

---

[4] A. Balal, 'Comments on some strategic considerations in organising farmworkers', unpublished, 1989.

such generous state support. This raises the aggregate cost structure of commercial farming, a significant cause of inflation since the 1970s.

For a long time, too, the government protected local producers of farm supplies, like chemicals and farm machinery, from competition by cheaper overseas goods. As a result, the cost of many agricultural products is high and rising. This fuels South Africa's high inflation, and makes exports uncompetitive on the world market. These problems have been exacerbated by the glut of agricultural products on the world market, and the consequent low prices of many agricultural commodities.

Despite the cost penalties, state support has encouraged the development of a highly diversified agricultural economy in South Africa. With the exception of a few non-essential food crops — coffee, tea, rice — white farmers produce a remarkable range of the country's agricultural needs, both of food and raw materials. This is largely owing to the fifty years of state subsidies and support for white farmers. But the economic cost has been great, the environmental results destructive, and the human and social consequences disastrous for most black people living in the countryside.

The ecological limits

A country's ecology sets the limits of its potential agricultural production. Only some 12 per cent of South Africa's surface area is suitable for growing crops. Rainfall decreases sharply from east to west across the country, and only in the eastern half is there enough rain to grow crops without irrigation.

The most severely ecologically damaged parts of the country are in the dry west, where overgrazing and attempting to grow crops in areas too dry for them have resulted in devastating soil erosion and bush encroachment.

In the eastern half of the country, cultivation is only possible where the soil is suitable and the land flat enough. Some soils are highly erodable, and can only be ploughed if properly protected from erosion. Thus, almost all areas of the country depend on mixed farming — growing crops and keeping animals on the same farm.

The pattern of agriculture

There are, in effect, three concentric circles in the single system of South African agriculture. The 'core' of the system is the highly productive commercial sector, which comprises about a third of white farms. This core has three types of farm: livestock, highly mechanized arable, and labour-intensive plantations. As a group, core farms supply about three-quarters of South Africa's agricultural produce.[5]

---

[5] H. Hattingh, 'Skewe inkomeverdeling in die landbou', Lanvokon, '86 Conference, Feb. 1986, Pretoria.

Next is the less developed sector, still white-owned. Here, agriculture retains non-capitalist elements, particularly the use of tenant labour rather than wage labour. Many of the farms are small or occupy ecologically marginal land, carrying on poor cropping or low-value sheep or cattle ranching. Often the white farm-owners do not live on the farm. Some farms are run by black managers who may receive low wages, or in some cases none at all. However, such employment provides a place to stay and some land to cultivate or graze.

Finally, there are the ten homelands. Almost all land is communally held — individually owned land is rare — and distributed by chiefs or headmen on the basis of one family, one plot. Plot size varies, but in most cases they fail to meet the subsistence needs of their occupiers, who depend on family members engaged in migrant labour. Homeland inhabitants make up about a third of South Africa's population, but supply less than 7 per cent of the country's annual agricultural production. As a result of removals and evictions from white areas — often of farm-workers rendered redundant by mechanization — the number of rural landless is growing.

A depressed agriculture

Since most of the land is pastoral, stock farming is usually the only viable type of agriculture. Much of the cultivated land is marginal, inappropriately used and increasingly degraded. Even where land is suitable for cultivation, it is often under-utilized — because people lack the basic capital to buy the equipment needed to take advantage of fertile ground. So, even in optimum circumstances, yields are low and farmers become demoralized. They are caught in a vicious circle of a deteriorating environment and deepening poverty.

Relocation and overcrowding

The worst homeland overcrowding and poverty is in relocation areas. On their original land, such communities may have farmed quite successfully, combining migrant labour with peasant agriculture to produce a reasonable standard of living. In some relocation areas they live in huge rural settlements; though promised land, they were allocated none.

Because of South Africa's massive unemployment, many of those removed to homelands have found it impossible to find jobs. Often their only skill is farming, but there is seldom land available for them to farm, and they swell the destitute ranks of the rural landless. So they try to eke out an existence by cultivating the tiny plots of land on which they are housed.

An ecological disaster

South African agriculture as practised at present is rapidly and severely degrading the environment.

Several processes are at work here. In more arid areas, especially the bushveld, land better suited to game farming has been stocked with domestic animals like sheep and cattle. They overgraze the grassland, encouraging bush encroachment, and wind and water erosion. Another destructive process is caused by white farmers ploughing up large areas of grazing land in an attempt to grow more profitable field crops. This has created dust-bowl conditions, especially in the southern Free State and on the margins of the Karoo. In higher rainfall areas, shallow, erodable types of soil unsuitable for cultivation have also been ploughed, with disastrous consequences. Even soil suitable for cultivation may need conservation measures, such as erosion banks and water channels, to preserve its quality.

The floods of 1987 provide a further example of ecological devastation arising from current agricultural practices. South Africa has extremes of climate — in this case the heaviest rainfall on record followed a prolonged drought. River catchment areas had been denuded of grass cover by overgrazing. Vleis and swamps — which act as natural sponges — had been drained and ploughed up, while river-beds and large dams were silted up with eroded soil. As a result, when excessive rain fell, overgrazed land could not absorb the large amounts of water which rushed into the river system, carrying soil with it. The volume of floodwater caused many silted rivers to break their banks, destroying fertile land. Ironically, the worst damage was down-river from the rains, so that flooding was worse in areas where there had been no rain.

The government gave aid, but will not tackle the cause of the disaster: white farmers' exploitative farming methods and overcrowding in the homelands.

A more recent form of land abuse is overuse of chemicals, whether insecticides, herbicides or chemical fertilizer. Already the nitrate and phosphate content of river water in some areas has risen to near poisonous concentrations because of excessive use of chemical fertilizers.

Unoccupied farms

In many districts, especially those in ecologically damaged areas, white farmers have been abandoning their farms, unable to make a living from them. This is not a new phenomenon. In 1960, 24 per cent of Free State farms and 42 per cent[6] of farms in northern Natal were unoccupied. But

---

6 S. Greenberg, *Race and state in capitalist society*, New Haven: Yale Univ. Press, 1980.

the problem of abandoned land has returned with the advent of serious drought in the 1980s, despite government attempts to keep white farmers on the land through incentives or drought relief payments.[7]

The present system is the product of the apartheid state's attempt to structure agriculture and manage the way the rural population lives through a programme of social engineering.

Although white farmers own and control the vast majority of South Africa's farms and utilize wage labour as the basis of social relations, there is a continuing struggle over land rights in less productive/developed areas. Squatting and labour tenancy have not been eliminated and in the areas that they survive (for example, north-east Transvaal and northern Natal), tenants cling to their access to land, especially to grazing rights. Grazing rights are the central element of land reform.

Any attempt to undo the present system must aim to end its exploitative nature, and replace it with one in which workers can share in the way agriculture is structured and in the wealth it produces, without destroying the land.

In looking at future possibilities, agriculture must aim to become sustainable. Sustainable agriculture is a system which:

▷ provides a place for rural people to live and produce their food and fuel;

▷ provides employment for rural people;

▷ provides food for the urban population;

▷ provides industrial raw materials;

▷ earns foreign exchange with the exports it produces; and

▷ (perhaps most important) protects the environment and makes it possible to pass on land to the next generation in better condition than it was received.

South African agriculture certainly produces food, industrial raw materials and exports. But it provides employment for only a small proportion of the rural population. Nor does it meet their food or fuel needs, or provide them with adequate homes.

The physical, political, economic and social obstacles to the homelands developing a sustainable agriculture, or even the ability to support their populations, are huge. To have any hope at all, the target of land reform in such areas must be subsistence producers. Without their understanding and willing participation, any strategy will flounder.

---

[7] RSA Dept. of Agriculture, *Annual Report, 1983*, Pretoria: Govt. Printer, 1984.

Short-term options within the present political system

While at present the future of the rural population looms bleak, their demands are becoming more clearly formulated. Some unionized workers on large estates want the land nationalized, then handed over to production co-operatives under worker control. Workers on smaller farms generally want at least a family plot to farm so as to feed their families. In the homelands the most common demand is simply for more land. Fundamental changes to the way land is owned and distributed will have to wait for a change of regime and a new, democratic government.

Any land reform plans should include the establishment of development zones both close to cities and near homelands, which would become models for agricultural resettlement. Prime targets for such projects must be land already owned by the state or large corporations, or their cost would be prohibitive.

There are a number of immediate objectives whose success or failure will influence what happens later in a post-apartheid South Africa. So it makes sense to consider possible short-term changes before going on to make suggestions about long-term policies.

The 1913 Land Act

There are calls for both the Group Areas Act and the 1913 Land Act to be abolished, allowing all South Africans to own or occupy land wherever they choose. Ending racial restrictions on land ownership, while an important principle to fight for, in itself is not a solution since few of the impoverished rural millions can afford to buy or even rent farms.

Abolishing racial barriers to land ownership is unlikely to result in large numbers of black people entering commercial agriculture. More likely, more people will occupy nominally white-owned farms which have been abandoned as unprofitable. Such squatter-tenants may be farm-workers from the area, or the landless unemployed drifting from the homelands in search of a livelihood. Either way, lacking capital and infrastructure, they will be able to eke out only a bare subsistence.

The Urban Foundation recommends that the government buy up white farmland near cities or homelands and make it available to landless blacks either on a leasehold or freehold basis. Its proposal indicates that business interests are aware of the injustice of the present patterns of land distribution — and that the free enterprise lobby recognizes that a state programme is needed for any land reform.

However, the present government is unlikely to consider such a programme in the foreseeable future, given its concern for right-wing farmer reaction. The Holgat farm is a case in point. A trust set up by the South African Council of Churches bought the farm in 1987 to give the dispossessed residents of the Mogopa 'black spot' land to live on and farm. Following local white farmers' representations to government, Holgat was expropriated before anyone had moved on to the land.

Any government attempts at land reform are likely to be met with stiff opposition from white farmers, who are resisting changes even to laws relating to conditions of employment. So, present land reform is likely to be limited to some special areas.

One immediate advantage of ditching the 1913 Land Act would be to end the threat of removal hanging over 'black spot' communities — they could even expand their landholdings, whereas at present they have only the government's word that it will not recommence removals. Some of these communities are in line for state-initiated development projects, which are intended to neutralize their hostility to the government. But with the Land Act gone, it would become possible to undertake progressive agricultural pilot projects with the rural poor outside the homelands, at present the only place Africans have legal tenure of farm land.

Security of tenure is important to any attempt to improve peoples' conditions through better production. Once residents of the few remaining 'black spots' have been guaranteed residential rights, they can develop appropriate agricultural programmes, whether collective, co-operative, communal, individual or family based.

Places with this potential for development include KwaNgema in the south-eastern Transvaal, where 400 families subsist as peasant-workers; Driefontein, a much bigger farm which adjoins KwaNgema; Mathopestad in the western Transvaal; and the much smaller Motlatla nearby. In Natal there are Reserve Eight and Doornkop, and in the eastern Cape, Kwelera and Newlands, among many others, offer similar possibilities. Some communities are already running successful farms, though the majority are under-utilized. However, development will not be without problems. Many of the communities have conservative and hierarchical local political structures.

Options for the churches

Church farms also offer a number of positive options. Many could be placed under the control of the people who work them. Though only on a small scale, a fund of experience of co-operative and collective farm management could begin to develop. The churches are not major landowners, but they do own small amounts of land all over South Africa.

In the early decades of this century, the land of many missions and religious orders was well and skilfully farmed. But church farming activity has declined in the past thirty years. Today, many church-owned farms are leased to white farmers. Others house rent-paying black tenant families, who live under constant threat of removal if the owner church were to bow to pressure from the government — and white congregations — and accept the apartheid doctrine that black tenants do not have the right to occupy land in white rural areas. In many cases white commercial farmers, often congregation members, want to take over the estates.

In the case of farms leased to white farmers or companies, the owner church receives rent or a share in the lessee's crop. These farms, like others in white South Africa, offer workers low wages and poor working conditions.

Debate about the churches' rural land policy has become part of a wider debate as to how they should respond to the growing struggle against apartheid and economic exploitation. Some church leaders view land ownership as a headache and would like to sell their surplus land on the commercial market. Clearly, selling or leasing church property to white farmers would not help change in South Africa, while it would certainly harm the black tenants or workers.

Some churches are trying to use their land to assist rural development. The Anglican Church commissioned a study to help it decide what to do with Springvale, its 1 200 hectare farm near Pietermaritzburg, stipulating security of tenure for the one hundred tenant families on the farm. The Indaleni Methodist Mission Development Centre, too, has set up a number of development projects on its old mission station near Richmond in Natal.

In 1985 the Catholic Bishops of Natal commissioned a nine-month research survey to determine how their church's land in Natal could best be used. Until then, decisions about how Catholic church land was used were taken on an *ad hoc* basis. The survey concluded that it was the church's duty to give its black tenants security of tenure, and that it should negotiate with them how the land should be used. Church land without black tenants should be made available to progressive organizations for development projects.

Two such projects, on Catholic-owned land in the Orange Free State and Natal, started before the survey. One is Sheridan farm, made up of 800 hectares owned by the Catholic Diocese of Bethlehem. It is a mixed farm, with maize, wheat, beef cattle, sheep, dairy and asparagus sections. Twenty full-time workers are employed and forty-two families live on the farm. Many women work seasonally. Until August 1985, it was a typical white farm: a white monk told workers what to do and paid them a small monthly salary. Then the Bishop of Bethlehem decided on an experiment in worker control at Sheridan.

After consultation, a project co-ordinator, responsible to a board appointed by the church, was employed along with two other organizers. Workers from each crop section of the farm formed a section committee to manage farming and marketing the crop and to buy the necessary supplies.

The church signed a three-year lease, which paid only nominal rent. When this period has expired, the project will be reviewed.

In its first season, the farm met its basic target, which was to maintain productivity. However, progress has been slower in terms of organization and consciousness. People whose lives had been spent working for white farmers found it difficult to accept that they were now in control of their farm. They still see the church as the owner, and the project co-ordinator as the manager. However, a village committee was formed which shifted decision-making from the minority of full-time workers to the farm community as a whole.

The Catholic Church has also leased Blackwoods, a small 24-hectare farm near Howick in Natal, to the Sarmcol Workers Co-operative (Sawco). This coop was made up of workers dismissed after a strike at the BTR Sarmcol factory in Howick. About twenty-five of these workers began farming; they had valuable organizational experience as unionized industrial workers, though they began with little or no experience of farm work. Although the coop has grown vegetables successfully, lack of management and marketing skills has so far prevented the farm from being economically viable. Coop members see improving their knowledge and gaining skills as essential to reaching this goal. In making land available for pilot projects, the churches can make an invaluable contribution towards the future of the rural poor.

The homelands

Contrary to what is widely believed, land in the homelands is as good as the average in South Africa as a whole. It has a similar or slightly better proportion of arable to pastoral land: 13 per cent of it is arable, as opposed to 11 per cent in South Africa as a whole. However, much of the arable land is on slopes and needs to be protected from erosion.

Abused and overcrowded though it may be, this land is a valuable resource. It is rendered unproductive by the political and social systems which dictate how it is used.

Homeland agricultural policies

In theory, each of the ten homelands has an independent Department of Agriculture. But the guiding hand of Pretoria can be seen in the similarity of the ten 'separate' policies.

Homeland agricultural policy promotes the methods and technology used in white agriculture. Farmers are told that modern technology is the solution to their agricultural problems, and are advised to use pesticides, expensive chemical fertilizers and hybrid seeds — which most of them cannot afford. They are not advised to take advantage of resources available to them, such as manures, mixed cropping, adapted seeds and intercropping — a variety of techniques better suited to subsistence agricultural needs which could help them improve their small yields.

The crucial issue of subsistence agriculture is neglected, though a government concerned with the welfare of its people as a whole would concentrate on upgrading and making subsistence agriculture viable. If most of the producers who work one-family plots were enabled to produce small surpluses, it would benefit far more people than the present policy, which encourages a small minority of richer producers and launches large government-owned commercial agricultural schemes.

Unsuccessful subsistence agriculture presents homeland authorities with a dilemma. They wish their territories to appear economically self-sufficient. This is impossible while their major resource, the land, is improperly used. But the very structure of homeland administration limits the ways that people can participate in agriculture. Headmen receive bribes and political support in return for allocating land, so it is in their interests to divide the available land between as many people as possible. Efficient land use would involve landholders negotiating with each other to allocate resources effectively, a process local chiefs find threatening as it short-circuits their authority.

In any case, homeland policy defines successful agriculture as that which produces marketable surpluses, cash profits, and hence the tax revenue which keeps the inflated bureaucracy going. All homeland governments have agricultural extension services which play a major role in their attempt to improve agriculture. Because of the profit orientation of official agricultural policy, extension officers are instructed to devote most of their attention to full-time farmers. These are usually richer peasants or traders and those associated with the tribal authority, who as a result have access to more land.

Homeland commercial schemes

Rather than undertaking a broad-based agricultural policy, homeland governments continue to pour resources into ambitious commercial farming schemes. These are usually managed by government agricultural corporations, of which there is one in each territory.

The bureaucrats and technocrats in these corporations do not base their planning on the needs of ordinary villagers, with whom they have little contact. Rather, their plans are often drawn on a grand scale, requiring centralized management and large-scale capital investment. Tea plantations in the Transkei and in Venda were planned to yield maximum returns from intensive commercial farming. Land was confiscated to establish the estates, which has led to overcrowding and has reduced local production of subsistence crops.

In other cases, recently incorporated trust land has been used to establish commercial schemes rather than being redistributed to feed the immense land hunger of ordinary people. An example is the Zebediela citrus estate in Lebowa. Running such schemes is the major function of homeland agricultural corporations, though they also direct projects which involve ordinary villagers.[8]

Commercial agricultural schemes which involve ordinary villagers commonly do so to their detriment. Small landholders usually lose control of their land as a result of such projects. The numerous village schemes run by the Transkei Agricultural Corporation are typical, as are those implemented by its equivalents in other homelands, notably the Lebowa Landbou Maatskappy, and Agricor in Bophuthatswana.[9]

Typically, the local authority (the chief or headman) together with the manager of the scheme (an employee of the agricultural corporation) informs people that their plots are all included in a single scheme and will be planted with certain crops, under supervision of the manager. The scheme manager alone decides how to cultivate — usually by extensive mechanized ploughing — and what to plant — usually a single cash crop. At the end of the season he presents each landholder with a bill for ploughing and inputs provided. Should any landowner make a net loss after he has sold the crop and paid the bill, he must pay for it out of income generated elsewhere. To add insult to injury, farmers may be forced to plant crops they consider unsuitable for local conditions at the wrong time.

In another common variation on official attempts at commercial farming success, homeland agricultural corporations confiscate fertile land from small plot-holders to use for plantations. These usually grow non-food or export crops — coffee, tea, sisal, fruit and cotton are the most common. The government authority then offers low-paid plantation employment to the former landholders. Thus people not only lose the right to work their own land for subsistence purposes, but are also exploited by being forced into low-paid agricultural work. When the schemes fail, the state tends to call in management consultants from the private sector rather than reconsider the scale and organizational principles of its interventions.

Some homeland-run commercial schemes have been considered successful, at least in terms of gross product. But most survive only because of massive state subsidies. Until 1982, for instance, the Ditsobotla project in

---

8 J. Keenan, 'Agribusiness and the Bantustans', in *SA Review*, Johannesburg: Raven Press, 1984.

9 G. R. Cloete, 'Maize production schemes in the Transkei', in *Environmental and Development Agency: Land and People*, vol. 1, South Africa (now EDA), Johannesburg, 1987.

Bophuthatswana was held up as a model of successful government intervention.

The project began in the late 1970s when the area of arable land belonging to a village on trust land was increased, allowing each family a larger plot of about fifteen hectares. However, the landholding families did not farm their plots: Agricor, the Bophuthatswana agricultural corporation, selected a group of about fifteen villagers to work as contractors and farm the land on behalf of the other villagers. They were advanced the finance and equipment which would enable each to farm 100 hectares intensively. While the project produced a good deal, those villagers who did not become contractors had to continue to seek a living as migrant labourers. Most of the income from the project reverted to Agricor.[10]

Ultimately, the scheme collapsed, both because of drought and because of debt resulting from the high-cost inputs Agricor recommended. In 1987 its liabilities of the Ditsabotla scheme were estimated at R100 million.

Probably the most successful stimulus to peasant agriculture was a grower scheme launched in KwaZulu, not by a state agency but by the South African Sugar Association. It made finance available to peasant growers without insisting on minimum plot sizes or changes in land tenure, and encouraged the sugar mills to provide the necessary infrastructure. The assured market for this cash crop and its flexible labour demands (which could accommodate continued migrant labour) made the scheme popular. Nearly 8 000 small growers participate.

Most large, ambitious schemes have been spectacular failures, even in areas with a high potential for production. Examples include an irrigation scheme at Tugela Ferry in KwaZulu and at Qamata in the Transkei. An authoritarian state, it seems, has been quite unable to find ways of co-operating with subsistence producers. Any consultation with locals, at best, is with the tribal authority; there is seldom communication with the actual target group.

Projects are imposed from the top down, often in ignorance of local needs and interests. Large schemes involve major disruption to plotholders' lives and rights. Contracts between tribal authorities and agricultural corporations may effectively dispossess landholders of their land for up to five years, and many landholders fear they will never regain control of it.

Small-scale schemes

Small schemes have a better potential for success, since people find it easier to participate because of their more human scale. A few small-scale schemes

---

[10] M. Roodt, 'Capitalist agriculture and Bantustan employment patterns' in *SA Review*, Johannesburg: Ravan Press, 1987.

in homeland villages do attempt to meet people's food needs. These may be promoted by government agencies or, as is increasingly the case, by non-government organizations concerned about malnutrition. Some of the more successful are communal gardens, in which individuals are allocated plots in an area of irrigable land set aside for this purpose. These are to be found in many homeland villages. The way such projects are organized is crucial to whether they succeed, who they benefit and how long they last.

Unfortunately, gardens are usually run under the auspices of the tribal authority or a group close to it. Poorer residents are often excluded from control as they do not belong to the élite group. Frequently disputes arise between the membership and the élites who run the schemes, so after some years valuable land may be lying idle because social disputes paralysed the project. Sometimes, schools lay out communal gardens, but these schemes also are open to abuse. In one instance, the teachers in Bochum in the northern Transvaal were taking all produce grown by pupils, a move hardly designed to encourage them to continue their agricultural activities.

Other schemes may focus on helping people to get maximum production out of the family plot. Projects which tailor their methods to the skills and resources of the poorest villagers are more likely to succeed than those which encourage people to rely on expensive inputs, a strategy which tends to exclude the poorest villagers or drive them into debt.

Some small schemes which provide irrigated plots to families have been reasonably successful. Examples are to be found near Umzimkulu in the Transkei and in Gazankulu near Letaba, where families have been able to supply their food needs and produce a small marketable surplus. Many of these successful subsistence projects, however, are in danger of being taken over by homeland governments who wish to grow cash crops.[11]

A community project

Because of their complicated, conservative and corrupt hierarchies, the homelands offer limited possibilities for developing new forms of land use, village organization and production. The lives of common people are usually strictly controlled, and almost all villages lack agricultural infrastructure and means of access to markets.

However, the Luncedo Farm Centre project based at Sunduza in the Herschel district of the Transkei is an example of organized village production.[12]

Like most Herschel villages, Sunduza is heavily populated. There are about six hundred families, each with a residential plot 50 metres long

---

[11] D. Cooper, 'Looking at development projects' in *Work in Progress*, no. 26, Southern African Research Services, 1983.

[12] A. Mvelase, 'Land use and the community: a case study', *Environmental and Development Agency: Land and People*, vol. 1, South Africa (now EDA), Johannesburg, 1987.

and 50 metres wide. Fewer than two hundred own livestock and about four hundred have fields of between one and two hectares.

Most Herschel families do not have the resources to farm successfully. They cannot get credit, while seed and fertilizer are difficult to obtain, and there are no marketing structures for selling produce. Most Sunduza men are migrant workers and 95 per cent of Herschel families depend for survival on members who work in white mines, factories and farms. Only pensioners, small children, the disabled and women live permanently in the village. But although migrants spend most of their time outside the village, regular visits and report-backs ensure that they are active and important in community affairs.

An agricultural field-worker began working in Sunduza in 1980. The villagers' immediate priority was to find a way to plough their fields. Few people had the oxen needed for ploughing, so many fields lay fallow and families went hungry. A farmers' association was formed. The priority of its first fifty members was to buy ox-drawn planters and cultivators to hire out, and then to raise the funds to buy two tractors. Members agreed on a ploughing schedule, what was to be charged for ploughing, and undertook to collect the money. They also agreed to use the tractor to set up a milling service.

The project aroused keen interest in the district. Associations were formed in four other villages. The five associations together made up the Luncedo Farm Centre. Centre policy included equal sharing among members and between villages, free membership so that everyone could join, and payment for services. The centre's organizing committee had to learn new skills: bookkeeping, running a credit scheme, organizing ploughing schedules, running meetings, maintaining machinery, and ordering seed, trees and plants.

There was some conflict with the tribal authority, whose members expected special privileges and free services. Also, because it focused on field crop production, the scheme did not benefit the landless poor, about a third of the population. Equal participation by women in decision-making was also difficult to achieve.

The over-used and eroded soil, combined with a lengthy drought in the first half of the 1980s, presented severe problems. But the project gave farmers new ideas and techniques. It provided transport for produce, milling for crops, and ordered good seed and a variety of fruit trees. The project helped villagers get far more food from their fields, since tractors plough deeper, better and faster than ox-ploughs. This enables more families to plough in the short period after the first summer rains. Under southern African conditions this is necessary for good yields from dry-land farming.

In the first years of the project, the tractors ploughed fields for about three hundred Sunduza families and about two hundred fields in other villages. Farmers planted maize, sorghum, beans and wheat according to the season and their personal preference. Once organized in farmers' associations, those who wanted to grow winter crops demanded that cattle-owners keep their animals away from the usually fallow winter fields, so that winter wheat could be planted.

The farm centre project started by offering its services on credit so that even poor farmers could participate. It was hoped that people would produce enough surplus to sell and thus pay back their debts. But, in fact, even families with good yields consumed all they produced, and there was no surplus to sell for cash.

Soon the farm centre faced large outstanding debts and the committee refused further credit until old debts were paid off. Membership dropped, especially during the 1982–5 drought, which caused many crop failures. High inflation and a weak rand led to huge increases in costs, including those of the centre's tractor charges, at a time when many migrants were being retrenched because of recession. Since people could not afford to use the tractor services, they became reluctant to participate in running the farm centre. Only richer farmers continued to use the centre's services. To combat this, the farmers' associations opted to continue raising funds from outside the village to subsidize ploughing costs.

When the project was initially planned, charges for replacement were built into the cost structure of the tractor service so that the project would ultimately become self-supporting. In practice, it is not near self-sufficiency. After five years, even with the subsidy, the centre has only about R20 000 in its savings account: a new tractor costs about R40 000 and the old one is due to be replaced.

Initial costing when the project was planned was based on the price of mechanization on white commercial farms, since at the time there was no example of mechanization in a homeland village. Experience has now shown that costs in this situation are far higher than on commercial farms, because of small field size, poor-quality and eroded land, and distance from service centres.

But the greatest unforeseen problem was the sharp rise in prices of agricultural equipment. In the last six years, the cost of tractors and other equipment has trebled. The farm centre did not escape the difficulties which led white farmers to accumulate huge debts.

Crops produced in the villages went to increase family food supplies, rather than to the market. So, while the project succeeded in improving subsistence production, it could not recover its costs. At worst, it could be argued that the money spent on the centre produced far more food than the same amount could have supplied if spent directly on food aid.

Role of the Development Bank

According to the Development Bank of Southern Africa, the major source of development capital in South Africa, both large-scale corporate models and support for subsistence farmers in the homelands should be considered. But to date almost all its development aid has gone to corporate farming. Unless the Development Bank or homeland governments formulate very different approaches, there is little chance of the situation improving for subsistence producers.

The major beneficiaries of development efforts at present seem to be the multinationals involved in the supply of inputs like seed, fertilizer and tractors, and supporters of homeland élites like those chiefs, bureaucrats, shopkeepers and teachers who benefit personally through larger landholdings or bribes extracted from those who depend on them for land or services.

The new Development Bank policy of small farmer support still assumes full-time farming. This does not recognize the reality of most homeland families, who rely on income from many outside sources to survive. It also does not take account of the position of women in homeland society.

Although the small farmer policy may be a better option than large-scale schemes for meeting the needs of homeland producers, it still does not cater for the needs of most homeland residents.

Private ownership

There are strong pressures on homelands to create a free market in land. The legislation exists and this will lead to greater inequalities as a class of wealthy landowners squeezes more people off the land.[13]

Sanctions

Anti-apartheid groups overseas have for decades been urging people to boycott South African exports, including agricultural products. It is hard to tell what effect this has had. Between 1970 and 1980, the value of agricultural exports increased from R431 million to R2 052 million. By 1984, it had fallen to R1 842 million, primarily because of drought. Then, because of the drop in the value of the rand at the end of that year, the rand value of agricultural exports more than doubled. Volumes have also risen. For example, in 1986, 3 000 tons of high-priced Cape fruit was air freighted to Europe, as opposed to 2 000 tons the previous year.[14]

It is likely, though, that the present level of boycotts, partial though they are, may at least slow down export growth, and contribute to a continued

---

13 M. Sarakinsky and J. Keenan, 'Agricultura and the Bantustans', in *SA Review no. 4*, Johannesbug: Ravan Press, 1987.

14 RSA Dept. of Agricultural Economics and Marketing, *Abstract of agricultural statistics*, Pretoria: Govt. Printer, 1987.

sluggish performance of the South African economy in the early 1990s. South African farmers are certainly particularly worried that sanctions — or the threat of them — may put them at a disadvantage in competing with the rapidly expanding agricultural exports of other southern hemisphere countries like Australia, Chile and Brazil. If South African farmers, already using backdoor export routes through neighbouring countries, are forced to sell at a discount, their incomes would drop drastically.

The international community, it seems, cannot agree to impose comprehensive mandatory sanctions. In theory, a full-scale international boycott of South African farm produce could create havoc in the agricultural economy, as well as having a knock-on effect on agricultural supply industries and processing and packaging plants.

Workers would not be the only ones to suffer. Though the effect on the South African economy of a comprehensive boycott of agricultural exports would not be as severe as one of precious metals, it would hurt an important constituent of the ruling élite. Land values could be expected to fall dramatically and banks, already overexposed in their credit to farmers, could suffer heavy losses. The tractor and farm machinery sectors are already in severe recession, and farmers' loss of revenue from exports could further damage them. The effect on pesticide and fertilizer sales would be similar.

Even partial sanctions could lead to a major pullout by farm-related multinationals, which dominate the sale of all inputs to farmers. International refusal to sell South Africa some of the imports it needs would be inflationary. Farmers use a great deal of imported chemicals and machinery — and while they would probably continue to get them in spite of sanctions, prices would rise dramatically.

South African industry can increase its import substitution, but at a price. Costs of farm equipment and inputs thus seem set to continue rising. Steep increases in the prices of farm machinery would cause even the commercial agricultural sector to remain less mechanized than its European equivalent. But it would take decades for this to have a major impact on profitability.

To date, the sanctions lobby has succeeded in invoking the General Agreement on Trade and Tariffs against South African farmers' use of prison labour, and other gains — extending the Labour Relations Act to cover farm-workers immediately comes to mind — could conceivably be wrung from farmers' organizations by international pressure.

The partial sanctions imposed to date have not had much impact. Even if they do become more stringent, sanctions appear unlikely to cause the present government to fall in the foreseeable future, though over decades they might wear down the country's infrastructure. The trade-off between sanctions and unemployment has complicated implications for South African opposition organizations, especially those which organize workers.

The sanctions lobby targeting South African agricultural produce would do well to debate and explore the most constructive options with local bodies organizing on farms, so as to avoid tactics counter-productive to progressive organization in South Africa.

Long-term options in a post-apartheid South Africa

Any post-apartheid government will face immense problems in reorganizing South Africa's rural areas. A clear political commitment to rural people will be needed to prevent yet another replay of a common and destructive pattern: a new government pouring most of its resources into the towns, which are usually more politically organized, while ineffective and undemocratic programmes are imposed on the countryside. How far this is avoided will depend on how much democratic political organization has taken place in the rural areas.

As it takes power, a new government will have one major agricultural priority: to maintain production. Food shortages in the cities would cost it political support, threaten stability and cause harmfully high inflation. Factories would also need their supplies of raw materials to continue to maintain industrial production and employment. Therefore, each step a new government takes to reform or revolutionize agriculture will almost certainly have to be considered in the light of whether it will maintain or, better still, increase production.

Only if there is extensive grassroots organization in homeland rural areas — where, after all, a third of South Africa's population now lives — will it be possible democratically to develop a new local government to replace the tribal authority system. Because by far the most land is communally owned, community-level schemes which begin by helping villagers meet their food and fuel needs are likely to be the most popular and effective way of organizing.

Even after liberation, the homelands will probably continue to be crowded compared to the rest of rural South Africa. Many of those now living in them will wish to continue there, as they have invested savings and built houses on their small pieces of land and are committed to a rural way of life. Nonetheless, investment in improving rural social conditions and economic viability will be essential to prevent the social dislocation and political instability that will follow if millions of people suddenly decide to urbanize. A policy which aims at stimulating rural production and processing of agricultural products would help slow down migration and stabilize rural communities.

Some shift in the balance between urban and rural populations — at present about 50:50 — can be expected, with the urban sector gaining.

With appropriate state investment in urban housing, some migrant workers' families will opt to join them in the towns. The degree of urbanization from the homelands is impossible to predict, since it will depend on economic and political conditions before and at the time of a change of regime.

Supporting subsistence production

Rural investment in the homelands must aim to provide such basic infrastructure as health facilities, decent schooling, better roads and transport services. Organized community groups should be encouraged to meet their own needs where possible. Important among these are wood for fuel and building, water supply, sanitation, and erosion control programmes.

The way support for subsistence agriculture is deployed will be vital. Marketing systems should be developed to buy, store and transport any surpluses produced. This would not involve extravagant expenditure on silos and new rail links, but rather extend white coop facilities to include a network of small depots to which small producers can deliver grain in bags. This could first be used to supply local millers, though for longer-term storage grain would have to be moved to larger depots. Such a system, combined with a rational pricing policy, could begin to generate surpluses from what are now sub-subsistence areas.

Extending the white coop network should also include those systems which provide credit and cheap agricultural inputs such as tools, equipment, seed, fertilizers and pesticides. Simply to request the coop system as it is now organized to serve the homelands is unlikely to be effective. A new government is unlikely to have enough cadres with the technical and managerial skills to take over the coops, so negotiation with their existing managements will be necessary.

Equally, subsistence producers will need appropriate extension advice and training in methods suitable for subsistence agriculture. Even consultative extension workers willing to work on a small scale will need a considerable amount of retraining. The present homeland extension service should be well placed to supply trainees, as many extension officers are directly experiencing the frustration of offering inappropriate advice. Their retraining will need to include community participation methods as well as technical know-how. A new government will also have to deal pragmatically with extension workers, because they are often caught between the demands of their present employers and the needs of the communities they supposedly serve.

Low-cost techniques, such as animal rather than tractor power, should be used as far as possible. Intercropping and organic methods of controlling pests should be taught as replacements for imported chemicals, where possible. Through discussion, local knowledge of soil, seed, climate, animals

and pasture should be elicited, where necessary supplemented, and promoted. The policy guideline for both infrastructure and input programmes
should be to avoid large-scale high-tech projects in favour of many local inputs — to opt for twenty local dams rather than one mega-dam, for
instance.

However important, a supportive infrastructure will not be enough in
the long term. A fundamental change in the way production is organized must take place if most homeland villagers are successfully to engage
in subsistence production. Peasant production will have to shift from its
present system of individual family-based plots to collectively organized
village production. While individual production and marketing should not
be restricted, in time the village must become the productive unit and the
decision-making and planning processes must become collective. Only this
will make appropriate land use possible, allowing the best arable land to be
cultivated intensively while land at present ploughed, but in fact suitable
only for grazing, will be used as such. This appears the only way to halt the
dangerous downward spiral of ecological destruction.

Without massive popular grassroots political organization this cannot
be done. If a post-apartheid government does not have a strong base of
rural organization and support, it will most likely be forced to compromise
with the existing tribal and homeland local authorities where the existing
authorities can muster local support. The alternative is to risk widespread
violence as local magnates and their dependents fight to retain their powers
and privileges. In this situation, probably the most a new government could
do would be to offer resettlement to the rural landless, while improving the
infrastructure of those with access to homeland land.

Resettling the rural landless

Marginal white farms, often under-utilized or with absentee landlords, are
the obvious first target for a resettlement programme. A new government
will probably not have a free hand to expropriate land, as a change of regime
in South Africa is likely to follow some kind of a negotiated settlement
rather than outright military victory. As in the case of Zimbabwe's Lancaster
House settlement, the government will probably be restricted to taking over
land on a 'willing-buyer willing-seller' basis, at least in the early years.

If land for resettlement must be paid for, it makes sense first to target
under-utilized land, which will cost least. All over South Africa's 'white'
areas under-utilized or abandoned farms are to be found. There are also
pockets of state-owned land leased out to white farmers. More farms are
likely to be abandoned if guerilla activity in white farming areas escalates
and the agricultural recession intensifies, though it is unlikely that as high

a proportion will be abandoned as in Zimbabwe. Farms in border areas surrounding the homelands should be considered a priority for resettlement. Research is needed to determine the extent of state- and privately-owned under-utilized land.

Much under-utilized land, however, is ecologically marginal and not highly productive, so the units on which people are resettled must be large enough to be successful. There is some danger in targeting only farms in less fertile areas for resettlement, since they are often already too small to be viable. These units should rather be combined to make potentially successful farms. A communal or collective model has greater potential for success than individual family plots.

In devising resettlement schemes, government planners must take into account the fact that the lives of the rural poor in both homeland and white areas are inextricably bound up with migrant labour — and will be for some time. Hence a new government should accept that total dependence by resettled communities on the land must be a long-term objective rather than a condition of their access to land.

It must be remembered, too, that under-utilized land is not uninhabited. A considerable black farm-worker population already lives on these farms. In under-utilized areas resettlement programmes will thus increase the populations. As a result, extreme care must be taken to encourage appropriate farming methods.

Since these areas are largely pastoral, animal husbandry will predominate. As far as possible, overstocking must be avoided. This cannot be enforced punitively but must be achieved through community education, incentives and stock improvement schemes. A market which gives black livestock owners a fair price for their sales will contribute to increasing the offtake of animals from overgrazed land and redirect livestock owners' stock-owning ambitions towards quality rather than quantity.

Much white marginal land is bushveld, so productivity can be maximized by keeping a mix of different domestic animals and by combining domestic animals with game. The object is to mix grass-eating grazers, such as sheep and cattle, with goats and game, which browse on bush as well as eating grass. Particularly in the case of pastoral farming, it is important that a state animal health programme be maintained to prevent the catastrophic epidemics which can destroy whole farming regions. The more such a service consults with farmers, the more successful it will be.

Political structures to integrate resettled families with established farmworker communities will be essential. Equally important is a democratic approach which involves local producers in planning. Peripheral farms must never be actually or potentially overpopulated: planning must take rates of population growth into account.

Resettlement programmes in marginal areas must supply settlers and locals with the infrastructure and resources they will need for successful production. These are similar to those needed in the homelands, which have already been outlined. The long-term target of this policy would be an agricultural economy based on marketing livestock, which also aims to meet its food needs. Since dry-land production in these marginal areas is extremely risky, state-funded irrigation will almost certainly be needed to make food cultivation reliable.

Who would have claims on land for resettlement? People living on farms should have a right to the land on which they are settled, but the historical rights of people who have been displaced would also have to be taken into account. Perhaps the major group to be considered would be communities who are still together and who had their land in so-called 'black spots' expropriated.

A land reform programme needs to have clear objectives and a clear policy. Land reform laws should try to create the conditions in which claims to land can be fairly heard. They should create a forum for argument and counter-argument on land, rather than a state body handing out land according to its own criteria.

Should a resettlement programme stress allocation of family plots, or collective farming, or both? The Zimbabwean experience indicates that family-based peasant farming can produce surpluses quickly, given a supportive infrastructure and pricing policies. Collective farms have been less successful, because they often lacked capital as well as the more complex management, planning and accounting skills needed to run larger, more intensive units.

Collectivization in southern Africa often fails. Reasons include lack of skills and capital, autocratic state management, bad technical planning, and inappropriate, expensive mechanization. Planners who aim to increase productivity by collective production would do well first to consult the preferences of those involved, carefully scrutinize experiences of collectivization gained elsewhere, and only then begin with cautious experimentation.

Pricing policies

A flexible pricing policy for staples is potentially an extremely effective development strategy, though rigidity can create shortages of some products and gluts of others, which is almost invariably inflationary. A government has two good reasons to intervene in a market: the need to stimulate production of a particular commodity, and to prevent hoarding and profiteering, where either producers or distributors have enough control of the market to do so.

The present government controls prices of most agricultural commodities, though only in a few cases to keep prices down. Most price-controlled goods — notably dairy products, sugar and meat — benefit producers for political reasons, something which inflates prices. Where there are enough producers and distributors to compete effectively, as in the case of South Africa's present markets for fresh vegetables and fruit, produce markets should be unregulated.

In present-day South Africa, too, a disturbingly small number of conglomerates control the distribution of most staple foods and essential industrial raw materials. Without government intervention, they would have monopolistic control of crucial markets. Since this situation is likely to worsen in the foreseeable future, a new government will probably have to regulate prices of essential commodities such as grains (wheat, maize, sorghum), dry beans, groundnuts, cotton and sunflower seed. Meat, dairy products and sugar are more doubtful cases.

Planners setting the prices of staples should introduce a bias which favours smaller farmers and subsistence producers. The simplest way to do this is to pay a slightly higher price for the first five tons provided by each producer, an intermediate price for the next twenty tons per producer, and a lower but market-related bulk price for the balance. The aggregate retail price must be determined by total demand, so that while it manipulates the relative advantage of different producers, government does not subsidize the producer price of staples — as the present inflationary policy does. If farmers are in desperate need because of drought or natural disasters, direct assistance is better than pricing subsidies.

The core of commercial farms

A new government may be tempted to take advantage of the present division in white agriculture between the commercial core and the marginal periphery, and leave the productive core intact while resettling the landless on unsuccessful white farmland. This would have the advantage of allowing the core to continue to provide most of the food needs of the urban population, supply raw materials to industry, and generate export revenue. At the same time, the subsistence sector can be reorganized to produce, if not surpluses, enough for its own needs.

But this simple solution is likely to prove ultimately unsatisfactory. The agricultural core is as productive as it is mainly because it controls such a large proportion of South Africa's most fertile land. In the long term, a real land redistribution programme must involve some change in who controls the resources of the fertile, productive core farms that make up about a third of white farm units.

In the interests of national stability, it is essential that production levels be maintained. However, if conservative white farmers' dominance of agriculture is allowed to continue without check, any government faces continually being held to ransom by this group, and thus unable to fulfil its development objectives for the rural poor. But a policy of large-scale expropriation would, of course, arouse a storm of white opposition and a flight of capital. The fact that the economic and political costs to the state would be high must be considered when deciding whether and when to target the core areas. A new government must be careful when introducing changes into the commercial farm sector. The aim should be not only to maintain production, but to increase the productivity of the land, while encouraging more people to live on it.

Simply returning land to the tiller will be impractical. Many highly productive farms involve the use of considerable fixed and movable assets. They are capital-intensive production units that would be very difficult to divide without damaging their productivity. These units require large amounts of capital and complex management skills to be run as they are at present.

A more rational farm policy would encourage a diversity of crops on a single farm, with greater integration of livestock and arable production. Such organic agriculture would not solve all farmers' problems, but it would dramatically reduce input costs and increase demand for labour. It would also ensure more consistent, if not higher, yields per hectare. The danger of total crop failure through drought — which can be expected in one out of seven seasons — is significantly reduced by planting diverse crops suited to the local bioclimate, and by ceasing to plough the worst soils.

At present, most white farmers do not intensify production in this way because monoculture is simpler to manage. However, some of the best-managed private and corporate farms are profitable because they do diversify and maximize their land use.

In the past decade the number of core farms has decreased, while on average units have become larger. Unexpectedly, however, this concentration has not led to increased productivity per unit of land:[15] medium-sized family farms remain more productive than mechanized mega-farms. This is because medium-sized units are often managed more intensively, using more labour and a diversified structure of production, which suits land capability best. Consequently, many mega-farms are under-utilized in terms of productive potential and could support more people. With good planning and management, it is possible to increase productivity, even in the core.

Under the umbrella of a sophisticated land redistribution policy a range

---

[15] 'Agriculture', a supplement to *Financial Mail*, 17 Sept., 1982.

of structures of production will evolve, according to the needs, organizational level and skills of those involved. It will not be sensible to try to impose a standard model of production on the diverse farm communities which, backed by government, will be taking control or making their mark on agricultural production. A rigid policy of collectivization is unlikely to be successful, for example. Rather, farm communities should be encouraged to develop systems of management appropriate to them. The way the state intervenes in the commercial core will make a crucial difference as to how far production there becomes both more humane and more efficient.

Consult, train and plan

Fruitful two-way communication between farm- or district-based worker committees and state planners will be indispensible. Such committees may evolve from union structures or from village committees. But the essential policy framework should be one which maximizes the number of people successfully living on the land. Allocation of state resources and pricing policies for agricultural commodities should aim to enable rural standards of living to rise, ultimately to match urban ones.

However, the state's role should be one of support for grassroots initiative, rather than of direct intervention. A new government will urgently need to back progressive organization of farm-workers, not only as workers but also as communities, and to encourage farm communities to participate in local and national government. A network of organizers specifically trained to work with farm communities in different parts of the country may provide essential input. Such organization, if successfully carried out, could become the base from which to reorganize production in at least some parts of the commercial agricultural sector.

However, considerable differences in rural income will probably continue for some time because of the great skill differential between managers and workers, and between skilled and unskilled labour. Policy should be biased toward equalization of both skills and income. Because of the present division of labour between farm-workers and managers, the skills of the former alone will not be enough to maintain production. Training is a crucial long-term factor. Farm-workers need to gain at least some of the indispensable managerial, organizational and technical skills essential for success in restructuring commercial production.

Any future state engaged in radical land reform will have to take extreme care to provide the inputs of capital, techniques and organizational skills which will make it work, rather than dissipate support by half-hearted attempts doomed to failure. Until a future government has the skilled organizers and technicians, the resources and the political will to make land reform work, it may be best to leave core agricultural production in the hands of its present owners.

Developing a sustainable system

An agricultural policy like the one sketched out above should result in increased agricultural production, both since under-utilized land will be farmed more intensively and because productivity on commercial farms should increase. At first, and as their standard of living rises, much of the surplus would be consumed by rural people who are at present on the edge of starvation. State planners should aim to promote exactly this development. But, in time, increased agricultural production should begin to lower urban dwellers' food costs and those of industrial raw materials. This will in turn boost industrial development.

In these circumstances it becomes possible to envisage South Africa developing a sustainable system of agriculture. While it would increase both the standard of living of rural people and agricultural productivity, it should also conserve soil and water and improve the environment. It can be attained only by policies and planning which are as concerned with human as with economic factors.

Acknowledgement

This chapter is drawn from David Cooper, *Working the land: a review of agriculture in South Africa*, the Environmental and Development Agency

IV

Strategies of change

20 The apartheid legacy

John Kane-Berman

> *With the government's committal to political and socio-economic reform, the apartheid debate in South Africa has shifted from having to argue the case for equality to focusing on appropriate strategies to reduce material inequalities between black and white. This chapter examines the process of socio-economic liberalization that is under way, with the objective of enhancing debate on strategies that will help to put the fragmented society together again on a more equitable basis.*

Introduction

The last two decades have witnessed the steady erosion of apartheid in the socio-economic field. Political apartheid has, however, simultaneously been both loosened and tightened; while the 1983 Constitution incorporated coloured and Indian people into parliament, it maintained the exclusion of Africans.

The government has for some years been formally committed to the elimination of what it calls 'unnecessary' racial discrimination. More recently it has also said, in the words of Mr P. W. Botha, that 'political reform would serve no purpose without socio-economic reform'.[1] Whereas at one stage it was government policy to discourage or even prevent the construction of houses for Africans in the white-designated area, the provision of such houses is now an important policy objective. (See Chapter 13.) The old policy of starving black education of funds has also been abandoned in favour of a policy of providing equal educational opportunities for all.[2] (See Chapter 10.) Black business, once subject to crippling restrictions,[3] is now officially encouraged.

---

[1] South African Institute of Race Relations, *Social and Economic Update*, vol. 1, 1987, p. 2.

[2] J. Kane-Berman, *Soweto: black revolt, white reaction*, Johannesburg: Ravan Press, 1978, pp. 183–203; and *Race Relations Survey*, 1986, pp. 409–17.

[3] Kane-Berman, *Soweto*, pp. 61–2.

This shift in government thinking means that debate can now focus on appropriate strategies to reduce material inequalities between black and white, instead of having to argue the case for equality. The backlogs are sometimes vast — for example, according to some estimates the black housing shortage is 1,82 million units.[4]

Determining to what extent material backlogs in South Africa are the legacy of apartheid rather than a function of the country's stage of economic development is a futile exercise. They are obviously in part the consequence of the discriminatory policies already referred to, but they are also a function of economic development, which in turn is partly a function of discriminatory policies.

The real issue, now, is how the backlogs in black amenities would be eliminated. This is a far greater challenge to South Africa then merely repealing the remnants of discriminatory legislation.

The purpose of this chapter is to examine the process of socio-economic liberalization that is under way in South Africa, with a view to enhancing debate about strategies to accelerate reform. The chapter will also attempt to measure the backlogs in various fields and the progress made in eliminating them.

However, the apartheid legacy is not only to be found in the social and economic field: it is to be found also in the structure of the state. It will therefore also examine the forces that are helping to put a fragmented society back together again, and will also identify policies that will foster constitutional change.

Apartheid is not merely a matter of segregation but is the organizing principle of the state. Therefore, dismantling apartheid involves not only such relatively straightforward matters as removing social segregation imposed by law, but also entails the rewriting of the country's constitution.

The erosion of apartheid

What has been eroded?

Apartheid has been steadily eroded in the social, educational and commercial fields. The process of erosion in the residential field is well under way, and one of the severest forms of apartheid, the pass or influx control system, has been abolished.

Sport

Under Dr Hendrik Verwoerd, Prime Minister from 1958 until his assassination in 1966, sport was rigidly segregated. He said that South African teams

---

[4] *Social and Economic Update*, vol. 6, 1988, p. 28.

visiting New Zealand could play against a mixed team of whites and Maoris, but made it clear in 1965 that Maoris would not be allowed to play in South Africa.[5]

In 1967 the next Prime Minister, Mr John Vorster, agreed that a visiting team from New Zealand could include Maoris. This had happened in the past and no problems had arisen.[6]

As the Right would put it, it was then that the rot set in. Today South African sport is substantially mixed. Blacks and whites not only play against each other, but also in the same teams, and there is no apartheid among spectators, in the change-rooms or in the bars.

There can be little doubt that the steady disintegration of sports apartheid is largely due to the international sports boycott of South Africa, but the country is no nearer to returning to international competition than it ever was. The conditions for South Africa's re-admission to international sport are now much tougher, and indeed go far beyond sport.

The chairman of the United Nations' Special Committee Against Apartheid, Major-General Joseph Garba, stipulated four conditions in 1987 for South Africa's re-admission: equal access for every citizen to public and private sports facilities; abolition of the homelands; a unitary education system; and the end of economic apartheid.[7]

Social segregation

Social segregation beyond the sporting arena has also been extensively eroded. Restaurants, hotels, cinemas, theatres, suburban trains, public lavatories, beaches, parks, museums and libraries have all been to a larger or lesser extent desegregated.

Industry

Starting in about 1973, the industrial colour bar has also been steadily eroded. Government policy had been that Africans could not be trained even for semi-skilled work in the white-designated area, but this was relaxed and provision was made in the 1974 Budget to subsidize training.

Statutory restrictions on the jobs that blacks may perform in commerce and industry finally disappeared in 1987, when the Mines and Works Act of 1911 was amended to allow blacks to qualify for certificates of competency in the mining industry, without which a wide range of jobs were closed to them.[8] Although the statutory prohibition has disappeared, both employers

---

5 South African Institute of Race Relations, *Race Relations Survey*, 1965, pp. 311–12.

6 *Race Relations Survey*, 1967, pp. 318–20.

7 *Race Relations Survey*, 1987/8, p. 269.

8 South African Institute of Race Relations, *Quarterly Countdown*, vol. 7, 1987, p. 28.

and black unions in the industry claim that new regulations providing for minimum educational standards could be used to exclude many black workers.[9] The first few blacks have nevertheless received their certificates of competency. If the removal of earlier restrictions is also taken into account, there are now 5 000 blacks doing jobs previously reserved for whites in the mining industry.[10]

The erosion of the industrial colour bar includes the diplomatic corps[11] and the public sector. In 1989 the first black person was employed as a pilot on South African Airways.[12] Blacks have also sat as acting judges, although they have been criticized by some blacks for doing so.[13]

Despite the steady erosion of the colour bar, certain aspects of discrimination remain. Black medical students are barred from entering gynaecological and obstetrics wards in white teaching hospitals,[14] while there are no doubt many sections of both the public and the private sector where blacks are discriminated against, even where no law exists.

The colour bar has also been removed from the industrial relations system. When black trade unions revived in the early 1970s, they faced hostility from both the state and employers. The director of the Steel and Engineering Industries Federation of South Africa (Seifsa), for example, said in 1973 that there would be no negotiation with black unions in that industry.[15] At the end of 1976 the Vorster government banned nearly thirty union officials.[16] Despite this hostile climate, the unions survived and by 1979 'were becoming a permanent and prominent feature of the industrial relations scene', according to a commission of inquiry which in that year recommended the extension of statutory trade union rights to Africans.[17] The Wiehahn Commission's recommendations were largely accepted by the government, and with effect from 1 October 1979 Africans have had the same union rights as workers of other races had long enjoyed.

Black business

Restrictions on black business have also been relaxed. In 1968 it was decreed that black entrepreneurs in the townships in the white-designated

---

[9] *Quarterly Countdown*, vol. 11, 1988, pp. 29–30.

[10] N. Steenkamp, presidential address to the 98th Annual General Meeting of the Chamber of Mines, 21 June 1988.

[11] *Race Relations Survey*, 1986, p. 728.

[12] *Sunday Times*, 7 May 1989.

[13] *Race Relations Survey*, 1987/8, p. 550.

[14] *Sunday Times*, 1 March 1987.

[15] *Financial Mail*, 21 Dec. 1973.

[16] *Star*, 7 Jan. 1977.

[17] Depts. of Labour and of Mines, 'Report of the Commission of Inquiry into Labour Legislation', RP47/1979,

area could not open more than one shop or conduct business 'for any purpose other than that of providing for the daily essential domestic requirements' of the township residents. The official policy was to encourage black business and professional people to offer their services in the homelands instead.

Some of the restrictions were lifted in May 1976[18] and a whole range of other controls in January 1989. Nor are black businessmen confined any longer to black townships. The Group Areas Act was amended in 1984 to allow the desegregation of trading areas.[19] By the end of February 1989, ninety-three free trading areas in central business districts had been opened to all races. However, Africans are able to occupy, but not own, property there.[20]

Property

Racial restrictions on property ownership have also been relaxed. It was long-standing policy to deny Africans home ownership rights in the white-designated area.

Urban-areas legislation was based on the philosophy that there was no place for Africans in the white-designated area except 'in so far as and for so long as their presence is demanded by the wants of the white population'. The law accordingly gave local authorities power to restrict the numbers of Africans entering their areas to the number required by white employers.[21]

In 1975, however, the government began to reverse the 'temporary sojourners' policy. A thirty-year leasehold policy was introduced in some townships, which was not so much a new right as the restoration of one lost in 1967.

Further relaxation of the policy followed business lobbying in the wake of the upheavals in Soweto and elsewhere in June 1976. A 99-year leasehold system was announced in April 1978, although it was stated that 'there is no intention to grant home ownership to blacks in urban areas'.[22] Home ownership was, however, granted in 1986.[23] At the time of writing, about

---

Part 1, p. 2.

[18] Kane-Berman, *Soweto*, pp. 61–2.

[19] *Race Relations Survey*, 1986, p. 11; and *Race Relations Survey*, 1985, pp. 97-98.

[20] *Social and Economic Update*, vol. 7, 1989, p. 6.

[21] Kane-Berman, *Soweto*, pp. 71–2.

[22] Kane-Berman, *Soweto*, pp. 191–200.

[23] *Race Relations Survey*, 1986, p. 349.

100 000 of the 367 000 formal houses in African townships in the white-designated area have been sold to their occupants under a government-promoted housing sale since 1983.[24] Most were bought on lease rather than in freehold. Black home ownership rights in the white-designated area remain subject to the Group Areas Act. They may be exercised only in townships proclaimed for Africans, or in future free settlement areas in terms of the Free Settlement Areas Act of 1988.[25]

Residential segregation

The Group Areas Act is one of the major apartheid laws that remains in force, although it has been extensively eroded. *De facto* residential deseg-regation has been under way for ten or twelve years.[26] The Free Settlement Areas Act is designed to accommodate this new reality by providing for the proclamation of certain *de facto* racially-mixed areas as official mixed areas. Initially the government intended enforcing the Group Areas Act much more strictly in areas not so proclaimed, but it withdrew the proposed legislation.[27]

In 1985 the Prohibition of Mixed Marriages Act of 1949, which outlawed marriages across the colour line, was repealed along with Section 16 of the Immorality Act of 1957, which prohibited sex across the colour line.[28] Mixed couples are still disadvantaged under the Group Areas Act, however. They may live together lawfully only in proclaimed free settlement areas; in other suburbs they would have to obtain permits.

Influx control

The other major aspect of apartheid that has been eroded is the influx control system, which was designed to limit the number of Africans in the white-designated area to the minimum number compatible with the demands of white employers. The pass laws pre-date Union and have indeed been the focus of protest for more than a century.

According to a government official, 17,12 million Africans were arrested for pass law offences between 1916 and 1981[29] (an average of 721 every day for 65 years). During that period these laws were progressively tightened.[30] As late as 1979 legislation was enacted to increase the fines payable by

---

24 *Race Relations Survey*, 1983, p. 230; and *Business Day*, 14 Nov. 1988, 10 Jan. 1989.

25 *Quarterly Countdown*, vol. 11, 1988, pp. 17–19.

26 C. Pickard-Cambridge: 'The greying of Johannesburg — residential desegregation in the Johannesburg area', Johannesburg: South African Institute of Race Relations, 1988.

27 *Quarterly Countdown*, vol. 10, 1988, pp. 28–30; and *Quarterly Countdown*, vol. 11, 1988, pp. 16–17.

28 *Race Relations Survey*, 1985, pp. 4–5.

29 *De Rebus*, July 1986.

30 Kane-Berman, *Soweto*, pp. 72–8.

anyone employing an African who did not have permission to work in the white-designated area.[31]

In 1986, however, having been persuaded that the pass laws had become unworkable, the government repealed them.

Education

Segregation also has been extensively eroded in the education field. The colour bar imposed on universities in 1959 has been lifted and they are now free to admit students on academic merit alone.[32] About 22 per cent of the students at the formerly whites-only English-language universities are now black.[33]

Since 1988 the government has no longer applied a racial quota to students at technikons, whose governing councils may now determine their own admission policy.[34] Private schools also have desegregated, and in March 1989 about 13 per cent of the pupils in white private schools were black.[35]

How and why has erosion occurred?

As already indicated, the main reason for the steady desegregation of sport by both sports administrators and government is the international sports boycott. The other changes have been in response to internal pressures. Moral pressure, including pressure from the Afrikaans churches and from various liberal lobby groups, caused the repeal of the miscegenation laws.

Perhaps the most important internal pressure was the drying up from 1970 of the white skilled-labour surplus, necessitating the training of blacks to fill jobs requiring greater levels of skills. As we have seen, the government intended limiting black training to semi-skilled jobs, but this concession led to a series of other concessions, among them the indenturing of Africans as artisans and the removal of all racial job restrictions in commerce and industry.

The economy's need for more trained blacks in turn necessitated spending more money on black education. The budget for African education has risen from R70 million in 1971/2[36] to R3,4 billion in 1987/8, an increase of more than 4 700 per cent.[37]

---

31 *Race Relations Survey*, 1979, p. 393.

32 S. Saunders, 'Freedom, the universities and the future', 1987 Presidential Address, South African Institute of Race Relations, Johannesburg, 1987, p. 7.

33 *Race Relations Survey*, 1987/8, p. 181.

34 *Hansard*, 23 Feb. 1988, question cols. 70–2.

35 *Business Day*, 10 March 1989.

36 *Race Relations Survey*, 1971, p. 252.

37 *Race Relations Survey*, 1987/8, p. 150.

The increasing number of blacks in skilled jobs strengthened the bargaining power of the black trade union movement. Unions were a functioning reality in factories before official recognition was granted. African workers won legal union rights by organization and action on the factory floor — illustrating how movement away from discrimination can come about before the law is changed.

Perhaps the best example of this is the fate of the pass laws. Hundreds of thousands of black South Africans rendered them unworkable simply by voting against them with their feet and moving from country to town regardless. So also the legislation to legalize racially-mixed suburbs was enacted only after such suburbs had developed anyway.

By joining unions, by ignoring the pass laws and the Group Areas Act, ordinary black people brought about new *de facto* situations on the ground which parliament then subsequently catered for by changing the law.

Simply by organizing themselves and taking action, blacks have not only substantially undermined apartheid, but also created new rights — the right to have their unions registered by law, the right to move from country to town and the right to trade being the most obvious examples.

The right to strike was established in the same way. Strikes by Africans were prohibited under War Measure 145 of 1942, which was still in force in the early 1970s when a series of strikes broke out in Durban. The first few months of 1973 saw more than 60 000 African workers involved in 160 strikes. The law was clearly a dead letter, and by the middle of that year legislation had been enacted to legalize African strikes once various cooling-off procedures had been adhered to.[38]

South Africa has no bill of rights, although the government in 1986 instructed the South African Law Commission to investigate the idea. The commission duly recommended the adoption of a bill of rights and indeed prepared a draft bill, which was published in March 1989.[39] (See Chapter 3.)

In the meantime, black people are creating new rights for themselves, from the bottom up, as it were. Perhaps the fact that various groups have won rights in this way rather than having them handed down from above will have the effect that they will fight to preserve them against future attempts by any government to remove them.

The manner in which these rights have been won may help to ensure the survival of pluralism in South Africa.

A number of strategic lessons emerge from this. Firstly, South Africa has

---

[38] *Financial Mail*, 23, 27 March, 15 June 1973.

[39] *Sunday Star*, 12 March 1989.

shown itself capable of non-revolutionary transformation. Union rights were won in a struggle that was bitter and involved a great deal of hardship, but minimal violence. The desegregation of various educational institutions similarly occurred without violence, as did the abolition of influx control and the erosion of the Group Areas Act. Nor was violence involved in the erosion of the industrial colour bar.

Violence did play a role in the acquisition by Africans of home ownership rights. Until it was shocked into action by the upheavals in Soweto and elsewhere in 1976, the business community was largely complacent about conditions in black townships. The launch of the Urban Foundation at a conference of businessmen in Johannesburg in November 1976 was a direct response to the violence in Soweto. Initially the Foundation sought to deal with problems such as the housing shortage without involving itself in politics, but it soon broadened its objectives and committed itself to working for fundamental change.[40] The foundation played a major role in securing home ownership rights for Africans.

Although the Soweto violence clearly provided the main impetus, the government had already begun to change its policy on black permanence in the white-designated area, in that the restoration of a limited form of leasehold in a limited number of areas was announced at the beginning of 1975.[41] Some of the restrictions on African business were lifted in May 1976.[42] Education policy had also begun to change prior to the Soweto violence. It was in 1971/2, for example, that the per capita state spending gap on black and white pupils began to narrow, after having widened steadily for about fifteen years.[43]

The second strategic lesson to emerge from these changes is that blacks and whites alike have adjusted to new realities with remarkable ease — giving lie to the argument that legally imposed racial segregation is necessary to prevent racial friction.

Although there have been a number of racial incidents on beaches and in *de facto* grey areas, these have been the exception rather than the rule.

Post-apartheid South Africa, in other words is not something that will be legislated into existence by some future government. It is already being forged wherever one looks as people of all races learn to live, work and play side by side on an increasing scale with a minimum of fuss. Ordinary South Africans, by their own actions and ability to adjust to the actions of others,

[40] Kane-Berman, *Soweto*, pp. 155–8; and *Race Relations Survey*, 1984, pp. 107–8.

[41] Kane-Berman, *Soweto*, p. 192.

[42] Kane-Berman, *Soweto*, p. 62.

[43] Kane-Berman, *Soweto*, pp. 186–8.

are putting a racially segmented society back together again.

Thirdly, the role of the government in relation to society has changed. Whereas Dr Verwoerd and his predecessors sought to shape society in a particular way, the hallmark of the Botha years has been ideological breakdown in the corridors of power as one after another apartheid law has been rendered unworkable.

Instead of being the major actor, the government has often been a mere spectator — and sometimes a spectator deliberately looking the other way. Indeed, reform in South Africa has proved to be less of a programme worked out and implemented by the government than a process in which the government has sometimes simply been dragged along by the actions of others.

The strategic lesson is obvious: those seeking change should not simply demand that the government bring it about, but should seek ways of bringing it about themselves on the ground.

Fourthly, ordinary people have a vital role to play in transforming South Africa: they have already demonstrated their ability to change society behind the backs and under the nose of the government and political organizations opposed to it. The erosion of the Group Areas Act and the disintegration of influx control were brought about by hundreds of thousands of ordinary South Africans acting spontaneously, in pursuit not of any defiant political objectives, but of their own self-interest — mainly, in these cases, by looking for jobs and accommodation.

Fifth, their success, along with the success of black unions and of the growing number of black participants in the informal sector of the economy — shebeen kings and queens, taxi drivers, and hawkers — has been a self-empowering process, not the result of some programme of 'black empowerment' launched by others.

What is left of apartheid?

Although apartheid has been substantially eroded in many fields, a great deal still remains. Discriminatory legislation pre-dating Union still remains, while apartheid measures have been passed not only by parliament but by provincial and local authorities.

Political apartheid

Besides being contained in the constitution itself, political apartheid is imposed by numerous statutes which include all laws providing for separate racially-based administrative and political systems. Nor should the various 'status acts', in terms of which 7–8 million Africans lost their South African citizenship when the Transkei, Bophuthatswana, Venda, and the Ciskei (the TBVC territories) became constitutionally separate states, be overlooked.

The Restoration of South African Citizenship Act of 1986 enables only about a fifth to a quarter of these denationalized people to regain their South African citizenship.[44] Putting South Africa back together again would involve making provision for the remainder to regain South African citizenship unless they chose not to do so.

Various 'colour-blind' apartheid laws also require amendment. These include the Aliens Act of 1937 and the Admission of Persons to the Republic Regulation Act of 1972, which make denationalized Africans subject to disabilities of foreigners. So far, administrative exemptions have meant that little use has been made of these statutes to re-impose influx control, although fears in this regard were widely expressed when the Abolition of Influx Control Act was passed.[45]

Discriminatory laws

As already indicated, although apartheid in many fields is disappearing, crucial forms of it remains. These include the Group Areas Act and the Black Land Act of 1913, which prohibited interracial transfers of land. Also still on the statute book is the Population Registration Act of 1950, which provides for the classification of the entire population of South Africa according to certain defined racial categories and their subdivisions.

The repeal of the Group Areas Act is likely to follow, not precede, its irretrievable breakdown on a larger scale than is already the case. In abandoning plans in 1988 to enforce the Group Areas Act much more strictly outside free settlement areas, the government has in effect conceded that the Act has become unenforceable.

The National Party is also beginning to reconsider the principle of rigidly imposed statutory racial classification.[46]

Socio-economic apartheid

Apartheid in the social and economic field that is still in operation includes discriminatory state old-age pensions. Although for several years the percentage increases given to blacks have been greater than those given to whites, blacks still receive lower old-age pensions than whites. The maximum monthly pensions payable from October 1987 were as follows: whites R218, Indians R167, coloured people R167, Africans R117.[47]

Another aspect of discrimination is that blacks have relatively fewer facilities than they need and whites more than they need, but blacks are

[44] *Race Relations Survey*, 1986, pp. 94–5.

[45] *Race Relations Survey*, 1986, pp. 343–4.

[46] *Quarterly Countdown*, vol. 12, 1989, pp. 7–8.

[47] *Race Relations Survey*, 1987/8, p. 441.

prevented from sharing the excess white facilities. In the last ten years, 196 white government schools have been closed because they are no longer needed by whites,[48] while there are 279 000 empty places at white government schools.[49] This means that 7 427 classrooms in white schools are standing empty, while in 1987 the shortage of classrooms at black schools was 37 781.[50] Yet, the government continues to refuse to allow black children to take up the vacancies in white schools, even where such schools have asked to be allowed to admit them.[51]

However, the country faces greater problems than this. Among them are crippling skills shortages, a high rate of illiteracy, extensive malnutrition and growing unemployment. The burden of joblessness and poverty does not fall exclusively upon blacks — unemployed whites were, for example, taken on as casual labour during a strike on the railways by blacks in 1987, only to be dismissed when the strike was settled,[52] while Operation Hunger began receiving requests from urban white families for relief in 1985.[53]

Another problem is income maldistribution. Income from property is seriously distorted: a merchant bank calculated a few years ago that 98 per cent was in white hands and 2 per cent in coloured and Indian hands, the African share being nil.[54] African land ownership is confined to the homelands, collectively comprising about 14 per cent of the country, and recently acquired sites in townships in the white-designated area. Even allowing for coloured and Indian land ownership, it can be argued that 80 per cent of South Africa's land is in the hands of whites, who make up 14 per cent of the population.[55]

There are other serious distortions: Soweto, designed to be a self-sufficient self-governing local authority, is little more than a dormitory township for Johannesburg, much of whose prosperity depends on spending in its central business district by Soweto residents. Only in recent years has provision been made, through the establishment of regional services councils, to reverse this effective subsidization of the rich by the poor.[56] The councils are designed, among other things, as mechanism for the transfer of funds

---

48 *Citizen*, 11 March 1988, 17 May 1989.

49 *Business Day*, 26 April 1989.

50 *Race Relations Survey*, 1987/8, p. 160.

51 *Hansard*, 7 March 1989, question cols. 259–65.

52 *Race Relations Survey*, 1987/8, p. 675.

53 'Operation Hunger corporate survey', supplement to *Financial Mail*, 7 Oct. 1988.

54 *Financial Mail*, 21 Feb. 1985.

55 *Race Relations Survey*, 1987/8, p. 11.

56 *Race Relations Survey*, 1985, pp. 78–9.

from wealthier to poorer areas. The first such councils came into operation in 1987.[57]

Racial zoning has led to other distortions: black families who once lived reasonably close to the city centre were forced to move to new black townships further away. Thus the poorer section of the community often lives furthest from the centres of employment.[58]

The policy of apartheid has been a major cause. The country's housing shortage would not be as great if home building had not been stunted during the 1960s and 1970s as an influx control measure. Shortages of black classrooms and teachers would likewise not be as great had the government not pegged the exchequer's allocation to African education at R13 million in 1955 and maintained this for fifteen years.[59]

Desegregation alone (however essential) would not eliminate the shortages. These have been determined not only by internal policies and internal resources, but have also been a function down the years of international commodity prices and world growth trends.

The rate of economic growth is also affected by skilled manpower shortages, themselves a function not only of growth but also of education policies. Had growth been higher, more money might have been available for black education, but if the general level of education of black people had been higher, growth would have been higher.

Attempting to identify the causes of these inequalities is thus rather pointless. So also are attempts to quantify the costs of apartheid. It is argued that having fourteen legislatures (parliament, three own affairs chambers; and ten homelands assemblies) is an example of the cost of apartheid. The United States has fifty-one legislatures (congress and the fifty states), but presumably this is the cost of democracy!

The real economic costs of apartheid are not to be found in adding up budgets or looking for obvious waste. The real cost is an opportunity cost: lost economic growth resulting from the stunting of black education, foreign capital droughts resulting from political instability, itself a result of apartheid.

Some 40 per cent of South Africans have no education at all compared to fewer than one per cent of Japanese.[60] Japan has virtually nothing in the way of minerals, so it developed by exploiting its human resources. South Africa exploited its minerals, but failed, because of apartheid, to exploit its

---

[57] *Race Relations Survey*, 1987/8, p. 121.

[58] Kane-Berman, *Soweto*, p. 60; and *Social and Economic Update*, vol. 5, 1988, p. 48.

[59] Kane-Berman, *Soweto*, pp. 59–60, 187–8.

[60] *Business Day*, 21 Jan. 1988.

human resources. So perhaps a better way of measuring the cost of apartheid is to subtract South African GDP per capita from Japanese GDP per capita. The difference — $16 929[61] — is the per capita cost of apartheid!

Absolute backlogs

Jobs

Unemployment is a major problem. According to the Nedbank group, non-agricultural employment grew by only 166 000 between 1980 and 1986 — during which period the economically active population increased by 1,6 million.[62] The Minister of Manpower said in October 1987 that up to 6 million South Africans could be unemployed by the year 2000.[63]

According to the Minister of Health and Population Development, South Africa's population growth rate of 2,3 per cent a year, means that a real growth rate of 5 per cent annually is required to provide work for the 1 000 people entering the labour market each day. At 3 per cent growth only half these people would have formal jobs.[64]

South Africa has threadbare social security. Only about 8 per cent of the people officially enumerated as unemployed draw unemployment benefits[65] and these are very limited; only people who contributed to the Unemployment Insurance Fund while employed are eligible for benefits. People who have not been employed, among them many young people joining the labour market each year, get nothing from the state.

Some observers set a great deal of store by the employment-generating capacity of the informal sector. (See Chapter 14.) An official of the Small Business Development Corporation believes that the proportion of people entering the labour market each year and going into the informal or small business sector could be as high as 70 per cent, the rest either being absorbed by big business and the formal sector or remaining unemployed.[66]

Skills

One of the constraints on growth is the shortage of skills. In 1980 adult literacy among whites was estimated at 97 per cent; among Indians at 80 per cent; and among coloureds at 60 per cent. African literacy was estimated at 45 per cent. This means that about 5 million adults were illiterate, although

---

[61] *Financial Times*, 12 June 1989.

[62] Nedbank Group, 'Guide to the economy', Aug. 1987.

[63] *Race Relations Survey*, 1987/8, p. LVIII.

[64] *Citizen*, 27 Oct. 1987.

[65] *Race Relations Survey*, 1987/8, pp. 294, 302.

[66] Small Business Development Corporation, 'Roots of enterprise', *Leadership*, June 1988, p. 74.

some estimates put the figure at 9 million. Despite this, little is being done to promote adult literacy in South Africa.[67]

Only about 11 per cent of the South African work-force consists of skilled manpower, compared to 40 per cent in Western industrialized countries.[68] The Director-General of Manpower predicted that the need for professional, technical and highly skilled manpower in the twenty years to the end of the century would amount to 897 000, but that supply would fall short by 442 000. The increase in the demand for unskilled labour would be one million against a projected supply of 3,8 million.

He said that the roots of the labour problem were in the country's traditional education system. A drastic shift from over-emphasis on formal academic education to technical and occupational education was urgently needed.[69]

This view had earlier been expressed by Professor J. P. de Lange, who headed an investigation into South African education for the Human Resources Research Council. He said that 80 per cent of children at white secondary schools and 99 per cent at black secondary schools were taking academic subjects, when the figures should be about 30 per cent. The other pupils needed to take courses directed at business and technical needs.[70] In 1988 there were four times more students at universities than at technicons.[71]

Backlogs in black education facilities persist over and above the classroom backlog already referred to (see Chapter 10), but the country's capacity to produce the necessary skills is itself constrained by skills shortages, among them the fact that a large proportion of teachers in African schools have not completed their own schooling. The proportion of African teachers now officially classed as professionally qualified has increased from 78 per cent to 81 per cent; however, a great many of them possess only a Standard 8 certificate and a teaching qualification.

Moreover, although there has been a large increase in the number of Africans matriculating, only a minuscule proportion obtain university entrance passes in mathematics.[72] In the Johannesburg area, for example, only forty-one of the 1 558 Africans who wrote higher-grade mathematics in 1987 passed. The vast majority of African pupils do not even study maths or physical science.[73]

---

[67] E. French, 'Adult literacy in South Africa — a history to be made', *Africa Insight*, vol. 18, no. 1, 1988.

[68] *Citizen*, 7 March 1989.

[69] *Business Day*, 30 Sept. 1988.

[70] *Business Day*, 22 June 1988.

[71] J. Hofmeyr and R. Spence, 'Bridges to the future', *Optima*, vol. 37, No. 1, March 1989, p. 38.

[72] *Social and Economic Update*, vol. 6, 1988, p. 12.

[73] Hofmeyr and Spence, 'Bridges to the future', p. 37.

Housing

According to the Urban Foundation, the black housing shortage is 1,82 million units — 800 000 in the white-designated area, 125 000 in the independent homelands and 892 000 in the non-independent homelands. In addition, 2,9 million more houses will be needed to accommodate the natural population increase by the year 2000.[74]

Among the major constraints on reducing this backlog are the shortage of land and the inability of most black people to finance their own housing. Some progress nevertheless appears to have been made and additional land is being proclaimed. Additional land proclaimed by the end of 1988 is used for housing, some 28 per cent of the present housing shortage in the white-designated area can be eliminated.[75] Moreover, the proportion of Africans who can do without a housing subsidy has risen from 16 per cent in 1987 to 29 per cent, while those who need a full subsidy dropped from 75 per cent to 45 per cent.[76]

Electricity and water

According to government statistics, 95 per cent of African households in the Free State, 93 per cent in Natal, 87 per cent in the Cape and 79 per cent in the Transvaal do not have electricity.[77] The state-owned Electricity Supply Commission (Escom) announced a scheme in 1987 to electrify all black areas.[78]

Only about a third of the houses in Soweto and the neighbouring township of Diepmeadow have access to running water within the house, and only 20 per cent of the population of the Transkei have access to a safe water supply (piped water from a purification system).[79]

Infantile mortality

Between 1981 and 1985 the infantile mortality rate among whites dropped from 13,3 to 9,3 per thousand, among Indians from 18,8 to 16,1 and among coloured people from 59,2 to 40,7. Among Africans, the rate remained at 80 per thousand.[80]

---

74 *Urban Foundation Annual Review*, 1988, p. 4.

75 *Social and Economic Update*, vol. 7, 1989, pp. 35–6.

76 *Social and Economic Update*, vol. 7, 1989, pp. 31–2.

77 *Social and Economic Update*, vol. 6, 1988, p. 17.

78 *Social and Economic Update*, vol. 7, 1989, pp. 22–3.

79 *Social and Economic Update*, vol. 3, 1987, pp. 45–6.

80 *Race Relations Survey*, 1987/8, p. 808.

Grappling with the legacy

The final part of this chapter will suggest the kinds of strategies that could be used to tackle South Africa's problems of injustice, inequality and deprivation in the social, economic and political fields.

Abolishing apartheid

The demand has sometimes been made that apartheid should be abolished before constitutional talks can begin. This is impossible since abolishing all apartheid laws would mean abolishing the constitution itself. This would leave the state in limbo while negotiations about a new constitution were in progress.

Many apartheid laws clearly could be repealed without undermining the administrative structure of the state. As far as the structure of the state is concerned, however, the law introducing a new apartheid-free constitution, based on comprehensive negotiation, would presumably at the same moment enact the new and repeal the old constitution.

Bill of rights

Sifting through the vast volume of legislation to identify and repeal discriminatory provisions would be immensely time-consuming. The same objective would be easier to achieve through the enactment of a bill of rights overriding all discriminatory laws. (See Chapter 3.)

A model which could be followed, with suitable adaptations, is the bill of rights adopted by the KwaZulu–Natal Indaba in 1986. It provides that laws within provincial jurisdiction that are inconsistent with the bill of rights may be declared void by the Supreme Court on application thereto after the lapse of a year from the date of its coming into effect.

Land distribution

The maldistribution of the country's land needs to be addressed. A senior official of the Development Bank of Southern Africa has called for the Land Acts to be re-examined as they hamper the growth of 'emerging black farmers'.[81] According to one study, the availability of arable land in the homelands is so limited that only subsistence agriculture can be practised on a household basis.

However, this may not necessarily imply that rural black people in the homelands will demand a redistribution of agricultural land as opposed to access to land, housing, services and employment in the urban areas.[82] This

---

[81] *Business Day*, 12 Nov. 1987.

[82] M. Cobbett, 'The land question in South Africa: a preliminary assessment', *South African Journal of Economics*, March 1987, pp. 63–77.

should make it easier from a political point of view for the Land Acts to be amended to enable Africans to buy land in rural areas — which is the logical follow-up to the introduction of home-ownership in urban areas in 1986.

Education

So far, twenty-five white government schools — twenty-two in the Cape, two in the Transvaal and one in Natal — are reported to have sought to desegregate themselves.[83] Although the government has recently reiterated that it will not allow white government schools to be opened,[84] pressure for it to do this, at least partially, is certain to increase.

While the government has provided for the legalization of racially-mixed residential areas, it does not have a workable policy for the education of black children lawfully resident in these formerly white areas. However, it many be inching towards one and is now talking about 'strongly subsidized' private schools in these areas.[85]

Housing

South Africa's housing problem is so great that the country does not have the resources to solve it by building conventional houses. A fundamental change of approach is required. It will involve provision by the state not of housing but of adequate land and security of tenure to enable people to erect their own houses, making use of whatever materials they find appropriate.

The state will have to focus less on housing construction and more on building access roads and providing water, sanitation and refuse removal services.

'Squatting' is already a widespread phenomenon in South Africa, the Urban Foundation estimating that the country could have as many as 7 million squatters — better described as people living in informal circumstances.[86]

Although the government is still committed to the removal of squatters in certain areas — for example, 220 000 in the Cape[87] — there are clear indications of a change in policy. The Prevention of Illegal Squatting Amendment Act of 1988 increased the penalties for illegal squatting and extended the powers of the state to remove squatters. On the other hand,

---

83 *Sunday Tribune,* 21 May 1989.

84 *Citizen,* 8 March 1989.

85 *Business Day,* 13 June 1989.

86 *Star* and *Sunday Tribune,* 7 August 1988.

87 *Quarterly Countdown,* vol. 11, 1988, p. 24.

it provided for the establishment of informal towns that could later be converted into conventional towns.[88]

The then Minister of Constitutional Development and Planning said in December 1988 that informal housing would in future have to be accepted as a temporary but integral part of South Africa's housing pattern. Informal towns would in time be upgraded as the residents' financial means increased.[89] Serviced sites for squatters have already been proclaimed.[90]

Wages

The differences in earnings between white and African in South Africa are the result of many factors, among them differences in the level of skills, the relatively recent advent of black unionization, the industrial colour bar, and supply and demand. (See Chapter 6.) In recent years the ratio of white to African earnings has narrowed. In manufacturing, for example, the ratio has narrowed from 4,2:1 to 3,6:1.[91]

This trend is likely to continue, given, among other things, the success of black unions, which, in 1987 for example, ensured that black union members were the only group in the economy whose wages kept up with inflation.[92] With effect from 1 March 1988 all pay disabilities in the public service were eliminated.[93] Moreover, the Industrial Court has ruled that racial discrimination in wage rates is an unfair labour practice.[94] Given these developments, there is no need for the government to intervene to remove inequalities in pay.

Unemployment

A more serious problem is unemployment. This clearly cannot be dealt with properly unless South Africa achieves much higher rates of economic growth, which necessitates both a resumption or foreign capital inflows and the expansion of the country's exports. The former will depend very largely on foreign views about political stability in South Africa, while the latter will require continued efforts to circumvent trade boycotts.

Government spending

A major part of the reason for the increase in government spending in

---

88 *Quarterly Countdown*, vol. 10, 1988, pp. 37–38.

89 *RSA Policy Review*, April 1989, p. 35.

90 *Star*, 25 Oct. 1988.

91 *Race Relations Survey*, 1981, p. 138; and *Race Relations Survey*, 1987/8, p. 332.

92 *Business Day*, 4 Dec. 1987.

93 *SA Digest*, 18 Sept. 1987.

94 *Business Day*, 29 Feb. 1988.

recent years has been its efforts to reduce backlogs. Spending on education, for example, has increased from 6,4 per cent of the national budget in 1969/70 to 18,6 per cent in 1987/8. Spending on defence, police and prisons has declined from 24 per cent of the budget to 21,2 per cent during this period.[95]

The privatization of state assets is now seen as a means of helping to finance expenditure on development. The former State President told parliament in February 1988 that the proceeds of privatization would go towards paying off the public debt, building infrastructure in development areas, and creating capital funds for the development of small business.[96]

Political solution

The structural conditions for negotiation between black and white for a new constitution are now better than they ever have been. The failure of widespread township violence in 1984 to 1986 to threaten the stability of the state has caused a loss of faith in revolutionary strategies. The fact that African National Congress (ANC) bases in Angola had to be closed and their personnel moved in terms of the settlement plan for South-West Africa/Namibia is also a setback for revolutionary strategies. The ANC is coming under increased pressure from the Soviet Union to opt for negotiation as opposed to violence.[97]

On the other hand, the government has accepted that the homelands do not provide a complete constitutional solution and has committed itself to ending white domination, replacing it by a constitution based on power-sharing. Legislation to establish a national constitutional-negotiating forum was passed in 1988. Government indications that it is considering the release of Mr Nelson Mandela suggest a shift from imposed to negotiated solutions, since a number of black leaders have said they will not enter into constitutional talks as long as he remains in prison.

However, the gap between what blacks are demanding and what whites are willing to concede remains very wide. The standard black demand is for majority rule in a unitary state, although both Inkatha and the ANC have indicated a willingness to consider federal proposals. The government, however, is not only opposed to majority rule, but appears not even to accept that there is a black majority in South Africa, apparently still adhering to the view that blacks are made up of a number of different tribal minorities.

An extension of their own affairs system operating among white, coloured and Indian peoples to Africans in the white-designated. The idea

---

95 *Race Relations Survey*, 1987/8, p. 423.

96 *Star*, 5 Feb. 1988.

97 *Star*, 20 April, 1989.

seems to be that decisions on matters of general or common concern will be made in a forum in which no single race dominates by virtue of numbers, and where the representatives of each race group would have a veto. It is unlikely that major black political organizations could support a white veto, however.

Can a compromise be reached between the two dominating forces of black aspirations and white apprehension? There are some encouraging signs. The first multiracial constitutional conference ever held in South Africa was the KwaZulu–Natal Indaba, convened in Durban in April 1986. Its purpose was to work out a non-racial constitution for government at second-tier level in Natal and KwaZulu as a single unit within South Africa as a whole.

The Indaba, which contained representatives of a fairly wide spectrum of black and white opinion, dealt with the issue of minority fears by providing for minority groups to have vetoes in a proposed provincial legislature, on language, cultural and religious matters only. Any disputes about whether the proposed legislation affected these interests and could therefore be subject to veto by any one group would be settled by the courts[98] in terms of a bill of rights (which outlaws racial discrimination).

The Indaba's proposals are unlikely to be implemented in their present form, since the government objects to them in certain important respects. Negotiations about possible amendments are likely to ensue. Whatever the outcome, the Indaba, whose discussions lasted for eight months, proved that political compromise was possible in South Africa across a fairly wide spectrum of viewpoints, and also that negotiation can produce satisfactory results.

One of the problems in convening national constitutional talks would be determining who the representatives of black opinion would be. Whites have no such problem, since general elections show clearly the relative strengths of the various white parties. The relative strengths of various black political organizations at any constitutional negotiating table would also have to be determined by an election under free conditions in which all political groupings claiming to represent blacks would have to be allowed to participate. This requires the release of all political prisoners and lifting of the bans on various organizations.

No constitutional talks at national level are yet in sight, since some of the pre-conditions laid down by black leaders who would be key participants, such as the release of political prisoners, have not yet been met by the government.

---

[98] KwaZulu–Natal Indaba, 'Constitutional proposals', Durban, 1986.

National constitutional negotiations would presumably have to include representatives of people in the four independent homelands, should they wish to be constitutionally reunited with the rest of the country. Political organizations and leaders in these areas would therefore have to be allowed to participate in the election of representatives of black opinion.

Conclusion

This chapter has tried to show that the problems South Africa faces as it enters the last decade of the twentieth century go far beyond the repeal of racially discriminatory laws. They are problems that confront many developing countries, with their high rates of population growth and limited financial resources.

The continued enforcement of apartheid, particularly in the political field, makes solutions even more difficult to find than they might otherwise be.

It may be argued that the closing years of the twentieth century are likely to see a blurring of racial divisions in South Africa and a widening of economic cleavages within the black population. On the one hand, there will be a growing number of better educated, better-housed and better-paid Africans, whose living standards move closer and closer to those of whites and not infrequently overtake them. Typically, these people will include members of trade unions, managers and administrators, civil servants, and an entrepreneurial class concentrated mainly in the informal sector.

On the other, there will be a large black underclass — the unemployed, the illiterate and the malnourished — living in both towns and rural areas. Financial and economic neglect of the homelands would make the black underclass even larger and push some of its members into starvation.

A study of wage and income trends between 1980 and 1988 showed that the South African population grew by 18 per cent, real wages per employee by 11 per cent, and modern sector employment outside agriculture by 6 per cent. The implication is a fall in real per capita income. What appears to have happened is that the wage gains from the limited economic growth over the 1980s were concentrated in the hands of a labour force representing a shrinking proportion of the population. The incomes of households with access to modern sector employment would have risen in real terms, but an ever increasing proportion of households would have become dependent on informal sector activities to subsist.[99] Continued wage rises will probably improve the material situation of employed blacks substantially, but the

---

[99] M. McGrath and M. Holden, 'The 1988/89 budget', in *Indicator SA*, vol. 6, no. 1–2, Summer-Autumn, 1989.

numerical importance of people without jobs is likely to rise.[100]

In answer to its foreign critics the South African government, and indeed many whites who do not support the government, repeatedly claim that blacks in South Africa are better off than those elsewhere on the continent — one of the reasons, they say, why several hundred thousand blacks from neighbouring countries, notably Botswana, Lesotho, Malawi, Mozambique and Swaziland, work legally or illegally in South Africa.

Apartheid has ensured that high white living standards have been obtained at the cost of blacks. With its present resources and rates of growth, it seems highly unlikely that South Africa can raise average black living standards to the levels that whites have enjoyed. The gap is being narrowed and will continue to be narrowed, but by a lowering of white and a raising of black standards.

Parity requires both an increase in social expenditure on blacks and a dramatic reduction in expenditure on whites; to have reached parity in 1976 at the average level of all races would have implied a more than 70 per cent reduction in white benefits from government expenditure.

As Professor Servaas van der Berg has observed: 'Apartheid has allowed white standards to be set at a level far exceeding the resources of the country, if these standards were to be extended to other groups'. The problem that South Africa faces is 'how to adjust expectations of whites (and other groups) downwards to a level commensurate with South Africa's resources as a developing country'.[101]

The legacy of apartheid goes beyond material inequalities and distortions to distorted expectations. It is natural for whites to expect that their living standards will not decline, and it is equally natural for blacks to expect that equality will bring them up to the levels they observe among whites. Yet both sets of expectations are unrealistic.

It is hard to imagine who has the more difficult task: white political leaders explaining this to their followers, or black political leaders explaining it to theirs.

---

[100] S. van der Berg, 'Long-term economic trends and development prospects in South Africa', *African Affairs*, vol. 88, no. 351, April 1989, p. 196.

[101] Van der Berg, 'Long-term economic trends', pp. 199–200.

21 Business and politics: towards a strategy

Philip Frankel

> In some business quarters there is growing scepticism over the ability of government to generate creative ideas appropriate to the immediate challenges facing South Africa. The private sector, as the engine room of the economy, has a right and duty to contribute to the country's socio-political development. This chapter outlines the opportunities available to business for it to facilitate the transition to a post-apartheid era in which it still has a meaningful role.

Continuity and change

If there is a single factor behind what one commentator has aptly termed the 'unhappy bed-fellowship' between business and government over the years, it is the long-stated belief in the private sector that the Nationalist government is largely incapable of comprehending the economic consequences of its single-minded pursuit of political ideology.[1]

The eventual triumph of economic over political forces has never been fully incorporated into the ideological culture of Afrikaner nationalism. On the contrary, state patronage and an anti-materialist world view has encouraged the somewhat glib view that political structures can be ideologically erected, shaped, manipulated and changed with relatively little restraint by economic forces.

It is out of this divergence over the independence of politics in society that fundamental conflicts over the use of developmental resources have frequently appeared in the business–government dialogue. Long delayed and then unenthusiastic state recognition of the need for an expanded pool of trained black labour to meet the ever-changing demands of South African capital is at least partially derived from an ingrained ideological conviction that economic pressure for differentiation and growth can be deflected, if not subordinated, by political volition.

---

1 H. Hartmann, *Enterprise and politics in South Africa*, Princeton: Industrial Relations Section, Princeton Univ., 1962, p. 20.

A similar culturally-impregnated belief in the power of political will is also at the base of long-standing conflicts between state and business over the development importance of foreign capital. Governmental decision-makers, most of whom are the product of Afrikaner culture since 1948, generally have tended to regard external investment as altogether too un-dependable and politically demanding. They have, therefore, with some exceptions, never fully identified with traditional business anxiety that re-liance on local capital must restrict private investment, limit the consumer market, adversely affect the balance of payments and generally lead to a much slower (and politically explosive) rate of economic growth.

As a consequence, in the circumstances of 1960, 1976 or even post-1984, policy-makers within the state, on the whole, responded with far less alarm to the outflow of capital investment than their business counterparts, who see free enterprise as crucial for economic expansion.

Business–government relations have never been, nor seldom are, entirely conflictful. While there are noticeable differences in the way that South African business and government define the political world, their social style and institutional interests, points of contact and agreement have often arisen out of the social function of business to generate wealth and the reciprocal function of the state to define its distribution in the political context.

However, the deployment of social resources to the advantage of the eco-nomy has long remained an outstanding question on the agenda. Likewise, business perceptions of government reform strategy as slow, impractical and possibly even dangerous under the present State of Emergency are part of a conventional wisdom stretching back to Sharpeville and Soweto. In 1960, for example, Harry Oppenheimer expressed a sense of urgency in his prediction that 'we must accept . . . a black political majority in the future'.[2]

This view, with its ancillary calls for the abolition of institutionalized racial discrimination to the advantage of economic activity, is still the political credo for much of the business community.

There are indications that business is increasingly frustrated by govern-ment policy and that it is becoming more professional in its own approach to politics — despite the continuities in its political philosophy. Many of the issues on the political agenda of the private sector have been rendered obsol-ete by the passing of time and now have a somewhat redundant character. This includes calls for South Africa as a single economic entity, legalized black union representation, and the abolition of passes.

---

[2] 'Statement by the Chairman', *Report of the 31st General Meeting of Members of Rhodesian Anglo-American Ltd.*, 8 Dec., 1960.

Nevertheless, the basic attitude of business in its negotiations with government today is distinguishably different from those of previous years when business was, for the most part, inherently less definite and insightful in its feelings toward politics, state policy and political alternatives to apartheid. Overall, there is a far more activist conception of politics emerging in business circles. This is apparent in annual reports, chairperson's statements, and press releases emanating from private sector sources.

Contemporary business is far less sectorial, more socially responsive and trans-ethnic than previously.

The fairly widespread tendency of business in the 1950s and 1960s to define black South Africans as mere labour units, or to argue that political incorporation requires 'reasonable' levels of education and property ownership, is today generally unacceptable.

The private sector has come to appreciate the inseparability of politics and economics in contemporary South Africa and the improbability of real social change without pre-conditional or accompanying alterations in the apartheid framework. Barlow Rand chairman, Mike Rosholt, for example, has criticized business for believing that 'we can tackle socio-economic reform and political reform thereafter'.[3] In 1985, Gavin Relly, Chairman of Anglo American, reflected the feelings of many other South Africans in the business community when he stated categorically that 'the impact which industry and commerce can make on the GNP is determined by a combination of private enterprise, induced economic growth and political alteration/reform which releases the forces of free enterprise'.[4]

Since then, growing numbers of prominent business leaders have taken these political cues to lobby for direct business involvement in government decision-making structures which allow business an operational role in the dismantling of apartheid.[5] This new self-confidence in the political arena, is evident in Anglo executives' insistence that 'organised business talk to government . . . in the strongest possible fashion'.[6]

Many people in business are insisting that the issue is not whether business should participate in the political process, but more specifically how it can best contribute to the creation of more democratic and non-racial forms of South African society. The private sector, as Chris Ball (then of First National Bank) noted, is the 'engine room of the economy', and by virtue of this, 'has not only the right but indeed the duty to the community

---

[3] Quoted from 'Special Report, Barlow Rand', *Financial Mail*, 13 Feb., 1981.

[4] *Leadership* vol. 4 no. 3, 1985, p. 13.

[5] C. Ball, 'The business of reform', *South African Indicator*, vol. 2, no. 4, Jan. 1985.

[6] See, for example, C. Arterton and H. Hahn, *Political participation*, Washington: American Political Science Association, 1975.

at large to make a positive contribution to socio-political development in South Africa'.[7]

Indeed, in some business quarters there is growing scepticism at the ability of government to generate creative ideas appropriate to the immediate challenges facing South Africa. In these circumstances, the more activist business elements in the Urban Foundation's Private Sector Council (PSC), and, to a lesser extent, Assocom and the Federated Chamber of Commerce (FCI), soon to merge, have begun to develop their own tentative conceptions and plans for the transition to a post-apartheid era.

Politicization, it should be added, involves the ability to concretize political ideas, and the FCI Business Charter, as well as Assocom's Lombard Report, both of which express the growing concern of business to participate in the task of defining the transition to post-apartheid society, are significant milestones in articulating a more concise business programme for political transformation. They reflect a growing sense of unease at the erosion of democratic values and civil liberties in the increasingly authoritarian context of the third State of Emergency in the country. While the history of business in defence of these liberties is not untarnished, there is an awareness in the private sector today (at least at senior executive level) that the violation of human rights by apartheid is a major reference point for mobilizing political and economic action against South Africa internationally.

Many of the major provisions of the Business Charter take their cue from provisions contained in the Universal Declaration of Human Rights. By the same token, the FCI's Charter of Social, Economic and Political Rights expresses deep concern with the impact of what it terms 'growing economic and political isolation and the drift of South Africa into a repressive siege society', on 'fundamental democratic values and human rights', many enshrined in the United Nations Charter.[8]

There appears to be a two-track response to state policy. In the economic arena, the Business Charter echoes the broader feeling in private sector circles that an 'unleashing' of the economic forces of the country must necessarily include tax reform, deregulation, strict control on public spending and a whole series of fiscal measures to enhance structural investment and reduce the serious problem of national inflation. The political component of this programme — involving major inroads into institutionalized discrimination — also appears to meet at least some of the demands for reform and broader participation at national level articulated by international opinion.

---

[7] Ball, 'The business of reform'.

[8] Federated Chamber of Industry, *Charter of social economic and political rights*.

The programme envisaged by business ostensibly involves both short- and long-term strategic action. In the short term, the FCI and other employer organizations, such as the Urban Foundation, place exceptional emphasis on the extension of freehold title and other measures designed to alleviate the black housing crisis under the accelerating conditions of 'positive urbanization'. The alleviation of these social problems requires major restructuring in race relations and administrative structures at a local level.

In the longer term, the mainstream of South African business would presumably feel comfortable with a process of political reconstruction that eliminates the last major vestiges of institutionalized racial discrimination and brings state acceptance of the positive features of black trade unionism. The private sector has generally steered clear of prescribing to government with whom it should enter into dialogue in developing a new constitution. However, there is a widespread and growing perception that negotiations with representative elements in the black community are essential to the effective reorganization of political participation.

The more assertive business elements in the English community — notably Anglo American, the Premier Group, First National Bank and a number of multinationals based in South Africa — also believe that the process of negotiation must include a package of concessions by the state comprising, but not necessarily limited to, the release of political prisoners, cessation of the State of Emergency, abolition of Group Areas legislation, and some sort of commitment by government to genuine power-sharing at central level.[9]

Within this context, even the more conservative segments of English business are prepared to accept the vague but important notion of the private sector as catalyst or mediator between the major actors in the local situation.[10]

Toward a political strategy

The political mobilization of business is the result of complex developments within the business community itself. For one thing, the nature of South African capitalism has changed over the years to demand new and more sophisticated resources capable of servicing the production needs of an increasingly advanced and differentiated economy.

On the international front, the diversification of South African capital has made local business increasingly sensitive to pressures and influences on world markets, particularly from companies with offshore interests,[11]

---

[9] FCI, *Charter.*

[10] FCI, *Charter.*

[11] D. Kaplan, 'The internationalisation of South African capital: South African direct foreign investment in

and particularly when international economic opinion has opted for disinvestment and economic action against apartheid. The modernization of South African capital has also stimulated the importation of high-tech management techniques for training middle- and upper-level executive staff. This has subsequently promoted corporate responsibility ethics in the businessmen community.

Finally, business involvement in political activity is the direct result of developments in black and Afrikaner politics. The political rise of business is totally incomprehensible if viewed in isolation from the enormous pressures for business action exerted by an increasingly powerful, organized and politically articulate black labour movement. The rapid emergence of a black middle class with ostensible stakes in the capitalist system has also activated business to endorse political reform which meets the aspirations of the black bourgeoisie. Changes within the class structure of Afrikanerdom have led to the growth and consolidation of functional ties between Afrikaner and English business which transcend traditional ethnic divisions and, in principle, open up new channels of influence for business in the heartland of the Afrikaner community.

Whether business has utilized these channels to the best of its ability is a moot point. It is generally recognized that South African business has accepted the need for substantial economic and political reform for almost a decade. Yet, as business critics allege, private sector involvement in politics may be ingenuous or incompetent in fulfilling its anti-apartheid constraints, and in the last analysis has produced little in the way of social change.

Business has tended to steer clear of prescriptive formulae for moving away from apartheid and — with rare exceptions (notably the Lombard Report) — has preferred to defer to government the task of filling in the details and technical features of reform policy. This reliance upon the technical skills, rationality and ultimately, goodwill, of the state in making policy adaptions is a major source of the suspicion surrounding private sector interventions in politics. It is also, one might add, an important measure of the inexperience and naïvety accompanying the political efforts of business.

Even if business had a clearer conception of its medium- to long-term political goals, it still needs to develop the means to transform political objectives into concrete social action. Despite debate over many years in many forums, the business community still lacks an operational arm to exert political pressure on government. The so-called Action Programme accompanying the FCI's Business Charter is largely devoid of any effective

---

the contemporary period', in *Southern African studies: retrospect and prospect* (proceedings of a seminar), Edinburgh: Centre for African Studies, Univ. of Edinburgh, May/June 1983.

suggestions regarding implementation. This failure to act on declarations is an important point of conflict precluding more effective collaboration between white and black business.

If business is to play a more integrated and influential political role, it needs to have a more definite understanding of what it wants, the costs it is prepared to absorb, and the type of leverage it needs to exert.

It is, of course, unrealistic to believe that business can actually lead the way to political change in South Africa. While the last few years have seen increasing forays of business into the political arena, there are a variety of forces at work to undermine the capacity of the private sector to initiate/support reform initiatives. These constraining forces on business power include the lack of a tradition of political intervention; widespread ignorance about the workings of the political process; an economy punctuated with occasional alluring prospects of growth; and, in the last analysis, the race and class tie which binds business to some attentuated version of the present apartheid order.

Business is ultimately concerned, by definition, with the pursuit of profit, and the nature of its political involvement is always shaped by this cardinal consideration. In this respect, South African business is no better or worse than its counterparts in other economies.

There are, in the circumstances, solid and understandable grounds for the notion that business has not done all that it technically could to herald some sort of post-apartheid society. Despite the 'natural' constraints on the private sector as a political actor, there are still a variety of under-utilized channels into which it might move in substantiating its claim to effective political participation.

There is, for example, considerable work remaining to be done by business to encourage desegregation, industrial democracy and the expansion of opportunities in the areas where it has direct control, that is, in the relatively sheltered environment of the workplace.

This is not to diminish the important role which management has already played in constructing a viable system of industrial bargaining. (Many commentators would, in fact, like to see this policy of negotiation replicated in the political field.) Nor does further work along these lines involve what Mike Rosholt has termed 'the abdication of business responsibility to manage'.[12]

However, the industrial relations arena in South Africa is far from functional or equitable, and there is much to be done by the private sector before it can speak piously of transferring the values of the workplace to the wider realms of society.

---

12 *The Star*, 10 Nov. 1987.

Business needs to take much more action in educating white management at middle- and lower-levels in the political values and processes at work to transform South Africa into a non-racial, more democratic society. Business should also take urgent and long overdue action to enhance black participation in the corporate economy. This could be achieved through extended and more intense black management development projects to complement the progress already achieved in training technicians and artisans. Various avenues to black participation include cash participation in profit-sharing schemes leading to employment share-owning programmes (ESOPS); the reorganization of corporate structures to allow the work-force more leverage over pension funds; and social responsibility initiatives.

Ultimately, business needs to take a far more protective and assertive role over its workers at the various points where the shopfloor encounters the hostile political environment. This means supporting workers in their struggle for civil liberties. It also entails providing moral and practical assistance to workers in taking advantage of their new rights in a climate of shifting legislation.

If business is to exercise its influence in the political process, it must move beyond the shopfloor and actively promulgate political values before a wider public audience. If it is to protect its stakes in some future political order, it needs to come to terms with the fact that corporate responsibility is a long-term social investment rather than a type of grudgingly-given charity, and to act with urgency to create a climate conducive to the elimination of remaining discrimination in employment practices.

Business has moved tentatively in this direction through corporate support for non-racial schools and housing. Yet it could act with much more vigour to make the implementation of various apartheid laws more difficult for government. More assertive action to provide family housing for the work-force would, for example, strike at the very heart of the migrant labour system, leading to the irretrievable integration which government spokesperson see as cancelling out the practical possibilities for implementation of future Group Areas legislation.

An agenda of this order implies a number of sub-commitments. In the first place, it requires the private sector clearly, consistently and publicly to identify with the various institutional and informal forces at work for change, both at home and internationally. This means taking every possible opportunity to distance itself from government policy — while recognizing that circumstances may arise where it is strategically necessary to praise government for its actions.

This raises issues of criteria for social change and development: it is necessary for business to distinguish between what is reform and what is not. The private sector must look to a much greater investment in research and debate which defines standards for change and subsequently monitor their progress.

A workable post-apartheid system will be unavoidably different from the present order. Business should therefore seriously re-evaluate its commitment to unrestrained free enterprise principles in favour of various alternative formulae for economic development which advocate both growth and distributional goals. This means recognizing that many black South Africans who associate the end of capitalism with the end of apartheid are unlikely to change their views, regardless of programmes promoting the advantages of capitalism.

In adjusting to political realities, business must accept that most blacks want to participate in designing management strategies — especially corporate responsibility programmes, most of which lack worker participation and are laced with paternalism. If business is to re-learn politics, it is important that it recognizes black initiative and leadership in and outside the workplace.

The political reorganization of business also implies changes in public language. This means moving away from the apologetic rhetoric which has often characterized political intervention by business in favour of an approach which is direct and demanding in its assertions of the right of business to make claims against the state in the political arena.

This approach should be aimed at minimizing the capacity of government to portray the private sector as dis-unified and self-interested by asserting its solidarity. Repeated calls by business as a whole for reduced government activity in the workings of the marketplace and in allocating resources and social freedoms are important sources of economic propaganda which can also reduce production costs, inflation and restrictions on small and informal business so as to foster 'the participation of . . . the less developed population groups in the market economy'.[13]

The leaders of the private sector should move towards interweaving what they say and do with the broader forces working to raise the standards of living of all South Africans.

The private sector has a function to assert its political rights as the primary element in the community responsible for the production of wealth and making of public policy. There is a long and enduring tradition dating back from Verwoerd through Vorster that business should 'keep out of politics'. Government has often used this notion to steer business into technical issues associated with economic reform, arguing that the state is primarily responsible for the political role of the distribution of wealth.

---

[13] Report of the Committee for Economic Affairs at the President's Council, 'Mechanisms which restrict the functions of the free market orientated system in S.A.', 1984.

Business leaders such as Mike Rosholt have signalled to government that in South Africa today there are no longer any clear distinctions between political and socio-economic issues, that very few matters of political significances do not in some way impinge on the economy and the business person and that, in the final analysis, business has no option but to work for the removal of all barriers to economic growth, even if some of these barriers have a political flavour.

It should be made explicit that private sector support for government policy depends on government according more credibility to business forums of opinion. Business must also assert the conditionality of its support for political reform as part of the price which government must pay to attract business expertise and organizational support for its own efforts to create political change through economic development. This means moving away from an essentially passive and reactive role to that of a genuine initiator in the transition away from apartheid.

To transcend the division between putative and actual power, between the net influence of business and that which it uses, the private sector should develop what some commentators have termed an 'organisational content and strategic intent',[14] that is, the psychological and practical means to position itself and extract costs from the state. To achieve this, business needs to develop the various institutional mechanisms at its disposal to project its political interests.

Some type of umbrella forum is needed whose purpose it is to identify and project the political interests of the private sector over and beyond the more directly functional concerns of such organizations as the FCI and Assocom.

If business is to influence public policy, it must have access to political or politically-related information. There are indications of a substantial loss of direction in government game-plans for reform, increasing the possibility for business penetration into the higher arenas of public policy — subject to the proviso that business has at its disposal the necessary researched and policy relevant information.

The private sector could be more effective in identifying the social costs and risks involved in perpetuating neo-apartheid forms of policy or policy alternatives to apartheid presently advocated in state circles. It also needs to identify gaps between the realities and standard formulae for governance. It could help the state identify priorities for allocating social resources and, in the last analysis, provide information on policy alternatives which could circumvent points of impasse.

---

[14] *Business Day*, 29 Oct. 1987.

Finally, and perhaps most importantly, research sponsored by business communities needs to be of a monitoring nature, based on the need to provide continuing policy-relevant information pin-points where reform policy is effective or ineffective in generating social change.

With a few exceptions, there are large gaps between the limited political information at the disposal of the private sector and the massive social knowledge of the state. This undermines the persuasive power of business leaders in negotiation situations and allows government to dominate proceedings. The new research agenda for business requires both practical and abstract knowledge, which counters the present situation where the public sector talks and the private sector listens.

The private sector should achieve an equilibrium between abstract calls for non-racialism and democracy and more limited, immediate goals relating to day-to-day policy and political problems, so that it can prescribe policy alternatives to government.

Research supported by business sources needs to take special account of black South Africans in its design and implementation. It should also be aimed towards political education within its own constituency, extending beyond the handful of chief executives currently projecting business interests in socio-political change into governmental circles.

Outside this narrow realm, top management is uncomfortable in a political role and within middle and lower management political impulses are weak or non-existent. This is partly because of the limited tradition of corporate responsibility in South African business circles and partly because of the risks attached to political participation under current conditions. Neither of these forces, which inhibit business integrating and mobilizing resources in political activity, can be countered effectively in the short and medium term. Nevertheless, the private sector should still make every effort to extend political education among the ranks of upper and lower management, possibly through increased use of outside institutions such as business schools, which are already functioning in this arena to produce a more socially conscious generation of business people and the ever-expanding legions of management consultants, who should be encouraged to place more emphasis on corporate and political responsibility.

Under the present State of Emergency many people in the business community, at all levels of the executive hierarchy, have lapsed into political apathy in the face of what appears to be restored social order accompanied by short-term economic growth.

In this situation they are unlikely to enter readily into political alliances with other sympathetic pressure groups. They should, however, consider forging short-term alliances on specific issues. The establishment of the

PSC as an umbrella body uniting various fragments of business in project-ing private sector interests to government is an important development. The decision to consolidate Assocom and FCI into a single organization representing commerce and industry is also significant — although there are a variety of potent arguments and interests in commerce and industry which would prefer that they be kept apart.

While the existence of the National African Chamber of Commerce (Naf-coc) is unavoidable, and probably desirable in certain respects, given the structural features of the political economy, there are a variety of channels which could still be activated by the private sector to bring a fuller weight of black business to bear on the broad front of private sector activity.

Business should also identify and integrate Indian and coloured business as a means of initiating an internal coalition within the private sector.

Much the same can be said about English and Afrikaner business. Leaders in both sectors need to capitalize on common functional concerns of a modernizing economy to co-ordinate socio-political action. While it is un-realistic to believe that Afrikaner business will in future cast aside the sus-taining mixture of ethnic affiliation and state patronage to make common cause in politics with English capital, nonetheless, the new corporate, func-tional and technocratic spirit abroad in Afrikaner business offers a variety of unexplored opportunities for short-term coalitions on common issues. This is particularly true at the level of large-scale Afrikaner enterprise where some of the larger corporations are no longer dependent on sources of state patronage, as they were earlier in their development.

Subject to the proviso that English business develop political coalitions in areas of concern such as Regional Service Councils (RSCs), urbanization, local government and the like — the business community could gain a very powerful resource at the epicentre of Afrikaner society.

Business should be more than a bridge-builder or catalyst for change. While the private sector can play an important role as a channel for political communication between various power groups in South Africa, it should move beyond its position as a conduit to giving practical support to sectors whose political agendas are reasonably sympathetic to its own.

Within this range are such key political movements as Inkatha, the United Democratic front (UDF) and even the African National Cogress (ANC) — all of whose agendas can accommodate tactical involvement with business in the process of encouraging political change and negotiation. Inkatha provides opportunities for more broad-ranging liaison — most noticeably Chief Buthelezi's opposition to disinvestment. Similarly, the role of busi-ness in adding local-level negotiation in the Eastern Cape can be used to consolidate links between the private sector and the UDF.

While there are fundamental differences between business and ANC perceptions of the political world, this does not preclude dialogue between the two, as evidenced by the 1985 Lusaka meeting. A relative shift from military to political struggle is leading a proportion of ANC leadership toward negotiation — if not necessarily negotiation with the South African government. This strategic/tactical rearrangement means a net increase in the opportunities for important pressure groups, such as business, to make contact with the ANC and establish relations.

While the interests of labour and capital are generally opposed, there are opportunities for tactical co-operation. A common opposition to basic apartheid structures has allowed business and black labour to build up a fairly viable system of industrial relations, often in the face of government intervention. They would be strengthened were business to put up stronger resistance to further government intrusion into the industrial relations arena.

This could take the form of more definite opposition to legislated action against the unions and the violation of individual rights under the provisions of the State of Emergency. While there are many instances of action already taken along these lines, business could effectively legitimate its investment in the industrial relations system by voicing a deeper concern with, for example, the new Labour Relations Act, or with the continued detention and harassment of union leaders. There must be more consultation between management and union leaders, and the industrial relations system needs to be developed to allow for this communication.

The recent establishment of ESOPS by several companies is particularly important in incorporating the black work-force into the system and advancing worker interests. Plans by some twenty-six South African companies to implement these worker share-schemes have been criticized by the unions and outside commentators who see them as attempts to increase productivity and depress worker demands under the veneer of shopfloor welfare. Yet, the move toward making ESOPS an integral feature of corporate life is an important step in aligning South African free enterprise with most advanced capitalist countries.[15]

While the Congress of South African Trade Unions (Cosatu) is understandably dismissive of minority shareholder arrangements, it is equally concerned with the co-optive potential inherent in worker participation in the share market. Its leaders have nevertheless indicated that equity sharing in the form of worker trusts — presumably along the lines of Scandinavian 'wage-earner funds' under union control — could advance worker control over the economy.

---

[15] *Weekly Mail,* 9 Oct. 1987.

This introduces the possibility of some type of coalition between organized management and workers, provided business is willing to entertain more effective union participation in the process by which ESOPS is defined and initiated. Conditional to this is that business provide assurance that proposed equity sharing schemes are not a substitute for negotiations over the 'living wage' currently demanded by Cosatu; that corporations undertake not to link the introduction of worker shares with an increase in company share capital; and that organized labour be given representation and executive roles in determining the price of shares and their distribution.

The private sector has not fully exploited all the possibilities for political influence inherent in the party and parliamentary systems, where the advent of tricameralism has fundamentally changed the logic and stakes of political power at legislative level. Despite the decline in parliamentary opposition, there is still capital to be made through closer affiliation with individual Democratic Party (DP) leaders.

The National Party can attract considerable financial support from both English and Afrikaner capital, particularly as the new State President, F. W. de Klerk, lays claim to a new reformist image. Business might consider more broad-based support for the DP as the upholder of South Africa's liberal free-enterprise tradition, particularly support for research into socio-political issues which reinforce its parliamentary position.

More generally, the business community has failed to capitalize on the inherent contradictions of the Tricameral Parliament embodied in the principle that decisions are the result of consensus, particularly consensus in the Joint Standing Committees (JSCs) of parliament.

In the tricameral system today, there are various forces at work to polarize relations between the white Assembly and the two 'junior' houses. Most of these tensions are projected into the strategically-situated joint committees in whose deliberations the principle of consensus decision-making is becoming progressively harder to realize. The standing committee system was designed specifically to invite public participation in major policy issues: this means there are enormous and still largely neglected opportunities for interest groups, such as business, to shape opinion on policy.

The consensus principle means that if and when business can sway either the coloured or Indian standing committee members to its viewpoint, it can, in principle, stalemate the entire legislative process, since the State President is normally reluctant to reject the findings of joint committees — because this exposes the transparency of power-sharing under the tricameral arrangements.

Mostly, the private sector has preferred to stand back from active involvement in the tricameral system, either because business leaders are sceptical of the technical and ethical principles of government embodied in the new parliamentary arrangements or because of a lingering feeling that active lobbying to cultivate political support in parliament is not in accord with the better principles of democratic government. Yet, close and consistent contacts between business and the legislative arm are accepted practice in all the major democratic systems of the world and there is no substantial political or moral reason why a similar network should not be replicated here.

The private sector's present methods of lobbying the legislature — the odd telegram or isolated protest to parliament in the face of impending legislation — is ineffective in protecting business and society from what is often arbitrary legislation. Its compatriots in Europe and America have established, specialized relationships and organizations whose singular purpose is to muster policy-related information with a view to shaping legislation, as well as feeding it through the legislative network in a way which assures maximum impact for business on the terrain of public policy.

In pursuit of this goal, the private sector clearly needs to move beyond the present arrangement where business comes together to negotiate with government on infrequent occasions, either in the odd institutional setting or through informal individual contacts between business and government leaders. The private sector has to develop a more coherent and sustained system whose ongoing rationale is to seek out and exploit every available pocket of sympathy for business interests in governmental circles.

This means a far more determined effort by progressive business organizations to use the political advantages inherent in the multiplicity of institutions in the public sector. Given the present shift of power and decision-making away from the legislative arm of government to other executive organs, business lobbyists should direct their activity both within the Tricameral Parliament and other extra-parliamentary institutions.

In addition, there is, in principle, no strategic reason why the private sector cannot build on its connections as an integral part of South Africa's growing military-industrial complex. Total strategy, according to its designers, involves co-ordinated action in all fields and has been described as 'a guarantor of the free enterprise system' by its military proponents.[16] Business needs to exploit the compatibilities of interest between itself as the producer of wealth and the military as the protector of state security by taking a far more active role in the workings of the National Security Management System and the various other organs in the extensive network already in place for business and government and the military to liaise over national matters.[17]

---

[16] See Glenn Moss, 'Total strategy', *Work in Progress*, Feb. 1980.

[17] On this network, see P. Frankel, *Pretoria's praetorians — civil–military relations in SA*, Cambridge: Cambridge Univ. Press, 1984.

The danger is that business may become the tool of the security apparatus through compliant service on bodies such as the JMCs (Joint Management Centres), which have been widely criticized. Private sector involvement on these publicly unaccountable organs of the State Security Council (SSC) has already reaffirmed a common view in black society of an unholy alliance between the military and capital. At the same time, the SSC is increasingly becoming the arena within which the major decisions of state are taken. Thus, it is only on this terrain that business can make an immediate impact on public policy.

Business can play a far more interventionist and affirmative role in bureaucratic struggles within the state, enlisting support from sympathetic elements in the parastatals who have important channels of influence into the state bureaucracy and from technical contacts within the state bureaucracy. The Department of Constitutional Development and Planning, despite its role in political development, has proved largely alien territory for the small business lobbyist.

Such lobbying demands a variety of diverse resources. These include professional consultants who can exploit the various power points within the state. It demands willingness from business to invest human and material resources in every avenue which leads to public decision-making. And it requires more professional participation in specialized committees and commissions established by the state.

Business is also responsible to a vast extra-parliamentary constituency, which is important in the process of social and political development.

In the first place, the private sector needs to balance its special commitment to advancing the interests of the black middle class with a broader and intrinsically more popular agenda that embraces the community in and outside the industrial relation system. While there are many gains attached to building a black middle class with political and economic stakes in the capitalist system, private sector activity in this area must be seen against a broader background. Although strategically placed, the black middle class is small and likely to remain a minority élite, whatever the pattern of economic growth and development. There are, in any case, few intellectual or historic grounds for the still-widely articulated view in business circles that this group 'have a stake in stability and in providing a counter to the process of radicalism'.[18]

On the contrary, unless business and other constituencies can stimulate political change which will absorb the status claims of an upwardly mobile black middle class, there is every likelihood that this group will provide the leadership for radicalism and hostility to capital. Even if this

---

[18] Quoted in J. Saul and S. Gelb, 'The crisis in SA', *Monthly Review*, 1987, p. 45.

were not so, it is strategically inadvisable for the private sector to perpetuate what the broad mass of South African blacks see as a crass effort to
co-opt black leaders into the existing system on the basis of pragmatic class
considerations.

Many of the schemes initiated by the private sector to encourage black
business and economic participation will have no effect beyond the select
circle of the black middle class, nor will they provide the broader masses
with any appreciable benefits. They are no substitutes for the minimum
living wage demanded by the unions.

Under the circumstances, business needs to reassess its priorities in forging black ties. It needs to identify who benefits from its various programmes of social upgrading and assess the philosophy and motivations
often latent in these programmes.

More positively, there should be increased black participation across the
sociological spectrum in designing and implementing corporate responsibility and social justice schemes. The appointment of more black community
representatives from outside the managerial middle classes of black society
to non-executive positions on boards of directors is one of many mechanisms which would consolidate ties with a more grassroots black South
Africa.

Conclusion

There are major constraints on business instituting its political role as has
been described in this chapter. Some of the limiting factors are integral to
the business community itself, while others are inherent in the sociological
context in which it perforce operates.

It is situated between an authoritarian state indisposed to receive advice
from a pressure group outside the ruling party, and mass society sceptical
of its sincerity. For business to make its contribution to social change an
immense outlay in time, human energy and, above all, finances will be
required. It is all very well to talk of massive allocations for the housing,
education and training of urban workers. But, if business is to give positive
urbanization real content, it will have to absorb these costs or at least
come to some equitable arrangements or partnership for sharing them with
government.

There are various areas in which business can build its political role in
the near future. The private sector is increasingly, if reluctantly, cognizant of
the political connotations of the industrial relations system so laboriously
constructed over the years — and this suggests an important departure point
for the future relations between management and worker.

Perhaps, more importantly, there is support in business leadership for the notion that genuine social reform requires mechanisms for the redistribution of wealth in some fashion, and that these processes of redistribution require political reform. The concentration of capital since the 1960s means that relatively small circles of business people are strategically placed to influence the political role of a much wider constituency. Provided this leadership cadre is willing to become more politically active, there is hope that business could come to occupy a position on the high ground of social change.

22   City politics comes of age: strategic responses to local government restructuring[1]

Mark Swilling

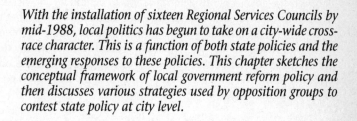

With the installation of sixteen Regional Services Councils by mid-1988, local politics has begun to take on a city-wide cross-race character. This is a function of both state policies and the emerging responses to these policies. This chapter sketches the conceptual framework of local government reform policy and then discusses various strategies used by opposition groups to contest state policy at city level.

Introduction

As states become more complex, causing decision-overload, there is a growing realization that democracy is best achieved by decentralizing political decision-making and empowering local communities.

The reason why democratization through decentralization is so widely favoured is simple. It helps local communities feel:

▷ that they can participate in decision-making structures that are seen as accessible;

▷ that these structures can influence the allocation of resources; and

▷ that tangible gains can flow from participation.

The result is a more efficient allocation of resources and more effective management of social structures. The central state can unload the decision-making burden on to local and regional governments that are better placed to take account of circumstances posed by local conditions. This makes local government the key level of government — a necessary pre-condition for a workable democracy.

---

[1] This chapter was completed in October 1988, and is therefore out of date. No attempt has been made to update it in order to incorporate the changes introduced by F. W. de Klerk. In particular, the release of the detainees, scrapping of the NSMS, and the constitutional negotiation initiatives are notable changes that make much of the argument in this chapter redundant. Nevertheless, this chapter does capture the strategies pursued by the 'seurocrats' during their heyday, and the responses that were being devised by parliamentary and extra-parliamentary anti-apartheid forces. Many of these strategies are still very much applicable today. To this extent, this chapter remains relevant to current debates.

South Africa's local government reform strategy is framed by consociational theory. This holds that political stability is ensured by fragmenting power vertically into cultural pillars that are simultaneously autonomous and coexist in a single nation-state.

In practice, this consociational contract has given rise to our strange local government regime, which is premised on ethnic primary local authorities (PLAs) and multiracial Regional Services Councils (RSCs). A recent review of this reformist option argues that it does not facilitate decentralization, democracy or substantive de-racialization.[2]

Given the government's determination to defend its consociational policies against federal and majoritarian alternatives, it follows that the social forces behind the alternatives to government policy share an interest in oppositional strategies that will replace apartheid with non-racial democratic alternatives. But before these alternatives can be assessed, it is essential to understand the full extent of state strategy and the place local government occupies in this strategy.

Local government reform and national security

Local government reform policy occupies a point where national security and constitutional reform policies intersect. Security strategists argue that the revolutionary climate will be eliminated when local government is normalized. Constitutional planners argue that the new local structures are the building blocks for a future South African democracy.

The stakes, therefore, are high when it comes to ensuring the success of local government reform. The state's security and constitutional policy depend on success at this level.

National security strategies, as expressed through the actions of the National Security Management System (NSMS), are aimed at restoring law and order in the townships, and winning the hearts and minds of the black population by introducing reforms to remove the underlying socio-economic grievances that revolutionaries exploit.

The Joint Management Centres (JMCs) (the base units of the NSMS) are attempting to break up communities, extract the leadership and put the pieces together again in the image of the state. This cannot, however, be achieved without making concessions to meet at least some popular demands. These concessions make up the welfarist dimension of state strategy at the local level, and include the following:

▷ infrastructural upgrading;

▷ housing development;

---

2 G. Tötemeyer and C. Heymans, *Government by the people?*, Kenwyn: Juta, 1988.

▷ local government reform;

▷ scrapping of influx control; and

▷ populist co-option in squatter camps.

In short, the state is meeting key popular demands, but on its own terms and while the popular leadership are in jail. These demands include housing, better services and financial support for local government.

For security officials, the welfarist concessions are just as important as the repressive measures, although less effective in the short term. The time-lag between the promise of concessions and their effect on communities leads to rising expectations which, for those who subscribe to the conservative explanation of revolution, can fuel revolutions. Welfarist concessions, therefore, must be coupled to harsh repression to lower expectations and to eliminate revolutionaries.

The delicate balance between using just the right amount of repression without triggering a counter-reaction and identifying the most explosive grievances that need to be addressed is maintained by the JMCs through co-ordinated control of intelligence, coercion and developmental resources. Inevitably, the reality is far more complex. Persistent popular dissent and inadequate resources for upgrading are just two problems that confront security officials.

In 1984 the constitutional planners announced that the Black Local Authorities (BLAs) would be included in the RSCs to facilitate the redistribution of resources to African as well as coloured and Indian areas.

This inclusion, in response to the political and fiscal consequences of their exclusion, was the direct result of popular resistance and mobilization: the United Democratic Front (UDF) and the major trade union federations took on the state in the early 1980s precisely on the grounds that the new constitution would be rejected because it excluded the African majority and because townships could not be self-financing.

Alternative perspectives and strategies

The municipal elections of 1988 were intended to establish the PLAs as uniformly-elected local authorities. The newly-elected representatives to the own affairs structures then nominated representatives to the RSCs.

From the state's point of view, the legitimation of this system did not rest on high polls, but rather on the multiracial decision-making process it is supposed to facilitate. Or, to express this strange logic differently, if state structures lack legitimacy because of separate racial forms of representation, then it follows that multiracial representation in joint structures will generate legitimacy.

To respond to this multi-layered, indirect form of government, appropriate strategies and tactics will need to be devised. The naïve assumption that the new local state structures are merely cosmetic reforms and therefore irrelevant must be jettisoned. No matter how inadequate these structures are, they will re-shape the terrain of conflict and struggle in ways that will require a more sophisticated approach to city politics. This new terrain will be created by the *de facto* effects of the new local state system. These can be summarized as follows:

1. The gradual transfer of power from the PLAs to the RSCs may mean that the city will come to be governed by a single metropolitan power centre rather than a multiplicity of disconnected ethnic authorities.

2. Metropolitan government transcends group areas division. Group Areas boundaries will still affect electoral mechanisms and residential patterns, but not decisions over the distribution of hard services.

3. Township rents and service charges will not be increased to finance capital development projects because these will be paid for by RSC levies on business.

4. The new system is intended to hide the mechanisms for extracting surplus from residents. Instead of communities paying higher rents and service charges to single identifiable township-based authorities, residents will carry the cost of the levies on business as individual consumers and wage earners.

5. Decisions about state expenditure in the city are intended to take place beyond public scrutiny. Working in conjunction with JMCs, RSCs will probably direct resources according to the counter-revolutionary and security imperatives of the JMCs. What these imperatives are and how priorities are decided upon will remain unknown.

6. The power of PLAs may be reduced. Given that real decisions will be taken at RSC and JMC level, the PLAs of all groups — including whites — will have a decreasing say in running the city.

7. It is intended that community groups will play a less important role.

8. State propaganda will probably try to create the illusion of multiracial and legitimate government. A popular consciousness may emerge in all communities that understands the need for a single, open city. Even if this is coupled to a rejection of the legitimacy of the RSCs in the black areas, means to express this consciousness will be required. Put another way, calls for extending the objectives of township strategies to white areas may become an important political campaign.

9. Future urban planning will be undertaken by RSCs on a metro-regional basis creating cross-community rather than community-specific effects

(for example, the proclamation of buffer zones as housing development areas).

10. By making RSC income for development dependent on levies from business, city development becomes tied to business cycles and the astuteness of RSC accumulation strategies.

Some common themes emerge from these points that suggest the local state's scope of action has been redefined to facilitate the following:

▷ cross-group area, city-wide intervention;

▷ multiracial representation via ethnic PLAs;

▷ an integrated urban fiscal system including a measure of redistribution from white to black areas; and

▷ diminished democracy.

Racial boundaries will no longer be used to secure the political separation of whites from other races, but rather to define the composition of the citizenry as a unity of separate and identifiable groups. It is not race as such that secures the dominance of the white minority in this system, but rather their wealth, because of the way representation is linked to user charges. It may be useful to call this re-racialization — a principle that flows directly from the theory of consociationalism.

A critical choice will have to be made on how to respond effectively to the PLA/RSC structures and the new urban system.

The uniqueness of the local level rests on three conditions:

1. Basic goods and services required for urban living are provided and maintained at local level of government.

2. The local level is experienced directly daily by the local population.

3. Local constituencies may be divided by race and wealth, but their common cultural environment and place in the city means they occupy a common living space and economy. This could form the basis for one city, open city campaigns.

The PLA/RSC system takes these conditions as starting points and will try to use them to realize the state's consociational security objectives. This chapter considers four strategic options for contesting the city and challenging the state's objectives:

1. local election strategies;

2. mass township-based resistance;

3. local coalitions; and

4. local-level negotiations.

Local election strategies

There are two broad oppositional strategies. Firstly, there is the parliament-ary position that argues for participation — mobilizing opposition from within the electoral process rather than leaving the system to be manip-ulated at will by the government.

Secondly, there is the extra-parliamentary opposition that argues for the complete dismantling of the PLA/RSC system. This is coupled to a boy-cott strategy — mobilizing opposition against the entire local state system, including the electoral process.

The participationist and boycott strategies derive from different policy positions on social change. Liberal opposition parties like the former Pro-gressive Federal Party (PFP) and the present Democratic Party (DP) saw participation in parliament as the only practical way to control the mech-anisms for dismantling apartheid. Boycott tactics were seen as reactive and ultimately unproductive because they cannot be translated into proactive policies.

Those parties that participated in the House of Delegates and House of Representatives did so for different reasons. The Labour Party (LP), for ex-ample, justified participation on the grounds that this was the best way of 'wrecking apartheid from within'. The notion that being in government was necessary to control the levers of social change was never dominant. Nor have the coloured and Indian parties succeeded in turning their con-stituencies into a voting population with a political culture centred on the electoral process.

Boycott strategies were generated by equally coherent conceptions of so-cial change. The extra-parliamentary movements that fall under the rubric of the UDF and the Congress tradition proceed from the assumption that the South African state is rooted in colonial conditions, serving the inter-ests of the white minority. All attempts by the state to create representative structures (Bantustans, community councils, the Tricameral Parliament and other advisory bodies) have been designed to divide along ethnic lines the oppressed majority.

Proponents of the boycott strategy would argue that election boycotts are a necessary strategy, not just an *ad hoc* tactic, for they are the most effective method of intensifying the unity of the oppressed, and building them into a movement committed to a united, non-racial democracy.

The various strategies used by the different anti-apartheid groups de-rive from policy positions on social change that will not be fundamentally revised in the short term. As far as the policies underlying participation are concerned, conditions have changed that both reinforce and under-mine them. The growing power of what Sampie Terreblanche calls the 'securocratic state' has drastically undermined the significance and power of parliament. This has detracted from the DP's argument that change is possible through parliament. However, it has strengthened the LP's strategy: although change has become increasingly difficult to promote in parliament, blocking Nationalist legislation has become easier, and has become an effective method of exposing the centralization of real power in the executive.

Conditions have not altered sufficiently for the extra-parliamentary movements to question their strategy. The present state is still perceived as essentially colonial and therefore the basic need for a boycott to maintain the unity remains.

There is a remote possibility that the call for a non-racial municipality being made by business, liberal parties and extra-parliamentary organizations may be conceded by the government. The Local Bodies in Free Settlement Areas Bill has already conceded this in principle.

If this does become general policy, it may well be the kind of shift at local level that will result in serious consideration of participation by extra-parliamentary organizations, justified on grounds that a non-racial municipality was originally a people's demand that the regime has now been forced to concede. It would have to be followed by a lifting of the Emergency and the unbanning of organizations that are recognized as bona fide representatives of the majority.

Mass township resistance

From 1976 to 1986, mass township resistance was the single most effective method of contesting the goals, meaning and function of the city. Social movements emerged to contest every aspect of urban control: land-use regulations, Group Areas, housing policies, squatter laws, influx control, labour mobility, trading regulations, health care facilities, child care, transport systems, education and welfare measures for senior citizens, the unemployed and the disabled.

Township resistance developed from small-scale protests into deep ruptures between community and state. An anatomy of township protest shows a definite pattern, as summarized in the text that follows.

Grievance expression

The first signs of community protest emerged when grievances were expressed about appalling living conditions in the community. When these were not addressed by councillors, some eminent persons would present the grievances to local officials in the form of a petition or simply a verbal articulation of problems.

Official rebuke

In case after case the authorities either ignored, rebuked or repudiated the petitioners. Officials frequently responded with excuses that rested on un-proven bureaucratic assertions rather than reasoned discussion of demon-strable facts.

Mobilization of counter-power

Active elements in the community resorted to the mobilization of counter-power, for one reason because they had virtually no access to higher ech-elons of the state through the media, intermediaries, political parties or intellectuals.

Mobilization and organization

Grassroots organization spread country-wide. The web of cross-cutting or-ganizational structures that bound these communities was carefully built up from below. The UDF and its allies helped articulate common national political goals that expressed the connection local communities had al-ready made between official refusal to deal with local grievances and the constitutional structure that deprived them of political rights.

Demonstrating power

Once the basic foundations of grassroots organization had been established, it became necessary to mount campaigns that would demonstrate the com-munity's power. Despite the ultra-radical insurrectionary rhetoric of the time, in reality the boycott weapon was limited to facilitating popular demonstrations of community power. A sustained armed presence never emerged to alter the balance of military power.

The spiral of repression and resistance

Right through the 1980s activist's initiatives to organize communities were matched by efforts of security policemen to detain leaders and infiltrate and intimidate the communities.

The conflict between the social movements and the state was exacer-bated rather than ameliorated by repression. Faced with violent resistance to their demands, all the communities could do was redouble their efforts to strengthen grassroots organization. This, in turn, intensified the level of repression and so the cycle continued. Escalating violence was the product of the process rather than a revolutionary strategy.

Constructing dual power

When the 1985 State of Emergency was declared, the activists found them-selves sandwiched between the militarism of the youth squads and the tactics of the security forces. Criticized by the youths for being too moder-ate, hunted and detained by the security forces, they responded by forming street and area committees — decentralized structures capable of withstanding repression and bringing the youth under the control of their parents.

Stalemate and negotiations

The rupture between state and people led to a stalemate. Stalemates, however, can lead to negotiations when there is a shared perception of stalemate. Although national negotiations are unlikely, local-level negotiations have taken place because of this realization, but only in those areas where the concept of obtaining concessions through bargaining rather than insurrection was more dominant in the minds of the leadership.

Although township social movements have varied in size from a handful of concerned residents to mass movements, they have succeeded in shaping a popular consciousness about city form and function that challenges the basic assumptions of state policy. Under the direction of national organizations such as the UDF, alternative conceptions of the community have been generated. Implicit in the struggles for housing, land, services, better education, cheap transport and urban welfare are some common themes around which a conception of the post-apartheid city could coalesce:

▷ *Democratization*: In contrast to the logic of RSCs and JMCs, local township organizations have implemented a decision-making structure based on street and area committees that facilitates, in turn, a participative political culture.

▷ *Redistribution:* Questioning the ethnic division of local government finance, township organizations have demanded the re-unification of the city into a single urban political economy to facilitate the redistribution of urban wealth.

▷ *Non-racialism:* By rejecting the need for separate municipalities for each racial group, township organizations have probably been the most forceful movement behind the demand for non-racial municipalities.

▷ *Coalition building:* Transcending the traditional compartmentalization of city-life into separate sectors (for example, sport, culture, politics, church, business, etc.), township organizations built their power by uniting these sectors into colourful multi-faceted coalitions.

▷ *Negotiations:* As already discussed, township organizations have also demonstrated a desire to negotiate solutions.

Because township movements were so effective in contesting the city, they became the prime target of state repression after the declaration of the 1986 State of Emergency. Despite the obvious damage to the organizational underpinnings of township resistance, the political consciousness that has sustained popular mobilization remains. Mass township resistance will continue to contest both the city and the general racial oppression that enables the state to use the city for its own purposes.

The principles of participatory democracy, redistribution, non-racialism, negotiation and coalition are likely to form the policy options of the extra-parliamentary democratic movements.

In the short term, any local government policy initiated by either government or the private sector that ignores these principles must reckon on encountering another township challenge such as that of 1984–6. In the long term, realistic policy options that express the interests of the black majority will have to take seriously the logic and political culture of mass township resistance.

Local coalitions

In places like Cape Town, Pietermaritzburg, Port Elizabeth, East London, Port Alfred, Pretoria and Durban loosely structured coalitions of white liberal groups have tried to build support for some sort of non-racial arrangement.

Traditionally excluded from the local government establishment in most areas (except most notably in Cape Town), these elements proceeded from the assumption that a coalition with a sufficiently broad base could be established to counter the local conservative establishment. If they could unite liberal opinion and link this sector to black political groups, then traditional racial barriers that have always underpinned conservative dominance could be transcended.

During 1984–6, there was much talk in liberal and business circles about initiating local options. Pietermaritzburg and Cape Town were selected as guinea pigs.

Business groups, trade unions, major employers, local government officials, and community organizations were all approached to assess the viability of initiating a local option flowing from the Natal Indaba model.

The outcome of the Cape Town City Council's (CCC) local option was not a happy one. Squeezed between the intransigence of central government and suspicion and division in the black community organizations, the CCC's local option ground to a halt in 1985. It has, however, emerged in another form in 1988/9 as the Open City Campaign, which is linked to an ambitious participatory planning strategy aimed at involving community groups in setting the CCC's planning priorities.

Mass-based organisation and accountability structures are a pre-condition for such coalitions. The repression and detention of leaders in terms of the State of Emergency made it extremely difficult for leaders to participate in broad front initiatives during the period 1985–8.

There is, however, a more fundamental reason for the underlying power-lessness of local city councils. One academic observer of the CCC local option noted:

> In South Africa the need for the implementation and maintenance of the apartheid system has led to centralisation by the government of many functions which are often the domain of local authorities in other countries, e.g. education, welfare and the pattern of residential neighbourhoods. This means that there are not many substantial issues open for bargaining at local level. The CCC is not exactly a toothless body, but it is difficult to negotiate if there is not much to bargain about.[3]

Local-option initiatives failed for two reasons. Firstly, it soon became apparent that the local state was too tightly controlled and dominated by the central state for it to be used as an institutional base for alternative local strategies. Secondly, the major representatives of the oppressed majority made it clear that constitutional issues are national issues and cannot be negotiated at local level.

Since 1986 there has been growing interest in reviving local initiatives, but this time on a different basis. Gone is the naïve assumption that local solutions to national problems can be found. Instead, there is a shift from local option in favour of local coalitions. This implies the creation of city-wide coalitions of parties that share common tactical objectives. These may include the need for a non-racial municipality, abolition of group areas, housing development, election programmes, or simply the need to facilitate intra-city liaison between black and white groups.

In other words, what brings the coalition together is not the belief that immediate solutions are possible, but rather the desire to build broad-based opposition to specific issues (for example, group areas) and support for post-apartheid conceptions of the city, its administration and how its inhabitants should relate to one another. The coalitions, therefore, are a movement, not local conventions.

Three current examples of local coalition building are worth referring to:

1. In Cape Town, the city council recently commissioned a feasibility study into how a non-racial decision-making structure for the city could be established. Using this research technique to find common ground, the city council may be able to transcend the constraints of formal racist institutions and initiate a process of dialogue that may culminate in some sort of cross-race city-wide forum.

2. The Grahamstown Initiative, launched at a conference in September 1988 and attended by delegates from across the political spectrum —

---

[3] See R. Cameron's contribution in Tötemeyer and Heymans *Government by the people?*.

from National Party (NP) councillors to UDF civic activists — hammered out priorities for the future of Grahamstown. A permanent structure will now carry the initiative forward into practical campaigns and efforts.

3. In early June 1988, the National Democratic Movement (NDM), PFP and other concerned individuals launched a campaign entitled Manifesto: Pretoria 2000. Their manifesto states that Pretoria 2000 will 'focus on the central issue of what kind of city the Pretorians at large would really wish to live in by the year 2000 (and beyond)'.

Local coalitions around demands for a single open city are still fragile and hesitant. They have arisen out of white grassroots disillusionment with the formal party political system and a concern among black organizations that wider alliances are needed. Their most significant characteristics are:

▷ the identification of their aims with time rather than a racial outcome — this leaves the specifics of what each city will look like up to the negotiating process;

▷ the local focus, that is an appeal to a common local identity ('we Pretorians') that transcends racial identities; and

▷ the broad definition of the potential constituency of these coalitions.

The prognosis for these local coalitions, however, is not good. Three basic conditions need to exist before they can become a viable policy option:

1. Free association must be guaranteed: restrictions on black political activity will have to be removed.

2. Some way must be found to increase the autonomy and powers of local government so that fundamental racial divisions in the city can be removed by the local state if this is what the local consensus wants.

3. The government must make a policy decision to reverse the current iron-fisted denial of any local grassroots political processes.

Given that these conditions are unlikely, local coalitions may become the expression of grassroots intentions rather than working alternatives.

Local-level negotiations

Throughout the 1980s, particularly during 1985–6, local township-based organizations sought the help of local government and/or local business to resolve pressing local problems. The result was a process of conflict, negotiation and resolution that led many local activists to explore negotiation strategies in more depth. The following summary of this highly complex and uneven process is based on a study of thirty examples where these processes were evident.

All the negotiation initiatives took place as a result of unrest, turmoil and the destabilization of the status quo. Where power is distributed unequally and legitimate channels of popular political expression are absent, then the poorer classes have only the capacity to disrupt to bring their grievances to the attention of the ruling class. When this fails to draw a response from the state, then local power élites come under tremendous pressure to take the initiative.

Over and over again, white representatives of local government or business admitted that they agreed to negotiate because sustained levels of unrest were having a negative impact on the morale and political economy of their towns and cities. People in business were deeply disturbed by the consumer boycotts; local government technocrats were horrified that such anger existed about Development Board administration; municipal councillors wanted to restore peace to their cities; and many interests wanted to end the ongoing strikes, stayaways and stoppages that were crippling the local urban economy. With central state promising only more repression to weed out the agitators, the initiative inevitably came from within the local white establishment.

Black community organizations were aware that spiralling violent conflict, the brunt of which was borne by the youth, could not be sustained over time. As a result, they started negotiations. The rationale for this process can be summarized as follows:

1. Community leaders are obliged to address grievances and demands in practical ways, including bringing them to the attention of the authorities. However, they were in the unenviable position of having to demand concessions from the authorities without the advantage of access to state institutions through which these demands could be made. Not surprisingly, alternative methods were sought.

2. Once community organizations have taken political and ideological control of the township, they do not have coercive control. They therefore have a choice. They can take on the state and risk full-frontal confrontation, or reach a temporary accommodation with it. The first option would mean turning the townships into liberated zones. In the absence of a permanent people's army to defend these zones along lines seen in northern Mozambique during the anti-colonial war, the communities had no chance of winning a confrontation. The alternative, therefore, lay in demanding recognition as the representative of the community until the organizational power at national level was sufficiently strong to take on the state.

   This is a classic pattern of power distribution during times of intense conflict and struggle. The arrangement is usually transitional and will culminate in revolution only if the security forces cease backing the state (as in Russia). If the security forces remain loyal but are not used to destroy the alternative power structures, dual power can lead to negotiation and greater democratization as the rival points of power are absorbed on terms more favourable to the poorer classes. This is what happened to the American ghettoes, the South American squatter movements, the Spanish Citizens Movement during the 1970s, the Filipino protest movements after Marcos, Solidarity in Poland, and the Mau Mau in Kenya.

The implications of this process for South Africa are far-reaching. Although the social movements were smashed despite their desire to negotiate, a less repressive and a more democratic long-term alternative was available.

3. Like trade unions, once community organizations have created a mass base, this base needs to be sustained by winning, through struggle, short-term gains that improve aspects of daily living. Real material concessions are required to demonstrate the benefits of collective action. Until the early 1980s, community organizations tended to be élitist and without an organized mass base. The conventional wisdom was 'when you are weak, negotiate; but when you are strong, attack'. The organizational logic the union movement applied from 1979 was the reverse: 'when you are weak, organize; but when the majority are organized, negotiate and seek recognition.'

The reason for the opposing organizational logic was simple: unlike the unions, the élitist community organizations did not require concessions because they had no mass base to sustain. Radical rhetoric and mass meetings were sufficient. This all changed. The union logic now pervades the community organizations, which recognize that because the South African struggle is going to be long and drawn out, mass organization needs to be sustained over time. This cannot be done without winning short-term gains and gearing organization to struggle around immediate realizable goals without losing sight of the long-term objectives.

4. The most powerful argument against negotiations is the notion that they cannot take place at local level until state power at national level has been transferred to the majority. Strict purist interpretation of the non-collaborationist principle no longer has much support among those who accept that local-level negotiation will help strengthen organization over time.

5. The notion that negotiating with the state lends legitimacy to apartheid structures is rejected because, says one activist, 'just as trade unions that negotiate with management do not legitimise capitalism, nor should apartheid be legitimised simply because community organisations are

making short- to medium-term demands on local officials'.

Just as unions agreed to contest the terms of the management–labour relationship by entering the industrial bargaining system, so too have community organizations begun contesting the terms of the state–community relationship.

Implicit in this emergent process of local-level negotiations is an alternative urban management policy framework. The traditional wisdom in urban policy thinking assumes that urban conflict and politics can be managed best by local state institutions that replicate at city level the representative mechanisms that exist at central level. This notion of city government is highly developed in the liberal democracies. To be most effective, city government requires three conditions:

1. legitimate representative democratic institutions at central level;
2. a significant degree of autonomy for local government; and
3. mechanisms for direct participation in planning by grassroots constituencies.

None of these conditions exists in South Africa. Nevertheless, the cities are undergoing a fundamental transformation that will lay the basis for their future form and function, no matter what government is in power.

If the conditions for successful city government in the traditional urban policy mould are absent, what is the alternative? The industrial relations system may be relevant. In this arena there are conflicting interests that are no less intense or significant than those that exist in the city. However, unlike in the city context, the dominant interests — in this case management — have recognized the legitimacy of the structures that represent the subordinate interests, the workers. This is the only basis for bargaining in good faith.

In the cities, state policy contradicts this fundamental policy principle. Not only is the state, which should be the primary bargaining partner, totally opposed to recognizing the community organizations that represent the majority, but it has committed considerable resources to the task of forcibly eliminating these organizations.

Although local-level negotiations are rejected by the state, as organization recovers, these initiatives will re-emerge. In places like Durban, the Eastern Cape, the Eastern Transvaal and Johannesburg this has already started. If reformist sections of the state can organize a positive response to these initiatives, then using the local-level negotiations that took place as a precedent and borrowing from the industrial relations policy framework, the creation of urban bargaining forums may be conceivable.

These forums may be city-specific and could be arenas where the state and representative mass-based community organizations could bargain over the terms of urban living. Like the Industrial Councils in the industrial relations sphere, the decisions arrived at should be legally binding. An urban court may be required to arbitrate on certain kinds of disputes.

Conclusion: local political strategies and future policy options

There are three influential local government policy frameworks available at the moment.

1. the government's PLA/RSC option, that rests fundamentally on a consociational theory of society;

2. the federalist limited government option that envisages the maximum devolution of power to autonomous local and regional states, whose sovereignty in relation to central government must be constitutionally entrenched; and

3. an emerging social democratic policy framework that has support among a wide range of interests, from business on the right to the ANC on the left. (The Private Sector Council of the Urban Foundation is moving towards a local government framework that accepts the principles of non-racialism, democracy and redistribution without tying this to a federalist agenda nor, for that matter, to any explicit constitutional order. The recent Constitutional Guidelines of the ANC identify the devolution of power to strong local government as an important ingredient of the overall 'national democratic' constitutional framework.)

The four types of local political strategies identified in this chapter will be used in different combinations by social actors to achieve some variation of these three local government policy options.

The strategy that has the most potential for success is one that builds broad coalitions around purely anti-apartheid objectives and uses every means to realize this limited goal. There are more actors and interests who share an anti-apartheid objective than who share a common conception of a future beyond apartheid. If this strength combines in a broad front of elements that together use all possible strategies to contest the apartheid city — elections, local coalitions, local-level negotiations and mass resistance — then the result may well be effective and robust city movements.

Many groups, interests, parties and movements to the left of the government are already moving in this direction. Although this is part of an overall national strategy to broaden their base, how they operate at city level may determine their effectiveness and coherence at national level.

All interests to the left of the NP will need to make two fundamental choices: first, a tactical policy decision on whether or not to participate in broad front coalition politics; and second, a longer-term policy on how to intervene and operate at the level of city politics.

Acknowledgements

I would like to thank Lisa Seftel and Janet Cherry for their useful comments on earlier drafts of this paper. However, responsibility for the arguments and conclusions in this paper lie entirely with myself.

Select bibliography

Blunt, P., 'Conditions for basic need satisfaction in Africa through decentralised forms of decision making', *The Journal of Applied Behavioral Science*, vol. 20, no. 4, pp. 403–21.

Brus, W., *The politics and economics of socialism*, London: Routledge and Kegan Paul, 1973.

Cobbett, W., Glaser, D., Hindson, D. and Swilling, M., eds., 'South Africa's regional political economy: a critical analysis of reform strategies in the 1980s', in South African Research Services, *South African Review no. 3*, Johannesburg: Ravan Press, 1986.

Dahl, R., *Dilemmas of pluralist democracy*, London: Yale Univ. Press, 1984.

Du Plsanle A. and Lombard, J., 'Removal of discrimination against blacks in the political economy of the Republic of South Africa', Assocom Memorandum, 1985.

Lijphart, W., 'Power-sharing in South Africa', *Policy Papers in International Affairs no. 24*, Berkeley: Univ. of California, 1985.

Louw, L. and Kendall, F., *South Africa: the solution*, Ciskei: Amagi Publications, 1986.

Swilling, M., 'Living in the interregnum: crisis, reform and the socialist alternative', *Third World Quarterly*, vol. 9, no. 2, 1987, pp. 408–37.

Watson, V., 'Towards new forms of local government in a future South Africa', in Tötemeyer and Heymans, *Government by the people?*, Kenwyn: Juta, 1988.

23 Black strategies for change in a constrained society

John D. Brewer

Black politics in South Africa stands at the crossroads. It can go underground and engage in illegal, clandestine activity, moving increasingly towards terrorism. Or it can adopt non-violent strategies, working to a large extent within the system for change. This chapter argues that the goverment bears the primary responsibility for making it possible for black political groups to choose this option, and outlines the various non-violent strategies available. It argues that black South Africans have not yet reached the last resort.

Introduction

Black politics has been strengthened by the legal space allowed it prior to the States of Emergency. Therein lies a paradox. There is a danger that the gains made in political mobilization and consciousness will diminish unless black political groups can continue to politically engage the state, but the legal and extra-legal constraints on their political activity are now the most severe in the country's history. Draconian legislation, and ruthless and violent conduct by the security forces also limit the possibilities for mass insurrection. Moreover, conservative governments are in power in the West and they remain to be convinced that they should intensify international pressure to aid and facilitate mobilization inside South Africa. In such circumstances, black politics stands at the beginnings of a descent into paramilitary-style terrorism, which is a strategy for change which needs to (and can) be avoided.

Black politics in South Africa stands at the crossroads. It can go underground and engage in illegal, clandestine activity, moving increasingly towards terrorism; or it can adopt non-violent strategies, working to a large extent within the system for change.

This chapter argues that the government bears the primary responsibility for making it possible for black political groups to choose this option, and outlines the various non-violent strategies available. It argues that black South Africans have not yet reached the last resort.

John F. Kennedy once said that 'those who make peaceful revolution impossible will make violent revolution inevitable'. In a society in which black South Africans have so few legal opportunities to protest against apartheid, an analysis of their possible strategies for change must begin by recognizing that the obvious choice is one between peaceful and violent means. This in turn defines the choice before the government and its supporters.

It is no longer — nor has it been for a long time — a case of whether or not to introduce change, but of how it will be brought about. The end result must be a transformation of South Africa: the choice is how to achieve it.

The conduct of the government is the single most important influence on whether blacks opt for peaceful or violent strategies for change. The government can either propel blacks in desperation towards violence or encourage negotiation. The conditions for violence are present in South Africa; the government, more so than other actors, has within its making the conditions for peace.

Since the 1976 uprisings the underlying base of black politics has been strengthened to an extent that it is difficult to see blacks becoming quiescent again, despite the confined space for legal political activity. The constraints imposed on them offer a potential legitimacy to terrorist-style violence. This chapter outlines alternative strategies by which blacks can push for change non-violently. It also identifies the set of choices before the government to make it possible for blacks to opt for peaceful strategies for change with reason and justification.

The descent into terrorism can be prevented, but it will be argued that the government bears the primary responsibility for this choice.

Structural changes in black politics

In the heady days of the insurrection in South Africa between 1984 and 1986, black politics seemed at its zenith. Political rhetoric reflected this optimism, but references to easy victories have diminished since the imposition of the States of Emergency. In February 1988 the government prohibited political activity by seventeen anti-apartheid organizations, including the United Democratic Front (UDF), effectively banning all peaceful political protest outside state-sponsored political platforms.

Despite this, black politics is stronger than it ever has been; the state has merely suppressed some of the more accessible organizational manifestations of protest. This strength lies in a series of changes, realignments and alliances within black politics, affecting the level of mobilization, political consciousness and organizational skill of black South Africans, and is independent of the institutional structures which give expression to it.

Since 1976 there has been a transformation in black politics. While the problems black South Africans face are old and familiar, the circumstances in which they confront these problems are new; so too are the alliances employed to achieve them, changing the nature of the 'revolutionary terrain' in South Africa.[1] The deracialization measures introduced by the government have been foremost among these new circumstances and have affected black politics in many ways.[2]

Forty, or even thirty years ago, many of the reforms would have been heralded as very significant indeed. That they are viewed as inadequate by most black people confirms how radicalized blacks have become.

In 1960 the Defiance Campaign came to an end with the banning of the leading political organizations. By contrast, the State of Emergency twenty-five years later is unlikely to dissipate the mood of opposition because it has become so diffused throughout the whole of black life. Black opposition to apartheid is expressed in the rich indigenous poetry emerging from literary groups in the townships, in sport, religion, street daubings, in dance and song, worker activism, schools and consumer boycotts. It occurs in the urban townships and increasingly in formerly conservative rural areas.

Organizations may be hamstrung, but the diffusion of resistance has meant that political quiescence has given way to a willingness to confront the government in whatever way is possible, resulting in the politicization of ordinary aspects of everyday life.

At one level, mass collective action has the value of registering collective anger. But, in the long term, collective action should be judged by whether it raises political consciousness and leads to organizational forms of opposition. Despite the current restrictions, the political activity of the 1976–86 period has been effective in expanding the constituency for change, in incorporating formerly politically conservative sections, especially in the rural areas, in encouraging people to make political sacrifices, and in facilitating the expansion of immediate concerns into a more generalized challenge to apartheid.

This maturation in black political consciousness was also demonstrated in the tactical and organizational sophistication shown by political and community groups prior to the States of Emergency. A variety of organizations were formed to channel protest and make it concrete and their operation showed tactical agility. Black South Africans realized the futility

---

[1] H. Adam and K. Moodley, *South Africa without apartheid*, Berkeley: California Univ. Press, 1986; J. D. Brewer, *After Soweto: an unfinished journey*, Oxford: The Clarendon Press, 1987; J. D. Brewer, 'Internal black protest' in J. D. Brewer, ed., *Can South Africa survive?* London: Macmillan, 1988; R. Cohen, *Endgame in South Africa*, London: James Currey, 1986; S. Johnson, *South Africa: no turning back*, London: Macmillan, 1988; and J. Saul and S. Gelb, *The crisis in South Africa*, London: Zed Press, 1986.

[2] Brewer, 'Internal black protest'.

of working independently, and there were organizational links between students, trade unionists and political movements. Although many of these organizations have now been mollified, the significant feature is the structural realignment in black politics that lay behind this organizational capacity.

After the banning of the main political movements in 1960, politics was pursued through clandestine means. The movements in exile were largely inactive inside South Africa. With Black Consciousness, in 1969 there emerged activists who refused to participate in government-sponsored platforms but who retained a commitment to pursue opposition through peaceful and overt political activity.

Black Consciousness dominated black politics in the 1970s but it has been replaced as the dominant element by the traditional theme of non-racialism associated with the 1950s and now espoused by the UDF and its affiliates. These organizations successfully reintroduced the African National Congress (ANC) into internal politics, and it has become as important as it was before its banning in 1960, one index of which is the number of organizations and bodies which have met with ANC officials in exile.

There are many reasons why the ANC and the theme of non-racialism have re-emerged to become so popular in internal politics. Despite its isolation from the internal struggle after its banning, there was always a residue of support for the organization, but the prominence of its military activities since 1979 has given the ANC a prestige which in internal politics legitimated the non-racialist stance of the UDF and its affiliates. There was also recognition of the ANC's historic role by emerging political activists.

The growing intensity of the political struggle inside South Africa convinced the ANC of the limitations of an exile-based strategy built primarily around sabotage. The idea of non-racialism became a unifying theme which allowed the ANC to associate with some of the organizations playing an active role in internal black politics.

The realignment is significant. It links the predominantly middle class and professional support of Black Consciousness with the working-class support of the ANC. It provides the ANC with an internal wing, so that internal political movements reap the benefits of the ANC's international reputation. This alliance also makes class and labour issues more important to internal politics,[3] opening up the trade union movement and the workplace as means to pursue opposition. The new strength of black politics lies in these changes. Moreover, the realignment is independent of the organizational structure which gives expression to it.

Precisely because black politics was becoming more effective, the government moved to restrict black political activity. However, the state cannot

---

[3] T. Lodge, 'The UDF: leadership and ideology' in Brewer, *Can South Africa survive?*.

suppress all forms of political protest; there are few means available to overcome consumer boycotts or the expression of protest through everyday activities.[4] Nonetheless, while the mood of resistance is strong, the organizational thrust which gives voice to it has been culled.

This containment is unlikely to be lasting. Suppressive police and army tactics are counter-productive and militate against moribundity because the conduct of the security forces in quelling protest is treated by blacks as a litmus test of the state's commitment to change, encouraging the inference that the government is not serious about reform.

History also shows that after previous bannings blacks emerged and re-grouped stronger than before — sometimes very quickly, as after the 1977 bannings; sometimes longer, as happened after the restriction of 1960 — but regroup they did. In the long term, suppression has always been circumvented, but the example of the 1960 bannings also illustrates that the wait can be lengthy.

The potential for violence

One option is for black politics to go underground and engage in illegal, clandestine and increasingly terrorist-type activity.

This was what some activists meant when they said that the 1988 restrictions meant war. Another route is passivity and acquiescence. The banning of the major political organizations in 1960 acts as a model for both views, for this repression marked the long period of political self-effacement among black South Africans inside the country, and the transformation, however slowly, of black political organizations into guerrilla movements in exile.

Of the two options, the first is the more likely, at least in the short term. The severity of the constraints imposed on political activity since 1986 gives a potential legitimacy to this turn.

Moral conventions teach that violence is evil and a threat to civilized society. Yet all governments operate with the notion of the 'just war': international relations are premised on the idea that states will threaten or use violence when it serves national interests. The state has an effective monopoly of the means of violence and is recognized as the guardian of the public's interest and safety, factors which also legitimize the state's use of force against its own citizens, as with capital punishment.

It is easy to envisage circumstances in which it would be morally unpalatable for the state to desist from violence. Violence by citizens against their government is not so readily sanctioned. Yet contemporary events

---

[4] J. Scott, *The weapons of the weak*, New Haven: Yale Univ. Press, 1985.

reveal that members of a wide cross-section of societies in the modern world consider it acceptable to take up arms against their political rulers. The roots of violence are found in divisions which strain relationships and destroy a sense of community. Wherever disease, poverty, destitution, unemployment or discrimination serve to deepen division, they also cause violence.

However, explanation and justification are different processes, and understanding the roots of violence does not of its own give authority to its use: widespread practice does not lend legitimacy to common conduct. Some of the maxims which do justify violence against the state include the following:

▷ when the state imposes a general rule which is widely recognized to be detrimental to the majority of its citizens;

▷ when the state acts in defiance of widely accepted rules, with no recognizable benefit to the majority of its citizens;

▷ when there is no common moral code which can be used to apply pressure and sanction on the state;

▷ when violence is the last political resort and there is no other recourse available to the powerless;

▷ when force is used to quell or respond to violence by the state;

▷ when the social and moral purpose served by violence has greater priority and acceptability than the moral value placed on peace and stability; and

▷ when human suffering, and the social and moral costs of force, are less than those which would arise from failure to act violently.

The application of some of these conditions to South Africa can be challenged on the grounds that they involve relative evaluations. Nonetheless, the conduct of the South African government provides ample justification for its black citizens to resort to violence against it:

▷ It abrogates the loyalty which by right all states are owed by applying rules unfairly and selectively to its black citizens which do not operate for whites and which are unequal and detrimental in their effect.

▷ It shuns the appeals blacks make to moral and humanitarian arguments for change.

▷ It limits the options by providing so little opportunity for blacks to engage in peaceful political protest.

▷ It uses force against them and imposes suffering on them.

The States of Emergency alone would be sufficient reason for black violence against the government, let alone the state's failure to eliminate the fundamental injustices and inequalities of apartheid.

However, it does not necessarily follow that force is practical as a strategy for change. At one level, it divides people even further by making the use of violence an obstacle to reconciliation and negotiation. It automatically destroys the search for a common code between victim and aggressor by which to achieve peace in the future.

Further, black South Africans have so little capability for effective use of force, in terms of weaponry and support bases in neighbouring states, that violence is unlikely to be on a scale that will break the political impasse or quell the state's violence. This view assumes there will be no military intervention in support of blacks by the super powers, their surrogates or neighbouring countries, as there was in Namibia. Indeed, hopes for this in South Africa are very unrealistic.[5]

Violence on its own has been effective only in those societies where the ruling élite had already lost its political will and was collapsing in on itself. Although not without its problems and divisions,[6] the South African state remains determined, resolute and ruthless.[7]

It is also extremely doubtful that South African liberation movements could be turned into paramilitary-style organizations because of the absence of a prolonged tradition of military resistance in South Africa and the ANC's life-long commitment to political mobilization. This has hindered the ANC's use of violence in the past. Current thinking in the ANC, for example, is against the use of indiscriminate violence and injury of innocent civilians.

Even if there were no political constraints on the use of terror — and there is a group of younger radicals in the ANC which favours an escalation in the ruthlessness of violence[8] — the violent overthrow of the South African state by terrorism or insurrection is unlikely. The imbalance between the military strength of the state and its opponents is too great, and the necessary strategic conditions for guerrilla warfare are absent.[9] Moreover, the state's monopoly of the means of violence ensures that it can inflict greater suffering on blacks than if they desisted from violence.[10]

An escalation of black violence against whites is likely to alienate support in conservative governments in the West, if not also popular support. The

---

[5] G. Berridge, 'The super powers' in Brewer, *Can South Africa survive?*

[6] Brewer, 'Internal black protest'.

[7] H. Giliomee, 'Afrikaner politics 1976–86', in Brewer, *Can South Africa survive?*.

[8] S. Davies, *Apartheid's rebels*, New Haven: Yale Univ. Press, 1987.

[9] J. Herbst, 'Prospects for revolution in South Africa', *Political Science Quarterly*, 1988, p. 103.

[10] J. Herbst, 'Prospects for revolution'; S. Johns, 'Obstacles to guerrilla warfare: a South African case', *Journal of Modern African Studies*, 1973, p. 11; Brewer, *After Soweto*; and P. B. Rich, 'Insurgency, terrorism and the apartheid system in South Africa', *Political Studies*, 1984, p. 32.

loss of this support would reverse the trend towards the internationalization of black politics and lead to the diplomatic isolation and exclusion of the ANC. The partial political and diplomatic acceptances of the PLO is not a contrary example because it occurred only once the organization renounced terrorism.

The state's relative immunity to violence would result in its redirection against fellow blacks, simply because black opponents would be easier targets. This is something Mandela recognized and warned against when speaking from the dock in the Rivonia trial. Given that the government represents intra-black violence as mindless anarchy against which it is the main defender, an escalation in violence will serve the domestic and international interests of the regime as well as further fragment black politics.

In short, the moral sanction for violence exists in South Africa, but its practical prospects of success are poor. There remain other strategies by which blacks can strive for change.

Black South Africans have not yet reached the last resort. However, the likelihood of their choosing peaceful strategies is slim unless the government realizes that this decision depends on choices of its own. The government can do much to help blacks opt for non-violence by making this choice one that can be reasonably justified.

Possible strategies for the future

Two terms commonly used to describe the current situation in South Africa are 'impasse'[11] and 'oppressive stalemate'.[12] Both imply a redistribution of the balance of power inside South Africa to the extent that black interests and demands can no longer be entirely ignored, but not so far as to place the state in imminent threat. Stalemates can last a long time, so in itself a situation of impasse is not a catalyst for change. If terrorism is unlikely to end the stalemate and insurrection is impossible, where does black politics go from this juncture?

One strategy is for black political groups to disengage from political confrontation in favour of mobilization around educational and social issues, so that political liberation becomes sublimated into social welfare. This strategy alone will not transform South African society, but it will prepare black South Africans for that shift when it comes.

To accelerate the process, black political groups must continue to confront and engage the state. Four tactics seem feasible. They are not mutually exclusive and their effectiveness is enhanced when combined. In each case,

---

[11] J. D. Brewer, 'Five minutes to midnight' in Brewer, *Can South Africa survive?*.

[12] S. Marks and S. Trapido, 'South Africa since 1976: a historical perspective' in Johnson, *South Africa: no turning back*.

some of the costs and benefits of adopting the strategy are identified, as are the critical choices involved.

Formation of a popular front

To obtain the maximum political leverage, anti-apartheid organizations need to form a broad, popular-front coalition. The most striking features of current black politics are its internal fissures and the violence that has accompanied the polarization. The cleavages are complex and transcend the obvious conflicts between the strategies of collaboration and non-collaboration, for there are equally strong divisions within each.

Those who support the strategy of collaboration differ over what degree of association is legitimate and what reforms are necessary to win further participation in state-sponsored political machinery. An example of this is the conflict between Inkatha and the coloured and Indian parties which decided to participate in the Tricameral Parliament, leading to the break-up of the South African Black Alliance. The registered unions, as more reluctant collaborators, often find themselves opposed to those who more willingly adopt the strategy, but they are also divided among themselves over such issues as the optimal organizational scale, union democracy and politicizing the workplace.

Within the strategy of non-collaboration, the conflict between racial exclusivity and non-racialism is a major source of division. There are tactical differences over the question of armed struggle and differences over principle, such as that represented by the socialism of the National Forum and the social democracy of the Freedom Charter.

Internal schisms are natural where there is space to express political ideas, but are a luxury when the state is attempting to crush black political mobilization. Divisions turn blacks inward and against one another, whereas whatever leverage they have should be marshalled for a united assault, leaving dissension until the post-apartheid election, much on the Zimbabwean model.

The benefits of coalition are many and show themselves in domestic and international politics. It would halt faction fighting between supporters of black political movements, and so overcome the ambivalence this creates in Western attitudes towards South Africa's liberation. Co-operation at an organizational level would also clearly identify both the nature of the struggle and the protagonists, and so concentrate international support.

A popular front would cement links between supporters at grassroots, transcending class, regional, generational and ethnic cleavages. Events in black politics during the 1980s illustrate the tactical advantages that followed the formation of coalition groups like the UDF, the National Forum and the Congress of South African Trades Unions (Cosatu), and the associations between them, as exemplified by the co-operation between the UDF and Cosatu.

These pragmatic alliances expanded the constituency working for change, incorporated into the struggle large segments of the population, linked political and trade union mobilization to encourage the articulation of workplace and community issues, and undercut some important social divisions in South African society. Workers were united with the middle class urban groups and the unemployed, the young with the old, rural dwellers with those in urban areas, and migrant workers with settled employees. Expanding these alliances further would increase the potential for political mobilization.

Alliances already formed have created three identifiable power blocks within black politics: the UDF and Charterist faction of the ANC; Inkatha; and the orthodox Black Consciousness tradition of the National Forum and Azapo— each of which carries with it trade union federations and support among black workers. Talks have been held to widen the alliance still further. The ANC recently met with Inkatha, and the UDF and Azapo have discussed ways to overcome their differences. The political revival of the ANC inside South Africa, through a mobilization by the UDF and Cosatu, is such that other political leaders, including Buthelezi, cannot overlook it.

The support base of Inkatha is sufficient to ensure that it cannot be ignored, but Buthelezi will never be strong enough to become the dominant force in black politics,[13] for his power base is limited to rural KwaZulu and, to a lesser extent, international support and white opposition parties.[14]

Calls for unity have been issued frequently by leaders of all the main black political groups.

They face two key choices. First, whether or not to endorse the axiom that unity is strength. If they can find consensus on this, another choice is on the common denominators that would form the basis of a popular front. There are many possible points of convergence beyond the truism that they share an opposition to apartheid and a commitment to abolish it.

For example, Inkatha and the UDF/Charterist faction of the ANC have similar attitudes towards a bill of rights for South Africa, and some of the promises coming from the Indaba mirror the Freedom Charter and could well have been conceived by the ANC in exile. The ambivalence of

---

13 N. Massing, 'The chief', *New York Review of Books*, 1987, p. 34.

14 J. D. Brewer, 'From ancient Rome to KwaZulu: Inkatha in South African politics' in Johnson, *South Africa: no turning back*; and R. Southall, 'Buthelezi, Inkatha and the politics of compromise', *African Affairs*, 1981, p. 80.

some independent trade unions towards some forms of economic sanctions and disinvestment blunts any sharp contrast with the stance adopted by Inkatha, and speeches by some ANC leaders considerably soften its position on economic and cultural boycotts. The UDF's opposition to violence parallels that of Buthelezi's, although supporters of each have proved difficult to control.

All political groups support the strategy of close links with the trade unions and of politicizing the workplace; none support the Tricameral Parliament or accept that sufficient reforms have been introduced to initiate the process of further negotiation. All oppose social apartheid and residential segregation, and with one voice call for the incorporation of blacks into government and for all citizens to share equally in the privileges of living in one of Africa's richest countries.

Issues like these offer the prospect of forming expedient coalitions. There are differences of nuance and approach, and disagreements over principle would remain. The pragmatic benefits of unity might outweigh the satisfaction of purity in ideology and practice, and were a popular front to be formed, any group which remained outside would have to consider the risks of becoming isolated and marginalized.

Inkatha is the least likely to participate in the front, but thereby Buthelezi risks more than he does by joining, especially if the popular front can strengthen its links with the West and undercut Buthelezi's support there.

Increasing international support

For the international community to intensify its pressure on the South African government, the alliance between internal political movements and international actors must be strengthened.

The formation of a popular front would simplify the channels of communication between international agencies and internal organizations, and concentrate Western support and allegiances. But while foreign governments would welcome it if black political groups buried their differences, this alone would not necessarily be sufficient motive for them to increase the practical steps they would be prepared to take against South Africa.

Yet the constraints on political activity inside South Africa make this essential: internal black protest is not capable of realizing fundamental change on its own. However, the international community is unwilling to intensify sanctions and has not attempted to dislodge the diplomatic log-jam that has befallen South Africa since the abortive intervention of the Commonwealth Emminent Persons Groups, although this is in part due to the delicacy of negotiations over Namibia.

Increased global support might best be achieved by a radical change in strategy. The renunciation of violence is sufficiently dramatic to effect this shift. Conservative governments in the West find the ANC's use of terror the main obstacle to closer ties, and Inkatha's pacifist stance constitutes one of Buthelezi's chief attractions.[15]

If Mandela were to simultaneously accept the conditions imposed for his release and renounce violence (which seems by all accounts the only hurdle), this would reinforce the transition in Western opinion of the ANC, and his presence alone could have a series of unintended consequences, the effects of which are impossible to estimate but could well be positive. While it would be preferable if this were to occur without pre-condition set by the government, his renunciation of violence is worth the costs if it gets him out. At that point Mandela could function as the symbol of unity and be one of the main figures consulted about South Africa's future. He is probably the only person with the stature to persuade younger and more radical activists to desist from violence, although the government would need to ensure that he was protected from assassination by right-wing vigilantes, which seems the only problem arising from his release. His freedom alone would place South Africa on the Wests' agenda again, and little practical purpose is served by him languishing as a distant figurehead for the sake of the liberation movement retaining the right to occasionally use violence.

As already indicated, the prospect of achieving much through violence is poor. It could be countered that violence and terrorism, when combined with further economic sanctions, would weaken white morale, of which there is little doubt, but it could be argued that there will be no escalation in sanctions until the popular front foresakes force (and perhaps not even then). It is also true that pressure for sanctions intensified only after black violence, as happened in 1960, 1976 and 1984, but the South African government is never again going to allow black insurrectionary violence to escalate or be publicly relayed on the world's television screens. Those in the townships who now take up arms against the security forces die with the world unawares. Nor do Namibia and Zimbabwe offer contrary cases. Guerrilla warfare in Namibia was successful only because of the participation of the Cubans in Angola; and South Africa's security forces are stronger than were Ian Smith's in pre-independent Rhodesia, and their opponents militarily weaker. However, the renunciation of violence would offer (although not necessarily guarantee) much more.

Renunciation would strengthen the alliance with the West and increase the chances of international diplomatic and economic pressures being applied. Those who now oppose the application of further pressure would be

---

[15] The support voiced in the West for the violence and terrorism of the Afghan Mujehaddin or Nicaragua's Contras is not explained by the West's conversion to the principle of violence, but more by their ideological dislike of the governments that were subject to the violence. Clearly, the South African government does not provoke the same ideological distaste.

put on the defensive by being unable to use the spectre of terrorism as an excuse for inaction. It might also increase the pressure which interest groups inside Western countries would be prepared to put on their governments to intensify action against South Africa.

To this end, black political groups need to address themselves to a broader range of Western interest groups — not only anti-apartheid groups and ethnic minorities but also business, the church, trade unions, schools, the media, women's groups, local government and so on; groups in the centre as well as the periphery of Western political systems.

Black political groups must also resolve an ambiguity in their attitude toward economic sanctions: they need to make it absolutely clear whether the people they represent are willing to be hurt by their imposition, thus undermining a defence used in the West against further international pressure. This requires clarification of the forms and degree of sanctions which blacks themselves favour, and the types of investment and economic contact they wish to retain. For example, sanctions which affect technology, technological know-how and capital have great potential as levers on the government and also involve fewer costs for black workers.

In essence then, political machinery must be established whereby internal black political movements can mobilize at an international level where there are fewer constraints, in the expectation of increasing outside pressure on the government. An institutional framework is necessary for this, which would be easier with the formation of a popular front of black opposition groups. However, this move to an international terrain requires a number of pragmatic compromises in policy and practice that will strengthen the alliance with international forces. Unless these are made, black political groups will challenge the state with minimal support from the West — a daunting scenario under current constraints.

Political mobilization inside South Africa

Black organizations should continue to engage the state politically, despite the restrictions placed on them, rather than withdraw into covert activity and leave the state effectively unchallenged. This would ensure that the aspirations of black South Africans remain on the political agenda.

There are only two options for mobilizing inside South Africa. The first is to piggy-back on those organizations which survived the clamp-down or whose political activity was not expressly forbidden; the second is to utilize some of the platforms and initiatives established by the state.

The former obviates the taint of collaboration, but it offers a poor choice because the State of Emergency has left few organizations free to engage in political activity. Only the church seems capable and willing to provide a free ride, and while the church is already politicized, any escalation might lead to restriction against it. The forums it provides for confronting the state are also limited.

The decision that black political movements have to make, therefore, is whether politically to disengage, at least inside southern Africa, or mobilize and articulate issues using structures within the apartheid state.

These structures are of two sorts. There are semi-autonomous platforms which, although within the bureaucratic bounds of the state, are not directly controlled or managed by it. Their legitimacy, finance and operations are not exclusively dependent on the state. The registered unions constitute such a platform, as do Inkatha and the white opposition parties in parliament. While political unionism is virtually impossible without severe retaliation, black political groups could work through and co-operate more closely with Inkatha and the white opposition parties advocating reform.

In many ways Inkatha is in a unique position: it is relatively immune from banning and restriction because of Buthelezi's international standing. Inkatha could push to the limit its confrontational tactics, knowing that it has some measure of protection. The choice before Inkatha would be to switch the direction of its policies toward the democratic movement to gain legitimacy and overcome its ostracism; the choice before other political organizations is whether or not to make a pragmatic rapprochement with Buthelezi in order to engage the state politically.

The prospects of this happening are decidedly poor, however, for the structural position of Inkatha in black politics prevents it from escalating its pressure on the state, and the violence between supporters of Inkatha and the UDF has been so intense that it virtually rules out co-operation. This leaves but one avenue remaining — the official platforms under more direct state sponsorship such as the township councils of local government, the various consultative bodies established by the government, or a possible fourth chamber in parliament.

A concerted campaign by the popular front to control local and regional councils, and to participate in the national political debate by using platforms of negotiation, would have the following effects:

▷ The genuine leaders of the black community would at last be given a practical role in making decisions and distributing scarce resources of importance to black South Africans.

▷ This in turn would provide them with political leadership skills, training and education as well as the opportunity to politicize a constituency which could be used to press for further change.

Two sets of problems arise. The first are presentational: such strategy would be abused as both collaboration and capitulation. Pragmatic problems also exist because the government has enveloped these structures with a web of controls from which it might be difficult to disengage.

The allegation of 'working within the system' means one or both of two things: a physical location and operation in state-sponsored platforms, and ideological or policy support for some or all of the pillars of apartheid. However, a unified popular front could argue that it is not the platform which injures credibility but the policies articulated from it. Survey research shows that most of the black population would support participation in local government structures if these bodies were to be made effective and given jurisdiction over issues relevant to blacks.

Presentational problems can be overcome if participation is seen as the beginning of a process rather than its conclusion. Working through this machinery should not be regarded as any loss of revolutionary zeal, but as a short-term tactic to achieve pre-set goals. If it was no longer considered illegitimate to adopt this strategy, some of the practical problems associated with its use would fall away.

Forms of popular protest

Pressure on the government can be maintained and the political conscious-ness of blacks kept high by non-violent popular protests and everyday resistance.

Participation in structures which allow the state to be engaged at an in-stitutional level does not preclude the use of non-violent popular protests. There is already a wide diffusion of protest in South Africa — in poetry, song, religion, the workplace, schools, graffiti and so on. It is possible to deploy an extensive range of ordinary acts whose political content can be concealed. Examples are: industrial disputes, go-slows, civil disobedience over rents, rates and other local matters, consumer boycotts, and collect-ive protests against specific localized issues superficially divorced from the national debate on change.

There are also many acts for which it is difficult to apportion blame, except in a very generalized sense. A campaign of moral pressure could be mounted to persuade black police and soldiers to resign, for example. Various forms of economic sabotage could be employed. Particular events, people, products or state symbols could be boycotted. Hunger strikes over specific issues are also effective, as illustrated by their use in 1989 to bring about the release of detainees.

While none of this achieves the necessary transformation, it maintains an undercurrent of resistance which helps sustain the political consciousness of protesters and pressure on the state. Whatever effect may be achieved is enhanced many times when these tactics are co-ordinated with political engagement at institutional level. To be most effective, therefore, resistance needs to operate on two planes — the localized, micro and everyday level, and the macro, national level.

One of the strongest arguments in support of participation in state-sponsored structures of negotiation is that they provide (unfortunately) the only possible forum by which the everyday micro forms of resistance can feed into the national debate.

The most likely direction black politics will take in the present constrained environment is to become militarized and increasingly violent, and to restrict peaceful political engagement of the state to everyday forms of resistance. This is simultaneously both an easy and difficult option. It is a soft option for black political groups because it avoids them having to confront very problematic questions about strategy, policy, relations with each other and the West, and, perhaps most serious of all, about how general are the interests of the band of supporters they represent. At the same time, this path is difficult because the chances of achieving anything by it are negligible. Constraints operate as much on guerrilla warfare as political mobilization. The military might of the state is awesome, and although the state has its weaknesses, terrorist-type violence will strengthen rather than weaken the political position of the government, both internationally and domestically. The contention of this chapter has been that there is another yet more difficult direction and, in present circumstance, it yields the greatest prospects of success.

South Africa's State of Emergency is permanent. In a legal sense, the Emergency regulations have passed into ordinary law and politically the regime will never again allow black political groups the space which nurtured their progress between 1976 and 1986. Insurrection is impossible and conservative governments in the West are reluctant to impose further sanctions.

The non-violent strategies for change identified in this chapter represent what is possible rather than desirable; the politics of realism rather than idealism. Because the strategies are second best, they require difficult decisions and impose a heavy cost, for black political leaders have to choose whether or not to make a whole series of pragmatic compromises in policy and practice to reap the advantages, such as they are, of their use.

Choices for the government

Black political groups have no difficulty with the notion of negotiation, the problem is that what appears to be acceptable to the majority of whites looks like betrayal to most blacks. For this reason the decisions of black politics are predicated on a set of prior choices by the government. If blacks are to be convinced of the utility of peaceful strategies for change, the government needs to make this a decision which is reasonable and justifiable. Three requirements are imperative:

1. The bodies of consultation established for blacks by the state should be expanded and strengthened by devolving to them greater function and power so that they are genuine structures of negotiation.

2. All political prisoners and detainees should be released and amnesty given to political exiles to allow the black community's leaders to participate in the debate on change. Most of these are precisely the men and women of non-violence who are needed to make the transition to peace: their offence was political organization and mobilization, not paramilitary activity. Mandela must be the first to be released.

3. A shift in attitude is also necessary among whites. Political mobilization and articulation by blacks needs to be de-criminalized and recognized as providing the more secure basis for stability. This is a fair return for the renunciation of violence and participation in structures of negotiation.

The intervention of a third party is essential for these conditions to be negotiated and agreed multilaterally. The ANC will not renounce violence of its own accord, so that the participation of the West becomes necessary to achieve a peaceful solution. However, the ANC could signal its willingness, through informal channels, to renounce violence (as it did during the visit of the Commonwealth Eminent Persons Group) to increase the likelihood of involvement of a third party. Western countries should be encouraged to play this role.

However, this scenario is unlikely because the South African government does not yet recognize the need for it. Its present course increases the potential for terrorism, random violence and instability, which, if not life-threatening for the regime, will be damaging to all its citizens. The government must realize that peace has to be freely chosen rather than externally imposed if it is to be lasting, and that in the long term the severe restrictions on black political activity threaten stability rather than engender it. Courageous decisions lie before political leaders of all groups in South Africa if a permanent peace is to be found.

Acknowledgement

I am grateful for the comments of participants in the 1989 Southern African Research Programme at Yale University, and students on the 1989 International Relations Programme at Brown University.

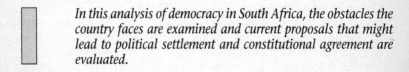

24   Towards a democratic transformation

Heribert Adam

In this analysis of democracy in South Africa, the obstacles the country faces are examined and current proposals that might lead to political settlement and constitutional agreement are evaluated.

Introduction

In the predominant outside view of South Africa there are expectations of a quick-fix solution. False analogies with conflicts elsewhere abound, reinforced by facile television images. If only stubborn whites could be induced to be flexible and see where their long-term interests lie (this thinking goes), a constitutional compromise formula could easily be found.

Conversely, if the African National Congress (ANC) could suspend violence, settle for power-sharing, accept group rights and enter into negotiations, this would resolve the predicament. Others' expect 'The Solution' to lie in the wholesale import of foreign models: 'The Swiss system is so extraordinarily appropriate for South Africa, even more so than for Switzerland itself, that we could take their constitution almost verbatim and transplant it into South Africa', write Louw and Kendall.[1]

I cannot be so optimistic about democratic transformation through the application of any single formula. The analysis that follows explores the meaning of democracy in the South African context by considering the obstacles it faces and critically evaluating existing proposals and experiments. It focuses particularly on the crucial debate about group rights. The process towards democracy — how to get there — is of more interest than the specific outcome of negotiations.

Designing an ideal South African constitution based on political equality, individual rights and the optional participation of all citizens in decision-making is easy. Yet it would be a futile exercise unless it took into account the specific historical context that has shaped South Africa's political evolution, as well as the commitments of the various social forces that help or impede the control of conflict democratically.

---

[1] Leon Louw and Frances Kendall, *After apartheid: the solution for South Africa*, San Francisco: JCS press, 1987, p. 121.

Invoking moral principles does not — by itself, at least — move constituencies or current power-holders who correctly expect to lose from the application of universal moral principles.

That said, a realistic democratic alternative, nevertheless, might inspire political initiatives. Whites will let go of apartheid more readily if they have a reassuring vision of what they are giving it up for. While almost everyone agrees that racial minority rule cannot be reformed but must be dismantled, little consensus exists as to what should replace it.

Majority rule, in the minds of most South African whites, is associated with reverse tyranny, economic decline and social dislocation. Unless substantial sections of the present power-holders can be won over to the idea of a non-racial democratic alternative, little progress seems possible, and further destruction and mutual brutalization in a simmering civil war almost inevitable.

In this impasse, debate about the post-apartheid order gains significance. It might demonstrate that people do not have to suffer the future but, on the contrary, could enjoy the future, provided they display the foresight to change policies.

Implications of democracy

Constitutions reflect power relationships rather than alter them. It would be naïve to think that a model constitution could be superimposed on an actual conflict and reconcile competing interests, thereby creating eternal harmony. A democratic constitution achieves something more modest: it merely constrains, and thereby minimizes, inevitable conflict.

It does so by channelling conflict into rule-governed modes of behaviour. These rules can be either imposed or widely agreed upon. If there is widespread consensus about the rules of political decision-making and the rights and duties of individuals, little or no coercion is needed. If, in contrast, one group dictates to others against their will, a whole machinery of force is required to make the rules stick.

This is not only costly for power-holders; often it simply does not work. It must be admitted, however, that imposed and enforced stability can endure for a long time if rulers have the resources and willpower to govern ruthlessly. An unjust regime is not necessarily an unstable one. In South Africa at present, the Emergency legislation has succeeded in restoring a superficial calm in the townships, although the causes of the protest have hardly been addressed.

Majority approval alone, however, does not necessarily produce legitimacy. The system of political rule must also be considered morally appropriate. Popular despotisms such as Nazi Germany may have mustered the consent of their people, but clearly remained illegitimate morally.

Majority rule alone does not necessarily guarantee democracy. In Northern Ireland and Sri Lanka, a pre-determined majority permanently dominates and excludes a minority. Consequently, many democracies place constraints on majority rule. The constitutional devices used are typically:
1. a guaranteed representation of all groups on the executive and legislature (power-sharing, grand coalitions);
2. a division of power between legislature and executive or between two legislative houses;
3. a devolution of power to semi-autonomous regions or groups (federalism); and
4. a minority veto on fundamental matters.

Such arrangements have become known as consociationalism.[2] The main problem in applying these proposals to South Africa is that they pre-suppose a relatively depoliticized public: an élite cartel of recognized leaders enters into controversial compromises and expects its loyal followers to accept them. This cannot be assumed in South Africa, where leaders need mandates that can be given only after free political debate. The restriction of political leadership makes this impossible. In the absence of free political activity and free elections, any black spokesperson faces the danger of 'outbidding' by rivals. Furthermore, racial group membership is controversial since it is imposed and not based on self-association.

South Africa constitutes only a partial democracy. It is a democracy for whites, for it excludes blacks from the only decision-making process that counts: white parliamentary executive politics. Coloured and Indian representatives in their separate parliaments are seen as clients of the white power-holders, and so carry dubious legitimacy in their own communities. They are dependent on white patronage and suffer the constant suspicion of co-optation.

The widespread perception that the existing South African system is illegitimate results from the exclusion of the majority, the legalized imposition of invidious racial classifications, and from the grossly unequal life chances which flow from this differential incorporation.

Three concepts of a South African nation

Constitutions reflect not only power relationships but the common values of a society, shaped by historical experience and current interests. Three different visions of a South African nation exist. They are difficult to reconcile because they are fraught with different implications for coexistence and conflict regulation.

---

2 Arend Lijphart, *Democracy in plural societies: a comparative evaluation*, New Haven: Yale Univ. Press, 1977; and Arend Lijphart, *Power-sharing in South Africa*, Berkeley, Inst. of International Studies, 1986.

1. The ultra-Right maintains that one South African nation does not exist, only different nationalities prevail, which should all be sovereign in their own territory.

2. The ruling National Party (NP) asserts: South Africa is a plural multiracial state, composed of separate but economically interdependent groups.

3. The ANC and liberals say: South Africa should strive to be a non-racial, common society where only cultural rights of self-defined groups should be recognized.

The differences between the three visions of South Africa can also be explained in terms of priorities. Roughly speaking, each group emphasizes one of the following: Group 1 stands for identity, Group 2 for security, Group 3 for prosperity. These ends are not mutually exclusive. Within each group all three goals are pursued simultaneously to varying degrees. But when they conflict, supporters of each group opt for their respective priority at the expense of the other values. Although they are inextricably interwoven, the priority value establishes the basis for different political choices and strategies.

How can the three visions, priorities and strategies be reconciled in a democratic institution? Given these predominant outlooks, can there be a democracy without democrats?

The question of group rights

The controversial question in South Africa is not whether ethno-cultural minorities should receive constitutional protection. Both the NP and the ANC agree on safeguarding linguistic, religious, educational and cultural rights of South Africa's 'different nationalities'. Both could also agree on a bill of rights which protects individuals as well as the cultural autonomy of minorities against the majority.

The sharp disagreement lies in whether a post-apartheid constitution should recognize racial groups. Is it legitimate for Afrikaners to want to institutionalize group claims on a racial basis rather than on an ethno-cultural one? Some academics have answered this question with an unequivocal 'yes', arguing that racial communities also have moral claims and rights that should be recognized in law and practice.[3]

The question goes beyond mere labels in South Africa, because race and culture do not always overlap. The institutionalization of race carries with it important political implications.

---

[3] S. P. Huntington, 'Reform and stability in a modernizing multi-ethnic society', *Politicon*, vol. 8, no. 2, Dec. 1981, p. 13.

Constitutional recognition of an Afrikaner cultural group would imply that everyone who speaks Afrikaans and/or adheres to Calvinism could join this grouping, should they so wish. Two million so-called coloured people, according to this logic, would be Afrikaners. The ruling NP (let alone the ultra-Right), however, defines an Afrikaner as a white person first and foremost. Against all genealogical evidence, or perhaps because of it, the government insists on the exclusion of the coloured people and other Afrikaner 'non-whites' from Afrikanerdom while, seemingly paradoxically, welcoming cultural aliens (English-speaking whites, other European immigrants) into the ranks.

Therefore, the principle of self-identification alone cannot solve the question of group rights. To be sure, permitting voluntary association would mean considerable progress compared with the present imposed group membership. Charles Simkins has proposed a practical way to achieve this without repealing the entire Race Classification Act: allow individuals to de-register their enforced racial classification.

The existence of such a 'colour-blind' group, however, would still not settle the offensive exclusion on the basis of arbitrary racial group boundaries by those who insist on a racial monopoly.

Clearly, the right of free association carries with it the right of disassociation. But should Afrikaners who insist on whiteness as an essential element of their Afrikanerdom be permitted legally to disassociate themselves from those who wish to define Afrikanerdom in non-racial, cultural terms?

Racial associations would be easier to tolerate if they were confined to the private sphere. But racial groups in South Africa inevitably clamour for recognition as public bodies and claim political rights and privileges for their racially organized formations. If they were denied that recognition because of their racial organizing principle, that would violate the right of self-definition of groups. Faced with this dilemma, Western democracies have generally tolerated racial groups, such as the Ku Klux Klan, but have used the criminal code to outlaw undesirable behaviour.

In South Africa, however, most white Afrikaners want more than to be tolerated in the private sphere. In the name of national self-determination they claim a public role as a racial group.

With racial exclusiveness, however, goes access to and denial of political power. The coloured people are excluded from Afrikanerdom not only because of bigotry. From the Nationalist Afrikaner perspective, the political inclusion of the coloured people on a common voters' roll would have jeopardized their parliamentary majority. Political inclusion would also have meant their sharing in the economic advancement of Afrikanerdom. Hence, tolerance of racial group claims in the political realm always amounts to much more than 'dignity' denied.[4]

There is another constitutional version of group rights that suggests a compromise in a bi-communal constitution. The Indaba model adopted a similar concept. It allows those who want to organize on a non-racial basis ('South Africans') the same rights and representation as those who want to exercise their political will as racial groups. Both blocs could then coexist according to each group's organizational preference, but they would share political power.

The Indaba model envisages a second chamber in which ten out of fifty seats would be allocated to those who do not wish to define themselves in ethno-racial group terms. Other models allow for both a racial and a non-racial house, or even one parliament with a racial and a non-racial party group.

Most of these proposals have (like the Indaba model) fixed quotas for each group in mind, irrespective of election results. Voting strength would be reflected only in a first chamber, elected on the basis of a colour-blind universal franchise.

In view of the election procedure for the United States Senate and other examples of fixed representation, regardless of constituency size, such an arrangement cannot be considered undemocratic *per se*. In South Africa, however, minority over-representation would cause deep resentment, as did the 20 per cent seats for 3 per cent of the population that was white in the original Lancaster House constitution for Zimbabwe. Nevertheless, the guaranteed representation and veto power of such sizeable minorities could be an item for serious negotiation.

Even more important would be minority representation in the military and civil service. The likelihood of a settlement in South Africa is very low unless the security anxieties of whites are met by some form of guaranteed participation in a future post-apartheid army.

In return for relinquishing exclusive political control, Afrikaner nationalists would most likely insist on a security fall-back in case the constitutional guarantees are violated. There is as yet no evidence as to what kind of compromise in this area would be acceptable to the ANC.

Would police be recruited from the communities they work in? Would an integrated army nevertheless tolerate ethnic units in practice? How would the officer corps be trained and recruited? Where would the present

---

4 Arend Lijphart, 'Ethnic factor and democratic constitution-making in South Africa', in Edmond Keller and Louis A. Picard, eds., *South Africa in southern Africa: domestic change and international conflict*, Boulder Colorado: Lynne Rienner, 1988.

Afrikaner colonels and policemen be employed and under whose command? Academics have focused the consociational debate on the constitutional arena, but have neglected to extend the search for potential compromise formula to the real centres of power in the economy and security apparatus.

Some advocates of bi-communalism and group representation rest their case on its alleged cross-racial appeal, pointing to 'significant numbers within the coloured and Indian communities which prefer to exercise their rights and make their claims on a communal basis'.[5] This popular projection of Afrikaner nationalism on to other groups remains questionable and is empirically doubtful.

Since the repeal of the Political Interference Act, a change in the South African party system towards ideological rather than racial formations is a theoretical possibility. If this fundamental change were effected, undoubtedly many more blacks would vote for white candidates than prejudiced whites can imagine. Far from remaining in frozen racial categories, the plurality of black attitudes and vastly different ideological outlooks would come to the surface.

Unlike the rest of Africa where one-party systems reflect homogeneous underdevelopment, the modern South African economy has brought about highly stratified interest groups. Racial classifications impose a deceptive homogeneity on the groups. Once freed of the artificial racial bonds, a multiracial, multi-party system would open opportunities for shifting coalitions and cross-racial alliances, according to common interests rather than skin colour.

If a black working class, which is free to organize, already spawns dozens of unions that cannot agree on strategies and ideologies, how much more so would this diversity apply to a free political realm! Long-term interests of the declining white numerical minority would be far better safeguarded through party solidarity with like-minded black citizens than through racial group representation.

Are African and Afrikaner nationalism comparable?

One of the greatest bogeys in the minds of the white minority is that of reverse tyranny. However, the ANC's non-racialism is not a tactical ploy.

---

5 Hermann Giliomee, 'Movement towards democratic bi-communalism as a way out of an impossible situation', Lecture at Queens Univ., Belfast, 22 Feb. 1988. See also Hermann Giliomee and Lawrence Schlemmer, eds., *Negotiating South Africa's future*, London: Macmillan, 1989; and Hermann Giliomee and Lawrence Schlemmer, *From apartheid to nation-building*, Cape Town: Oxford Univ. Press, 1989, p. 211, where it is argued that South Africa 'is primarily a struggle between Afrikaner and African nationalists'. For a critical discussion of this notion of a communal conflict, see my review of both books, 'The Polish path', *Southern Africa Review of Books*, Dec. 1989.

ANC executives admit that non-racialism was not uncontroversial and did not come easily in the light of racist experiences in all spheres of life.

Although it would have probably been more promising to lean towards the Pan African Congress (PAC) orientation of Africanist exclusivism and counter-racism to mobilize blacks, the ANC movement has stuck to its liberal tradition of universalism. The movement is now confident that this moral universalism remains sufficiently entrenched to withstand any future assault.

'The very strange fact that we have to struggle to maintain it has drilled non-racialism into the average ANC member so that it is almost second nature. It will not be easily erased. Any ANC leadership of the future that sought to abrogate non-racialism would need to de-indoctrinate that majority of the membership into rejecting it first',[6] wrote one of the organization's senior officials, Pallo Jordan. The same goes for Inkatha.[7]

While the ANC can claim the mantle of leadership as the oldest anti-apartheid movement as well as the organization with the most popular support country-wide, it clearly does not have a monopoly of principled opposition. Unlike SWAPO, it has never claimed to be the 'sole representative' of the black population, nor has it claimed to represent only blacks.[8]

The single most important difference between the ANC and its Afrikaner nationalist counterpart involves neither the use of violence nor socialism. The issue boils down to the recognition of racial group rights. The ANC maintains it will not compromise on this issue; it insists on guarantees of individual rights as sufficient to protect the collective interests of every South African. It refuses to make concessions to racial privileges, regardless of pragmatic calculations. A 'liberatory intolerance', the ANC argues, must be adopted toward any advocate of racial institutions — even self-chosen associations, in so far as they are racial.

Given the historically entrenched colour-consciousness in the apartheid land, does this stance necessarily make a future ANC government as authoritarian as its predecessor? How would a Mandela government cope with a substantial minority of race-conscious, ethnically inspired groupings, particularly the white ultra-Right?

Afrikaner nationalists, on the other hand, want veto power for whites as

---

[6] Pallo Jordan, 'Why won't Afrikaners rely on democracy', *Die Suid-Afrikaan*, Feb., 1988, p. 25.

[7] Although Buthelezi has been frequently accused of fanning tribalism, particularly of being anti-Indian, he has vehemently rejected the label 'Indian-hater': 'I have never had problems with the Indian community *per se*. I have only had problems with some Indian leaders who posture in their attempts to be blacker than the blackest South African.' (Letter to the editor, *Daily News*, 10 March, 1988.) Although using Zulu history and ethnic symbols as a mobilizing device, Inkatha's leadership has always stressed a 'race-free' South Africa as a goal.

[8] *Optima*, Sept. 1987, p. 132.

a group and guaranteed participation as a minority in government decision-making. The NP views universal franchise as permanent disenfranchisement of its constituency and the destruction of Afrikanerdom as a political force. From their perspective, the universalism of the ANC is self-serving; the movement can afford it, since it will always have a numerical majority in the country.

ANC spokesmen view this suspicion as a projection of white racism on to blacks. Afrikaners, on the other hand, point to the fate of Jews in the Diaspora. The ANC takes strong exception to this analogy, because it implies that an ANC government is capable of inflicting a holocaust. In response, critics of the ANC stress that good intentions by a non-racial leadership become irrelevant when the objective conditions arise for retribution and restitution for historical deprivation. In such conditions, they suspect, even a democratic government will be forced to adopt undemocratic policies.

The ANC's claims that it represents universal inclusiveness as opposed to the Afrikaner racial exclusiveness, is dismissed as a tactical ploy, albeit one motivated by good intentions. 'Your non-racial democracy', writes Hermann Giliomee (of the department of Political Studies at the University of Cape Town) to an ANC executive, 'is, after all, only an ideology which is to help your black nationalism come into power, and, if you succeed in that, to justify your regime.' The underlying fear is 'that your nationalist movement, as a result of circumstances, can be just as oppressive as my Afrikaner nationalism has become.'[9]

Given the mutual suspicions, the South African conflict clearly goes beyond a struggle over power and privilege. In the perceptions of the white side, at least, the conflict provokes existential anxieties about a loss of identity, a fear of lowered standards, of being swallowed by an encroaching Third World, and ultimate loss of control, deemed necessary for security and survival.

Is South Africa, therefore, an intractable communal conflict, comparable to endemic strife in plural societies elsewhere? Or has it enough of a common society — with shared languages, Christian religious culture and consumerism — to bind its citizens together, provided equal political rights and opportunities are created?[10]

The answer depends in part on one's faith and optimism. Empirical and comparative historical evidence can be marshalled for either proposition.

Making the assumption that ethnicity is a primordial given supports the

---

[9] Herman Giliomee, *Die Suid-Afrikaan*, Feb., 1988.

[10] This is argued in Heribert Adam and Kogila Moodley, *South Africa without apartheid*, Berkeley: Univ. of California Press, 1986, pp. 196–214.

pessimistic scenario: an intractable communal conflict. If politicized ethnicity, however, is construed as a fostered and manipulated attitude, an
outlook dependent on circumstances, it is conceivable that even Afrikaners
will shed their historical ideological baggage when immersed in new structural realities and when ethnicity is muted through changing patterns of
inter-group contact and interest-based association.[11]

In this view, held also by the ANC, Afrikaners are as rational as other
people: the South African conflict will lend itself to bargaining and compromise when both sides are approximately equal in power, when the costs
of apartheid maintenance exceed the benefits. There will be no negotiations
as long as no shared perception of stalemate exists.

Towards a political settlement

Once the power equation between the state and the opposition reaches a
stalemate in the perception of both antagonists, a political settlement can
be envisaged as a possibility of drawn-out negotiations.

There are two ways to reach a legitimate constitutional agreement.

An appointed commission of experts and representatives of all the relevant interest groups can work out a draft proposal. This constitutional
draft is then put to a referendum. A successful plebiscite brings the new
constitution into effect.

This procedure, however, remains suspect for groups who expect to be in
a minority position or to lose power under a new constitution. Such groups
usually boycott the exercise and thereby deprive it of legitimacy during the
drafting stage. This was the case with the well-intentioned Natal Indaba,
which was shunned by both the ANC/UDF (United Democratic Front) and
the NP, which adopted only observer status.

Generally speaking, commissions of constitutional experts labour under widespread scepticism; they are suspected of being sophisticated co-
optation devices controlled by the powers that be.

Democracy resists administration from above. If it appears to be a gift
from the rulers to the ruled, it lacks legitimacy because the 'gift' implies
the absence of moral equality. A sense of empowerment is psychologically
necessary for democratic consent. Thus, the proposed forum for constitutional negotiations has been stillborn. It will lack legitimacy, regardless of
who can be enticed to serve on it.

Only when a free citizenry defines the terms of its participation do the
rules people live by attain legitimacy. That is why a referendum usually

---

[11] Indeed, social science evidence from the American South in the 1960s suggests that 'stateways can change
folkways'. In other words, changing peoples behaviour through enforcement of new laws eventually — and
sooner rather than later — changes their attitudes.

precedes a new constitution. When, on the short-sighted advice of unrepresentative 'leaders', Pretoria in 1983 reneged on the promised referendum among coloured and Indian voters, the new constitutional proposals became fatally flawed. The contrast to white political activity could not have been greater. For whites, a referendum was held after an intense public debate.

A second procedure for reaching a legitimate constitutional settlement is the election of an assembly by direct, popular vote on the basis of proportional representation. This is more feasible for a divided society like South Africa. It carries its own direct political mandate and claims to legitimacy.

This constitutional heritage from the French Revolution and the liberal tradition would settle a vexing problem in South Africa: the conflicting and inflated claims of support for the different contenders. An election for a constituent assembly on the basis of universal franchise would restore the credibility of the political process and allow all sides to save face. Any group would be hard put to reject participating peacefully in the democratic exercise. During the lengthy transition to a new order, the current government would still be in full control until the new constitution had been accepted.

There could also be a stipulation that each political organization would nominate candidates with specified expertise (university education, legal background, work experience in the public realm) for the assembly rather than high-profile leaders.

This delegation of interest representation by previously lesser known figures would keep personal animosity or status considerations among leading spokespersons from interfering with the deliberations. It would also guard against the assembly deteriorating into a free-for-all publicity stunt. Moreover, one could allow for candidates to be nominated by their organizations but, once elected, not be personally tied to the organization's directives. Individual independence — like judges bound by judicial procedures and individual conscience only — would allow the process and chemistry of negotiations to work on the participants. The first test of the assembly would come when it devised its own working procedures.

The constitutional outcome of deliberations by democratically elected constitution-makers would be wide open. It may be that no Western model fits the unique circumstances of South Africa. No imported model ought to be held up as a yardstick; whatever is acceptable to the major constituent groups will be legitimate by definition.

As a conservative American has rightly pointed out: 'If England can have a queen and Americans a Senate that gives 40 times more influence to a voter in sparsely populated Wyoming than to a voter in California, then it seems to me that there is a broad range of "democratic" outcomes that can be envisaged in South Africa.'

Epilogue: towards the future

The pressure of events in South Africa recently, has given rise to further political developments. Here these events since the writing of the foregoing chapter are assessed.

The release of prominent political prisoners, the *de facto* unbanning of the ANC by allowing huge mass rallies, and the conciliatory rhetoric on the part of the new South African President, F. W. de Klerk, mean only one thing: both sides are moving towards negotiations rather than continued civil war.

While formal negotiations between the antagonists in South Africa are a long way off, and their aims are poles apart, informal contacts between the ANC and the Afrikaner establishment continue to take place since the historic Dakar meeting in July 1987. Even Mandela, despite his imprisonment, has met several cabinet ministers for exploratory talks about talks. It was Mandela who demanded the meeting with President P. W. Botha shortly before his resignation in August 1989. Normally state presidents do not meet their political prisoners unless they are forced to by a stronger rationale. Such has become the messianic standing of Mandela that he can now almost dictate the terms of his release. He will not leave jail unless conditions are ripe and he and his organization can play a meaningful role.

In the meantime, Mandela has been visited in his comfortable prison compound by most of the leading activists inside the country. As a result, a 76-page Mandela document outlines a new strategy in light of government initiative to draw the ANC into negotiations. Some government planners hope to expose the ANC as 'unreasonable' in this process, perhaps split the organization and use rivals for a multiracial internal settlement. This then, it is envisaged in Pretoria, would lead to the re-admission of the country into the international community and the lifting of sanctions.

The Mandela strategy anticipates such manoeuvring. By carefully co-ordinating his role with the exiles in Lusaka and the internal leadership, maximum unity is ensured, Above all, Mandela counsels his followers to strive for internal unity of all black groupings, including Bantustan leaders who are usually denounced as collaborators. Already Chief Minister Enos Mabuza of KaNgwane has frequently consulted with Lusaka. Recently, the military leader of Transkei, General Bantu Holomisa, seems also to waver in his loyalty to his sponsors in Pretoria. There is talk about the re-incorporation of this 'independent' state into South Africa. For the first time again, massive ANC demonstrations have been allowed in Umtata. The first Bantustan could well become a solid power base of the ANC.

The outstanding question remains whether Buthelezi's Inkatha will be re-admitted into the ANC as well. In this respect the fragile intermittent peace talks in Natal go well beyond their regional significance. While Mandela strongly advocates the inclusion of the Zulu movement into the ANC, where Buthelezi had his political home before their split in 1979, many younger ANC executives in Lusaka oppose such a development. While this question remains unresolved, the mutual killings in Natal continue.

In a perceptive new book,[12] veteran journalist Allister Sparks argues that with the banning of the ANC in 1961 and its turn to armed struggle, the oldest and most legitimate anti-apartheid movement virtually opted out of politics. At its consultative conference in 1985 the ANC still envisaged negotiations only about the hand-over of power. At present, Sparks points out, we witness the re-entry of the boycotting opposition movement into politics. This process is not about surrender of one side or the other, but new alliances, bargaining and compromise.

The ANC's continued commitment to armed struggle should be no obstacle to such a development. It has been largely a symbolic exercise anyway. The few bombs or mines, which mostly go off at night as a reminder, also helped the government to mobilize its constituency against a 'terrorist threat'. But the symbolic armed struggle mainly benefited the ANC for another reason than threatening a firmly entrenched opponent. It gave an essentially moderate ANC leadership an aura of militancy. Thus the frustrated township youth could be kept in the non-racial camp rather than having them drift away into a nationalist counter-racism and anarchy. Were the ANC to renounce violence formally, as the government demands, it would commit political suicide. The ANC must also insist on tangible preconditions for negotiations being met in order to demonstrate to a sceptical constituency the benefits of negotiations.

The crucial sticking points of the eventual bargaining will be Pretoria's insistence on guaranteed racial group rights, at least for a long transitional period. The fallacy of this stance lies in a dwindling minority setting itself up for continuous hostility. In addition, constitutional racial minority status will prevent whites from mentally adjusting to being part of Africa. Only a small liberal minority of whites realizes that a protection of values which many other racial group members share will be a far better guarantee of individual white security than racial group rights. Alas, when the chips are down and the pressure for a negotiated compromise is on, a Zimbabwe-type guarantee of minority representation, regardless of numbers, will probably emerge nonetheless. Afrikaner nationalism and white security anxieties are simply too strong to be ignored completely.

In the most optimistic scenario of minority representation, a common voters role would at least allow voting across the colour bar: whites could

---

12 Alister Sparks, *The mind of South Africa*, New York: Knopf (forthcoming).

vote for a non-racial, black-led ANC and blacks for a white-led NP, which would essentially represent conservative interests. That would be a departure from the Rhodesian model. Since many blacks share a capitalist law-and-order orientation, the opening of the NP to voters from non-white groups would allow it to break out of its racial ghetto. Under such conditions, entrenched minority party guarantees, which would apply to all political parties under a system of proportional representation, could indeed be justified.

Three other contentious areas of compromise stand out:

1. recognition of property rights with only limited redistribution of wealth;
2. state guarantees for cultural rights, especially subsidized mother-tongue instruction in Afrikaans language schools; and
3. guarantees of physical security by keeping police and army units under community control.

In all three areas a potential compromise formula is conceivable. Since the South African conflict is over power and privilege, it is bargainable and negotiable. That distinguished the dismantling of racial domination from far more intractable communal or religious conflicts elsewhere.

However, once apartheid is abolished and all South African citizens are enfranchised equally, normal and real politics only begins. The material inequality among the population groups is so staggering and the development needs are so massive, that any government of whatever ideological persuasion or racial composition faces a formidable challenge. Perhaps only a broad coalition government of national unity with as wide a backing and consensus as possible can tackle this task. Only such a national pact would be able to keep in check the separatist ultra-Right as well as the extremist demands for immediate nationalization and redistribution on the Left.

Index